DOCTOR ILLU

DOCTOR ILLUMINATUS

A RAMON LLULL READER

Edited and Translated by
Anthony Bonner

with a new translation of
The Book of the Lover and the Beloved by
Eve Bonner

PRINCETON UNIVERSITY PRESS
PRINCETON, NEW JERSEY

Published by Princeton University Press, 41 William Street, Princeton, New Jersey 08540

In the United Kingdom: Princeton University Press, Chichester, West Sussex

The preparation and publication of the original cloth edition of this volume (1985) was assisted by grants from the Translations Program and the Publications Program of the National Endowment for the Humanities. Publication of the cloth edition was also aided by a grant from the Paul Mellon Fund of Princeton University Press

Library of Congress Cataloging-in-Publication Data
Llull, Ramón, d. 1316.
    [Selections. English. 1993]
    Doctor illuminatus: a Ramon Llull reader / edited and translated by Anthony Bonner, with a new translation of The book of the lover and the beloved by Eve Bonner.
        p.   cm.—(Mythos)
    "This reader is a reduced version of the Selected works of Ramon Llull published by Princeton University Press in 1985"—Pref.
    Includes bibliographical references and index.
    ISBN 0-691-03406-0 (alk. paper)—ISBN 0-691-00091-3 (pbk.: alk. paper)
    1. Philosophy—Early works to 1800. 2. Theology—Early works to 1800. 3. Apologetics—Early works to 1800. 4. Mysticism—Early works to 1800. I. Bonner, Anthony. II. Title. III. Series: Mythos (Princeton, N.J.)
B765.L82E5   1993
189'.4—dc20   93-13696

First Princeton Paperback edition, for the Mythos series, 1993

Princeton University Press books are printed on acid-free paper and meet the guidelines for permanence and durability of the Committee on Production Guidelines for Book Longevity of the Council on Library Resources

10 9 8 7 6 5 4 3 2 1

Printed in the United States of America

Todo objeto cuyo fin ignoramos, es provisoriamente monstruoso.

J. L. Borges, *Una vindicación de la cábala*

Burlarse de tales operaciones es fácil, prefiero procurar entenderlas.

Ibid.

Lullum, antequam Lullum noscas, ne despicias.

A. Oliver in *Raymundi Lulli Opera Medica*

Table of Contents

List of Illustrations and Tables

Preface to the Abridged Edition

THIS READER is an abridged version of the two-volume *Selected Works of Ramon Llull* published by Princeton University Press in 1985. If there I tried to give a representative selection of Llull's thought and of his place in the history of European thought and literature—a task already almost hopeless in a man who wrote some 265 works on every subject conceivable—then in this selection of a selection all I can reasonably hope to give is a small taste of the man's work. To that end I have chosen part or all of four works. The first consists of excerpts from the *Book of the Gentile and the Three Wise Men,* Llull's principle work in the field to which he dedicated his life, that of apologetics. The last is the *Ars brevis,* the most famous formulation of the system around which all the rest of his thought revolved, and which has made him a precursor, however remote, of modern logic and computer science. In third place is his finest narrative work, a truly marvelous piece of political satire, the *Book of the Beasts.* All this is preceded by what constitutes almost a fifth work, Llull's (auto)biography as, apparently, told by him to the monks of the Chartreuse de Vauvert in Paris: this is the *Contemporary Life,* to which I added commentaries and historical interpolations to pad out the gaps in its narrative.

In the larger anthology, I had pledged myself to include only entire works which had not been previously translated into English. The removal of such constraints has made it possible to replace the mystical work in that anthology with the justifiably much more famous *Book of the Lover and the Beloved,* which is the second work presented here. The new translation, together with an introduction and notes, was done by my wife, Eve Bonner. My only role in this crucial part of the reader has been to help coordinate the notes with the rest of the anthology, and to write the bibliographical section at the end of the introduction to the work. I think and hope that with these four works the reader will get a good sample of the surprising range of Lull's capabilities.

The other change with respect to the longer anthology has been to reduce or omit altogether the bibliographical information in the notes, in view of possible readers more interested in entering into contact with Ramon Llull than in studying his works or thought in a scholarly way. Those interested in finding out where I got my information, however, can check the corresponding parts of the *Selected Works*.

Of the long list of people consulted and who gave advice for the longer anthology (see the preface there), three of them have very kindly repeated their services for the new translation of the *Book of the Lover and the Beloved,* reading part or all of the introduction thereto, or helping to solve problems of translation or interpretation. They are Jocelyn Hillgarth, Charles Lohr, and Jordi Gayà. Albert Soler has not only let us use the new critical text of the *Book of the Lover and the Beloved* that he has prepared for publication, but he has also gone over the introduction and translation to that work with a fine-toothed comb and offered countless useful corrections and suggestions. Finally, our editor at Princeton University Press, Timothy Mennel, has done a particularly careful and thoughtful job of seeing the book through the press. To all of them our sincerest thanks. Whatever faults remain are not theirs, but there quite certainly would have been many more without them.

Puigpunyent, Majorca   A.E.B.
March 1993

Acknowledgments

GRATEFUL ACKNOWLEDGMENT is made to the following libraries for permission to use reproductions from manuscripts in their possession: to the Landesbibliothek of Karlsruhe for Plates I–VII, and to the Biblioteca Universitaria of Bologna for Plates VIII–XII.

Abbreviations

ENC	*Els Nostres Clàssics* (Barcelona: Editorial Barcino).
Hillgarth, *Ramon Lull*	J. N. Hillgarth, *Ramon Lull and Lullism in Fourteenth-Century France* (Oxford: Oxford University Press, 1971).
MOG	*Raymundi Lulli Opera omnia,* ed. Ivo Salzinger, 8 vols. (Mainz, 1721–42; reprint Frankfort: Minerva, 1965).
NEORL	*Nova Edició de les Obres de Ramon Llull* (Palma, 1990ff.).
OE	Ramon Llull, *Obres essencials,* 2 vols. (Barcelona: Editorial Selecta, 1957–60).
ORL	*Obres de Ramon Lull,* ed. Salvador Galmés et al., 21 vols. (Palma, 1906–50).
OS	*Obres selectes de Ramon Llull (1232–1316),* ed. Anthony Bonner, 2 vols. (Palma: Editorial Moll, 1989).
ROL	*Raimundi Lulli Opera Latina,* ed. F. Stegmüller et al., vols. 1–5 (Palma, 1959–67); vols 6ff. (Turnhout, Belgium: Brepols, 1975–)
Sala-Molins, *Choix*	*Lulle, L'Arbre de Philosophie d'Amour, Le Livre de l'Ami et de l'Aimé, et Choix de textes philosophiques et mystiques,* trans. L. Sala-Molins (Paris: Aubier-Montaigne, 1967).
SW	*Selected Works of Ramon Llull (1232–1316),* ed. Anthony Bonner, 2 vols. (Princeton, N.J.: Princeton University Press, 1985).
Yates, *Art*	Frances Yates, "The Art of Ramon Lull. An approach to it through Lull's theory of the elements", *Journal of the Warburg and Courtauld Institutes* 17 (1954), 115–73; reprinted in her *Lull & Bruno: Collected Essays, Vol 1* (London: Routledge & Kegan Paul, 1982), pp. 9–77.

DOCTOR ILLUMINATUS

Historical Background and Life of Ramon Llull

Historical Background

RAMON LLULL is in many ways a perplexing figure. During his long life (1232–1316) he amassed a confusing number of claims to our attention: as a Christian philosopher in the Neoplatonic tradition; as the first of the great mystics of the Iberian Peninsula; as the first European to write prose novels on contemporary themes; as the first writer to use a Romance vernacular to discuss theology, philosophy, and science, and as one of the creators of literary Catalan; as a missionary, Christian apologist, and founder of a school of oriental languages for the purpose of training missionaries; and finally as the inventor of the "Art," a complex system, using semi-mechanical techniques combined with symbolic notation and combinatory diagrams, which was to be the basis of his apologetics in addition to being applicable to all fields of knowledge.[1] And behind all this there seems to lie a paradox, that of a figure coming from a small island in the western Mediterranean and from what nowadays is considered a minority culture, developing one of the most universalist of systems, one which he presented to popes, kings, sultans, and universities in Spain, France, Italy, and North Africa during his lifetime, and which brought him extraordinary fame throughout Europe in the Renaissance. If, however, we want to understand this apparent growth from geographical and cultural microcosm to macrocosm, we have to know more about Llull's background. For the small island of Majorca was strategically placed at the center of the commercial wheel of the western Mediterranean, and probably only a handful of thirteenth-century European cities were more cosmopolitan than Llull's birthplace, the island's capital. Moreover, the Catalan language and culture, to

[1] This initial characterization is taken largely from Pring-Mill's excellent summary in the 1967 edition of the *Encyclopaedia Britannica*.

which Llull gave such an impulse, were, within this wheel, not at all in a position of minority at the time.

To get some feeling for this situation, one must know a bit about the dramatic changes that took place in the Iberian peninsula in the beginning of the thirteenth century. Before then, and indeed from the beginning of the eighth century, the western Mediterranean had been, in Pirenne's phrase, a Muslim lake, and the Iberian Peninsula had been dominated by, or politically joined to, North Africa. The Spanish Christian kingdoms, locked into the space between the Muslims to the south and the mountains and sea to the north, were laboriously reconquering and resettling the center of the peninsula. During the twelfth century their progress had been slow, opposed as they were by two great North African Muslim empires, first of the Almoravids and then of the Almohads. At the same time, the Aragonese crown had been expending much of its foreign energies dabbling in the patchwork rivalries of the semi-independent principalities of southern France.

Then at the beginning of the thirteenth century, the Almohad empire collapsed, while the little principalities north of the Pyrenees were swallowed up by the northern French heavily backed by the papacy in its effort to stamp out the Catharist heresy and regain spiritual control of Occitania.[2] Looked at from the viewpoint of the Spanish Christian states, the result was a 180° reversal of the north-south power structure: a power vacuum to the north became a barrier, while the barrier to the south became a power vacuum, one into which all the Christian states stepped with extraordinary speed. In the space of twenty-two years (1226–48)[3] the Muslim possessions in Iberia were reduced to the petty kingdom of Granada.

The Aragonese monarchy, paralyzed by a royal minority, took longer than the other Christian states to go into action; but once it did, its speed was if anything even greater. In the space of only

---

[2] These changes were catalyzed by two crucial battles. First, in 1212, was that of Navas de Tolosa, in the mountain passes leading from Castile into Andalusia, where combined Christian forces from northern Spain and southern France overwhelmed a Muslim army. In the following year the battle of Muret was fought on the Garonne south of Toulouse, where a small northern French force backed by the Church defeated the combined forces of southern French nobility and the Aragonese crown (the king of Aragon himself died in the battle).

[3] That is, from the fall of Baeza (1226) to that of Seville (1248). The latter conquest gave Castile its first southern Atlantic port, which was soon to take on major importance in the economic life of the country.

sixteen years it moved south into the Balearic Islands (1229–35) and down the Mediterranean coast past Valencia (1238–45).[4] The extreme rapidity of this conquest entailed the sudden absorption of a large Muslim population, and a desperate search for settlers in an attempt to redress what was felt to be a serious social imbalance.[5]

As for the Aragonese monarchy that had led this portion of the conquest, it was a hybrid affair born of the marriage in the mid-twelfth century of the heiress of the kings of Aragon with Ramon Berenguer IV, count of Barcelona. Afterwards, each of their descendants styled himself King of Aragon *and* Count of Barcelona. Thus the son of Ramon Berenguer and the Aragonese princess was King Alfonso II of Aragon and at the same time Count Alfonso I of Barcelona (ruled 1162–96); their grandson was King Peter II of Aragon and Count Peter I of Barcelona (ruled 1196–1213);[6] and their great-grandson, as a result of presiding over the conquest of the Balearic Islands and Valencia mentioned above, was able to *add* titles, without being able to effect any real fusion between the two original ones, or for that matter between any of them. This was James I the Conqueror (ruled 1213–76, one of the longest reigns in European history), who was finally able to style himself King of Aragon, Majorca, and Valencia, Count of Barcelona and Urgel, and Lord of Montpellier.

The original joining of Aragon and Catalonia, however, remained dynastic and little else. The two regions had separate laws, customs, and privileges, and, as one historian has put it, any attempt to develop central institutions for the whole confederation was sure to meet with jealous resistance from both countries. In social structure the two areas were also different, Aragon being more rural, feudal, and landlocked, while Catalonia was more mer-

---

[4] The capital of Majorca was taken by assault on 31 December 1229, but the last pockets of resistance on the rest of the island were not cleared up until 1232. In that last year Minorca became tributary to the Catalan crown (it was not conquered until 1287; see below, n. 62). Ibiza was conquered in 1235. The campaign against Valencia began in 1232, the city itself surrendered in 1238, and the rest of the kingdom was not subdued till 1245.

[5] For Valencia, this imbalance was particularly dramatic (see the introduction to the *Gentile* below, p. 75). For Majorca it was less so, nor was there, because of the island's almost immediate economic boom, such difficulty in finding settlers.

[6] Catalan historians give their kings Alfonso and Peter one unit less than most other historians. Granted—as pointed out a bit further on—that the Catalans were dominant in every way in the Aragonese confederation, it seems unnecessary to prefer, in the purely ceremonial question of titles, the numeration as counts to that as kings. Note that this Peter II was the king killed at Muret (see n. 2 above).

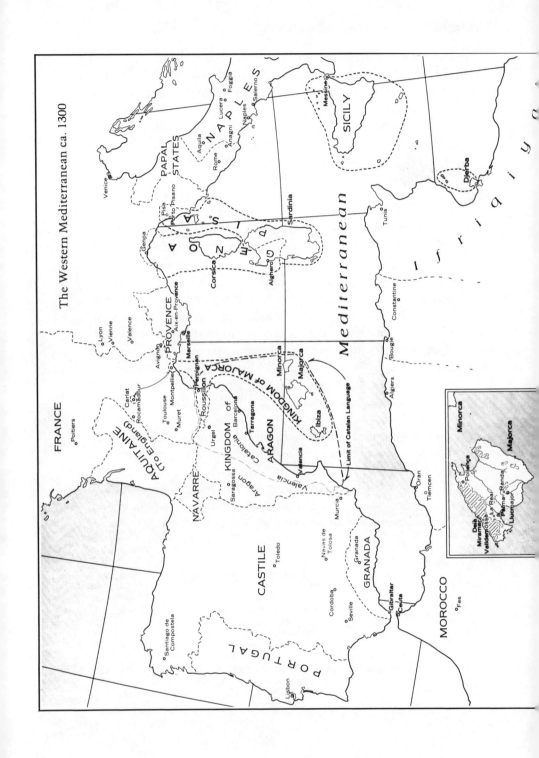

The Western Mediterranean ca. 1300

The Western Mediterranean, ca. 1300

THE MUSLIM STATES

1. Ifriqiyah, corresponding more or less to modern Tunisia and part of Libya, ruled by the Hafsids. For Ibn Khaldun it was the leading Islamic state of the period, and it was the most important area for Catalan commerce with North Africa.

2. A branch of the Hafsids succeeded, during the years 1285–1309, in establishing an independent emirate in the area around Bougie and Constantine (what is now eastern Algeria).

3. The central Maghrib—roughly the western two-thirds of present-day Algeria—constituting of the domains of the Abd-al-Wadid dynasty, whose capital Tlemcen and its port of Oran were important in the Majorcan gold traffic.

4. Morocco, ruled by the Merinid dynasty, although more in the Castilian zone of influence, yet maintaining its share of trade with Catalonia and Majorca.

5. Granada—all that was left of Muslim Spain—subsisting as a prosperous, independent state under the Nasrid dynasty until 1492.

THE CHRISTIAN STATES

Castile, which played only a minor role in the Mediterranean, although its newly conquered (1248) port of Seville was rapidly becoming an important center of trade.

6. Aragon with Catalonia and Valencia.

7. The Kingdom of Majorca, made up of three unconnected and dissimilar pieces: (1) the Roussillon, including Cerdanya and Capcir to the west, lying along the only really passable portion of the eastern Pyrenees, and a strategically important buffer region between France and Catalonia; (2) Montpellier, with its school of medicine and university, providing, mainly through its port of Lattes, the principal Mediterranean outlet for the commerce of France; (3) the Balearic Islands, of which Minorca had not been conquered from the Muslims until 1287.

8. France, the first power in Europe, and its capital, Paris, the intellectual center of the West.

9. Provence and Naples, separate areas under the single rule of the Angevin dynasty, first Charles I of Anjou and then Charles II the Lame (see Table 1).

10. Genoa and Pisa, rival maritime powers, the former controlling Corsica and a third of Sardinia, and the latter the remaining portion of Sardinia.

11. The Papal States, location of the papacy until 1305, after which it moved to France, and from 1309 on in Avignon.

12. Sicily, from 1285 to 1409 under a separate Catalan dynasty (see Table 1).

During Llull's active lifetime there was for the most part an equilibrium among these states. Historians have spoken of a Catalan empire, but Hillgarth has rightly pointed out that it was more apparent than real. The Catalans exercised a certain amount of what today would be called economic imperialism—especially in the Balearics, Sicily, and North Africa—and a certain sporadic naval hegemony, but for the most part those states, and even those dynastically tied to Aragon, competed with one another as quite independent units. Majorca, for example, not only was commercially dominant in Bougie, but had its own separate consulates in nine other towns of the Maghrib. More than anything, Llull's world was that of a Balkanized western Mediterranean, a kind of latter-day maritime *reinos de taifa*.

cantile, urban, and maritime in outlook. Lastly, the two areas spoke different languages: a dialect of Castilian in Aragon and Catalan in Catalonia.

The relative weight of these two regions, however, was very unequal. Even though the kingly title came from Aragon, and new kings were crowned in Saragossa, the demographic, economic, and cultural motive force behind the expansive strength of the kingdom came from Catalonia, and the effective economic, cultural, and administrative center was Barcelona. That it was the Catalans who overwhelmingly carried out the southward expansion is clear from the fact that their language was implanted almost everywhere in the newly conquered lands. It was also the Catalans who provided the strong mercantile class which, in close alliance with the monarch, provided a principal motive force of the expansion, and the importance of ports such as those of Palma[7] in Majorca and of Valencia was not lost on them. Nor did they stop there: soon most of the important North African trading centers were dotted with Catalan and Majorcan consulates.

Since the language of this expansion was Catalan, and since that was also the language of Ramon Llull, some facts about it must be made clear. Before the beginning of the thirteenth century, Catalonia lived very much within the cultural orbit of the brilliant troubadour world of southern France. In addition to the understandable attraction of that world, which was felt with almost equal strength in many other parts of twelfth-century Europe, two other factors contributed to the Catalan orientation. The first was its geographic proximity as a younger, as yet not so culturally defined, region; the second was a language which, even though of a separate Romance development, was not very far from Provençal. Catalonia, in fact, produced a considerable galaxy of troubadours, all writing in the standard Provençal koine. But then with the changed situation at the beginning of the thirteenth century came a severance of the umbilical cord. After that, southern France began to lose its attraction; it became a land of persecution from which people more and more frequently took refuge in Catalonia. At the same time the Aragonese crown, or rather the portion of it represented by the

[7] This is the Roman and modern name. In the Middle Ages the name was the same as that of the island, and was expanded to "the city of Majorca" if there was any possibility of confusion (the same situation still exists with Valencia and Ibiza).

Catalans, became a Mediterranean power, which in the next century would take its forces as far as Greece and Turkey; and it was precisely this imperialism that gave the Catalans a sense of their own identity. And it is a curious fact that this sense of identity was tied up not only with a feeling that they were carrying out a divine destiny, but also with a feeling for their language as an expression of that destiny. Moreover, the first monuments of the language are the chronicles that set down the exploits of the expansion, and the works of Ramon Llull, whose goal was to proselytize in the new lands; it is also noteworthy that one of the models in the formation of this language was that of the royal chancellery at the center of the ever-increasing web of administrative and diplomatic activity. It was this thirteenth-century prose that weened the language from the tutelage of Provençal and gave its definitive literary form; it was this language that the chronicler Ramon Muntaner vaunted as "the finest in the world."

By the time the initial expansive movement was over, Catalan was spoken in a pennant-shaped area stretching from the northern frontier of Roussillon in southern France westward to Andorra, and from there all the way south past Valencia to Alicante, in addition to the Balearic Islands.[8] Moreover, as a result of the dominant role of Catalan and Majorcan merchants in the western Mediterranean, it became a kind of lingua franca in the area. By 1300 it had become one of the international languages of diplomacy as well as of trade.[9] Nor was it surrounded as it is nowadays by a few national giants, linguistically speaking. The language units, like the political units, of the thirteenth-century western Mediterranean were much smaller and more equal in strength than they are now. All this is important for the reader to realize that Llull's use of Catalan (in addition to Latin) for a proselytism which was so international in aim was not the anomaly it might seem to modern eyes.

With regard to this internationalism, some points must be made

---

[8] In the fourteenth century it was also transplanted to Sardinia with the Catalan conquest of that island, and it is still spoken by the inhabitants of the town of Alghero (Alguer in Catalan).

[9] J. N. Hillgarth, "The Problem of a Catalan Mediterranean Empire 1229–1327," *English Historical Review*, Supp. 8 (London: Longman, 1975), p. 54, where he also says, "It was employed by Sicilian nobles, and, on occasion, by the Angevin King Robert of Naples. It was understood by the French popes of Avignon and could be used by a lay ambassador, who did not command Latin, to address a papal consistory."

about the island of Majorca, where Llull spent the first half of his long life. Its social structure was as different from that of its parent Catalonia as is that of any frontier area from its home base. Settlers came from all over Catalonia, and even from Aragon, as well as from Montpellier, Marseille, and other parts of southern France. There were also important communities of Genoese and Pisan traders. Muslims constituted perhaps a third of the population of the island.[10] Most were slaves as a direct result of the conquest, while some had been brought in subsequently by slave dealers. But there was also a certain number of free Muslims working as artisans, small traders, and tenant farmers. Numerically less significant, but very important in the economic, mercantile, and even diplomatic life of the island, were the Jews. They were of first importance to the crown as a source of revenue and as bankers; because of their knowledge of both the Islamic and Christian worlds and their respective languages, they made ideal ambassadors to represent the Catalan king in North Africa; lastly, they were leading intermediaries in the gold trade which, from tropical Africa, passed through Sijilmasa, Tlemcen, Oran, and Majorca. The fact that the island had such an excellent port situated almost exactly halfway between Barcelona and Algiers[11] placed it at the center of an extraordinary movement of ships and merchants to and from every port in the western Mediterranean, from as far away as Alexandria to the east, and Seville and the Atlantic coast of Morocco to the west. After 1280, Majorcans began to use the direct sea route to England through the Strait of Gibraltar; there is even a possibility that Majorcan sailors were the first to do so.[12]

The reader, however, must beware of imposing on this picture a modern image of a sunny, altruistic coexistence of different races and religions. Everything in the Middle Ages was more sharply contrasted. Commercial rivalries were more intense, piracy was the order of the day, relationships between subjugator and subjugated

[10] Historians' estimates vary from half of the population (perhaps 25,000 out of 50,000) to one-fifth (some 10,000). Two recent studies put the population as 40%.

[11] The Arab geographer al-Isidri said Majorca was one day's sailing from Barcelona and one from Denia (a port south of Valencia), two from Sardinia, and three from Bougie (in modern Algeria).

[12] The earliest known date for such trade refers to Genoese galleys trading with Flanders in 1277–8. In 1281 we find a Guillem de Bona of Majorca loading wool in London. It has been suggested that Majorcans might even have preceded the Genoese in such trade.

were brutally frank, and tolerance a matter either of economic interest or of momentary balance of power. But it all worked, and the impression is predominantly one of buoyancy and optimism, at least until the economic and social decline of the fourteenth century, which Llull did not live to see.

The First Thirty Years

Ramon Llull was born in 1232 or early 1233 in Palma, the capital of Majorca. His father, who had come from Catalonia with the conquering armies of James I just three or four years before, had also been called Ramon. The family name seems originally to have been Amat, and Llull a sobriquet that had slowly replaced it.[13] We are not sure whether the family was noble or of the merchant class, but the lands granted to the father after the conquest, as well as the son's later position at court, would indicate a noble origin. The former's wife, Isabel d'Erill, came to Majorca in 1231, when the island was already pacified, and their only son, Ramon, was born a year or two later.

His upbringing and education must have been typical of his class, which meant that it provided him with almost none of the intellectual training he was to need when his life took its definitive course. He seems to have written troubadour poetry and been attached to the court of James I, and particularly to that of his son, the future James II of Majorca, who was ten years Llull's junior.[14] He presents this part of his life as profligate, and he repents for it in sometimes moving Augustinian fashion in the *Book of Contemplation*.[15] In any event, his position as a courtier, with the resultant travels through Aragon, Catalonia, and Valencia, undoubtedly earned him considerable knowledge of the world.

[13] The old Catalan spelling was Ramon Lull or Luyl; in Latin sources it appears as Raymundus Lul, Lullus, or Lullius. This last form gave rise to the Spanish Raimundo Lulio and the English Raymond Lully. Ramon Llull is the correct form in modern Catalan (without accent; the form Ramón with accent is Spanish).

[14] The idea that as a young man he was a page in the court of James I comes from a report drawn up in 1373 by the Archbishop of Tarragona; modern scholars consider this report a forgery.

[15] Sala-Molins *Choix*, p. 19, n. 3, however, suggests one should take these confessions with a grain of salt, since at the end of the *Book of Contemplation* (ch. 366, 26) Llull admits to having exaggerated for effect, "like the troubadour who boasts of being in love so as to improve his poem."

Sometime before September 1257 he married Blanca Picany, by whom he had two children, Domingo and Magdalena. The acquisition of a family does not seem to have changed his life style much; many years later he commented laconically that he had been "married and with children, reasonably well-off, licentious and worldly."[16] We also know that, around that time, he was appointed seneschal (i.e., administrative head of the royal household) to the future James II of Majorca.[17]

And this is all we know of more than one-third of Llull's long life. He seems to have considered these years as wasted, valuable only as a negative example; in the autobiography that he recounted to his friends—as we shall see in a moment—he omits this part of his life altogether.

Conversion and Preparation

We know about the remainder of Llull's life[18] from a document almost unique among the literature of medieval thought. This is an autobiography known as the *Vita coaetanea* or "Contemporary Life," which, at the "instance of certain monks who were friends of his, he recounted and allowed to be put down in writing."[19] Most scholars assume that these friends were the Carthusian monks of Vauvert, a monastery formerly located approximately on what is now the southern part of the Luxembourg Gardens in Paris. From internal evidence it can be established that the work was composed at the end of August or the beginning of September of 1311, at the end of Llull's last trip to Paris. Not long after Llull's death it was included in the vast anthology called the *Electorium* that was put together by his disciple Thomas le Myésier.[20] This Latin version, copied (and later printed) many times,[21] was translated into Catalan

---

[16] See the text at n. 130 below.

[17] See §2 of the "Life" below.

[18] Or at least most of it: the "Life" has gaps of nine years (1265–74) and eleven years (1276–87), a five-year period (1302–7) dealt with in a most summary fashion, and the five years from the end of the narration to Llull's death (1311–16).

[19] See §1 below.

[20] For le Myésier and the *Electorium*, see "Lullism" (p. 61 below). The *Breviculum*, also described there, has an abbreviated form of the "Life" in and around the twelve miniatures, seven of which are reproduced here.

[21] The best edition is that in *ROL* VIII, 271–309. I have also consulted the translations into French in Ramon Sugranyes de Franch, "Ramon Llull, docteur des missions," *Neue Zeitschrift für Missionswissenschaft* 6 (Schöneck-Beckenried, Switzerland, 1950), and in Sala-Molins,

in the late fourteenth century, probably in Majorca.[22] Many earlier scholars preferred the Catalan version, but nowadays all scholars agree that the Latin version is older and more likely to be authentic, in spite of two or three specifically Majorcan details that the Catalan version was able to record from local tradition. It is the Latin version of the "Contemporary Life" we translate as follows, with interpolations to make it a continuous narrative,[23] and notes aiming to distill the large body of modern biographical research.

¶1. To the honor, praise, and love of our only Lord God Jesus Christ, Ramon, at the instance of certain monks who were friends of his, recounted and allowed to be put down in writing what follows concerning his conversion to penitence and other deeds of his.[24]

I

¶2. Ramon, while still a young man and seneschal to the king of Majorca,[25] was very given to composing worthless songs and poems and to doing other licentious things. One night he was sitting beside his bed, about to compose and write in his vulgar tongue a song to a lady whom he loved with a foolish love; and as he began to write this song, he looked to his right and saw our Lord Jesus Christ on the cross, as if suspended in midair. This sight filled him with fear; and, leaving what he was doing, he retired to bed and went to sleep.

¶3. Upon arising the next day, he returned to his usual vanities without giving the vision a further thought. It was not until almost a week later, however, in the same place as before, and at almost exactly the same hour, when he was again preparing to work on and finish the aforementioned song, that our Lord appeared to him on the cross, just as before. He was even more frightened than the first time, and retired to bed and fell asleep as he had done before.[26]

Choix; into Spanish in *Antología de Ramón Llull*, ed. M. Batllori (Madrid, 1961), vol. 1; into German in E.-W. Platzeck, *Das Leben des seligen Raimund Lull* (Düsseldorf, 1964).

[22] The standard edition of this Catalan version is that of Francesc de Borja Moll, *Vida coetània del Rev. Mestre Ramon Lull segons el MS 16432 del British Museum* (Palma, 1933). Particularly useful is the edition in *OE* I, 31–54, with elaborate notes by M. Batllori.

[23] I.e., filling in the gaps mentioned in n. 18 above.

[24] As scholars have pointed out, the phrase *conversio ad poenitentiam* has strong Franciscan connotations.

[25] Literally, "Seneschal of the table of the king of Majorca." The Catalan version has "Seneschal and major-domo," which are in fact synonyms. In English one could also use the word "steward." It should be noted that at this point James II was not yet king, but heir to the throne of Majorca.

[26] The Catalan version has this second vision appearing the night after the first. The version recounted in the text of the *Breviculum*, on the back of the miniature in which we see

Again on the next day, paying no attention to the vision he had seen, he continued his licentious ways. Indeed, soon afterwards he was again trying to finish the song he had begun when our Savior appeared to him, always in the same form, a third and then a fourth time, with several days in between.

¶4. On the fourth occasion—or, as is more commonly believed, the fifth—when this vision appeared to him, he was absolutely terrified and retired to bed and spent the entire night trying to understand what these so often repeated visions were meant to signify.[27] On the one hand, his conscience told him that they could only mean that he should abandon the world at once and from then on dedicate himself totally to the service of our Lord Jesus Christ. On the other hand, his conscience reminded him of the guilt of his former life and his unworthiness to serve Christ. Thus, alternately debating these points with himself and fervently praying to God, he spent the night without sleeping.

At last, as a gift of the Father of lights,[28] he thought about the gentleness, patience, and mercy which Christ showed and shows toward all sorts of sinners. And thus at last he understood with certainty that God wanted him, Ramon, to leave the world and dedicate himself totally to the service of Christ.

¶5. He therefore began to turn over in his mind what service would be most pleasing to God, and it seemed to him that no one could offer a better or greater service to Christ than to give up his life and soul for the sake of His love and honor;[29] and to accomplish this by carrying out the task of converting to His worship and service the Saracens who in such numbers surrounded the Christians on all sides.

Coming back to himself, however, he realized that he had none of the knowledge necessary for such an undertaking, since he had scarcely learned more than a bare minimum of grammar.[30] This thought worried him, and he began to feel very sad.

Llull composing his song and looking up at the five apparitions of the crucified Christ (Pl. II), says that the figure of Christ on the cross appeared larger, bloodier, and more wounded on the second night than on the first. This would mean that the increasing size of successive apparitions (drawn all together in one scene) in the miniature is not a matter of perspective as would appear to the modern eye, but rather a literal transcription of the text.

[27] Llull himself refers to these five apparitions of the crucified Christ in two poems, the *Desconhort* and the *Cant de Ramon*. The story so often told in past centuries of his conversion having been provoked by a lady whom he had been pursuing, and who finally allowed him to come to her rooms, where she undressed and revealed a breast eaten away by cancer, is a legend undoubtedly based on a somewhat similar episode in *Felix* (see *SW* II, 914).

[28] James 1:17.

[29] This desire for martyrdom is a constantly recurring theme in Llull's early works. See, for example, versicles 101, 141, and 323 of the *Book of the Lover and the Beloved*.

[30] I.e., very little Latin. See n. 39 below.

¶6. While turning over these doleful thoughts in his mind, suddenly—he himself did not know how; these are things only God knows—a certain impetuous and all-encompassing notion entered his heart: that later on he would have to write a book, the best in the world, against the errors of unbelievers.[31] Since, however, he could conceive neither the form nor manner of writing such a book, he was most amazed. Nevertheless, the greater and more frequent was his wonder, the more strongly the inspiration or notion of writing the aforementioned book grew in him.

¶7. However, thinking again, he realized that, even though in the course of time God might bestow on him the grace for writing such a book, he could still do little or nothing alone, especially since he was totally ignorant of the Arabic language, which was that of the Saracens.

It then occurred to him that he should go to the pope, to kings, and to Christian princes to incite them and get them to institute, in whatever kingdoms and provinces might be appropriate, monasteries in which selected monks and others fit for the task would be brought together to learn the languages of the Saracens and other unbelievers, so that, from among those properly instructed in such a place, one could always find the right people ready to be sent out to preach and demonstrate to the Saracens and other unbelievers the holy truth of the Catholic faith, which is that of Christ.[32]

¶8. Having therefore firmly made up his mind about these three intentions, that is to say: to accept dying for Christ in converting the unbelievers to His service; to write the above-mentioned book, if God granted him the ability to do so; and to procure the establishment of monasteries where various languages could be learned, as is explained above—early the next day he went to a church that was not far from there and, amid tears of devotion, fervently begged our Lord Jesus Christ to deign to bring about in a way pleasing to Him those three things which He himself had mercifully inspired in his heart.

¶9. After that he returned to his own affairs. Since he was still too imbued with his worldly life and licentiousness, he was quite lukewarm and remiss in carrying out the above-mentioned three projects for the next three

---

[31] The phrase between dashes is from 2 Cor. 12:2–3. The idea of "a book, the best in the world," was perhaps first carried out in the *Book of Contemplation*, and then certainly in the first work or works of the Art (see nn. 45 and 52 below).

[32] The idea of language monasteries for missionaries was not new—the Dominicans had already established some. It has been suggested that this orientation towards proselytism and apologetics might have been influenced by the disputation of Barcelona of this same year of 1263, which achieved considerable fame. For more details on both of these points, see the introduction to the *Gentile*.

months, that is, until the feast day of Saint Francis.[33] Then on that feast
day, a certain bishop preached in the Franciscan convent, explaining how
Saint Francis had abandoned and rejected everything so as to be more
firmly united to Christ and to Christ alone, etc.[34] Ramon, incited by the
example of Saint Francis, soon sold his possessions, reserving a small
portion for the support of his wife and children; and, in order to ask the
Lord and His saints for guidance in the three things the Lord had placed in
his heart, he set out for the shrines of Saint Mary of Rocamadour, Saint
James, and other holy places,[35] intending never to return.

II

¶10. Having carried out these pilgrimages, he prepared to set out for Paris,
for the sake of learning grammar there and acquiring other knowledge
required for his tasks. But he was dissuaded from making this trip by the
arguments and advice of his relatives and friends and most of all of Brother
Ramon of the Dominicans, who had formerly compiled the *Decretals* for
Pope Gregory IX,[36] and those counsels made him return to his own city,
that is, to Majorca.[37]

¶11. When he arrived there he left the grand style of life which he had
previously led and put on a lowly habit of the coarsest cloth he could
find.[38] And in that same city he then studied a bit of grammar,[39] and

---

[33] 4 October.

[34] This scene is depicted in the left half of the second miniature of Plate III.

[35] The first is the well-known shrine in the Dordogne; the second is Santiago de Compostela, in northwest Spain. Between the two it would have been only natural for Llull to have followed the well-known pilgrims' route, in which case the "other holy places" would have been the many shrines and churches on the way. The center and right panels of Pl. II from the *Breviculum* depict Llull's visits to these two shrines.

[36] Saint Ramon de Penyafort (ca. 1185–1275) compiled the *Decretals of Gregory IX* (pope from 1227 to 1241), which were formally promulgated by the Vatican in 1234. He was master general of the Dominican Order from 1238 to 1240. For his involvement in missionary work, see the introduction to the *Gentile*. As for the reasons for the aging Dominican's advice, we can only guess that there were still remains on Majorca of an earlier missionary school, or that in such a frontier society missionary problems would be nearer to hand than in the closed academic world of the Paris university.

[37] See n. 7 above.

[38] This emphasis on clothing "de panno vili" is characteristic of the Franciscan Spirituals (as well as of the Sufis). It might have been this contrast with his former courtier's raiments that caused the mockery of friends mentioned in the Prologue to the *Gentile*. On the right half of the second miniature of the *Breviculum* (Pl. III), Llull is receiving this habit from the same bishop who preached the sermon (some two years before! The miniatures, perhaps for reasons of visual distribution, are not in chronological sequence).

[39] I.e., of Latin. A considerable amount of ink has been spilled as to how well Llull ever learned Latin. The consensus nowadays seems to be that he learned it well enough to read it, write it, and even lecture in it effectively, although inelegantly and not without occasional grammatical errors (hence the modesty of some of his statements, and his preference for writing in Catalan and having better-trained people translate his work into Latin).

having bought himself a Saracen, he learned the Arabic language from him.[40]

Between that sentence and the next of the "Life" there intervene nine years of study, the crucial formative years about which we know nothing except by inference and deduction. That Llull's training must have been more than purely linguistic, as the auto-biography implies, is clear; that he was more than the somewhat innocent self-taught mystic and literary figure earlier scholars tried to present is also clear.

The list of works and authors that Llull mentions in the earlier stages of his production, although brief, is not uninteresting. There is the Bible, the Koran, and the Talmud, as well as Plato and Aristotle. Of Aristotle's works he cites in the *Doctrina pueril* no less than ten: the *Metaphysics*, *Physics*, *De coelo*, *De generatione et corruptione*, *Meteorologica*, *De anima*, *De somno et vigilia*, *De sensu et sensato*, *Historia animalium*, and the spurious *De plantis*. In another early work there is a possible citation of Anselm of Canterbury and Richard of Saint Victor. He also seems to have been familiar with the Latin tradition of logic as represented by the *Summulae logicales* of Peter of Spain.

Scholars have suggested that it was in the Cistercian monastery of La Real near Palma that Llull could have become acquainted with these (and surely other) works, partly because he mentions this monastery twice in the "Life" (see below), and partly because this would explain a slight doctrinal retard on Llull's part, his Augustinianism, a certain anti-Aristotelianism, and perhaps his mystic exaltation. Other scholars have suggested the Cistercian college of Valmagne at Montpellier.

It may also have been in Montpellier at this time that Llull acquired his medical knowledge.[41] From the *Principles of Medicine* we know that he was acquainted with the medical writings of Avicenna, Matthew Platearius, and Constantine the African. The first of these he undoubtedly encountered in the translation already

[40] Most scholars assume that, after hearing the bishop's sermon in the autumn of 1263, he must have spent about 2 years, or at least 1½, on the settling of his affairs, the long pilgrimage, the stay in Barcelona, the buying of the slave, and the establishment of a new life of study. Llull would therefore have begun his studies in 1265, which accords roughly with statements made in later works.

[41] Montpellier, the second city of the Kingdom of Majorca, was then the seat of the most renowned medical school in Europe.

available in European medical circles.[42] Quite another matter is his direct contact with Moslem culture through the slave he purchased.

First of all we know that he learned Arabic well—well enough to be able to dispute with Muslims and well enough to write major works in that language.[43] As to his knowledge of Arabic culture and Islam, he mentions, as we said above, the Koran; we can see from Book IV of the *Gentile* that his knowledge of the Muslim religion was reasonably sound; and the *Book of the Lover and the Beloved* was based expressly on Sufi models;[44] but the only Islamic author he mentions specifically, and in whose case we can be sure that his contact came directly from the Arabic, was al-Ghazzali. It was apparently during these years of intellectual apprenticeship that he wrote a compendium (in Arabic; this version is now lost) of al-Ghazzali's logic, which he then translated into Latin (under the title of *Compendium logicae Algazelis*), and finally into Catalan verse (the *Lògica del Gatzel*). Aside from this early venture into the purely logical side of al-Ghazzali's writings, there must have been other connections—one cannot help thinking—with this Islamic thinker whose teachings had played a central part in the spiritual life of the Almohads and whose doctrines were in essential ways close to those of Llull.

It was also, in all probability, towards the end of these nine years of intellectual apprenticeship that he wrote the vast *Book of Contemplation*, also first written in Arabic, which contains the germs of most of Llull's later thought, and which perhaps constituted his first attempt at writing the "best book in the world."[45]

Nine years later it happened that, while Ramon was away, his Saracen slave blasphemed the name of Christ. Upon returning and finding out about it from those who had heard the blasphemy, Ramon, impelled by a great zeal for the Faith, hit the Saracen on the mouth, on the forehead, and

---

[42] As for Averroes, whose name comes up frequently in the works written in Paris during the years 1309–11, Llull is dealing more with the ideas circulating there under the banner of Averroes than any actual works; see §43 of the "Life" below.

[43] See *SW* I, 19, n. 74, for a list of these works.

[44] See the introduction to that work for more details.

[45] Cf. nn. 31 and 52. Hillgarth, *Ramon Lull*, p. 30, refers to it as "the greatest work he wrote and one of the most extraordinary books of the Middle Ages." M. Batllori in his *Ramon Llull en el món del seu temps* (Barcelona, 1960), p. 12, calls it the *summa* of medieval mysticism, comparable to Aquinas's theological *Summa* and to Penyafort's *summa* of Canon Law. One can also follow Llull's own development through the vast extension of this work (some million words), from the more direct, personal style of the first books, to the algebraic notation of the later books, a clear prefiguration of the Art.

on the face. As a result the Saracen became extremely embittered, and he began plotting the death of his master.

¶12. He secretly got hold of a sword, and one day, when he saw his master sitting alone, he suddenly rushed at him, striking him with the sword and shouting with a terrible roar: "You're dead!" But even though Ramon was able, as it pleased God, to deflect his attacker's sword arm a bit, the blow nonetheless wounded him seriously, although not fatally, in the stomach. By means of his strength, however, he managed to overcome the Saracen, knock him down, and forcibly take the sword away from him.

When the servants[46] came running to the scene, Ramon kept them from killing him, but allowed them to tie him up and put him in jail until he, Ramon, decided what would be the best thing to do. For it seemed harsh to kill the person by whose teaching he now knew the language he had so wanted to learn, that is, Arabic; on the other hand, he was afraid to set him free or to keep him longer, knowing that from then on he would not cease plotting his death.

¶13. Perplexed as to what to do, he went up to a certain abbey near there.[47] where for three days he prayed fervently to God about this matter. When the three days were over, astonished that the same perplexity still remained in his heart and that God, or so it seemed to him, had in no way listened to his prayers, he returned home full of sorrow.

When on the way back he made a slight detour to the prison to visit his captive, he found that he had hanged himself with the rope with which he had been bound. Ramon therefore joyfully gave thanks to God not only for keeping his hands innocent of the death of this Saracen, but also for freeing him from that terrible perplexity concerning which he had just recently so anxiously asked Him for guidance.[48]

Illumination; Beginnings of the Art

III

¶14. After this, Ramon went up a certain mountain not far from his home, in order to contemplate God in greater tranquillity.[49] When he had been

[46] The Latin word *familia* can mean either "family" or "servants, household." Since, however, one presumes from §9 above that he was at this point living apart from his family, and since the Catalan version translates the word as *companya de casa*, I have preferred "servants."

[47] The Catalan translation, perhaps following local tradition, specifies that it was the abbey of La Real.

[48] This story is beautifully represented in three separate scenes in the third miniature of the *Breviculum* (Pl. IV).

[49] The Catalan text, again more precise on local tradition, specifies that this was Mount Randa, a solitary hill rising 1,800 feet above the plain some fifteen miles east of Palma.

there scarcely a full week, it happened that one day while he was gazing intently heavenward the Lord suddenly illuminated his mind, giving him the form and method for writing the aforementioned book against the errors of the unbelievers.[50]

Giving thanks to the Almighty, he came down from the mountain and returned at once to the above-mentioned abbey,[51] where he began to plan and write the book in question, calling it at first the *Ars major*, and later on the *Ars generalis*.[52] Within the framework of this Art he then wrote many books (as we will see below)[53] in which at great length he explained general principles by applying them to more specific things, in accordance with the capacities of simple people, as experience had already taught him.

When he had finished the book written in the aforementioned abbey, he again went up the same mountain. And on the very spot where he had stood when God had shown him the method of the Art he had a hermitage built,[54] where he stayed for over four months without interruption, praying to God night and day that by His mercy He might bring prosperity to him and to the Art He had given him for the sake of His honor and the benefit of His church.

¶15. While he was staying in this hermitage, there came to him a handsome young shepherd of cheerful countenance, who in one hour told him as many good things of God and of heavenly matters, especially of angels, and other things, as another ordinary person—or so it seemed to him—would have taken at least two entire days to recount.

Seeing Ramon's books, the shepherd got down on his knees, kissed

[50] The scene is depicted in the upper left-hand corner of the fourth miniature of the *Breviculum* (see Pl. V). The "form and method," as is clear not only from the phrase itself, but also from the work written as a result of its discovery (see the next paragraph), can refer only to the structure of the Art (for which see the next chapter, on "Llull's Thought"). This is of capital importance. The theological, philosophical, and natural conceptual framework was already present in the *Book of Contemplation*; the problem was how to give it all *form* and make it *demonstrable* to Muslims and Jews. Llull's conviction that the Art was given to him by God is clear not only from other passages of the "Life" (§16, 18, 19, 22, 23, 24), but also from many passages in his works. It was this experience, of course, that earned him the title of *Doctor Illuminatus*. The usual date given for this event is 1274, which would mean that Llull was about forty-two when he *began* the principal part of his life's work.

[51] The Catalan translation (as well as some of the Latin sources of the "Life") again specifies that it was the abbey of La Real.

[52] *Ars major* is the subtitle of the first work of the Art, the *Ars compendiosa inveniendi veritatem* or *Brief Art of Finding Truth*. *Ars generalis* is a generic name Llull used from 1294 on in referring to works of the Art, or to the Art itself, even though no individual work bore that title until the *Ars generalis ultima* of 1305–8. As for this being the new edition, as it were, of "the best book in the world," see n. 31 above.

[53] A reference to the list of works appended to the "Life" in the *Electorium*; cf. n. 123 below. For the specific works referred to—that is, those written within this cycle of the Art—see below "Llull's Thought," p. 48.

[54] The Oratory of Cura, cared for by Franciscan friars, now occupies the spot on Mount Randa where Llull is thought to have built his hermitage.

them fervently, and watered them with his tears. And he said to Ramon that those books would bring many benefits to the Church of Christ. The shepherd also blessed Ramon with many blessings of a prophetic nature; and, making the sign of the cross over his head and over his whole body, he left.

When he thought about all this, however, Ramon was astonished, for he had never seen this shepherd before, nor had he heard mention of him.[55]

¶16. Later on, upon hearing that Ramon had written several good books, the king of Majorca sent for him and had him come to Montpellier, where he was staying at the time. When Ramon arrived there, the king had his books examined by a certain Franciscan friar, and especially certain meditations he had composed as devotional material for every day of the year, with thirty individual paragraphs assigned to each day.[56] These meditations the friar admiringly found to be full of prophecy and Catholic devotion.

In that same city Ramon then wrote a book based on the Art he had been given on the mountain, and this book he called the *Ars demonstrativa*, and he read it there publicly. He also wrote a *Lectura* on this same work, in which he explained how primary form and primary matter constitute the elemental chaos, and how the five universals, as well as the ten predicaments, descend from this chaos and are contained in it in accordance with Catholic and theological truth.[57]

¶17. At that same time Ramon also obtained an agreement from the above-mentioned king of Majorca that a monastery be built in his kingdom, that it be endowed with sufficient property, and that thirteen Franciscan friars be sent there to learn Arabic for the purpose of converting unbelievers, as was stated above. To them and to those succeeding them in the same monastery, the sum of five hundred florins was to be provided every year from the aforementioned property for their maintenance.[58]

[55] This second illumination—or second stage of the previous illumination—with the appearance of the mysterious shepherd, is depicted in the central part of the fourth miniature of the *Breviculum* (see Pl. V).

[56] A reference to the *Book of Contemplation* with its 366 chapters (an extra one for a leap year), each divided into thirty paragraphs.

[57] The *Ars demonstrativa* is the work translated in *SW* I. The *Lectura* is a reference to the *Lectura super figuras Artis demonstrativae*, the middle portion of which (printed separately as the *Liber chaos* in *MOG* III) is what is being discussed in the latter part of the paragraph. The text of the "Life" seems here to have combined two separate sojourns of Llull in Montpellier: that of the previous paragraph, which must have taken place around 1274–5, and this one, around 1283–4 (for which see p. 21 below).

[58] This is a reference to the monastery of Miramar, situated on the magnificent, rugged northwest coast of Majorca. It is presumed that Llull's request to the king took place in 1275, and that the first community of Franciscans began their study of Arabic there towards the beginning of the next year. The foundation was confirmed by a papal bull of 17 October 1276, issued by John XXI (the logician, Peter of Spain).

Once again the "Life" makes a leap in time, this one of eleven years.[59] Formerly Lullists filled up this interval with accounts of travels all over central Europe, the Near East, and Africa (as far afield as Ethiopia and the empire of Mali), but nowadays most scholars reject these travels or regard them as doubtful at best. For our purposes it is perhaps more important to understand that it is at the end of this period that we see Llull emerging on the international scene, precisely after the scene had undergone some important changes.

The first change was domestic, but not without international repercussions. In 1276, the year of the foundation of the monastery of Miramar, King James I died, bequeathing the central portion of his kingdom—Aragon, Catalonia, and Valencia—to his elder son, Peter III (II of Catalonia), and the peripheral areas—the Balearic Islands, Roussillon, and Montpellier—to his second son, James II. This second, heterogeneous, unconnected amalgam of three bits of territory constituted the kingdom of Majorca, which was to live a more or less independent existence until reabsorbed by the Aragonese crown in 1349.[60]

The second change involved the Sicilian Vespers of 1282 and their enormously complicated aftermath. First, and most obviously, the bold seizure of the island by Peter III (called Peter the Great by the Catalans) caused the Angevins of Sicily to be replaced by a separate Catalan dynasty, the only important member of which, for Lullian history, was Frederick III (1296–1337), the nephew of Llull's patron, James II of Majorca (1276–1311).[61] It is important to understand, however, that like Majorca, in spite of Sicily's dynastic ties to Aragon, by Frederick's time it constituted a truly independent kingdom, with no administrative or military control exercised by the parent nation.

Perhaps the greatest consequence of the Sicilian Vespers was to bring down on the relatively small state of Aragon-Catalonia-Valencia the formidable combined hostility of the Angevins of Naples-Provence, of their cousins the kings of France, and of the

---

[59] That is (barring the problem of n. 57 above), from 1276 to 1287.

[60] See the map and §7 of the explanation on the back of the map. I say "more or less" because of the annexation of the Balearics to Aragon during 1285–98, for which see below.

[61] See the genealogy in Table 1. For Llull's connection with Frederick of Sicily, see p. 42 below.

papacy, from whom the Angevins had held Sicily in fief. In the ensuing struggle, the geographically incoherent little kingdom of Majorca was in a most unpleasant position: if its king, James II, sided with this powerful trio, he risked losing a third of his kingdom—the Balearic Islands; if he sided with the apparent under-dog, Aragon, he risked losing two-thirds—Roussillon and Mont-pellier. *Realpolitik* combined with a mistrust of his ambitious brother, Peter III of Aragon, made him choose the former course. So when the French invaded Catalonia in 1285 and were, to every-one's astonishment, driven out again with great losses, James was promptly stripped of the Balearic Islands. For thirteen years he lived in Perpignan and Montpellier, until, as an indirect result of the Treaty of Anagni of 1295, the Balearics were returned to him in 1298.[62]

This situation had considerable repercussions on the life of Ramon Llull from 1285 onwards. Already in 1283 we find him in Montpellier writing his great novel, *Blaquerna* (which includes the *Book of the Lover and the Beloved*), and shortly after that, probably also in Montpellier, beginning the second cycle of the Art, compris-ing the *Ars demonstrativa* and the *Lectura super figuras Artis demon-strativae*. As a result of his royal patron's loss of Majorca, it is quite likely that between 1283 and 1287, when the "Life" takes up again, Llull did not return to the island. After that, and except for a very brief visit there in 1294, we do not find him visiting Majorca again until 1300. This new situation doubtless also played a role in the abandonment of Miramar.[63] But from the kingdom of Majorca in the larger sense Llull was never far away for long, for he continued using Montpellier as a base during his numerous travels.

It is also indicative that in this changed political situation we now find Llull entering into relations with the kings of France and Na-ples, the allies of his patron and the enemies of the king of Aragon. Indeed, Llull seems to have had no relations with the king of Ar-agon until, significantly, the year 1299.[64]

With respect to Llull's subsequent travels, two facts are of inter-

---

[62] Another result of the war of 1285 was that the Catalans, fearing other possible "treason-able" activities in the midst of their Mediterranean sphere of influence, conquered the island of Minorca, which was included in the territories returned to James II in 1298.

[63] Probably some time between 1292 and 1295.

[64] Except possibly for a visit on the brief trip of 1294 mentioned above.

TABLE 1. KINGS OF ARAGON, SICILY, FRANCE, AND NAPLES

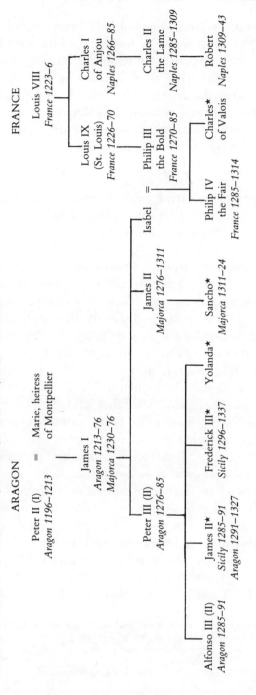

NOTE: This table is limited to those important for understanding Llull's life and the relevant politics; it omits the complicated situation of the rule of Sicily in 1291–6. Persons marked with an asterisk were married to offspring of Charles II the Lame (Yolanda to King Robert himself); their spouses' names are omitted because the fact of the interrelation of the two houses is more important than the details (for which see Batllori, *Món*, p. 38). For the variant numbering of Peters and Alfonsos, see "Historical Background and Life," n. 7; for those of James of Majorca and Frederick of Sicily, see ibid., n. 99. "Aragon" before dates of rule means king of Aragon, count of Barcelona and, from 1238 on, king of Valencia.

est. First, the only non-Mediterranean place to which he ever traveled was Paris. Second, if we draw a wavering line from Paris through Montpellier and Majorca down to Bougie, in North Africa, the only occasions after 1287 when Llull ventured west of this line were a brief visit to Barcelona in 1294, a stay in Perpignan and Barcelona in 1299, and several months in Barcelona in 1305. The Iberian peninsula evidently was to play almost no part in Llull's later life.

International Aspirations and Psychological Crisis

IV

¶18. After this he went to the Papal Court, to see if he could persuade the pope and the cardinals to establish similar monasteries throughout the world for teaching various languages. But when he arrived at the Court, he found that the pope, called Honorius, had recently died.[65] He therefore left Rome and made his way to Paris, there to communicate to the world the Art which God had given him.

¶19. Ramon arrived in Paris in the time of the Chancellor Berthaud, and at the special order of said chancellor he read a *Commentary* on the *Ars generalis* in one of his lecture halls.[66]

Having read this *Commentary* in Paris, and having observed the attitude of the students there,[67] he returned to Montpellier, where he once again

[65] "Similar" to Miramar, mentioned in the previous section of the "Life" (§17). Llull's hopes might have been raised by the fact that the pope in question, Honorius IV, had already (January 1286) tried to promote the teaching of oriental languages at the University of Paris. Honorius died in April 1287.

[66] The *Electorium* has two marginal notes here, presumably in le Myésier's hand. The first says "First journey to Rome; first journey to Paris; first time he lectured," and the second identifies the Chancellor as Berthaud of St. Denys, who took up this post in December of 1288. The third scene of the fourth miniature of the *Breviculum*, with le Myésier depicted as a student, is doubtless meant as an illustration of these lectures (see Pl. V). The *Commentary* mentioned in the text is undoubtedly the *Compendium seu commentum Artis demonstrativae*. It was during this same stay in Paris that he wrote *Felix* (which includes our *Book of the Beasts*), from which we can infer that it was then that he had his first interview with King Philip IV the Fair, the nephew of James II of Majorca (see the Genealogy [Table 1]).

[67] The implication is that these first Parisian lectures of Llull's were by no means a success. The communication gap, already large, was apparently made larger by the language of the correlatives (see n. 83 below); in the very *Commentary* mentioned here he apologizes for using such an "Arabic manner of speaking" (*modus loquendi arabicus*; see *MOG* III, 450 = Int. vi, 160). The greatest problem, however, as is clear from the next sentence of the "Life," came from the proliferation of figures and terms of the Art at this stage.

wrote and lectured on a book, this one entitled the *Ars inventiva veritatis*.[68] In this book, as well as in all others he wrote from then on, he used only four figures, eliminating—or rather disguising, because of the weakness of human intellect which he had witnessed in Paris—twelve of the sixteen figures that had formerly appeared in his Art.[69]

Having duly accomplished all these things in Montpellier, he set out for Genoa, where, staying but a short time, he translated into Arabic the above-mentioned book, that is, the *Ars inventiva*.[70] With this accomplished, he made his way to the Papal Court, attempting, as on previous occasions, to have monasteries established throughout the world for the teaching of various languages, as was said above.[71]

But seeing that he could accomplish little of what he wanted there as a result of obstacles put in his way by the Papal Court, and after giving the matter due consideration, he returned to Genoa. His idea was to take passage there for Saracen lands, so as to see whether at least alone he could accomplish something among them by debating with their wise men, using the Art given to him by God to prove to them the Incarnation of the Son of God, as well as the Blessed Trinity of Divine Persons in the highest unity of essence, in which these Saracens do not believe, but rather blindly assert that we Christians worship three Gods.

¶20. Since it soon became known among the Genoese that Ramon had arrived, with the intention of traveling to the land of the Saracens in order to convert them, if he could, to the faith of Christ, the people were most edified by this, hoping that through him God would accomplish some significant good among the said Saracens. For the Genoese had heard that Ramon himself, after his conversion to penitence, had received by divine

[68] Another marginal note in the *Electorium* adds the date of 1289 next to this return to Montpellier. Llull might merely have gone *through* Montpellier on his way to a general Franciscan chapter in Rieti that summer, and even perhaps visited Rome again, then returning to Montpellier to write and lecture. With the *Ars inventiva veritatis*, probably written at the beginning of 1290, begins the ternary phase of the Art (see p. 48 in "Llull's Thought" below). The *Art amativa*, finished on 9 August of the same year, was probably also written in Montpellier. He was certainly still there on 26 October, when he was given a letter of recommendation by the general of the Franciscan Order, Raymond Gaufredi, authorizing him to teach the Art in the Franciscan convents of Italy.

[69] See the introduction to the *Ars brevis* for more details on these changes.

[70] This means that Llull probably had the forthcoming trip to North Africa already in mind. None of the Arabic versions of Llull's works have survived.

[71] On this second (or perhaps third; see n. 68 above) visit to Rome, where he doubtless arrived towards the beginning of 1291, Llull probably entertained high hopes of obtaining some kind of backing from Nicholas IV, the first Franciscan pope. Presumably influenced by the fall of Acre, the last Christian stronghold in Palestine, in May 1291, he wrote his first work trying to promote a crusade, the *Libre de passatge*, containing the *Tractatus de modo convertendi infideles*, preceded by a *Petition to Nicholas IV*.

inspiration on a certain mountain a sacred science for the conversion of unbelievers.

But just when the Lord was thus visiting Ramon with an outburst of joy on the part of the populace, which for him was like a kind of dawn, He suddenly began to try him with a very serious affliction.[72] For when the ship and everything else were ready for sailing, as we mentioned before, with his books and other belongings already on board, there came to him on several occasions a kind of fixed idea that if he traveled to the land of the Saracens they would slaughter him the moment he arrived, or at the very least they would throw him into prison forever.

Therefore Ramon, fearing for his skin, like the apostle Saint Peter during the Passion of the Lord,[73] and forgetting his previously mentioned intention to die for Christ in converting the unbelievers to His worship, remained in Genoa, held back by a kind of paralyzing fear, abandoned to himself, by permission or dispensation of God, perhaps to prevent him from becoming too vain or presumptious.

But after the ship had set sail from Genoa, Ramon, on account of the huge scandal against the faith created in the eyes of the people by his not leaving, suffered such remorse of conscience that he fell into a profound despair, firmly believing that he would be damned by God. This thought brought him such inward pain of heart that outwardly his body became wracked with fever and he became gravely ill. And languishing thus in Genoa for a long time, without revealing to anybody the cause of his grief, he was brought almost to nothing.[74]

V

¶21. Finally, when the feast of Pentecost arrived,[75] he had himself carried or led to the church of the Dominicans, and when he heard the friars singing the hymn *Veni Creator*, he said to himself with a sigh, "Ah! Is it possible that this Holy Ghost could save me?" And in this feeble state he was led or carried to the friars' dormitory, where he threw himself down on a bed. While lying there, he looked up at the highest point of the ceiling, and he saw a tiny light, like a pale star, and from the general area of the star he heard a voice which said to him: "In this order you can be saved."

And thus Ramon sent for the friars of the house and asked to be clothed

[72] Job 7:18. The text of the "Life" is much closer to the Vulgate than to the King James version.

[73] Matt. 26:69–75; Mark 14:66–72; Luke 22:56–62; John 18:17.

[74] Ps. 72:22 in the Vulgate; 73:22 in the King James version, where "And I was brought to nothing" is, as in the newer Vatican Latin version, rendered as "So foolish was I."

[75] Or Whitsunday, which in 1293 fell on 17 May. Earlier authors maintained that these events took place in 1292, when Whitsunday fell on 29 May.

at once in their habit; but the friars put off doing it because the prior was away.

¶22. Upon returning to his own lodgings, Ramon remembered that the Franciscans had accepted the Art which God had given him on the mountain much more willingly than the above-mentioned Dominicans.[76] Whereupon, hoping that said Franciscans would promote the Art more efficaciously for the honor of our Lord Jesus Christ and for the good of the Church, he thought that he would leave the Dominicans and enter the Franciscan order.

While turning these things over in his mind, there appeared next to him, as if hanging on the wall, a band or cord like those that the Franciscans wear around their waists. And when he had been consoled by this vision for scarcely an hour he looked farther off and saw overhead that same light or pale star he had seen earlier while lying in bed at the Dominican convent. And he heard the star say, as if threatening him: "Did I not tell you that you could only be saved in the Dominican Order? Be careful what you do!"

¶23. Ramon, therefore, considering that on the one hand he would be damned unless he remained with the Dominicans, while on the other hand his Art and books would be lost unless he remained with the Franciscans, chose (which was most admirable of him) his own eternal damnation rather than the loss of the Art which he knew he had received from God for the salvation of the many and especially for the honor of God himself.

And thus, in spite of the disapproval of the aforementioned star, he sent for the Guardian of the Franciscans, whom he asked to give him their habit. The Guardian agreed to give it to him when he was nearer death.[77]

¶24. Therefore, although Ramon had lost hope of God's wanting to save him, he all the same decided to confess superficially and to make out a will, so that neither the friars nor the people would consider him a heretic.

When, however, the priest brought Christ's body before him and, standing in front of him, offered it to him, Ramon felt as if a strange hand were twisting his face from a position looking straight ahead to one look-

---

[76] See, for instance, Gaufredi's letter of recommendation mentioned in n. 68 above.

[77] "Guardian" is the Franciscan title for the superior of a convent. Whether in fact Llull ever joined the Franciscans is unknown. In favor of his having become a member of their Third Order is the evidence of the artist of the *Breviculum*, a statement to that effect by the inquisitor Eymerich, the fact of his having been buried in the Franciscan Church of Palma as opposed to that of his own parish, and a tradition that goes back at least to the fifteenth century. That he was not yet a member of the order in 1304 is clear from a passage of the *Liber de praedicatione* (*ROL* IV, 360), where he refers to the "followers and brothers" of Saint Francis and does not number himself among them. None of this evidence is very conclusive; the only thing certain is that Llull was very close to the Franciscans in thought and spirit.

ing towards his right shoulder, and it seemed to him that at the same time Christ's body, which the priest was offering him, passed over to the opposite side, that is, toward his left shoulder, and that it said to him: "You will suffer the punishment you deserve if you now receive me." But Ramon, firmly sticking by the decision he had taken, namely that he would rather be eternally damned than have his Art perish because of his bad reputation—that Art revealed to him for the honor of God and the salvation of the many—now felt as if a strange hand took his still turned head and twisted it straight again. In this position, seeing Christ's body still in the priest's hands, he straightway fell off his cot onto the ground and kissed the priest's foot. And in this way he then received Christ's body, so that, beneath such pretended devotion, he would at least save the above-mentioned Art.

What a wondrous temptation, or rather, it would seem, dispensation of divine trial! In olden times, the patriarch Abraham "against hope believed in hope";[78] this man, however, obstinately preferring that Art or doctrine, by which many people could be converted to understanding, loving and worshiping God, to his own salvation—like the sun which, though covered by a cloud, nevertheless keeps on burning—despairing of God in a wondrous way beneath a certain darkness of mind, proved that he loved God and his fellow man infinitely more than himself, as can be clearly gathered from the foregoing account.[79]

¶25. While Ramon was still detained by this grave feebleness of body and soul he heard a rumor that there was a galley in port about to leave for Tunis. Upon hearing this, as if awakening from a deep sleep, he had himself and his books carried at once to the ship. But his friends, seeing him at death's door and feeling sorry for him, dragged him off the boat against his will, which made him very unhappy.

First Missions

VI

Nevertheless, not long afterwards,[80] finding out about another ship, of the sort the Genoese commonly call a bark, preparing to go to the above-

---

[78] Rom. 4:18.

[79] The extraordinary events of §21–4 were omitted from the early eighteenth-century editions of the "Life," presumably because they were considered doctrinally or psychologically embarrassing. Until fifty years ago there were scholars who doubted the authenticity of these passages, but more recent scholarship is surely right in finding the descriptions too detailed, unusual, and unflattering to be inauthentic. Llull himself referred to the episode some three years later in the *Tree of Science*.

[80] All the Latin sources except two lack the negative; but in the circumstances and in view of the "a few days later" of the Catalan version, this is probably the correct reading.

mentioned Saracen city or kingdom, that is to say, Tunis, he had himself, along with his books and whatever else he needed, carried to this bark, against the will and advice of his friends.

As soon as they had left port and the sailors had the ship under way, Ramon suddenly became joyful in the Lord, and through a merciful illumination of the Holy Ghost, he regained not only the health of his enfeebled body, but also the hope which, beneath his former darkness of mind, he had thought forever lost. And this to such an extent that within a few days, to the amazement of everybody traveling with him and even of himself, he felt in as good a state of mind and body as ever before in his former life.

¶26. Giving due thanks to God, they soon afterwards entered the port of Tunis, where they disembarked and entered the city.[81]

Ramon, after slowing gathering together, day by day, those most versed in the Mohammedan religion, said to them, among other things, that he knew the foundations of the Christian religion well in all its articles, and that he had come with the idea of converting to their sect if, having heard the foundations of their religion, that is to say, that of Mohammed, and having debated with them over this matter, he found them more valid than those of the Christians. And when men more knowledgeable in the Mohammedan religion started coming to him daily in greater numbers, explaining the foundations of their religion so as to convert him to their sect, he was easily able to answer their arguments, saying:

"It is proper for every wise man to hold to that faith which attributes to the eternal God, in whom all wise men of the world believe, the greatest goodness, wisdom, virtue, truth, glory, perfection, etc.,[82] and all these things in the greatest equality and concordance. And most praiseworthy is that faith in God which places the greatest concordance or agreement between God, who is the highest and first cause, and His effect.

"However, as a result of what you have set before me, I see that all you

---

[81] For Tunis, see the explanation on the back of the map. It is important for the reader, however, not to imagine Llull's trip there as a stepping *totally* into a foreign world. It was a place familiar to Genoese, Pisan, and Catalan merchants. The Catalans, for instance, had their own *funduq* there, a kind of merchants' inn with warehouse and Christian chapel, and they usually had a consul to help sort out their legal and commercial problems. The sultan's militia, moreover, was composed of Catalan mercenaries; the idea being that since they would be less prey to the factional feuds so common to North African politics, they would have greater personal loyalty to the sultan. So Llull undoubtedly had friends and people willing to help him there; he was only alone when he ventured into the dangerous area of preaching directly to the Muslims.

[82] This list of divine dignities, or attributes of God (for which see "Llull's Thought," p. 50 below), is somewhat patchy (in addition to varying among the sources of the "Life" here). The scene of Llull's arrival in Tunis and subsequent discussions with the Muslim doctors is beautifully depicted in the ninth miniature of the *Breviculum*, all the speeches of which are taken directly from this section of the "Life" (see Pl. I here).

Saracens who belong to the religion of Mohammed do not understand that in the above and other similar Divine Dignities there are proper, intrinsic, and eternal acts, without which the dignities would be idle, and this from all eternity. The acts of goodness I call bonificative, bonifiable, and bonifying, while those of greatness are magnificative, magnifiable, and magnifying, and so on for the other aforesaid and similar Divine Dignities.[83]

"But since, as I already see, you attribute those acts only to two Divine Dignities or Reasons, that is, to wisdom and will, it is thus clear that you leave the other above-mentioned dignities, that is, goodness, greatness, etc., in a state of idleness, consequently placing inequality as well as discord between them, which is not right. For by means of the substantial, intrinsic, and eternal acts of the Dignities, Reasons, or Attributes, taken equally and concordantly, as they should be, Christians clearly prove that in one completely simple Divine Essence and Nature there exists a Trinity of Persons, namely the Father, the Son, and the Holy Ghost.

¶27. "This I will be able to do with the help of God, using clear arguments based on a certain Art divinely revealed, as it is believed, to a Christian hermit not long ago, if you would care to discuss these things calmly with me for a few days.

"You will also be shown, if it pleases you, in the most rational way, by means of this same Art, how in the Incarnation of the Son of God, through the participation, that is to say, union, of Creator and creature in the single person of Christ, the first and highest cause agrees and accords with its effect in the most rational way; and how this becomes apparent in the greatest and noblest degree in the Passion of Christ the Son of God, which He voluntarily and mercifully deigned to suffer in the humanity He had taken on in order to redeem us sinners from the sin and corruption of our first forebear, and to lead us back to that state of glory and divine fruition on account of which and for the final purpose of which the Blessed Lord created us."[84]

---

[83] These are the famous Lullian correlatives, which were quite as unusual in the original Latin (or Catalan)—*bonificativum* (*bonificatiu*), *bonificabile* (*bonificable*), and *bonficare* (*bonficar*)—as they are in present-day English; notice (n. 67 above) how in Paris he had felt obliged to apologize for this "Arabic manner of speaking." Notice, too, how they make their appearance in the "Life" precisely when Llull is first arguing with Muslims, and precisely, too (as becomes clear in the following paragraph, and as is often the case with the correlatives), in connection with proving the doctrine of the Trinity. These three correlative terms are best understood when associated with the triad of *potentia* ("power" or "potentiality"), *objectum*, and *actus*, or as it is sometimes put, with agent, patient, and action.

[84] Llull's speech in the last two sections gives his apologetic method in a nutshell: the use of the dignities and correlatives to prove the Trinity and the Incarnation, the two Christian dogmas which had proved the greatest stumbling block to Muslim and Jewish understanding of Christianity, and which no previous method had been able or willing to deal with in any reasonably convincing way. See pp. 49–51 below for more details, as well as *Gentile*, Bk. III, n. 6.

VII

¶28. When it seemed that Ramon was already enlightening the minds of the unbelievers on these subjects, it happened that a certain man of no little fame among these Saracens, who had understood Ramon's words and intention, begged and entreated the king[85] to order the beheading of this man, who was trying to subvert the Saracens and who with audacity and temerity was attempting to destroy the Mohammedan religion.

A council was convened, and at the instigation of the above-mentioned notable and of several other councilors, the king's will was already inclining towards Ramon's death. One of the councilors, however, a man of prudence and knowledge, tried to prevent such a crime by persuading the king that it would be dishonorable for him to kill such a man, who, even though he was attempting to spread his Christian religion, nevertheless seemed to possess abundant maturity of goodness and prudence; and he added that in the same way a man who dared to enter Christian lands for the sake of imprinting the Saracen religion on their hearts would be considered a good Saracen.

The king, therefore, giving in to these and similar words, desisted from executing Ramon; he did, however, immediately order him to be expelled from the kingdom of Tunis. When he was taken out of prison, however, he suffered many insults, blows, and vexations at the hands of the multitude.

¶29. At last he was taken to a Genoese ship which was about to set sail. And while he was on his way there, the king decreed that he was to be stoned to death if he were again found in the country.

Ramon was immensely unhappy about this, for he had already arranged for the baptism of some men of considerable reputation as well as many others whom he was aspiring to lead to the full light of the orthodox faith before his departure. While this man of God found himself afflicted by the pangs of this dilemma, it happened that the ship to which he had been taken set sail for its own land.

When he saw this, Ramon felt that tribulations were pressing in on him from all sides. For if he left, he saw that the souls which he had already prepared for Christian worship would slide back into the trap of eternal damnation; but if he ventured to stay, he was already familiar with the madness of the Saracens who were quite prepared to kill him.

Nevertheless, all aflame with the love of God, he did not fear to face the dangers of death if only he could obtain some effect of salvation for these souls. And getting off the ship that was leaving, he secretly boarded another one that was entering the same port, for he hoped to be able to find

---

[85] Abu-Hafs, the Hafsid Sultan of Tunis (1284–95).

some way to get on land without the hindrance of their brutality and violence, so that in the above matter he could carry out the good work he had begun.

¶30. While this was the way things stood, it happened that a certain Christian, similar to Ramon in bearing and dress, was walking through the city, and the Saracens seized him, thinking he was Ramon. When they were about to stone him, the man in question cried out: "I am not Ramon!" Looking into the matter, they found out that Ramon was on the ship, and the other man managed to escape from their hands.

Ramon remained there three weeks, but seeing he could do nothing in the service of Christ, he left for Naples,[86] where he stayed, lecturing on his Art, until the election of Pope Celestine V.[87]

VIII

¶31. After this, Ramon went to the Papal Court to obtain from the pope something he had long desired for the sake of the faith of Christ, as was said above, and there he wrote some books.[88]

Some time later, Pope Celestine V was succeeded by Pope Boniface VIII, whom Ramon entreated with all his might to have some useful things done for the Christian faith.[89] And even though he suffered considerable anguish following the pope from one place to another, not for a single moment did he desist in his attempts, assuming the pope doubtless

[86] Llull must have returned to Europe sometime during the last three months of 1293, since the best MSS of the *Taula general* state that it was begun in mid-September in Tunis and finished in mid-January of 1294 in Naples. It should be mentioned that it is at about this time that Llull begins to date his works, usually also giving the place in which they were written, thus permitting us to follow his career more closely. Simultaneously, references to his Art now cease to be to specific works, but more generically to an *Ars generalis* (see n. 52 above).

[87] In addition to lecturing prior to Celestine's election (5 July 1294), we know that on 1 February Llull received permission to preach to the Saracen colony established at Lucera (near Foggia) by Emperor Frederick II some years before, and that on 12 May he was granted a safe-conduct to visit the Muslim prisoners in the Castel dell'Ovo in Naples.

[88] The "Life" omits a rapid trip to Barcelona, where we find Llull on 30 July, and to Majorca, where he dedicated the *Arbre de filosofia desiderat* to his son, whom he had not seen in a long time. The phrase "went to the Papal Court" could mean that Llull went to Aquila, where Celestine V was crowned and remained at least until the beginning of October, or it could simply mean that after his trip Llull went back to Naples, where the pope resided from then till December. In any case, Celestine V, a hermit made pope against his will, was a figure in whom Llull, together with other reformers such as the Franciscan Spirituals, placed great hope. Of the two works Llull addressed to him, in order to obtain "something he had long desired," the first was his *Petitio Raymundi pro conversione infidelium*, which is usually called simply the *Petition to Celestine V*; the second was the *Flowers of Love and Flowers of Intelligence*, translated in *SW* II.

[89] On 13 December, Celestine V resigned. Boniface VIII was elected on 24 December in Naples and crowned a month later, on 23 January 1295 in Rome. To him Llull addressed a *Petition to Boniface VIII*, identical in true title and almost identical in content to the previous one. He also addressed to him a work on the Articles of Faith called the *Apostrophe*.

would deign to listen to him, since he was not petitioning for his own benefit or for some prebend, but rather for the public good of the Catholic faith.

¶32. At last, however, seeing that he could obtain nothing from the pope, Ramon made his way to the city of Genoa, where he wrote some other books.[90]

He then went to see the king of Majorca, and after having had an interview with him,[91] he went on to Paris, where he gave public lectures on his Art and composed many books. Later on he had an interview with the king, entreating him with regard to certain things of great usefulness for the holy church of God.[92]

But seeing that he could obtain little or nothing with respect to such things,[93] he returned to Majorca, where he stayed for a time, trying by means of both disputations and sermons to bring the innumerable Saracens living there to the path of salvation. He also wrote several books there.[94]

¶33. While Ramon was laboring at these tasks the news happened to be spread abroad that Cassan, the emperor of the Tartars, had attacked the kingdom of Syria and was trying to bring it all beneath his dominion. When he heard this, Ramon, having found a ship about to embark, sailed

[90] This lack of success of an Art, which for Llull was undeniably God-given, was not only puzzling but profoundly discouraging. He gave vent to this discouragement in a moving poem called the *Desconhort*, probably written in September 1295, and to a lesser extent in the Prologue to the *Tree of Science*, begun at the same time. As for the stay in Genoa, we know nothing about the books he wrote there.

[91] Since James II had not yet recovered Majorca (see p. 21 above), Llull's audience with him probably took place either in Montpellier or Perpignan.

[92] In Paris he wrote a dozen works, among them the *Tractatus novus de astronomia*, the *Declaratio Raymundi per modum dialogi edita contra aliquorum philosophorum* against the extreme Aristotelianism of the Arts Faculty of the Paris University, and the *Tree of the Philosophy of Love*, to name only a few of the most important. As for Philip the Fair, this was probably Llull's second interview with him (see n. 66 above).

[93] Bringing on a second bout of discouragement, poured out this time in the *Cant de Ramon*, perhaps the most beautiful poem Llull wrote, and certainly one of the gems of medieval Catalan literature.

[94] On his way to Majorca, he stopped in Barcelona, where he wrote the *Dictat de Ramon* (along with a *Commentary* on it) and the *Oracions de Ramon*, dedicated to James II of Aragon (not to be confused with his uncle, James II of Majorca) and his queen, Blanche of Anjou. On 30 October 1299 he obtained permission from the king of Aragon to preach "in the synagogues of the Jews on Saturdays and Sundays, and in the mosques of the Saracens on Fridays and Sundays, throughout our lands and dominions." Since the king of Majorca was at this point a vassal of the king of Aragon, this permission was doubtless valid in the Balearics, hence the "disputations and sermons" there. Note that Llull's return to Majorca was probably conditioned by the island's finally having been restored—in August 1298—to his friend and patron, James II of Majorca.

to Cyprus, where he discovered that this piece of news was completely false.[95]

Seeing himself frustrated in his intent, Ramon tried to find some other way in which he could employ the time granted him by God, not in idleness, but rather in work acceptable to God and beneficial to his fellow man. For he had stored in his vigilant heart that advice of the Apostle who said: "Let us not be weary in well doing: for in due season we shall reap, if we faint not";[96] and of the Prophet who said: "He that goeth forth and weepeth, bearing precious seed, shall doubtless come again with rejoicing, bringing his sheaves with him."[97]

¶34. Ramon accordingly went to the king of Cyprus[98] and eagerly entreated him to exhort certain unbelievers and schismatics, namely Jacobites, Nestorians, and Muslims, to come to hear him preach or to dispute with him. At the same time he begged the king of Cyprus to send him, once he had done what he could for the edification of the above-mentioned people, to the sultan, who was Saracen, and to the king of Egypt and Syria, so that he could instruct them in the holy Catholic faith. The king, however, was not interested in any of these things.

Then Ramon, trusting in "he who preaches the word in great virtue,"[99] set to work among them with sermons and disputations, with the sole help of God. But, persisting as he did in preaching and teaching, he fell sick with a serious bodily illness.

Two people waited on him, a clergyman and a servant, who, not setting God before themselves[100] and forgetting their salvation, plotted to strip with their criminal hands this man of God of his belongings. And when he

[95] The "emperor" was Ghazan, the Mongol khan of Persia, who in December 1299 and January 1300 conquered most of Syria—Aleppo, Homs, and Damascus. What was false was the rumor, apparently throughout Europe, that Ghazan had conquered Jerusalem. What was not so much false as disappointing, for Llull at least, was that almost immediately after this brilliant campaign, Ghazan was forced to abandon Syria in February 1300 to deal with troubles on his border with Turkestan, thus allowing the Mamelukes to reoccupy the country. It was disappointing because the Mamelukes, having taken the Holy Land from the Crusaders, were, for Western Europeans at least, the villains of the time, while the Mongols of Iran, as possible allies against the Mamelukes and, more for Llull, as possible converts to Christiantiy, were in great favor.

[96] Gal. 6:9.

[97] Ps. 125 (126):6.

[98] This is Henry II, of the French family of Lusignan, last king of Jerusalem (1286–91) and king of Cyprus (1285–1324) during the island's period of greatest splendor as the chief Latin emporium in the eastern Mediterranean.

[99] Ps. 67:12 in the Vulgate. The corresponding passage of the King James version (68:11) is somewhat different: "The Lord gave the word: great was the company of those that published it."

[100] Ps. 53:5 (54:3).

found out that they were poisoning him, he gently dismissed them from his service.[101]

¶35. Upon arriving in Famagusta, he was cheerfully received by the master of the Temple, who was in the city of Limassol, and he stayed in his house until he had recovered his health.[102]

After this, Ramon sailed to Genoa, where he published many books.[103] He then went on to Paris, where he successfully lectured on his Art and wrote several books.[104]

Last Missions

IX

In the time of Pope Clement V he left Paris and went to Lyon,[105] where he resided for a while and entreated the pope in favor of something of the greatest benefit for the faith, that is, that the pope himself found monasteries in which suitable devout men would come together to learn the languages of different nations, so that they could preach the Gospel to all the unbelievers in accordance with the Lord's command which says: "Go

[101] It was in September 1301, during this first part of his stay in Cyprus, at the monastery of St. John Chrysostom in Buffavento, near Nicosia, that Llull wrote, in Catalan, the *Rhetorica nova*, which he translated into Latin in 1303 in Genoa.

[102] This was the last grand master of the Knights Templars, Jacques de Molay, who, precisely when Llull dictated this "Life" in Paris, was in prison there, where three years later he would be tried along with other leaders of the order and burned at the stake. The narrative, however, is unclear here. How could Llull, upon arriving in Famagusta on the east side of the island, be received by de Molay, who was in Limassol, some sixty miles away on the south coast? Moreover, it leaves out a trip to the mainland, specifically to Ayas or Lajazzo (Yümurtalik in modern Turkish, the town on the Gulf of Iskenderun from which Marco Polo left on his famous journey) in Lesser Armenia (Cilicia), where Llull wrote the *Libre què deu hom creure de Déu*. There is even a possibility that he managed to visit Jerusalem.

[103] Suddenly the "Life" becomes very schematic here; the five years between Llull's departure from Cyprus in 1302 and his arrival in Bougie in 1307 are disposed of in fourteen lines. In May of 1303 we find him in Genoa, finishing the *Logica nova*. For the next two years he alternated between Genoa and Montpellier. As to the "many books," this is indeed the case. In addition to the *Logica nova*, the most important of these are his first work on sermons, the *Liber de praedicatione*, his major work on the theory of knowledge, the *Book of the Ascent and Descent of the Intellect*, and his most notable political tract, the *Liber de fine*.

[104] This trip to Paris, which the "Life" presents as being both successful and productive, is otherwise undocumented, nor do we know of any works written there during this period.

[105] This is the first French pope, Bertrand de Got, who was elected on 5 June 1305 and crowned on 14 November at Lyon, where he resided for three or four months. On his way down from Paris, Llull had spent the first months of 1305 in Montpellier, and the summer in Barcelona, where he received two grants from James II of Aragon and wrote the *Liber praedicationis contra Judaeos*, as well as the *Liber de Trinitate et Incarnatione*; in October he was present at the meeting between that king, James II of Majorca and Pope Clement V in Montpellier.

ye into all the world, and preach the Gospel to every creature."[106] But this petition was of little interest to the pope and to the cardinals.

¶36. From there, Ramon, after returning to Majorca, sailed to a certain Saracen land called Bougie.[107]

In the main square of the city, Ramon, standing up and shouting in a loud voice, burst out with the following words: "The Christian religion is true, holy, and acceptable to God; the Saracen religion, however, is false and full of error, and this I am prepared to prove."

Upon saying such things and using the Saracen language to exhort to the faith of Christ the multitude of pagans gathered there, many of them rushed at him with impious hands, wanting to stone him to death. While these people were raging at him, the high priest or bishop[108] of the city sent emissaries with orders to bring this man before him.

Once Ramon was before him, the bishop said, "What has made you indulge in such folly as to dare to attack the true religion of Mohammed? Don't you know that anyone who dares to do such a thing is liable to be put to death?"

Ramon answered, "The true servant of Christ who has experienced the truth of the Catholic faith should not fear the danger of physical death when he can gain the grace of spiritual life for the souls of unbelievers."

¶37. To which the bishop replied, "If you believe the religion of Christ to be true, and consider that of Mohammed to be false, give me a necessary reason to prove it." For this bishop was well known as a philosopher.

Ramon answered, "Let us both agree on a common point, then I will give you the necessary reason." Since this pleased the bishop, Ramon questioned him, saying, "Is not God perfectly good?" The bishop replied that He was.

Then Ramon, wanting to prove the Trinity, began to argue thus: "Every being which is perfectly good is so perfect in itself that it does not need to do good, nor ask for any, outside itself. You say that God is perfectly good from eternity and for all eternity, therefore He does not need to ask for, nor to do good outside Himself; for if He did, He would then not be perfectly and absolutely good. Now since you deny the most blessed

---

[106] Mark 16:15. Llull undoubtedly wrote a *Petition to Clement V*, but it has not survived. In November 1305 in Lyon, however, he began the last and greatest synthesis of the Art, the *Ars generalis ultima* (see §41 below).

[107] This trip is usually placed in the spring of 1307. At that time the splinter Hafsid kingdom of Bougie and Constantine (see the map and its accompanying explanation), ruled by Abu-l-Baqa Halid (1302–11), was very much a commercial fief of Majorca.

[108] *Antistes vel episcopus*, the mufti or cadi of the town. This and the ensuing scenes are depicted in the tenth miniature of the *Breviculum* (Plate VI), much of the text of which is taken from these sections of the "Life."

Trinity, let us suppose that it did not exist; in that case God would not have been perfectly good from eternity until He produced, in time, the good of the world. You do believe in the creation of the world, and therefore, when God created the world in time he was more perfect in goodness than before, since goodness is better diffusing itself than remaining idle. This, I claim, is your position.

"Mine, however, is that goodness is diffusive from eternity and for all eternity. And it is of the nature of the good that it be diffusive in and of itself, for God, the good Father, from His own goodness generates the good Son, and from both is breathed forth the good Holy Ghost."

¶38. Astounded by this reasoning, the bishop did not give a single counterargument; rather, he ordered him to be thrown into jail at once. A crowd of Saracens had gathered outside, waiting to kill him, but the bishop issued a decree that in no way should anyone conspire to kill this man, for he himself intended to subject this man to an appropriate death.

Upon leaving the bishop's house, and on the way to jail, Ramon was beaten with sticks and with fists, and forcibly dragged along by his beard, which was very long, until he was locked in the latrine of the thieves' jail, where for some time he led a painful existence. Later on, however, they put him in an ordinary cell in the same jail.[109]

¶39. The next day, however, the Mohammedan clergymen gathered before the bishop, asking that he be killed. After having begun the council by discussing the best way to do away with him, they decided to have him appear before them. And if they could establish that he was a man of science, then he would be put to death at once; but if he turned out to be a foolish and stupid man, they would let him off as a fool.

Upon hearing this, one of them who had sailed with Ramon from Genoa to Tunis and who had frequently heard his discourses and arguments[110] said to them, "Beware of having him brought here to the tribunal; he will bring up arguments against our religion that we will find difficult or impossible to answer."

They therefore agreed not to have him appear before them, and shortly thereafter they changed him to a less severe prison. Then the Genoese and Catalans residing there got together and asked that he be put in a more decent place, which was done.

---

[109] All this with a man now about seventy-five!

[110] Either the "Life" is wrong in mentioning Genoa and Tunis here, or the Muslim remembered Llull from his previous journey in 1293, fourteen years before. In any case, it gives us an interesting glimpse of Llull not neglecting a single opportunity to preach to Muslims, even buttonholing their doctors of the law on shipboard.

X

¶40. Ramon remained in jail there a half a year. During that time clergy-men or emissaries from the bishop would visit him frequently and seek to convert him to the Mohammedan religion, promising him wives, honors, a house, and large amounts of money. Founded as he was, however, on a firm rock,[111] Ramon, the man of God, said, "If you wanted to believe in the Lord Jesus Christ and would consider abandoning this mistaken religion of yours, I would offer you the greatest of riches and promise you eternal life."

Since they frequently insisted on these matters, it was agreed that each side would write a book in which each would confirm its religion by the most effective arguments it could find; the religion of the side which made use of the strongest arguments would be considered the truer one.

And when Ramon was already working hard on his book, it came to pass that an order was sent from the king of Bougie, who at the time was residing in Constantine, that Ramon was to be expelled from the country immediately.[112]

¶41. So he then boarded a ship anchored in the harbor, and the captain of the ship was given strict orders that this man was not to be allowed back on shore.

On the journey to Genoa, when the ship was near the Port of Pisa, about ten miles offshore, a great storm arose, and the ship suffered the violent blows of the tempest on all sides, until at last it sank. Some were drowned, while others, with the help of God, escaped; among the latter were Ramon and a companion of his, who, even though they lost all their books and clothing, and were almost naked, managed to make it to shore in a rowboat.

Upon arriving in Pisa, some citizens received him with honor. And there this man of God, although old and weak, persisting in his labor for Christ, finished his *Ars generalis ultima*.[113] Of this *Art*, as well as of other

---

[111] Matt. 7:25; Luke 6:48.

[112] The book on which he was working was the first (Arabic) version of the *Disputatio Raymundi christiani et Homeri saraceni*, lost in the shipwreck recounted in the following section, and rewritten (in Latin) in Pisa the following year. The Prologue and end of the *Disputatio* confirm some details of the story told here. For the king, see n. 107 above.

[113] Begun in Lyon in November 1305 (see n. 106 above) and finished in Pisa in March 1308. In January 1308, also in Pisa, Llull finished its companion work, the *Ars brevis*, translated here. Between the beginning of the larger work and the end of the smaller—that is, for all of 1306–7—we know of only one other work that Llull wrote: the first version of the *Disputatio* written in the prison of Bougie. This remarkably fallow period contrasts sharply with the renewed frenzy of literary activity that was to begin now and last until the end of his life. In Platzeck's chronological catalogue of 292 works, the *Ars generalis ultima* is numbered 146, which means that this man of 75 was now numerically only midway through his production. To be sure, none of these remaining works is of the length of some of the earlier works—see n. 1 to "Llull's thought"—but the fact of the matter is nonetheless astounding.

books of his, one could say that only those who aspire, not to the glory and empty philosophy of this world, but rather to a firm love and knowledge of God as the ultimate goal and supreme good, are worthy of its immense efficacy and delectable and perfect knowledge.

¶42. Having there finished the above-mentioned *Art* along with many other books,[114] and wanting to incite the Pisan community to the service of Christ, he proposed to their council that it would be good for their city to found an order of Christian religious knights devoted to doing continual battle against the treacherous Saracens for the recovery of the Holy Land.

Acceding to his pleasing eloquence and advice, they wrote letters to the pope and to the cardinals concerning this worthy project.

Having obtained these letters in the city of Pisa, he set out for Genoa, where he obtained similar letters. There many devout matrons and widows flocked about him, while the noblemen of that city promised him 25,000 florins in aid for the Holy Land.

After leaving Genoa he went to call on the pope, who was then residing in Avignon.[115] Seeing, however, that he could obtain nothing of what he intended there, he went on to Paris, where he gave public lectures on his *Art* and on many other works that he had written earlier.[116] A great crowd of masters as well as students came to these lectures. To them he not only expounded a doctrine reinforced by philosophical arguments, but also professed a wisdom wonderfully confirmed by the high principles of the Christian faith.[117]

[114] In Pisa he wrote eight works, including the last part of the *Ars generalis ultima* and the *Ars brevis* mentioned in the previous note, and the new Latin version of the *Disputatio* mentioned in n. 112. It is after this that Llull begins the post-Art phase of his production (see "Llull's Thought," p. 48 below).

[115] This is a tremendous simplification of Llull's travels and labors from mid-1308 to mid-1309. In May 1308 we find him back in Montpellier, where he finished the *Ars Dei*. During the summer he possibly met Clement V, as well as Philip IV, in Poitiers, to both of whom he says he "offered" that work. On 4 September, a letter from his Genoese merchant friend Christian Spinola to King James II of Aragon tells us that Llull was in Genoa at the time, and that he probably went on from there to confer with Arnold of Vilanova in Marseille. From October 1308 till April 1309, we find him again in Montpellier, where he wrote some eighteen works, including a letter to the king of Aragon and the important *Liber de acquisitione Terrae Sanctae*. It was therefore probably during the summer of 1309 that he had his audience at Avignon with Clement V.

[116] Llull probably arrived at the French capital in the fall of 1309, because by November of that year we find him finishing the *Ars mystica theologiae et philosophiae* there. He was to stay two years, till September 1311, a period that is extraordinarily well documented—we even know that he lived on the rue de la Bûcherie, on the Left Bank, one block inland from the quai opposite the Cathedral of Notre Dame. We have italicized the word *Art*, because rather than to the Art in general, it here undoubtedly refers specifically to the *Ars generalis ultima* and the *Ars brevis* (for which see the following note).

[117] Three documents bear witness to the success of these lectures. The first is one of 10 February 1310, in which forty masters and bachelors in Arts and Medicine attest that they

¶43. He saw, however, that as a result of what had been written by the Commentator on Aristotle, that is, Averroes, many had strayed considerably from the straight path of the truth, especially of the Catholic faith, saying that the Christian faith was impossible with respect to the intellect, although true with respect to belief. Since this was deplored by the community of Christians, Ramon therefore set out to disprove this concept of theirs by demonstrative and scientific means, managing to refute them in many ways. For if the Catholic faith is unprovable by the intellect, then it is impossible for it to be true. And on this subject he wrote several books.[118]

XI

¶44. After this, knowing that the holy father, Pope Clement V, was to celebrate a General Council in the city of Vienne during the calends of October of the year 1311, he decided to go to this Council to see if he could obtain three things for the restauration of the orthodox faith.[119]

The first was the establishment of an adequate place where men of devotion and vigorous intellect could be brought together to study different kinds of languages so as to know how to preach the doctrine of the Gospel to every creature.[120]

The second was that of all the Christian military religious orders a single order be made, one that would maintain continual warfare overseas against the Saracens until the Holy Land had been reconquered.[121]

The third was that the pope rapidly prescribe a remedy against the opinions of Averroes, who in many ways had proven to be a perverter of the truth, so that through the intervention of intelligent Catholics, who were not concerned for their own glory but rather the honor of Christ, an opposition be made to said opinions and to those holding them, which opinions seemed to block the way to the truth and to uncreated wisdom, that is, to the Son of God the Father.

---

have heard and approved of Llull's lectures on the *Ars brevis*. The second is a brief letter of commendation from Philip IV, dated 2 August of the same year. The third is a letter of commendation from Francesco Caroccioli, chancellor of the university, written on 9 September 1311, only a few days before Llull's departure from Paris.

[118] He wrote thirty-five works during these two years in Paris, many of them devoted to refuting the extreme Aristotelianism—known as Parisian Averroism—of the Arts' Faculty, which threatened to create a secular philosophy independent of Christian theology.

[119] For the Council of Vienne, see p. 41 below.

[120] Cf. Mark 16:15. This along with the following two requests also appear in three works Llull wrote at about this time: the *Liber natalis pueri parvuli Christi Jesu*, written in January 1311 and dedicated to the king; the *Petitio Raymundi in Concilio generali ad acquiriendam Terram Sanctam*, included in the *Liber de ente quod simpliciter est per se et propter se existens et agens* and written at about the same time as the "Life" was dictated (September 1311); the *Phantasticus* (for which see the opening of the following section), written shortly after the dictation of the "Life."

[121] This is similar to the request at the beginning of §42. The idea of the fusion of the military orders is one that Llull had been proposing for almost thirty years.

On this subject Ramon wrote a little book called the *Liber natalis*,[122] promising, moreover, that he had cogent philosophical as well as theological arguments against them, which arguments he discussed with the greatest clarity in other books.

This servant of God, true interpreter of the supreme truth and of the great profundity of the Trinity, wrote amidst his daily labors more than a hundred and twenty-three books.[123]

¶45. By now forty years had elapsed since he had first directed all his heart, all his soul, all his strength, and all his mind toward God.[124] In this period of time he had written books continually and with great diligence, whenever he had free time to do so.

He could justly have uttered the words of the prophet David, "My heart hath uttered a good word: I speak my works to the king. My tongue is the pen of a scrivener that writeth swiftly."[125] Truly his tongue was the pen of that uncreated scribe, that is the Holy Ghost, who gives "the word to them that preach good tidings with great power,"[126] of which the Savior spoke to the Apostles, saying, "For it is not you that speak, but the Spirit of your Father which speaketh in you."[127]

Wanting his books to be of general usefulness to everyone, he wrote many in the Arabic language, since that was a tongue he had learned.

His books were distributed throughout the world; but he had them collected principally in three places, namely, the Carthusian monastery in Paris, the house of a certain nobleman of the city of Genoa, and that of a certain nobleman of the city of Majorca.[128]

The Last Five Years

Llull must have left Paris soon after dictating this "Life," probably in the month of September 1311. A bit later we find him writing the *Phantasticus*, or, to give its full title, the *Disputatio Petri clerici et Raymundi phantastici*, which is the account of a dialogue with a priest

---

[122] See n. 120 above.

[123] In the *Electorium* the "Life" is followed by a catalogue of 124 works of Llull (the difference of one comes from two works listed under one heading).

[124] Cf. Matt. 22:37; Mark 12:30.

[125] Thus in the Vulgate (Douay) version of Ps. 44:2; the text of the King James version (Ps. 45:1) is slightly different.

[126] Thus in the Vulgate (Douay) version of Ps. 67:12; the King James version (Ps. 68:11) has, "The Lord gave the word: great was the company of those that published it."

[127] Matt. 10:20.

[128] These are, respectively, the Chartreuse of Vauvert, for which see p. 10 above; Perceval Spinola, of the same Genoese merchant family as the Christian Spinola mentioned in n. 115 above; and Llull's son-in-law, Pere de Sentmenat, for whom see n. 131 below.

he supposedly met on his way to the Council of Vienne.[129] Llull
accused the priest of being worldly and cynical, while the priest
accused Llull of being hopelessly impractical and idealistic—in
short, a *phantasticus*. Llull replied:

> I was married and with children, reasonably well-off, licentious and
> worldly. All of this I willingly left in order to honor God, procure the
> public good, and exalt the Holy Faith. I learned Arabic; several times I
> ventured forth to peach to the Saracens; and for the sake of the Faith I was
> arrested, imprisoned, and beaten. For forty-five years I have labored to
> move the Church and Christian princes to act for the public good. Now I
> am old and poor, yet my purpose is still the same, and the same it will
> remain, if it so please God, until I die.[130]

The Council of Vienne lasted from 16 October 1311, to 6 May
1312. There Llull obtained a partial but genuine success. Of the
three purposes expressed in the "Life," the first, for the establishment of schools of oriental languages, was fulfilled by Canon 11 of
the Council, which ordained the teaching of Hebrew, Arabic, and
"Chaldean" at Paris, Oxford, Bologna, Salamanca, and the Papal
Court to students who were then to become missionaries. The
second purpose was partially fulfilled, for although a new order was
not founded, the goods of the Templars, the brutal dissolution of
whose order had begun some five years before, were now transferred to the Hospitalers—a solution apparently acceptable both to
Llull and to the king of France. Only his petition against the Averro-
ists went unheeded.

In May we find Llull in Montpellier, where he wrote *De locutione
angelorum*, in which he confirms that he had personally presented
these petitions to the pope and cardinals at Vienne, and that two of
them had been conceded.

Probably in June Llull went on to his native Majorca, where he
was to stay almost a year, until May 1313. It must have been a very
different Majorca for him, for his old friend and patron James II had
died in 1311, and had been succeeded by his son King Sancho (1311–
24). Llull did, however, write seventeen short works there, and
drew up his will.[131]

---

[129] A city on the Rhone, just south of Lyon.
[130] Translated from *ROL* xvi, 15.
[131] These works have recently been published in *ROL* xvi, xv, and xviii. In the will,
published at the end of the last of these three volumes, Llull again mentions the three places he

In May 1313, at the age of 81, Llull set out on a new venture. First he went to Messina, one of the favorite residences of Frederick III of Sicily.[132] Llull had placed considerable hopes in this king. As early as 1296 he had sent him three works via his friend Perceval Spinola, and from May to September of the previous year of 1312 he had dedicated five works to him. Llull had thus been preparing the way for his encounter with this monarch, who had befriended Arnold of Vilanova and the Franciscan Spirituals even after the latter had been officially proscribed by the Council of Vienne. It is probable that Llull also learned of Frederick's plans for reform, which included the linguistic preparation of missionaries to Islam.

Llull stayed a year in Messina, where he wrote thirty-seven short works. He seems, however, to have had little success in obtaining help from the king for his forthcoming mission to Tunis, which must originally have been one of his principal reasons for coming to Sicily.

Help did arrive from another quarter, however, but as part of a political imbroglio in which Llull became at least marginally involved. In 1311 the throne of Tunis had been usurped by the courtier Abu Yahya Ibn al-Lihyani after years of scheming. But his success was only partial, and a younger member of the displaced Hafsid dynasty was able to set himself up in Bougie, with the clear aim of reuniting all of Ifriqiyah again—a wish he was to fulfil in 1318. In the meantime, al-Lihyani's position was not at all secure, and he found himself having to rely more and more on the Catalans, with whom he had had relations going back many years and who had indeed helped him to power. To ensure their continued interest in his cause, he had let it be known he might be interested in converting to Christianity. The kings of Sicily and Aragon had taken the bait, and for several years now there had been secret negotiations going on between the three.

That Llull was unaware of these negotiations, on a subject so dear to him, seems unlikely. What his specific role was, however, when he set out for Tunis in the autumn of 1314,[133] is unknown. It is

---

wants books of his to be collected, and it is here that we find out the name of his son-in-law (see n. 128 above).

[132] See the genealogy in Table 1 for Frederick's relationship to the kings of Aragon and Majorca.

[133] Some scholars have Llull take a roundabout route: Messina-Majorca (in May), Majorca-Bougie (August), and Bougie-Tunis (September), but this is to accomodate a docu-

significant that at the beginning of November, the king of Aragon
wrote three letters: one to Ibn al-Lihyani recommending Ramon
Llull, one to the sultan's interpreter, Joan Gil, also recommending
Llull; and one to Llull himself, informing him that he had written
the other two.

As a result of the sultan's peculiar game, it must have been an
unusual atmosphere Llull found himself breathing in Tunis: one
where the hostility of his former North African visits was replaced
by a certain perhaps uneasy receptiveness to Christianity, while the
Catalans were present in greater numbers than ever, not only in the
Sultan's militia and the usual merchant colony, but also as chap-
lains, envoys, interpreters, and so on.[134] Llull must have been able
even to dispute with Muslims and preach to them in comparative
peace. He had time there not only to write some twenty-five
smaller works, but also a larger *Ars consilii* apparently intended
for the sultan. We also know that during the summer of 1315
Llull wrote to James II of Aragon to have him send a former pupil, a certain Fray Simó de Puigcerdà, to translate some of his
works, and especially the *Ars consilii*, from Catalan into Latin.[135] If
Fray Simó arrived at all, it could not have been before late November 1315.

This would scarcely have been in time to be of much help, for
Llull's last works were written in December 1315 in Tunis, at which
point he disappears from history.[136] Most scholars agree that he
must have died sometime between then and March 1316, aged
eighty-three or eighty-four, either in Tunis, on the ship sailing
back, or, as seems likely from one piece of testimony, in Majorca.[137]
The only thing certain is that Llull was buried in the church of San
Francisco in Palma, at first in the sacristy, then beneath the pulpit,

---

ment first produced in 1612 to help in the process of canonization (by offering proof of Llull's
martyrdom; see n. 138 below), and which scholars now agree is a forgery.

[134] One scholar cites the anecdote of a Tunisian ascetic who one day shouted at the Sultan,
"O *faqih* Abu Yahya, what you are doing is unlawful. Allah has forbidden anyone to ask for
help of a polytheist." This might be a reference to Llull and advice offered to the Sultan in the
Ars consili, of which more in a moment.

[135] We have four letters written between 5 August and 29 October from the king to
various Franciscan officials trying to have the man sent to Tunis, a request which seems to
have met with considerable bureaucratic red tape.

[136] The works are the *Liber de majori fine intellectus, amoris et honoris* and the *Liber de Deo et de
mundo*, both dedicated to the sultan.

[137] The testimony is that of a fifteenth-century MS which claims to have gotten it from "a
very old book."

and at last, in 1448, in the beautifully sculptured tomb in a chapel to the left of the choir, where his body still lies.[138]

[138] Modern scholarship has shown that it was about the time this final tomb was constructed—in the middle of the fifteenth century—that the legend of Llull having been martyred in Bougie spread. It apparently began as a transposition of many of the details of Llull's previous two trips to North Africa, and principally that of 1307 to Bougie, and was based on the evidence of pious falsifications like that mentioned in n. 133 above. See *SW* I, 52, n. 201 for more details.

Llull's Thought

FOR THE PAST hundred years Ramon Llull has been known primarily as a man of action, a mystic, and a literary figure—as the founder of Catalan prose and one of Catalonia's greatest medieval writers. This picture is not wrong; it is incomplete. To try to understand the whole Llull is a difficult and somewhat complicated task, one that presents two initial hurdles.

The first is what might be termed the man's multiplicity. Llull is the author of a vast number of works—265 according to the latest catalogue of works—on countless subjects and in numerous literary forms.[1] The second is the very originality of his Art, which is at the center of this multiplicity and around which all the rest of his thought is organized. Not only is the Art visually peculiar, with its letters, charts, and movable wheels, but its functioning is at the root of an original method, and this very originality has caused Llull to use traditional terminology in a new way. There has been the natural tendency to want to fit his work into some preexisting category, and indeed the path of Lullism is strewn with the wreckage of such attempts.[2] It is the great merit of the brothers Carreras y Artau that they were the first to see the Art clearly as something sui generis.[3]

Aside from the sheer number of works, the product only of Llull's feverish energy, both of these problems have rational explanations within the context of Llull's aims. First we must understand

---

[1] 237 works preserved plus 28 lost works (these figures follow the more recent catalogue in *OS* II, 539–89). The catalogue in vol. II of Platzeck's work (see the Suggestions for Further Reading) has 292 works of which 256 are preserved. The Freiburg editors of the Latin works give a figure of 280 works, of which 240 are preserved (see *ROL* I, ix). The differences stem from questions of authenticity, grouping, etc. These works include short pamphlets, medium-sized works, seven works of around 150,000 words (the *Libre de demostracions, Liber de quattuordecim articulis fidei, Compendium Artis demonstrativae, Blaquerna, Felix*, the *Art amativa*, and the *Ars generalis ultima*), three works of around 250,000 words (the *Ars inventiva veritatis*, the *Lectura super Artem inventivam et Tabulam generalem*, and the *Liber de praedicatione*), one work of slightly over 400,000 words (the *Tree of Science*), and one of almost a million words (the *Book of Contemplation*).

[2] The traditional danger has been in wanting to see details of Llull's thought as similar to those of some predecessor or contemporary, and not always seeing that the overall result is something quite new and different.

[3] In their great two-volume work (see the Suggestions for Further Reading), and especially vol. I, p. 345.

that Llull was primarily and perhaps uniquely interested in *persuasion*, and this at all intellectual and social levels of society.[4] This interest accounts for the variety of forms he used, ranging from purely scholastic treatises addressed to the Parisian arts faculty to doggerel for the easier memorization of the rules of the Art; from the complicated treatises on the Art to charming dialogues like the *Gentile*, where the mechanism of the Art is disguised beneath the device of the "flowers" of a tree to make it more palatable to less sophisticated audiences; from long didactic novels like *Blaquerna* and *Felix* to collections of short mystical aphorisms, proverbs, questions and answers, and sermons.

Llull's shrewd estimation of the audience for which a work was intended also led him, like any good polemicist, to modify the tone he used in accordance with circumstances. Not only does he vary his style, say, from the endless chain of allegorical stories of *Felix* to the more insistently demonstrative arguments of the *Gentile* and the semi-algebraic shorthand of the *Ars demonstrativa*; he sometimes even shifts his political or social point of view for the sake of persuasion. One often feels that the oscillations between pacifism and bellicosity present in his crusading plans are determined to a certain extent by the temper of a particular moment or by the mood of a particular royal or papal court. One also feels that the tolerance or intolerance he shows—toward Jews, for instance—was very much conditioned by the audience he was writing for: what would have been normal in the pluralistic society of Majorca (the *Gentile*) becomes unthinkable in the intolerant surroundings of the French court (*Felix*).[5] Llull sought to persuade in order to save souls; consistency of personal social convictions was for him less important.

Closely related to this question of audience was another factor making for multiplicity: that of language. When writing for Muslims, Llull wrote in Arabic.[6] When writing for Christian lay audiences, he used his native Catalan, which, as I have pointed out, was

[4] To call him a popular philosopher, as some have done, is accurate in only a limited sense. Llull would very much have liked to persuade both the Islamic and Christian intelligentsia of his message, and one does not imagine works such as the *Ars demonstrativa*, the *Ars generalis ultima*, or the abbreviated form of the latter—the *Ars brevis* translated here—as being written for popular consumption.

[5] One has only to compare the empathy felt for the Jew in Book IV of the *Gentile* with the traditional antisemitism of *Felix*, Bk. I, ch. 11 (*SW* II, 711).

[6] Cf. the "Life," p. 16 above.

Sed er uobis auito iam qd uos omit qui estis sub lege macomeri ñ intelligitis in pñis diuinis dignitatib; actus ipos ē sublitm tuales mauiskcos t eous sine quibz ipe diuine dignitates omo tuissent ceriose euam ab ceno qd non decer.   Actus uo car di coz bonificaiuu bonificabile bonificare t sic de aliis omibz suo modo.   Sed qa uos estos actus pñis duab; soliumo dignitat ibz atrributio ur iam uides.   Sapientie uidelicet t uolutati maui festu est ex ler qd uos in omibz aliis dignitatib; diuinis amosuat   relinquitio saluer in bonitate magnitudine et auosirate   relinquitio saluer in bonitate magnitudine eternitate potestate glia uitrure uirture t pferione

er in cecio omibz; t perconsequis in cos ineqitate dissimilirudiné t discordiam ponitio qd in en te in se pfectissimo ñ licer. Sed si uelleno audire pratice per peado diuinas dignitares t actus car uobis manifeste ostendam. diuiná trinirate psonar. in bna sim plicissima essenta t natura. saluer pño t filio t spū sū.

PLATE I.   Llull's trip to Tunis in 1293 and his disputation with the
Muslims. From *Breviculum*, fol. 9ᵛ.

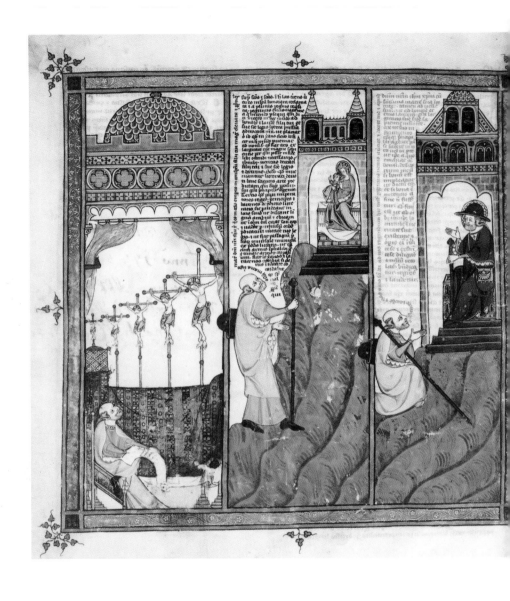

PLATE II.   Llull's visions of Christ and his two pilgrimages.
From *Breviculum*, fol. 1ᵛ.

PLATE III. Llull listening to a sermon and taking the habit.
From *Breviculum*, fol. 2ʳ.

PLATE IV.   Llull's dispute with his Muslim slave.
From *Breviculum,* fol. 3ᵛ.

PLATE V.   The vision of Mt. Randa and Llull teaching in Paris.
From *Breviculum,* fol. 10ʳ.

PLATE VI. Llull's trip to Bougie (1307), where he is stoned and imprisoned. From *Breviculum*, fol. 10[r].

Plate VII.   Llull and le Myésier discussing the latter's compilations.
From *Breviculum*, fol. 11ᵛ.

at that time a lingua franca in much of the western Mediterranean.[7] For a clerical audience he would of course either write directly in Latin or have a Catalan original translated into that language.[8] He also had some works translated into French, Provençal, or Italian. As a result of these translations, and as a result of the fact that many of the works were intended for more than one of the aforementioned audiences, a number of works are extant in more than one language, sometimes even in fairly different versions.

Another aspect of Llull's multiplicity, and that which perhaps has caused most confusion, is the wide variety of subjects and fields of knowledge he wrote about. Here we must keep in mind that when Llull wrote on philosophy, it was not as a philosopher, and when he wrote on science, it was not as a scientist. He was less interested in those subjects for themselves than as tools to further his main purpose, the conversion of unbelievers by means of a method based on the general principles that govern the natural order of the universe. For the sake of explaining this natural order as he understood it, he was forced to make incursions into all the sciences of his day; at the same time, since the principles he propounded were general, it was instructive to show how they applied to the particular sciences. Thus those particular sciences supplied him with both buttresses and display windows for his main system. This is why he wrote treatises on theology, philosophy, logic, and jurisprudence; scientific works (on medicine, astronomy, and geometry); mystical works and pedagogical works; works one could classify as sociological (such as his manual for knighthood),[9] polemical (such as his anti-Averroist tracts of 1309–11), or political (on crusades, missions, social reforms, etc.); and works on such specialized fields as the arts of rhetoric and of memory. Even the few more personal works he wrote are still concerned with this principal, and one could even say only, mission of his life.

A last aspect of Llull's multiplicity is what, for reasons that will become clear in a moment, one is tempted to call diachronic, that is, of his continuous evolution. If the theme which he spent his life

---

[7] Cf. the "Life," p. 7 above. In spite of these divisions of audience, Llull was still the first European to write philosophy and theology in the vernacular—in his case, of course, in Catalan.

[8] See the "Life," n. 39 above for Llull's knowledge of Latin.

[9] The *Book of the Order of Chivalry*.

developing with such an enormous number of variations never varied, the method of presentation did. And since Llull's originality lies precisely in this method, it is of first importance to realize how it developed.

To present this development in very schematic form, mentioning only the works translated here and a few crucial others, one can divide Llull's production as follows:

1. Pre-Art phase, ca. 1272–4, occupying the latter part of the nine years of study, but prior to the vision on Randa and the systematization of the Art. This period includes the various versions of al-Ghazzali's logic, as well as the *Book of Contemplation*.[10]

2. Quaternary phase, ca. 1274–89, from the vision on Randa to the unhappy first teaching experience at Paris. In this period the principles of the Art usually appear in groups of sixteen (hence the name). Algebraic notation is extensively employed and the four elements are used as a basis for analogical reasoning.

This phase may be subdivided into two cycles, which differ in structural details, but are mainly characterized by the grouping of a series of satellite works around a central work of the Art.

a. Cycle of the *Ars compendiosa inveniendi veritatem*, ca. 1274–83, which includes the *Book of the Gentile* and *Blaquerna* (with the *Book of the Lover and the Beloved*).[11]

b. Cycle of the *Ars demonstrativa*, ca. 1283–9, which includes *Felix* (with the *Book of the Beasts*).

3. Ternary phase, 1290–1308. The principles of the Art appear in groups of nine. As a result of the "weakness of human intellect," the number of figures is reduced and the algebraic notation vanishes from the actual discourse of the Art. The elements, too, lose their prime role as an analogical model. Rather than being divisible into cycles, this period shows a more or less continuous line of development from the *Ars inventiva veritatis* of 1290 to the *Ars brevis* and the *Ars generalis ultima* of 1305–8.[12]

4. Post-Art phase, 1308–15. Interest in the mechanization of thought is largely abandoned for concentration on specific logical

---

[10] See the "Life," p. 16 above.

[11] As well as the *Principles of Theology*, *Philosophy*, *Law*, and *Medicine* (this last translated in *SW* II), in addition to the *Doctrina pueril*, and the *Book of the Order of Chivalry* mentioned in n. 9 above.

[12] It also includes the *Tree of Science*, the *Proverbs of Ramon* often cited in the notes to this translation, and the *Flowers of Love and Flowers of Intelligence*, translated in *SW* II.

and philosophical problems. This period includes the Parisian anti-Averroist campaign of 1309–11, at the end of which Llull dictates his "Life."

We have spoken of the originality of the Art. This too has a rational explanation within the context of Llull's missionary aims. Since his purpose was to convert Muslims and Jews, he realized not only that any appeal to authorities was useless,[13] but also that he would have to try to offer some sort of proof for the Christian mysteries such as the Trinity and Incarnation.[14] The former problem had also been recognized by his Dominican predecessors (Penyafort, Aquinas, and Martí), but Llull felt strongly that their lack of success was due to their unwillingness to face up to the latter problem.[15] The attempt to prove the Christian mysteries by any usual means, however, involved the danger of rationalism. Llull was only too aware of this danger,[16] but he sidestepped it, avoiding any confrontation between faith and reason, by basing his arguments on a faith acceptable to all three religions—as well as on other considerations of a nature general enough to be equally acceptable to all three.[17]

The latter considerations were principally psychological (the three powers of the soul),[18] ethical (virtues and vices),[19] and scientific (the four elements and the medieval medical theory based on

[13] Because they just led to arguments over interpretation; see Llull's discussion of the matter in the text corresponding to the *Gentile*, Bk. II, n. 14.

[14] See the "Life," §26–7, and n. 84.

[15] In *seven* places in his works (the problem was clearly not unimportant to Llull) he tells the probably true story of the missionary (identifiable as Ramon Martí) bringing on himself the ire of the sultan of Tunis by dissuading him of the truth of Islam, but then being unable to persuade him of—or rather to prove to him—the truth of Christianity. For the specific setting of this story, as well as Llull's relations to Penyafort, Aquinas, and Martí in general, see the introduction to the *Gentile*.

[16] He discussed the problem of faith vs. reason in many works. An entire section (Dist. 36, chs. 238–54) of the *Book of Contemplation* is devoted to the subject, and later on he wrote two works, the *Disputatio fidei et intellectus* and the *Liber de convenientia fidei et intellectus in objecto*, specifically on this topic. See also versicle 198 of the *Book of the Lover and the Beloved* cited in the introduction to that work, p. 183.

[17] In this he was helped not only by the common Semitic origin of the three religions, but also by their having undergone the same Greek (i.e., Aristotelian and Neoplatonic) influences during the Middle Ages. This is the common ground of faith that occupies Bk. I of the *Gentile*.

[18] That is, memory, intellect, and will, the *acts* of which form Figure S; see Table 2 in the introduction to the *Gentile*. See also the introduction to the *Book of the Lover and the Beloved* for their importance in that work.

[19] See the *Gentile*, Tree 4 (as well as 2 and 5), and Figure V in Table 2 mentioned in the previous note.

them), in addition to many lesser bits and pieces of the Aristotelian world view common to the classical and medieval worlds.

Much more important and characteristic were the generally acceptable premises permitting Llull to base his arguments on a common faith. No Muslim or Jew, for instance, could disagree that God is one, that He is the first cause of all things, that He is good, great, eternal, and so forth. It was these latter divine attributes that Llull made into one of the cornerstones of his system. He called them properties, virtues, reasons (*rationes*), perfections, or, most often, dignities.[20] In the *Ars brevis* the list includes Goodness, Greatness, Eternity, Power, Wisdom, Will, Virtue, Truth, and Glory.[21] Then Llull made a series of affirmations about these dignities: they are not only concordant, but convertible with one another, involving no plurality in God's substance. Moreover, they are real; one scholar speaks of the archetypal, Platonic nature of Llull's universe and stresses his extreme realism, citing a passage where Llull uses the dignities to show that the universals really exist outside the soul.[22] Nor are these dignities "otiose," as Llull phrases it; they are active not only within God's essence (*ad intra*), but also in the created world (*ad extra*). Then midway through the cycle of the *Ars demonstrativa*, this gave rise to the doctrine of the threefold correlatives of action.[23] Soon, this doctrine also became applied to the created

[20] In addition to the usual meaning of the word, *dignitas* was also the common scholastic translation of the Greek *axioma*, and it may be that Llull chose the word because of this double meaning.

[21] See *Ars brevis*, Part I. This is the nine-version of the dignities found in the ternary phase of the Art. They form Figure A of the Art, under which, in Table 2 to the introduction to the *Gentile*, the reader will find the sixteen-version characteristic of the quaternary phase of the Art. For a long time there was considerable polemic as to whether these dignities were of Christian, Muslim, or Jewish origin. Nowadays, with less passion and more common sense, it can be seen that they correspond to a concept of the Names of God common to all three religions, stemming ultimately from the Old Testament and reinforced by early Neoplatonism. In Christianity they represent a tradition going back through Scotus Erigena to Pseudo-Dionysius and St. Augustine; in Islam they correspond to the *hadras*, and in Judaism to the *sefirot*. This does not mean, of course, that they have the same function in Llull as they have in Islam or Judaism.

[22] J.-H. Probst, *Caractère et origine des idées du Bienheureux Raymond Lulle* (Toulouse, 1912), p. 83, citing the *Quaestiones per Artem demonstrativam seu inventivam solubiles, MOG* iv, 113 = Int. iii, 97, where Llull shows that the five predicables (genus, species, difference, property, and accident) and the ten predicaments (substance, quantity, quality, etc.) are real. The later *Liber de quinque praedicabilibus et decem praedicamentis* is entirely devoted to proving the same thesis.

[23] For which see the "Life," n. 83, above.

world, which, having been fashioned in God's image, must also have, at each rung of its ladder, a similar -*tivum*, -*bile*, and -*are*. This active structure of being became the salient characteristic of Llull's metaphysics; such a total dynamic ontology was unknown in any other medieval thinker.

Moreover, creation was thus conceived as a similitude or likeness of the divine perfections. Or as Nicholas of Cusa put it, "The first foundation of the Art is that everything God created and made, He created and made in the likeness of His dignities." And just as for medieval man the world was a book in which one can learn about God, or a mirror in which one can see His image, for Llull the problem was accordingly reduced to one of finding the "signs which created beings give of his beloved."[24]

Or to put it another way, given Llull's realism and the exemplarist structure of his universe, the problem was one of adapting his arguments to this structure, to make the *modus intelligendi* conform as closely as possible to the *modus essendi*, so as to make evident ("to manifest," "to reveal" are, with Llull, usual synonyms of "to demonstrate") any particular truth. As Frances Yates has put it, Llull's was an "Art of thinking which was infallible in all spheres because based on the actual structure of reality, a logic which followed the true patterns of the universe."[25] It was a system based on the notion coming from Saint Augustine and running through Anselm and Bonaventure: *ordo et connexio idearum est ordo et connexio rerum.*

Now on this very broad base, it was Llull's idea to show that the Christian mysteries were part of the very structure of this universe, which would therefore be incomplete or imperfect without them. The arguments he used to "demonstrate" this relationship he called "necessary reasons." Taken by themselves they are, as many critics have pointed out, merely arguments of congruence; seen in proper perspective, however, they are the tip of an iceberg, the pinnacle of the vast ontological and analogical structure of the Art. And if we are to understand the Art, we must realize that, as Llull himself was careful to point out, it is neither logic nor metaphysics.[26] The best

[24] See the *Book of the Lover and the Beloved*, v. 57 (as well as v. 40).
[25] Yates, "Art," p. 117, as well as pp. 159 and 165 (pp. 12, 58, and 66 of her *Lull & Bruno*). See also the remarkable quotation from the *Proverbs of Ramon*, p. 55 below.
[26] See the discussion in the *Ars brevis*, Part x, n. 40.

clue to its nature may be found in the word *art* itself, which was the usual scholastic translation of the Greek τέχνη. It was thus a technique; it was not a body of doctrine, but a system.[27] Or to put it in contemporary terms, it was a structure. The very idea of showing that the system of the universe would be incomplete without the Christian mysteries is what nowadays we would call structuralist. So is the way in which Llull approaches philosophy or theology. He scarcely ever discusses a concept by itself, in the manner of Aristotle, Aquinas, or Scotus, presenting different sides of the question or what predecessors have said about it, and so on. Instead, he either presents it immediately as part of a cluster of concepts, its importance deriving from the place it occupies in a given gamut or from its relation to its limiting concepts; or he presents it in terms of how it functions. Above all, as I have already said, Llull presents us with a totally structured universe, the *modus essendi*, over which he lays another structure, that of the *modus intelligendi* deriving from and intimately related to the first.[28]

But these two *modi* do not actually constitute the Art; they are only its substructure. The Art's relation to these *modi* is threefold: (1) it specifies their foundation, (2) it uses them as a basis for a *modus operandi*, by which (3) it "finds" or "demonstrates" the truth—what one might call the *modus probandi*. As Llull phrases it: "The *matter* consists of the figures and terms of the Art itself. The *form* is to be found in the descent from a given universal to particulars, which descent consists in the ordered discourse of the acts of the soul by means of the mixture of the triangles of Figure T in the remaining terms of the figures. Through their ordered mixture the desired result is achieved, which is the necessary affirmation of the truth or negation of falsehood. This is what we declare to be the *purpose* of this Art."[29]

---

[27] The word *ars* normally referred to the manner of exposition or the technique of a science.

[28] The resulting edifice resembles a Gothic cathedral in its immensity, intricacy of design, and interrelation of parts. The reader can get a small taste of this in the *Ars brevis*, and a fuller one by studying the astounding web of interconnections among divisions and subdivisions of his most extended nontechnical presentation of the system in the *Tree of Science* (this can be done simply by making a schematic chart of the table of contents of the editions in *ORL* xi–xiii or *OE* i).

[29] *Lectura super figuras Artis demonstrativae*, Prologue, *MOG* iii, 205–6 = Int. iv, 1–2. He begins by saying that "like other sciences, the Art has a quadruple cause, to wit, its author, form, matter, and purpose. The author could be said to be God, to whose magnificence the

As for the *modus probandi*, a brief explanation of Llull's methods of proof or demonstration might be helpful. In the first place he used what Gilson, in connection with Saint Bonaventure, has called the "logic of analogy."[30] Sometimes it was comparative, sometimes it was, as Frances Yates has said, "a diagram of proportions having analogies with other proportions."[31] This is true especially concerning the operation of the elements when used as "metaphors" for the thing to be demonstrated.[32]

Closely allied with the analogical nature of Llull's reasoning is its ontological character. Taking the idea of evil as a privation, he fits this originally Neoplatonic notion into a scheme of concordance between goodness, truth, affirmation, and being on the one hand, and between evil, falsehood, negation, and nonbeing (or privation) on the other. Since the culmination of the ladder of being is God, it is but a small step to having the first series accord with perfection, "greater nobility," and merit, and the second with imperfection (or defect), "lesser nobility," and blame.[33] These then are used as criteria against which his analogical arguments are measured,[34] thus closing the gap between the *modus essendi* and the *modus intelligendi*,

---

Art is dedicated, while its immediate author is of no importance, since he is vile and sinful." The four causes correspond to the four Aristotelian causes: efficient, formal, material, and final. The phrase "acts of the soul" in the text refers to the components of Figure S (cf. n. 18 above). For Figure T, see Table 2 in the introduction to the *Gentile*, and *Ars brevis*, Part II, Section 2.

[30] Étienne Gilson, *La philosophie de Saint Bonaventure* (Paris, 1953), p. 184, in the chapter on *L'analogie universelle*, which is important for an understanding of this mode of thought. See also the interesting remarks of I. M. Bocheński in his *History of Formal Logic* (New York, 1970), p. 179, where he points out the relationship between medieval analogical reasoning and the concept of isomorphy in modern algebra, as well as the necessarily structural nature of this approach.

[31] Yates, "Art," p. 165 (*Lull & Bruno*, p. 66). The instrument used to carry out this comparative and analogical logic was Figure T (see Table 2 in the introduction to the *Gentile*).

[32] For Llull's specifically elemental exemplarism, the fundamental text is Yates, "Art," pp. 151–5 (*Lull & Bruno*, pp. 50–55). In the works presented here it plays almost no role, but in the larger anthology it is important in the *Ars demonstrativa* and the *Principles of Medicine*. See *SW* I, 67, n. 63 for references. It should also be noted that these analogical methods are largely abandoned in the ternary phase of the Art.

[33] Notice that the concepts of Being–Nonbeing, Perfection–Imperfection, Merit–Blame belong to Figure X; see Table 2 in the introduction to the *Gentile*.

[34] Another related technique is that of demonstration by degrees of comparison, in which Llull establishes an analogy between the positive, comparative, and superlative degrees of adjectives and the sensible, intelligible, and divine worlds on the one hand, and with the three proofs of *quia*, *propter quid*, and *per aequiparantiam* on the other hand. Often Llull uses the superlative degree alone (the *via eminentiae*), a technique the reader will find much used in the *Gentile*, and which took on great importance in the post-Art phase.

and permitting one author to refer to the Art as a "calculus of being,"[35] and another to describe it as "onto-theo-logical."[36]

The final point to be discussed in relation to the Art is the applications or uses for which it was intended. In the *Compendium artis demonstrativae*, he gives five of primary importance, which he divides into three of a more theological nature and two of a more scientific nature:[37]

1. "To understand and love God." In the *Ars demonstrativa* the sixteen "modes" are *preceded* by the statement that the primary aim of the Art is to know and love God. It is also the principal theme of *Felix*, and in general it is a topic on which Llull never tires of dwelling.[38]

2. "To be attached to virtues and to hate vices." This state is achieved by what Llull calls "accustoming," and it is the means of arriving at the knowledge and love of God. It is a process which checks passions or evil desires through the virtues of *temperance* (or *prudence*) until *fortitude* can take over, allowing *justice* to like truth and dislike falsehood. At the same time it is the only way to carry out one's duty in *being* man (note again the analogy between virtue and being, as opposed to vice and nonbeing). Lastly, it is by using the Art to love virtues and hate vices that permits one to dispel doubt in view of action.

3. "To confound the erroneous opinions of unbelievers by means of cogent reasons." This was the raison d'être of the Art. In another work he expanded on the theme, saying that "the subject of

[35] Mark D. Johnston, *The Semblance of Significance: Language and Exemplarism in the "Art" of Ramon Llull* (Ph.D. diss., Johns Hopkins University, 1978), p. 229: "Llull's own program served to reformulate the conventional elements of logic as a symbolic calculus of being . . . achieved . . . through the pervasive realism of his metaphysics."

[36] Eusebi Colomer, *De la Edad Media al Renacimiento: Ramón Llull–Nicolás de Cusa–Juan Pico della Mirandola* (Barcelona: Herder, 1975), p. 57: "Few medieval systems have come as near as Llull's to the Platonic and Hegelian ideal of a logic that is at the same time an ontology. And it could not be otherwise, since the order of being and of thought meet in God, in whose infinite thought reality is precontained in the idea. As a result the onto-logical nature of Llull's thought is essentially theo-logical, with which it fully achieves that onto-theo-logical structure which has rightly been indicated as characteristic of metaphysics."

[37] *MOG* III, 293 = Int. vi, 1. In Dist. III of the *Ars demonstrativa* this topic is discussed exhaustively, with the presentation of sixteen "modes" or areas in which it can be used; cf. *SW* I, 415ff.

[38] It is, for instance, the principal goal of all the conditions of the trees of the *Gentile* (see the Prologue, p. 89). In the beginning of *Felix* Llull even states that God "created this world and with great nobility and goodness gave it to men so that He would be much loved and known by them," (*SW* II, 659).

this Art primarily consists in demonstrating the truth of the holy Catholic faith through the use of necessary reasons to those who are ignorant of it, as well as reassuring those who already know and believe it, removing the doubts people might have concerning it, and confounding the errors of the infidels who despise it and busily do what they can to destroy it."[39] Notice the use of the phrase "necessary reasons" precisely in this context; Llull tends to use this term, which we have met before and will meet again many times, only in connection with proving the articles of faith.[40] Notice, too, how this application of the Art entails a variety of activities. In the *Ars demonstrativa* it appears under two headings, those of "Guiding" and of "Disputing."[41] The first is more or less the general heading for all the various facets of this application of the Art; the second is the specific method to be used for "confounding the errors of the infidels." Lest it be thought the latter method ever departs far from the structured, exemplarist Lullian universe, I offer the following statement from the *Proverbs of Ramon*: "Disputation requires an artificial order which is the image of the natural order of the powers of the body and of the soul."[42]

4. "To formulate and solve questions."[43] This is a constant of the Art, almost no work of which is without its final section giving questions (and answers) based on the subjects treated. Because of its generality, this aspect is closely connected with the next.

5. "To be able to acquire other sciences in a brief space of time and to bring them to their necessary conclusions according to the requirements of the material." As Paolo Rossi put it, this made the Art a "science of sciences," offering "a key to the exact and rational ordering of all knowledge, whose various aspects are comprised in and verified by it."[44]

These are, of course, tremendous claims. They did not, however, seem exaggerated to many in the generations that followed Llull—

---

[39] *Lectura super Artem inventivam et Tabulam generalem, MOG* v, 359–60 = Int. v, 1–2.

[40] There are exceptions, but they are rare.

[41] *SW* i, 425 and 433 respectively.

[42] Ch. 248, no. 2.

[43] *Ars compendiosa inveniendi veritatem, MOG* i, 433 = Int. vii, 1, and *Lectura Artis quae intitulatur Brevis practica Tabulae generalis, MOG* v, 301 = Int. iii, 1. See *Ars demonstrativa, SW* i, 430, on "Solving" for more details.

[44] Rossi, "Legacy," p. 185. See also Pring-Mill, "The Trinitarian World Picture," p. 233. (See the Suggestions for Further Reading for full bibliographic details.)

as we will see in the next section. It was only with the more empirical outlook which followed Galileo and Newton that they began to seem ungrounded. In our own age, with its reduced hostility to aprioristic modes of thought, with its greater interest in the philosophy of the Renaissance when Llull was a figure of such importance, with its interest in alternate forms of logic, with its search back to Leibniz and beyond for the roots of symbolic logic and computer science, the Lullian Art can be seen as a fascinating and even unique facet of man's attempt to explain the world about him and to order the pathways of his own processes of thought.

Llull's Influence: The History of Lullism

ALTHOUGH the point of this anthology is to present the Llull of his own time, as opposed to the often different personage later generations chose to see in him, the reader would all the same get a distorted picture if the force that Lullism represented in European thought from Nicholas of Cusa in the mid-fifteenth century to Leibniz in the mid-seventeenth were not even mentioned. Given, however, the extent and complication of such a history, all I will be able to do is just that—mention it, offer a bare indication of the leading threads.

Before going into Lullism proper, however, two questions should be cleared up. The first is the battle over Llull's orthodoxy, with his detractors accusing him of heresy and his followers trying to have him canonized. The second is the large amount of apocryphal literature, mainly on alchemy and the Cabala, that became attached to his name.

Questions of Orthodoxy

Goaded by the excesses of a group of Valencian Lullists influenced by many of the ideas of the Franciscan Spirituals, the Dominican inquisitor general of Aragon, Nicholas Eymerich (1320–99), began a campaign against the doctrines of Ramon Llull, and primarily against his supposed rationalism. The campaign culminated in 1376 with two events: The first was the publication in January of the *Directorium inquisitorum*, his notorious manual on inquisitorial methods, destined to become what might be called the standard work in the field. Among other things, it contained a list of a hundred errors of Ramon Llull, which was to become the standard list in *that* field. In the meantime a papal commission had been formed to look into Eymerich's accusations, and very shortly after his book appeared, that is, on February 6, a papal bull was promul-

gated censuring Llull and condemning twenty of his books.[1] This
aroused considerable anger at all levels of Catalan society, and the
king had Eymerich exiled. Even though Eymerich kept up his campaign from Avignon, Llull's followers began a campaign of re-
habilitation that was finally won in 1416, with the promulgation
by the Papal Court of what has become known as the "definitive
sentence," invalidating the bull of forty years earlier.

The second condemnation of Lullist doctrines came from an almost equally authoritative source—the Faculty of Theology of the
University of Paris. In 1390—the same year that Pierre d'Ailly became chancellor of the University—his pupil Jean Gerson (1363–
1429) caused the Faculty of Theology to publish an edict prohibit-
ing the teaching of Lullist doctrines. This was a result of various
circumstances, such as the new and extreme nominalism being
promulgated in Paris, the association of Llull's ideas with the mysticism of Jan van Ruysbroeck (which Gerson opposed), a distaste for
Llull's frequently involuted language, and the opposition (like that
of Eymerich) to Llull's supposed rationalism.

The damage these two condemnations did was enormous. The
second not only cut off what must have been a considerable interest
in Llull in Paris, but forced serious thinkers concerned with his
doctrines (Sibiuda, van den Velde, Nicholas of Cusa) to disguise
this fact in their published writings. The damage the first did was
perhaps even longer-lasting. Later Lullists were indeed able to show
that of Eymerich's hundred propositions, some were gratuitously
attributed to Llull, some were the result of an alteration of the
original text (Eymerich was a master of the out-of-context quote),
many were inoffensive, and the rest could be interpreted as being in
agreement with dogma. But in spite of the "definitive sentence,"
there lingered the feeling of something suspiciously heterodox
about Llull's doctrines. And all his enemies had to do in later years
to block attempts at canonization was to republish Eymerich's
work, thereby effectively bogging down the proponents in the
quagmire of a laborious defense. Veneration of Llull was, however,

---

[1] Part of the battle over Llull's orthodoxy has centered on the authenticity of this bull. His
partisans have always claimed it was a forgery, and it has certainly never been found among
the papal registers. Others, however, have upheld its validity on the ground that the Roman
Curia has always maintained its legitimacy, without which the "definitive sentence" of 1416
would make no sense.

permitted within the Franciscan Order and locally in Majorca by decree of Leo X (early sixteenth century), Clement XIII (1763), and Pius IX (1847); his feast day was set on 3 July.

Llull as Alchemist and Cabalist

The history of Lullian alchemy is just beginning to be written.[2] It seems to have begun in 1332, only sixteen years after Llull's death, with the appearance of the *Testamentum*, seemingly written by a Catalan living in London. This work, although using elements of Llull's thought and Art, does not pretend to have been written by him. The first work to do so was the *Liber de secretis naturae*, written towards the end of the century. This second work not only cites the first, but even cites those passages of genuine works in which Llull condemned alchemy, explaining that if the reader takes them at their face value, he hasn't understood their *real* meaning. Then towards the beginning of the fifteenth century legends of Llull the alchemist begin to appear. One simply states that, through the mediation of an English king Robert,[3] Llull learned the art of distillation from Arnold of Vilanova. Another states that, on the invitation of Abbot Cremer, he came to London (note the continued connections with England) to transform base metals into gold for Edward III, on the condition that the profits would be used to finance a crusade to the Holy Land. Seeing that the king was not carrying out his part of the bargain, Llull protested and was thrown in jail, or according to another version simply left England without revealing his secret. At about the same time these legends started circulating, the trickle of pseudo-Lullian alchemical works became a river so large that in the end a hundred or so works would be attributed to him. During the Renaissance and Baroque periods, the printed editions of pseudo-Lullian alchemical works considerably outnumbered those of genuine works. Indeed there must have been many circles in sixteenth- and seventeenth-century Europe where

[2] Almost single-handedly by the Italian scholar, Michela Pereira, whose *The Alchemical Corpus Attributed to Raymond Lull*, Warburg Institute Surveys and Texts 18 (London, 1989), sums up and lists her previous writings on the topic. Also much recommended for the way it sets Llull in the general history of alchemy is F. Sherwood Taylor, *The Alchemists* (London, 1952).

[3] Who never existed, but there is a possibility of confusion with Robert of Anjou, King of Naples.

the legendary Llull had thoroughly displaced the real Llull, or where the two at least lived side by side. Such, for instance, was the case of his great eighteenth-century editor, Ivo Salzinger, who was a "believer."[4]

The history of Llull the Cabalist is quite different and rests on a single work, the *De auditu cabbalistico*. Modern scholarship has shown that this work, which has long been recognized as spurious, was written by an Italian doctor and scholar, Pietro Mainardi (1456–1529) from Verona, who taught in Ferrara and in Padua. His point of departure seems to have been an attempt to carry out Pico della Mirandola's ideal of harmonizing the Lullian Art with the Cabala.[5] In any case, it was subsequently printed as a work of Llull, and as such it was given fame by Giordano Bruno and then printed in the famous Zetzner anthologies of Llull's works.[6] It was thus a more serious work, which received the consideration of important Renaissance figures who were also interested in the genuine Llull.

But before leaving this topic, the reader should be warned against separating too starkly the history of Lullism into the genuine and the spurious. Not only was the *De auditu cabbalistico* printed as a genuine work in Zetzner's enormously influential anthology, but Zetzner himself was also, in these same years, one of the principal European editors of alchemical literature, including, of course, that going under Llull's name. Secondly, intellectuals of the sixteenth and seventeenth centuries did not make our neat divisions between philosophy, "real" science, and the "occult" sciences. To give just a few examples, Copernicus, Tycho Brahe, Kepler, and Galileo were practicing astrologers; Leibniz was by no means uninterested in alchemy, and Newton was a practitioner of it; finally, many of the great thinkers of the time were devotees of hermeticism or Cabalism. Thirdly, within the history of alchemy, the pseudo-Lullian works are the most rational, having "very little in them which is allegorical or deliberately obscure. The picturesque array of green

---

[4] For Salzinger, see p. 69 below. Like all legends, that of Llull the alchemist dies hard, and one still finds works that trundle it out. But as Michela Pereira says at the beginning of the work cited in n. 2 above, "None of the alchemical writings traditionally attributed to Lull can now be plausibly ascribed to him. After the research done by nineteenth-century scholars . . . there is no longer any question of the works being authentic."

[5] In addition to trying to harmonize the arch–anti-Averroist, Ramon Llull, with the Averroism that Mainardi himself had imbibed in Padua!

[6] See p. 67 below.

lions and tail-eating dragons, the red man and his white wife, the king and queen, the gold and silver trees play in them but the smallest part."[7] Lastly, much of this pseudo-Lullian literature in fact used elements from his philosophy of nature and from his Art, which might, through this circuitous route, have influenced science, especially early chemistry.

Lullism Proper

The history of Lullism begins with a man who was not only a disciple of Llull's but also perhaps one of the most remarkable, tireless, and faithful transmitters of his doctrines. This was a canon of Arras, doctor in medicine and "socius" of the Sorbonne, Thomas le Myésier (d. 1336), whom we have already met in connection with the "Life."[8] His major contribution to Lullism consisted in compiling an anthology of Llull's thought and works that he called the *Electorium*, and this in four versions: a *magnum*, a *medium*, a *parvum*, and a *minimum*, of which the second and fourth are now lost.[9] The first, always referred to simply as the *Electorium*, is a huge manuscript now in the Bibliothèque Nationale in Paris.[10] The third, known as the *Breviculum*, roughly the same format but one-tenth the length, and now in the Badische Landesbibliothek in Karlsruhe, is justly famous for its magnificent series of twelve miniatures depicting various episodes from Llull's life.[11] Le Myésier's minor contribution to Lullism consisted in bequeathing his collection of Llull's manuscripts to the Sorbonne, thereby making a second cen-

---

[7] Taylor, *The Alchemists*, p. 94. The altered section here (altered with respect to *SW* I, 75) is a result of a new orientation which I tried to work out in "El lul·lisme alquímic i cabalístic i les edicions de Llàtzer Zetzner," *Randa* 27 (1990): 99–117. For Newton's interest in Lullian alchemy, see n. 36 below.

[8] See the "Life," p. 10 above.

[9] In the last miniature of the *Breviculum* (see Hillgarth, *Ramon Lull*, pl. XII) only the first three are shown, but the existence of four is attested by a marginal note in le Myésier's hand in the largest anthology.

[10] Ms. lat. 15450. It measures 363 × 280 mm. and has almost 500 folios (it originally had at least 560). For a detailed description, the reader should consult Hillgarth's *Ramon Lull*, pp. 348–97, and for a slightly briefer description (based on notes of Hillgarth) *ROL* v, 216–30.

[11] St. Peter, perg. 92. It measures 345 × 277 mm. and contains 44 folios (it originally had at least 61). It has recently been published in a magnificent facsimile edition, *Raimundus Lullus—Thomas Le Myésier, Electorium parvum seu Breviculum. Handschrift St. Peter perg. 92 der Badischen LB*, ed. Gerhard Stamm et al. (Wiesbaden, 1988), and completely transcribed in *ROL, Supplementi Lulliani* I. Seven of its miniatures are reproduced here.

ter, along with the Chartreuse of Vauvert, where students and copyists could work in later times.

We know something of the activities of a few other disciples in Paris,[12] and a few in Valencia in the 1330s,[13] but otherwise the history of Lullism during the fourteenth century is still largely unexplored. We know that Llull's doctrines must have continued to be taught in Paris, for otherwise Gerson would not have bothered to have them suppressed in 1390. They must also have been studied and taught elsewhere, since a great number of works were copied and translated into other languages. But to date this has only given us a few isolated names and unrelated bits of information.

In the fifteenth century, the increasing number of Llull's adherents are divisible into two currents of development. The first was centered in Catalonia, Majorca, and Italy, and involved figures relatively unknown in the general history of European thought, but who were important as teachers and propagators of Llull's thought or printers of his works. The instigators of this movement were the Lullian schools of Barcelona and Majorca. After their first contacts with Padua and Venice in the 1430s, the period of their greatest importance and influence began in the 1480s. It was then that Pere Daguí (or de Gui), chaplain to Ferdinand and Isabella, was teaching in Majorca; that his writings, and especially his *Janua artis magistri Raymundi Lulli*, which was to play such a role in the diffusion of Lullism, were printed;[14] and above all, that the works of Llull himself were first printed.[15]

The second current of development, in France, Germany, and also Italy, involved leading figures in the history of European

---

[12] Or rather one other disciple, Pierre de Limoges, who in addition to being a doctor of medicine like le Myésier, was also an astronomer. Also like le Myésier, he left his library to the Sorbonne, including five Lullian codices now in the Bibliothèque Nationale in Paris, which are among the earliest preserved, having been copied in Paris probably in the late 1280s. It was probably then—during Llull's first visit there—that the two were in contact, as opposed to the last two visits, when Llull's chief local disciple seems to have become le Myésier.

[13] This is the group which, in addition to turning out works falsely attributed to Llull, caught the eye of the Inquisitor Eymerich (see above under "Questions of Orthodoxy").

[14] It was printed in Barcelona 1482, Rome 1485, Barcelona 1488, and Seville 1491. Two other works of his were also printed in these same years in Barcelona and Seville.

[15] They are the *Ars generalis ultima*, Venice 1480; the *Ars brevis*, Barcelona 1481, Rome 1485, and Barcelona 1489; the *Tree of Science*, Barcelona 1482; and the spurious *Logica brevis et nova*, Venice 1480. These works by Daguí and Llull (genuine and apocryphal) make up the first fifteen numbers of the standard catalogue of early printed editions (by Rogent i Duràn; see p. 366 below), and thus constitute the works by which the Art was first divulged.

thought. Although men like Sibiuda, van den Velde, and Nicholas of Cusa were certainly influenced by Lullist doctrines or employed them in varying degrees in their own works, they rarely cited their source by name, often for fear of censure in the wake of Eymerich and Gerson. The earliest of these figures was the Catalan Ramon Sibiuda (?–1436) who studied and then taught at the University of Toulouse.[16] His *Liber creaturarum* (also called *Theologia naturalis*) was translated and commented on by Montaigne, and even influenced Pascal. Its encyclopedic aims, its realist and exemplarist metaphysics, and its proselytizing goal were of clear Lullian filiation.

The most important fifteenth-century figure to be influenced by Llull was Nicholas of Cusa (1401–64). Even though he seldom mentioned Llull in his writings, the large collection of Lullian works he copied, collected, and annotated is still intact at the hospital he founded in his native Kues. Many aspects of Llull's thought entered his philosophy and theology: the doctrine of the divine dignities, their mutual convertibility and their unfolding into the correlative triad, the creation as an image of the Creator, and the Incarnation as the object and final crowning of the creation. No other thinker influenced Cusanus as much, and it can probably be said that no other later thinker understood Llull so well.[17]

We mustn't leave Cusanus without mentioning his teacher at Cologne, the Fleming Heimeric van den Velde (ca. 1390–1460). Master and pupil seem to have stimulated each other's interest in the Majorcan thinker, and even though they shared an interest in the correlative doctrine, van den Velde was more influenced by the Art with its principles and rules. And even there it was more part of a general eclecticism on his part than a basic shaping element on the thought of a major figure, as was the case with his pupil.[18]

The other two figures usually cited as belonging to this second current of development are Bessarion (ca. 1403–72) and Pico della Mirandola (1463–94), but here the evidence merely shows that they

---

[16] His name was also written Sebonde and de Sabunde, along with eleven other variants!

[17] This paragraph has been revised in accord with Eusebi Colomer, "Nicolau de Cusa i el lul·lisme europeu quatrecentista," *Randa* 27 (1990): 71–85, where the reader will find all the bibliography on the subject since the corresponding paragraph of *SW* I, 78. See also the article by T. Pindl-Büchel in the same issue of *Randa*: 87–98.

[18] For van den Velde and a detailed exposition of the much discussed subject of who influenced whom between teacher and pupil and, above all, where Cusanus first became interested in Llull, see the Colomer article cited in the previous note.

were familiar with and, in the case of Pico, interested in Llull's Art.[19]

Toward the end of the century, however, Lullism takes on a completely different aspect: it leaves off the fitful, semiclandestine air it had before then, and assumes the role of first importance in European thought that it was to maintain until the seventeenth century. The first center from which this new influence spread out was Paris, and its first major representative was the humanist theologian Jacques Lefèvre d'Étaples (ca. 1455–1536). Lefèvre was familiar with Ramon Sibiuda and Nicholas of Cusa, so it was perhaps natural that he should have become fascinated with Llull; but, through his reputation, his extraordinary energy, his influential circle of pupils and above all his publications of Lullian works,[20] Lefèvre did more than any other person for the resurgence of Lullist studies. His interest in the Majorcan was chiefly in the mystical, ascetic, and moral side of his works, whereas that of his friend and best-known pupil, Charles de Bovelles (1479–1553), was more in Llull's metaphysics and rational theology. In addition to propagating Lullian doctrines in his own works, Bovelles was the first to publish a "Life" of Llull and to be in contact with Spanish humanist circles where Llull was then much in fashion.

This Spanish movement seems to have had its origin in the Majorcan school of Pere Daguí mentioned above. His pupil Jaume Janer was important, not only for his own writings, but also as founder of the Lullian school of Valencia, where he was the teacher of the humanist Alonso de Proaza. The best known of all the Majorcans of this period, however, was Nicholas de Pax. Both he and Proaza were in contact with Cardinal Jiménez de Cisneros (1436–1517), archbishop of Toledo and finally regent of Castile. Cisneros was himself an ardent Lullist, and in the University of Alcalá de

[19] Bessarion's Lullism is deduced from his close friendship with Nicholas of Cusa and from an anecdote concerning a hunting party, on which he is said to have asked where a hare had gone, only to have his host answer, "Apply the rule of C D K of the *Ars magna* and you will find the hare." This is, of course, the reply to the question of *Where?* in the *Ars brevis*, Part IV, Rule I. Note that such a joke would have been pointless unless the host had known the guest to have had a certain familiarity with the Art. As for Pico della Mirandola, he owned one or two copies of the *Ars brevis* and/or *Ars generalis ultima*, and he was interested in discovering a combinatorial method that would partake of both the Cabala and the *Ars Raymundi*.

[20] The Latin versions or new Latin translations of the *Libre de Sancta Maria*, the *Libre de clerecia*, the *Phantasticus*, the *Liber natalis pueri parvuli Christi Jesu*, the first two books of the *Book of Contemplation*, the *Book of the Lover and the Beloved*, the *Proverbs of Ramon*, and the *Tree of the Philosophy of Love*.

Henares, which he founded in 1508, he instituted a chair of Lullian philosophy and theology, whose first incumbent was Nicholas de Pax. Through Bovelles, who was a friend of the cardinal and corresponded with Nicholas de Pax, this group was in contact with the Parisian Lullist group.

But the most important contact between the two groups came from the Franciscan Bernard de Lavinheta (d. ca. 1530). This Basque from Béarn had studied in Toulouse and taught in Salamanca before coming to Paris.[21] At the University there he was the first, as a trained theologian, to teach the Art, thereby giving it the official sanction it had lacked for a century and a half. His publication of Lullian works at Lyon, Paris, and Cologne in 1514–18 was very influential throughout Europe.[22] His own *Explanatio compendiosaque applicatio artis Raymundi Lulli*, first published at Lyon in 1523, was enormously important, because its mixture of interest in the Art with encyclopedism, alchemy, and artificial memory was to become characteristic of the Lullism of this and the following century.[23] All it lacked was a treatment of Llull's system as an art of discourse, which was supplied by one of his pupils in a work called *In rhetoricam isagoge*, published in 1515.[24]

It was this now completed mixture that appealed to the first German commentator of the Art, Heinrich Cornelius Agrippa von Nettesheim (1486–1535). In his *In Artem brevem Raymundi Lulli commentaria*, written apparently in his youth but not printed till 1531 at Cologne, he presented the Lullian Art, to use Johnston's phrase, as "a pan-sophistic art of discourse."[25] Now the curious thing is that

[21] For new information on, and assessment of, this figure, see Michela Pereira, "Bernardo Lavinheta e la diffusione del lullismo a Parigi nei primi anni del' 500," *Interpres. Revista di Studi Quattrocenteschi* 5 (Roma, 1983–4), pp. 242–65.

[22] Of the sixteen works listed in Rogent i Duràn as published between December 1514 and April 1518 (nos. 52–68, discounting the doubtful no. 64), ten were edited by Lavinheta and one (no. 57) by a pupil of his.

[23] Lavinheta's work was reedited in Cologne in 1612 by Lazarus Zetzner (for whom p. 67 below), and in our day by E.-W. Platzeck (Hildesheim, 1975).

[24] The author was a certain Remigius Rufus Candidus of Aquitaine (if this was not a pseudonym). The work was printed under Llull's name, and as such it found its way into the Zetzner edition (see n. 31 below).

[25] See the thesis cited in "Llull's Thought," n. 35. Agrippa's commentary on the *Ars brevis* was perhaps the most widely read work in the history of Lullism; it was printed seventeen times between 1531 and 1651. When he wrote it, his enthusiasm for Llull was boundless, affirming that "the Art contains nothing trivial, it does not deal with specific objects; precisely for this reason it is to be regarded as the queen of all arts, an easy and sure guide to all sciences and all doctrines . . . Aided only by this Art, men will be able, without being required to possess any other knowledge, to eliminate all possibility of error and to find *de omni re scibili veritatem et scientiam.*"

this reduction of the Art to a rhetorical and dialectical formalism, to which Agrippa had given the finishing touches, was precisely what he himself criticized in his later *De incertitudine et vanitate scientiarum* (Cologne, 1530). There he said it was a method based on a few tricks for permitting somebody to talk on any subject and to get the best of his rivals; it was more for showing off one's cleverness and for ostentation of learning than for the acquisition of knowledge. In short, he has nothing but sneers for what he calls "loquacious Lullists," a species he himself had helped to invent.[26]

After this outburst of Lullist activity in the first three decades of the sixteenth century, there is a peculiar gap of some fifty years taken up largely by an editorial deluge of pseudo-Lullian alchemical works.[27] Then in the 1580s there is a strong resurgence of Lullism, this time in two well-defined centers.

The first involved the court of Philip II of Spain, who was himself an admirer of Llull. Not only were scholars at the court charged with collecting works of Llull, with drawing up catalogues, and with defending the cause of Llull's orthodoxy with the Papal Court, but one even finds that Pedro de Guevara, tutor of two of the Infantas, was himself an ardent Lullist who wrote two treatises on the Art. The King also supported the architect of the Escorial, Juan de Herrera, in the founding (1582) of a mathematical-philosophical academy in Madrid, in whose program the Art of Llull was to have a prominent place. In addition, Herrera wrote a curious *Tratado del cuerpo cúbico conforme a los principios y opiniones del Arte de Raimundo Lulio*, in which he tried to use the Art as a foundation for mathematics.

The other center involved a revival of the French-German connection of half a century before. Two lesser stars in this new galaxy of Lullists were Pierre Grégoire of Toulouse (1540–97), whose vast *Syntaxis Artis mirabilis*, which appeared between 1583 and 1587, was based on Llull and his commentators (mainly Lavinheta and Agrippa),[28] and the Venetian patrician Valerio de Valeriis, whose *Opus aureum*, a commentary on Llull's *Tree of Science*, was first

[26] And which was later to spell the death of Lullism; cf. p. 70 below.

[27] Of the thirty Lullian works printed between 1541 and 1578, for instance, seven are works on Llull (four of them by Agrippa), one is a publication of the *Ars brevis*, one a publication of the apocryphal *Art de confessió*, and the remaining twenty-one are pseudo-Lullian alchemical works! See my article cited in n. 7 above for more information on this gap.

[28] Scholars have fired amusing broadsides at the pretentiousness of this encyclopedia, but it should be remembered that Leibniz cited Pierre Grégoire as one of the precursors of his own *Ars combinatoria* (see n. 35 below).

published in 1589. By far the greatest figure of this generation, however, was Giordano Bruno (1548–1600), whose interest in Llull dates almost exclusively from his sojourns in France and Germany. His activities in this field, which he combined with his interest in other aspects of Renaissance philosophy, are too complex to be treated in any detail here. Suffice it to say with Frances Yates that "the three strands of the Hermetism, the mnemonics, the Lullism are all interwoven in Bruno's complex personality, mind and mission,"[29] and that, in addition to influences clearly discernable in his own thought, during the 1580s he wrote no less than seven works specifically on the Lullian Art.

The next generation produced the great encyclopedist, Johann Heinrich Alsted (1588–1638). In addition to publishing Lullist works by Lavinheta and Bruno and writing about Llull in many of his own works, he produced the *Clavis artis lullianae* with the intent of reconciling Llull's logic with that of Aristotle and Ramus and of defending Llull against his attackers.

Perhaps the most important event in the Lullism of this period, however, was not the appearance of any new figure or work but the publication of an anthology by Lazarus Zetzner of Strasbourg, entitled *Raymundi Lullii, opera ea quae ad adinventam ab ipso Artem universalem*, which, for the next century or so, was to become the standard work on Llull. It is therefore instructive in understanding seventeenth-century Lullism: it contained seven genuine works by Llull,[30] four other works falsely attributed to him,[31] four commentaries by Giordano Bruno, and the *In artem brevem* by Agrippa von Nettesheim.

The first edition of this anthology appeared in Strasbourg in 1598. It was reprinted in 1609 with the addition of the *Opus aureum* of Valerio de Valeriis.[32] This second edition was reprinted in 1617

---

[29] Frances A. Yates, *Giordano Bruno and the Hermetic Tradition* (London, 1964; Chicago, 1978), pp. x, 206, 324. Miss Yates said (p. 271) that Bruno even mentioned "among those who in solitude have achieved the vision and gained marvelous powers, Moses, Jesus of Nazareth, Ramon Llull, and the leisured contemplators amongst the Egyptians and Babylonians."

[30] They include the two most important works of the last period of the Art, the *Ars brevis* and the *Ars generalis ultima*; two polemical works, the *Liber lamentationis Philosophiae*, and the *Apostrophe*; and two logical works, the *De conversione subjecti et praedicati et medii* and the *De venatione medii inter subjectum et praedicatum*.

[31] They include the *Logica brevis et nova*, the *De auditu cabbalistico*, and the *In rhetoricam isagoge*, for which see respectively n. 15, and pp. 60 and 65 above. For a more detailed analysis of this anthology, see my article cited in n. 7 above.

[32] Also added was a brief, schematic *Tabula abbreviata commentariorum artis inventivae* by Agrippa von Nettesheim.

and again in 1651. Immediately after the second and fourth editions, Zetzner brought out Alsted's *Clavis artis Lullianae*, which is sometimes bound together with those two editions.

This mixture of Llull, pseudo-Llull, and Renaissance commentaries, emphasizing a general art of discourse, constituted the "package" in which Llull was presented to seventeenth-century readers, including Leibniz,[33] and it must be kept in mind when discussing their vision of Llull.

The next twist in the path came from perhaps the strangest character in the history of Lullism, the German Jesuit Athanasius Kircher (1602–80), scientist, mathematician, cryptographer, and student of Egyptian hieroglyphics. With the idea of perfecting Llull's Art, he published in Amsterdam in 1669 his vast *Ars magna sciendi*. This work begins by reforming the alphabet of the Art, inventing little symbols (a heart for *Concordantia*, a donkey for *Animalia*, etc.) and continues with what Martin Gardner calls a fascinating mixture of science and nonsense.[34]

A much more serious attempt to reform the Lullian Art was Leibniz's *Dissertatio de arte combinatoria*, published in 1666 when he was only twenty. Leibniz's relation to Llull is peculiar. The *Ars combinatoria* was of capital importance to him as one of the foundations of his universalist endeavors, and he acknowledged his debt to Llull as the first to have propounded such a method.[35] He later felt, however, that the Lullian Art was "a mere shadow of the true Combinatory," whose secrets Llull had scarcely penetrated.[36]

Leibniz's interests in a universal language, encyclopedism, and a general science constituted the side of his thought that was a continuation of Renaissance endeavors and that ultimately stemmed from Llull's Art as a system which would provide a key to universal

---

[33] It was apparently the first edition of 1598 that Leibniz read.

[34] "The Ars Magna of Ramon Lull," in *Logic Machines and Diagrams* (New York, 1958), p. 24 and n. 14.

[35] He also acknowledged as precursors Bruno, Agrippa, Pierre Grégoire, Alsted, and Kircher, among others. The debt to Kircher was to the the latter's *Polygraphia nova et universalis* (Rome, 1663), and to the work that Leibniz knew the older man was carrying out on his *Ars magna sciendi*. When it came out three years later, however, Leibniz was disappointed.

[36] One should also mention the interest in Llull evinced by Leibniz's great rival, Isaac Newton (1642–1727). From J. Harrison, *The Library of Isaac Newton* (Cambridge, 1978), pp. 183–4, we know that he owned eight volumes of Llull: a copy of the Zetzner edition of 1609, one of the *Ars generalis ultima* (Frankfurt, 1596), and six of the spurious alchemical works. Significantly, of these eight volumes, the two that are dog-eared and contain marginal annotations in Newton's hand are alchemical.

reality. Here, however, the relationship was much more remote. It was as if Llull had begun a tradition which had spread out into many strands, all of which Leibniz had tried to gather together again, albeit in a very different way, four hundred years later.

The last representative of German Lullism in the baroque period, Ivo Salzinger (1669–1728), was a person curiously athwart two eras. By his interest in Alsted, Kircher, and Leibniz, by his attempt to interpret the Art as a valid system of universal knowledge,[37] and by his attempt—perhaps the last serious one—to defend Llull as an alchemist,[38] he was the last of the sixteenth- and seventeenth-century Lullists; by the monumental Mainz edition of Llull's works for which he was responsible,[39] Salzinger was the first of modern Llull scholars, and the one who has perhaps done more for *that* cause than anyone since.

It would not be fair to give a history of Lullism without presenting his detractors, of whom there were many. With the advent of the Renaissance, his critics divided into two schools: those who continued to harry his reputation over questions of orthodoxy, and those who were opposed to him on purely philosophical grounds. The division came with the Spanish humanist Cardinal Fernando de Córdoba who, in the latter part of the fifteenth century, defended the Lullist Pere Daguí in Rome against charges of unorthodoxy, while at the same time attacking Llull mercilessly as a thinker in his *De artificio omnis et investigandi et inveniendi natura scibilis*, which itself presents a scheme of universal knowledge employing some devices from the Lullian Art.

At the beginning of the seventeenth century, with the rise of modern science with its more empirical, rational view of the world, it was only natural that Llull should fall from favor. Francis Bacon

---

[37] In his vast *Revelatio secretorum artis Raymundi Lulli* printed in *MOG* I, and its companion piece, the more succinct *Praecursor introductoriae in algebram speciosam universalem* printed at the beginning of *MOG* III.

[38] In his *Perspicilia Lulliana philosophica* printed in *MOG* I.

[39] The project took shape in Düsselsorf in 1710 with the backing of the Elector Palatine. A large manuscript collection (now in the Munich Staatsbibliothek) was assembled, but the death of the patron retarded work on the edition. A new patron, the archbishop and elector of Mainz, was found, and all the materials were transferred to that city, where the first three volumes appeared in 1721–2. In spite of the death of Salzinger in the spring of 1728 and that of the second patron six months later, the new editor, Philip Wolff, published Vols. IV–V in 1729 (or possibly 1730–1). In 1737 he brought out Vol. VI, and finally Vols. IX–X in 1741–2. For reasons that have remained mysterious (difficulties with the projected publication of alchemical works? Jesuit pressure?), Vols. VII and VIII never appeared.

called the Art "a method of imposture" whose object was "to sprin-
kle little drops of science about, in such a manner that any sciolist
may make some show and ostentation of learning." Once again,
however, we find Bacon following this with a description of a
universal science not without points of similarity to Llull's system.

The same could be said of Descartes, whose method, although so
essentially opposed to a system like Llull's, was not without certain
points of similarity to it. His chief contact with it, however, seems
to be anecdotal, and involves his distaste for the loquacity of an old
man he met in an inn, who said that by using the Lullian Art he
could speak on any topic for an entire hour, on a second topic for
another hour, and so on for twenty hours. It turned out, however,
that this old man had learned how to manipulate the Art by means
of Agrippa von Nettesheim's *Commentary*. Notice, in fact, how the
words "ostentation" and "loquacity," which appear in connection
with Bacon and Descartes, respectively, both appear in Agrippa's
comments cited above. What Bacon and Descartes were criticizing,
therefore, was more the Renaissance misuse of Lullism as an art of
discourse than Llull's Art itself.[40]

The more popular brand of anti-Lullism is best represented by
two literary texts. The first is from Rabelais, who has Gargantua
advise his son Pantagruel to master astronomy, "but dismiss divina-
tory astrology and the art of Lullius as fraud and vanity." The
second is Swift's portrait in *Gulliver's Travels* of the professor of
Laputa, whose machine for rotating hundreds of cubes with words
written on them to generate random sentences is thought to be a
satire on Llull's Art.

It was during the Enlightenment, however, that Llull's reputation sank to its lowest ebb, with scarcely anyone, outside of
Salzinger's little group in Mainz, a few Majorcan patriots and, curiously enough, a group of scholars in Russia and Poland, left to
defend him.[41] It was then too that he received his most famous and

---

[40] In addition to pp. 65 and 66 above, see Rossi, *Clavis universalis* (see the Suggestions for
Further Reading), pp. 142–6, where the texts of Bacon, Descartes, and Agrippa are compared.

[41] The most important of these Majorcans (before Father Pasqual, whom we will meet in a
moment) was the Jesuit Jaime Custurer (1657–1715), whose *Disertaciones históricas del culto
inmemorial del B. Raymundo Lullio* (Mallorca, 1700) was very influential. A contemporary and
correspondent of his was the Belgian Bollandist Jean Baptiste Sollier (1665–1740), whose *Acta
B. Raymundi Lulli* came out in Antwerp, 1708, and was then reprinted in *Acta Sanctorum* in the
following year. The other Majorcans were those responsible for the great flurry of printed

extended attack, at the hands of Benito Jerónimo Feijóo (1676–1764), the very Spanish monk and scholar who did so much to introduce the Enlightenment into Spain. In his *Cartas eruditas* he attacked Llull violently enough to arouse a host of counterattacks, which he then answered, only to arouse more. Out of this mass of rather useless polemic there arose one defender of Llull who backed up his arguments with scholarship rather than rhetoric. This was the Majorcan Cistercian Antonio Raymundo Pasqual (1708–91), who had studied for a short time in Mainz under Salzinger. His principal salvo against Feijóo was fired in the *Examen de la crisis del padre don Benito Gerónimo Feijóo*.[42] This led him further into Llull scholarship, resulting in his monumental *Vindiciae lullianae*,[43] which is still of considerable service to scholars. On his death he left in manuscript twenty other works on Ramon Llull, only one of which, the *Vida del Beato Raymundo Lulio, mártir y Doctor Iluminado*, has since been published.[44]

With Father Pasqual ends the history of Lullism proper. After him, with the publication of the Catalan works, begun with the poetry in 1859,[45] and the bibliographical work of Littré and Hauréau in 1885,[46] begins the era of modern scholarship.

---

editions in Palma between 1735 and 1760, in the wake of the Mainz edition. For the Russian and Polish Lullists, the most recent study of this curious phenomen is by E. Górski, "Apunte sobre el conocimiento de Ramon Llull en Polonia", *Studia Lulliana* 31 (1991): 41–52.

[42] 2 vols. (Madrid, 1749–50).

[43] 4 vols. (Avignon, 1778).

[44] 2 vols. (Palma, 1891).

[45] *Obras rimadas de Ramon Lull*, ed. Gerónimo Rosselló. This was not followed up till his three volumes of the *Obras de Ramón Lull* in 1901–3, and then finally with the more reliable *ORL* of 1906–50, principally edited by Salvador Galmés.

[46] In their article "Raymond Lulle, ermite," in *Histoire littéraire de la France*, Vol. 29 (Paris, 1885), so admirable bibliographically, and so objectionable in its attitude towards the Art.

THE BOOK OF
THE GENTILE AND
THE THREE WISE MEN
(abridged)

Introduction

THE *Book of the Gentile and the Three Wise Men* should be seen not only as Llull's most important apologetic and polemical work, but also as part of a long tradition of such works. To take the second aspect first, it was only natural that Judaism, Christianity, and Islam should feel defensive in each other's presence. All three were of Near Eastern Semitic origin, all three were revealed religions (or religions "of the Book," as the Muslims put it), and all three had major struggles trying to assimilate Greek thought. Moreover, ever since the Jewish diaspora and the Muslim conquest of so much of the Mediterranean basin, they lived in close proximity to one another or, as in the case of Spain, actually intermingling. The intent to convert others was natural under such circumstances.

Then in the thirteenth century the political situation in Spain brought on a new demand for apologetics. As I pointed out in the General Introduction, in the space of twenty-two years (1226–48), Muslim possessions were reduced from a third of the entire Iberian Peninsula to the area covered by the petty kingdom of Granada. This sudden absorption of new lands had a different effect on the crown of Aragon than on Castile. In the latter, a nation of 3 million conquered some 300,000 people in Andalusia, with the resultant increase of only 10 percent in population; whereas Aragon and Catalonia, with a combined population of half a million, found that in Valencia alone they had taken on 150,000 people, representing an increase of 30 percent. Ideologically, the reaction to this situation in the Crown of Aragon was a peculiarly specific one, set in motion by the Dominicans, at the instigation of their third master general, St. Ramon de Penyafort, and his disciple, Ramon Martí. A brief table of their activity in the field of missions, polemics, and apologetics should give some picture of the situation.

1250   Eight friars (including Ramon Martí) are sent to the *Studium arabicum* of Majorca, which had been functioning since 1242–5, or maybe even since 1232.[1]

---

[1] See my "L'aprenentatge intel·lectual de Ramon Llull," *Studia in honorem prof. M. de Riquer* II (Barcelona: Quaderns Crema, 1987), pp. 11–20, for the changes here with respect to *SW* I, 95.

1256–57   Ramon Martí writes his *Explanation of the Creed.*
1260   Ramon Martí writes his *Summa against the Errors of the Koran.*
1263   Ramon de Penyafort is present at the famous disputation of Barcelona, between Rabbi Moses ben Nahman (Nahmanides) and Fray Pablo Cristiá, which is held in the Royal Palace in the presence of King James I.[2]
1264   Ramon de Penyafort and Ramon Martí are members of the commission formed to supervise the implementation of restrictive measures adopted in the wake of the disputation.
1267   Ramon Martí writes his *Capistrum Judaeorum.*
1268–69   Ramon Martí, in Tunis, is unsuccessful in his attempts to convert the sultan, al-Mustansir.[3]
1270–72   Saint Thomas Aquinas, at the request of Ramon de Penyafort (a request transmitted by Ramon Martí, who had been a fellow student with Aquinas under Albert the Great), writes his *Summa contra Gentiles.*
1278   Ramon Martí writes his *Pugio Fidei adversus Mauros et Judaeos.*

This was the *general atmosphere* in which Llull conceived his apologetic and polemical mission; but his *concrete* relation to these three men and their writings is difficult to determine. We know that Llull met Penyafort, but we do not know how much or what sort of specifically missionary impulse the aging Dominican gave the young convert.[4] As for Ramon Martí, Llull surely knew of his teachings, but all we can say with reasonable certainty is that he seems to have disapproved of Martí's missionary methods.[5] As for Aquinas, any connection seems unlikely, especially since the latter's great apologetic works were still so recent when Llull, out of touch with Parisian scholastic developments, started elaborating his system (i.e.,

---

[2] For an excellent modern study—and reorientation of many crucial points—of the whole Christian-Jewish problem in medieval Catalonia, see Robert Chazan, *Daggers of Faith: Thirteenth-Century Christian Missionizing and Jewish Response* (Berkeley and Los Angeles: University of California Press, 1989).

[3] According to the *Liber de fine* (*ROL* IX, 267–8), this was when the incident recounted above in "Llull's Thought," n. 15, took place. Llull even states there that if Martí had been successful, Saint Louis's subsequent crusade to Tunis in 1270 would not have been the disaster it was, but rather the beginning of the recuperation of the Holy Land.

[4] See the "Life," §10 and n. 36 above.

[5] See "Llull's Thought," n. 15 above. The fact that Llull, much more given as he was to objective "examples" than to personal criticisms, repeats this story no less than seven times surely signifies a strong condemnation on his part of Dominican methods, or at least a strong implication that the Art could deal with precisely those problems that had caused the Dominicans' failure. For a recent survey of this question, see my "Ramon Llull and the Dominicans," *Catalan Review 4, Homage to Ramon Llull* (1990): 377–92.

the Art) for proving Christian doctrine, and started writing the *Book of the Gentile*. We do know, however, that at some point Llull became acquainted with the *Summa contra Gentiles*, as he cites it in a work written in 1309,[6] but when this contact took place is still unknown.

In discussing possible sources, we must not overlook the only clue Llull himself gives us, at the beginning of the work, where he says he wrote it "following the manner of the Arabic *Book of the Gentile*." This leads us to the *Book of Contemplation* written only a short time previously, where he thanks God for having "certified him in the Christian faith by reason of true proofs and true significations and manifest reasons, all of which he found in the *Libre de demandes e de qüestions*," which we find out from another passage, was also called the *Book of the Gentile*, and which, it turns out, explains "which of the three religions is the truer or better."[7] It seems most improbable that these citations do not refer to the same work. It seems equally improbable that Llull would be the author of a book concerning which he thanks God for having been "certified" in his faith because of what he "found" in it, and whose "manner" he follows.[8] Such a source would therefore have to be a work of Christian polemic written in Arabic, a category not as empty as the casual reader might at first think.[9] But scholars have as yet not come up with a specific work to which this might refer; when they do, an interesting step will have been taken in the clarification of Llull's sources, especially considering the importance he gives it.

In discussing possible sources and parallels, however, we must not forget, as mentioned before, Llull's very special outlook, with his almost mystical belief in the Art as an instrument of persuasion

---

[6] *De convenientia fidei et intellectus in objecto* printed in *MOG* IV. The date of the work, however is uncertain; most sources give 1309, but some give 1308 or 1304. Note that this is one of the seven works mentioned in the previous note as containing the anecdote criticizing Aquinas's former fellow student, Ramon Martí. In the *Excusatio Raimundi* of 1308–9 (printed in *ROL* XI) Llull also mentions Aquinas (along with Richard of Middleton and Giles of Rome).

[7] Chs. 77,3, 366,18, and 188,24 respectively.

[8] This seems confirmed by a *Libre de raons en les tres ligs* also cited in the *Book of Contemplation*, Ch. 11,28, which because of its similar content (it also "certifies that the Christian religion is truer and better than the others"), scholars have always assumed to be the same work. Here he thanks God for having "illuminated" him with its contents.

[9] See, for instance, the classic work in the field, M. Steinschneider, *Polemische and apologetische Literatur in arabischer Sprache* (Leipzig, 1877; repr. Hildesheim, 1966).

and conversion. For it is important to realize to what extent the *Book of the Gentile* is based on the conceptual structures of the Art.[10] To see this, it is perhaps best to give a table of the concepts of the seven basic figures of the Art at this stage of its development.

We have not given the graphic form of the figures, since that plays no role in the *Gentile*.[11] We have given the letters of Figure S because the components of the figure itself use them. We have added numbers in Figure X to show that this is a figure of paired (and often opposed) concepts: wisdom–justice, predestination–free will, perfection–imperfection, etc. Notice that the trees of the *Gentile* use seven of the dignities from Figure A, plus the virtues and vices from Figure V. The flowers of the trees are of course a pleasantly disguised version of the binary combinations—the *cambres* or "compartments" of this stage of the Art.[12] The acts of the Augustinian powers of the soul (Figure S) are ever present at this stage of the Art;[13] the triads of relative principles of Figure T, and the paired concepts of Figure X, to say nothing of the single-concept Figures Y and Z, turn up repeatedly in the text of the *Gentile*. This use of components of the Art will be pointed out in notes at the beginning of the work, after which the reader is free to find them for himself.

The *Book of the Gentile*, however, is not a work *of* the Art, but rather a popular presentation of Llull's apologetic arguments in accordance with the method and structure of the Art. It has no charts or symbolic notation, and the whole mechanism is sugar-coated by Llull's literary skill and his continual emphasis on the humanity of the four disputants. We have the Gentile's tears of sadness at the beginning and of joy at the end; the Jew's sorrow at the successive captivities of his race; and the Saracen's assertion of the temporal efficacy of his religion (resulting in the Muslim possession of the Holy Land). Then, too, there is the aspect of this work on which so many have commented, the exquisite courtesy of

[10] In the *Liber de Fine* (*ROL* ix, 285–6), Llull himself refers to the *Gentile* as a work of the Art, albeit a "special" one.

[11] Which the reader can see in *SW* i, in the illustrations following p. 318, whose lists, belonging as they do the *Ars demonstrativa*, differ slightly from those in this earlier cycle of the Art. The version of the ternary phase can be seen in the Prologue to the *Ars brevis* below.

[12] See Bk. i, n. 1, for more details and references.

[13] One of the basic elements of the *Book of the Lover and the Beloved*, for example, are the powers—or spiritual faculties—of the soul. See n. 5 to the introduction to that work.

TABLE 2. THE ALPHABET OF THE EARLIER ART

A	S	T	V	X
goodness	B memory remembering	God	faith	1 wisdom
greatness	C intellect understanding	creature	hope	2 predestination
eternity[14]	D will loving	operation	charity	3 perfection
power	E the act of **B C D**	difference	justice	4 merit
wisdom	F memory remembering	concordance	prudence	5 power
will[15]	G intellect understanding	contrariety	fortitude	6 glory
virtue	H will hating	beginning	temperance	7 being
truth	I the act of **F G H**	middle	gluttony	8 science[16]
glory	K memory forgetting	end	lust	1 justice
perfection	L intellect not knowing	majority	avarice	2 free will
justice	M will loving or hating	equality	accidie	3 imperfection[17]
generosity	N the act of **K L M**	minority	pride	4 blame
mercy	O the act of **B F K**	affirmation	envy	5 will
humility	P the act of **C G L**	doubt	ire	6 punishment[18]
dominion	Q the act of **D H M**	negation		7 nonbeing[19]
patience	R the combination of **O P Q**			8 ignorance

Y truth	**Z** falsehood

14 Whose equivalent in the created world is "duration."

15 "Will" sometimes appears as "love." Moreover, in creatures without the use of reason, "wisdom" appears as "instinct," and "will" as "appetite."

16 Or "knowledge."

17 Or "defect."

18 The Catalan *pena* also refers to the pain or punishment of Hell.

19 Or "privation."

the participants towards one another. Perhaps, as has been suggested, Llull simply wished to offer a model of how such discussions should be conducted. Perhaps he also hoped in this way to make his Christian convictions more acceptable to his Muslim and Jewish adversaries. His tact even leads him to introduce an ending most surprising in a piece of medieval polemical literature.

This mixture of the very abstract reasonings of the Art with the literary and psychological skills Llull could use so effectively is what gives this book its unusual flavor. This mixture is also, undoubtedly, what makes the book a success *as a whole*, without all of the individual parts being necessarily so successful. The reasonings of the Art, for instance, are more interesting in Books I and III, and less so in Books II (that of the Jew) and IV (that of the Saracen), where sociological considerations (i.e., Llull's presentation of popular Judaism and Islam) are more interesting. The Saracen's final description of Paradise, for example, is surprisingly beautiful when one considers that it was written by a man horrified at such a purely sensual conception of Heaven.

As was stated at the beginning, the *Book of the Gentile* is not only Llull's most important apologetic and polemical work, it is also his most general one. He wrote other works defending the Articles of Faith, all or in part,[20] or producing counterarguments to the doctrines of the Jews, of the Muslims,[21] or of dissident Christian sects,[22] but none of these presented the three major religions altogether, allowing each to give its arguments in detail.[23] For this

[20] For works written on the articles of faith, and also specifically on the Trinity and Incarnation, see Bk. III, nn. 3 and 6 below.

[21] For the Jews he wrote in 1305 the *Liber praedicationis contra Judaeos*, in the form of fifty-two sermons, presumably one for each week of the year. For the Muslims he wrote the *Disputatio Raymundi christiani et Homeri saraceni*, for which see the "Life," §40 and nn. 112 and 114 above. There is also the curious *Liber per quem poterit cognosci quae lex sit magis bona, magis magna et etiam magis vera* (printed in *ROL* XVIII) from 1313, written for Christian merchants trading in Muslim countries, enabling them to answer, and not be tempted by, the arguments of Muslims and Jews.

[22] For dissident Christian sects there is the brief *Liber de Sancto Spiritu*, written shortly after the *Gentile*, in which two Christians, one Latin and the other Greek, meet in a similar setting, with Lady Intelligence watering her palfrey by a spring (she even refers them to the *Book of the Gentile*). The Gentile himself, however, is replaced here by a Saracen who wants to know which of the two sects he should choose. Then there is the *Book of the Five Wise Men* of 1294, a dispute between a Catholic, a Greek, a Nestorian, and a Jacobite, with a similar Saracen confused as to which he must join if he wants to convert to Christianity.

[23] With the possible exception of the *Liber Tartari et Christiani*, but here Judaism and Islam are dispatched in a page or so each.

reason we may suppose that this work was conceived for use in Llull's missionary school at Miramar.

A good indication of the importance Llull himself accorded the work is the fact that he referred to it and recommended it to his readers sixteen times in ten later works.[24] That his disciple Thomas le Myésier shared the same conviction is evidenced by the pivotal role the work plays in the *Electorium*, where it forms the centerpiece of the central seventh part, toward which the rest of the anthology is directed, and which deals with "the knowledge and love of God and the salvation of all men."[25]

As for when Llull wrote the *Book of the Gentile*, the statement at the end of the Latin and Spanish medieval translations[26] (along with the evidence in the structure of the work itself), shows us that it is based on the *Ars compendiosa inveniendi veritatem*, and was therefore written after the illumination of Randa.[27] If it was written as a text for Miramar, this would place its composition between 1274 and 1276.

Manuscripts, Editions, and Translations

The popularity of the work is attested not only by the fact that it is preserved in a total of twenty-three manuscripts, but also by the fact that it was translated in the Middle Ages into Latin, French, and Spanish.

The French translation is preserved in a single manuscript, which, although dating from Llull's lifetime, is so hopelessly full of mistakes as to be almost useless.[28] The Spanish translation, done in 1378 by Gonzalo Sánchez de Uceda, also preserved in a single

[24] This number is surpassed only by citations of general and basic works of the Art (in addition to *Tree of Science*), made for evident methodological reasons. None of the other apologetic works come near to the *Gentile* in importance: the *Book of the Five Wise Men* is cited three times, and the others once or not at all.

[25] For the *Electorium*, see "Lullism," n. 10 above. Notice too that it is the only work allotted a representational illustration in that anthology—a magnificent two-page miniature.

[26] See the phrase in square brackets at the end of the Epilogue and the corresponding note.

[27] And within the first cycle of the Art, it has a particularly close relationship with the *Principles of Theology* (see "Llull's Thought," n. 11 above).

[28] The ms is Paris, Bibliothèque Nationale, fr. 22933, and it has been edited by Armand Llinarès in *Raymond Lulle, Le livre du gentil et des trois sages* (Paris, 1966), who in addition to making a valiant attempt to sort out its worst errors, has translated into modern French the large section missing from Bk. III.

manuscript, is of a far higher quality and in fact constitutes an important element for textual comparison.[29] The Latin translation, which dates from the time of Llull's first trip to Paris, is preserved in no less than sixteen manuscripts, clearly divisible into two families. The first family is headed by a manuscript which dates from the same first Paris sojourn (1287–9) and belonged to his first Parisian disciple, Pierre de Limoges.[30] The second family is headed by the *Electorium*, in which le Myésier basically took the text of the previously mentioned manuscript and adapted it to his anthology. This meant replacing the Prologue with other material, removing the introductory paragraphs of Books II–IV as well as the last third of the Epilogue.[31]

The Catalan edition is preserved in four medieval manuscripts, which, with the letters used to refer to them, are:

14th C.	**O**	= Oxford, Bodleian, Can. It. 147
	F	= Palma, Biblioteca Pública, 1071
	S	= Palma, Sapiència, olim F. 129
14th–15th C.	**D**	= Palma, Biblioteca Pública, 1025

The Catalan text was badly edited at the turn of the century by Gerónimo Rosselló, and unfortunately this has been the text re-edited and translated until recently.[32] This was why I felt I had to establish a new text for the *Selected Works*, the original Catalan of which has since appeared in the *Obres selectes*. A proper critical edition has now appeared as vol. 2 of the *NEORL*.[33]

[29] The MS, London, British Library, Add. 14040, has been edited by Herbert R. Stone in *A Critical Edition of the "Libro del gentil e de los tres sabios" [Castilian Text]* (Doctoral dissertation, University of North Carolina at Chapel Hill, 1965).

[30] Paris, Bibliothèque Nationale, lat. 16114. For this stay in Paris, see §19 of the "Life" above, and for Pierre de Limoges, n. 12 to "Lullism" above. The Latin text was edited in *MOG* I.

[31] For the *Electorium* and Thomas le Myésier, see "Lullism," p. 61 above.

[32] He did not know of the existence of the best MS, O, and made little use of the next best, F (possibly because it lacks the first eight folios), basing his text on S, which is less reliable than either, and comparing it with D, which has many mistakes and isolated, nonsensical readings. If he preferred a reading of the Latin version (of *MOG*), he would simply retranslate it into Old Catalan. This was the text used for the edition in *OE* I, and as recently as 1992 for the French translation of Dominique de Courcelles *Raymond Lulle: Le livre du gentil et des trois sages* (Combas, 1992). The other two translations that have appeared since the bibliography given in *SW* are: *Raimondo Lullo: El Libro del Gentile e dei tre Savi*, trans. Massimo Candellero (Turin, 1986), and a partial one in *Ramon Lull, Buch vom Heiden und den drei Weisen* (Freiburg, Basel, and Vienna, 1986).

[33] These new texts make it unnecessary to point out any but the most glaring errors of Rosselló's edition.

For this anthology I have abridged the text of the *Selected Works*, taking all of the Prologue and Epilogue, as well as all of the little introductions and epilogues to each book, thus not only preserving the continuity of the work, but also all discussions as to its purpose. As for the individual books, I have tried to conserve of each what seems most characteristic: a sample of the arguments of Bk. I, along with the arguments for the Trinity, Incarnation, and several other key Articles of Faith of Bk. III. As for the books of the Jew and the Saracen (Bks. II and IV) I have preserved those parts which do most to show us Llull's vision of these two religions. In each of these sections I have tried to include the most interesting exchanges of questions and answers between the Gentile and his interlocutors.[34] I hope this will be enough to give the reader an adequate idea of the techniques and outlook of a remarkable work of medieval Christian apologetics.

[34] Omitted sections have been indicated by the sign [...].

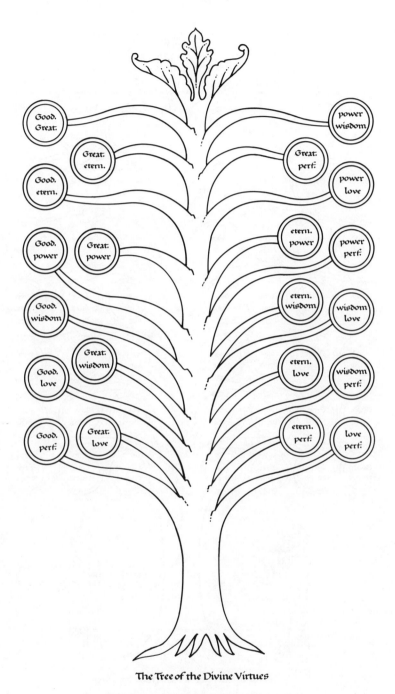

The Tree of the Divine Virtues

PLATE VIII.   *The Book of the Gentile,* Tree 1.
Adapted from Bologna, Bibl. Univ. 1732.

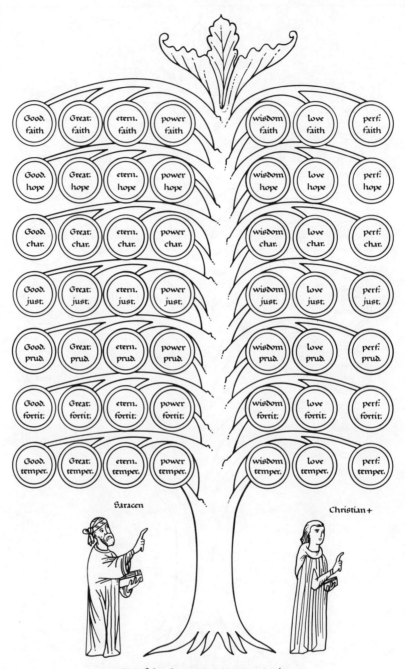

Good. faith	Great. faith	etern. faith	power faith		wisdom faith	love faith	perf. faith
Good. hope	Great. hope	etern. hope	power hope		wisdom hope	love hope	perf. hope
Good. char.	Great. char.	etern. char.	power char.		wisdom char.	love char.	perf. char.
Good. just.	Great. just.	etern. just.	power just.		wisdom just.	love just.	perf. just.
Good. prud.	Great. prud.	etern. prud.	power prud.		wisdom prud.	love prud.	perf. prud.
Good. fortit.	Great. fortit.	etern. fortit.	power fortit.		wisdom fortit.	love fortit.	perf. fortit.
Good. temper.	Great. temper.	etern. temper.	power temper.		wisdom temper.	love temper.	perf. temper.

Saracen

Christian +

Tree of the Created and Uncreated Virtues

Plate IX.   *The Book of the Gentile,* Tree 2.
Adapted from Bologna, Bibl. Univ. 1732.

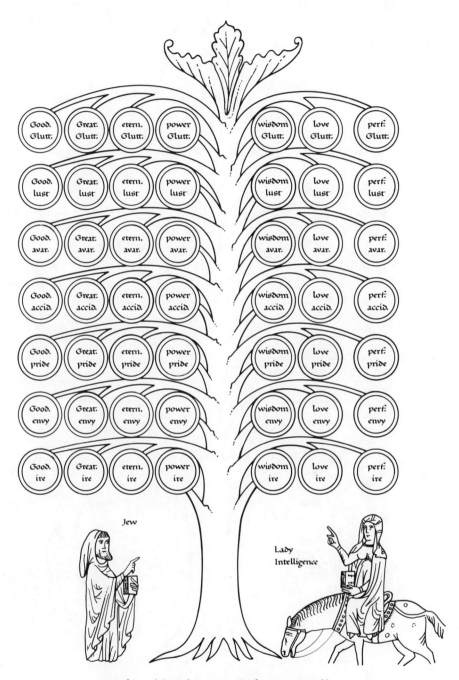

Tree of the Divine Virtues and the Seven Mortal Sins

PLATE X.   *The Book of the Gentile,* Tree 3.
Adapted from Bologna, Bibl. Univ. 1732.

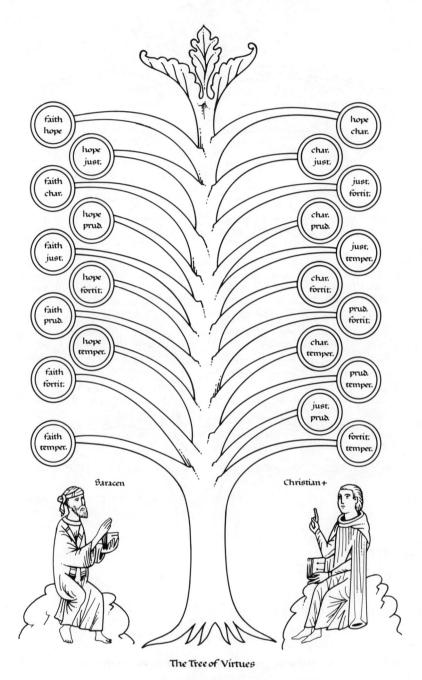

faith hope

hope just.

faith char.

hope prud.

faith just.

hope fortit.

faith prud.

hope temper.

faith fortit.

faith temper.

hope char.

char. just.

just. fortit.

char. prud.

just. temper.

char. fortit.

prud. fortit.

char. temper.

prud. temper.

just. prud.

fortit. temper.

Saracen

Christian +

The Tree of Virtues

PLATE XI. *The Book of the Gentile,* Tree 4.
Adapted from Bologna, Bibl. Univ. 1732.

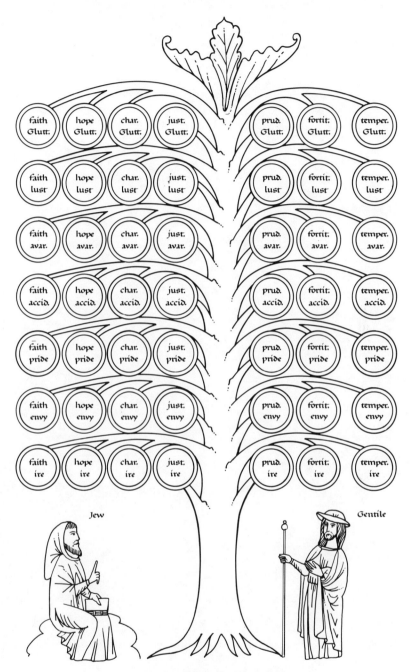

faith Glutt.	hope Glutt.	char. Glutt.	just. Glutt.		prud. Glutt.	fortit. Glutt.	temper. Glutt.
faith lust	hope lust	char. lust	just. lust		prud. lust	fortit. lust	temper. lust
faith avar.	hope avar.	char. avar.	just. avar.		prud. avar.	fortit. avar.	temper. avar.
faith accid.	hope accid.	char. accid.	just. accid.		prud. accid.	fortit. accid.	temper. accid.
faith pride	hope pride	char. pride	just. pride		prud. pride	fortit. pride	temper. pride
faith envy	hope envy	char. envy	just. envy		prud. envy	fortit. envy	temper. envy
faith ire	hope ire	char. ire	just. ire		prud. ire	fortit. ire	temper. ire

Jew   Gentile

The Tree of the Virtues and Vices

PLATE XII. *The Book of the Gentile,* Tree 5.
Adapted from Bologna, Bibl. Univ. 1732.

SUPREME HIGH GOD, honorable in all honor, with Your blessing, grace, and help, and with a view to honoring and serving You, I begin this book called the *Book of the Gentile and the Three Wise Men*.[1]

PROLOGUE

SINCE for a long time we have had dealings with unbelievers[2] and have heard their false opinions and errors; and in order that they may give praise to our Lord God and enter the path of eternal salvation, I, who am blameworthy, despicable, poor, sinful, scorned by others, unworthy of having my name affixed to this book or any other,[3] following the manner of the Arabic *Book of the Gentile*,[4] wish to exert myself to the utmost—trusting in the help of the Most High—in finding a new method and new reasons[5] by which those in error might be shown the path to glory without end and the means of avoiding infinite suffering.

Every science requires words by which it can best be presented, and this demonstrative science needs obscure words unfamiliar to laymen,[6] but since we are writing this book for laymen, we will here discuss this science briefly and in plain words. Trusting, however, in the grace of Him who is the fulfillment of all good, we hope to be able to enlarge on this book, using this same method, but with words more appropriate to men of letters, lovers of speculative science. For it would be an injustice to this science and to this Art not to demonstrate it with a suitable vocabulary, nor to explain it with the subtle reasonings by which it is best demonstrable.

---

[1] This is how the invocation is worded in the two best Romance MSS in which it appears. Rosselló's version is a free retranslation into Old Catalan of the elaborate and much expanded medieval Latin rendering!

[2] See the "Life," p. 8 above, for the Muslim and Jewish population of Llull's Majorca.

[3] This self-abasement is characteristic of Llull in his early works. In spite of its nature of a Christian *topos*, it might have an autobiographical element, as suggested in the "Life," n. 38.

[4] See p. 77 above, for this passage.

[5] That is, the Art and necessary reasons, for which see "Llull's Thought," pp. 51 and 55.

[6] Notice Llull's consciousness of the difficulties inherent in the vocabulary necessary for his Art. Cf. the "Life," n. 67.

This work is divided into four books. In the first book we prove
that God exists, that in Him are contained the flowers of the first
tree, and that the Resurrection exists. In the second book the Jew
tries to prove that his belief is better than those of the Christian and
the Saracen. In the third book the Christian tries to prove that his
belief is worthier than those of the Jew and the Saracen. In the fourth
book the Saracen tries to prove that his belief is worthier than those
of the Jew and the Christian.

By divine dispensation it came to pass that in a certain land there
lived a Gentile[7] very learned in philosophy, who began to worry
about old age, death, and the joys of this world. This Gentile had no
knowledge of God, nor did he believe in the Resurrection, nor did
he think anything existed after death. Whenever the Gentile
thought about these things, his eyes filled with tears and weeping,
and his heart with sighs and sadness and pain, for he was so fond of
this worldly life, and he found so horrible the thought of death and
the notion that after death he would be nothing, that he was unable
to console himself or stop crying, nor could he drive the sadness
from his heart.

While in the midst of these thoughts and tribulations, the Gentile
conceived in his heart the idea of leaving his land and going to a
foreign land, to see if he could find a remedy for his sadness. Once
there, he chose a path that took him into a great forest full of springs
and lovely fruit-bearing trees by which the life of the body could be
sustained. And in this wood there were many wild beasts and many
birds of different kinds, and he therefore decided to remain in that
secluded place to see and smell the flowers, and because he thought
that the beauty of the trees, of the springs, and of the river banks
might bring him some relief from the grievous thoughts which so
tormented and afflicted him.

When the Gentile was in the depths of the wood and saw the river
banks and the springs and the meadows, and that in the trees birds
of different kinds were singing so sweetly, and beneath the trees

---

[7] In the *Doctrina pueril*, ch. 72, Llull defines Gentiles as "people without religion, and who
have no knowledge of God," some of whom "worship idols, others the sun, moon, and
stars, others beasts and birds, and others the elements." The Gentile here, however, is
more of a philosopher; later on (see Bk. III, n. 10), he is even referred to as a "master" of
philosophy.

there were roe deer, red deer, gazelles, hares, rabbits, and many other beasts pleasing to the eye, and that the trees were laden with flowers and fruits of sorts which gave off pleasing scents, and when the Gentile tried to console and cheer himself with what he saw, heard, and smelled, there came to him the thought of death and of the annihilation of his being, and then pain and sadness increased in his heart.

While the Gentile was in the midst of these thoughts, by which his sadness was increased and his torments multiplied, a desire came to him to return to his native land; but he realized that such thoughts and sorrow as he suffered could not be driven from his heart without some help or chance occurrence. He therefore curbed his desire to turn back, and went on from spring to spring, from meadow to river bank, trying to find some pleasant sight or sound by which he could rid himself of his thoughts; but the farther he went and the more beautiful the places he found, the stronger the thought of death weighed down on him.

The Gentile picked flowers and ate fruit from the trees to see if the scent of one or the taste of the other would bring him some relief; but when he remembered that he had to die, and that a time would come when he would be nothing, then his pain, tears, and tribulations were multiplied.

Amidst these tribulations the Gentile did not know what course to take, because of the great anguish his thoughts had brought him. He knelt down and raised his hands and eyes heavenward, and he kissed the earth; and while crying and sighing most devoutly, he said, "Alas, wretched creature! Of what wrath or pain have you become captive? Why were you conceived and brought into this world, if you can find no one to help you amid your tribulations? And if there exists something which has in itself such virtue that it can help you, why does it not come and take pity on you? And why do you not drive from your heart those thoughts which never cease multiplying the grievous torments you suffer?"

After the Gentile had spoken these words, a desire entered his heart to leave, and to go from one place to another until he could find some relief. While wandering, like a man distraught, from one place to another through the wood, he came upon a lovely lane, which he decided to follow until he could find some solution to his state of anguish.

It happened that while the Gentile was walking along this road, three wise men met upon leaving a city. One was a Jew, the other a Christian, and the third a Saracen. When they were outside the city and saw each other, they approached and greeted each other in friendly fashion, and they accompanied one another, each inquiring about the other's health and what he intended to do. And all three decided to enjoy themselves together, so as to gladden their spirits overtaxed by studying. The three wise men went on so long talking about their respective beliefs and about the things they taught their students, that eventually they came to that same forest in which the Gentile was wandering. And they came to a lovely meadow with a lovely spring watering five trees, the same five trees depicted at the beginning of this book.

Next to the spring there was a very beautiful lady, very nobly dressed, astride a handsome palfrey, which was drinking from the spring. The wise men, upon seeing the five trees, which were most pleasing to the eye, and upon seeing the lady, who was of agreeable countenance, went up to the spring and greeted the lady most humbly and devoutly, and she most politely returned their greetings.

The wise men asked the lady her name, to which she replied that she was *Intelligence.* And the wise men asked her to explain to them the nature and properties of the five trees, and what was the meaning of the writing on each of their flowers.

The lady replied, saying: "The first tree, on which you see twenty-one flowers, represents God and His essential, uncreated virtues, which virtues are written on the flowers, as you can see.[8] This tree has, among others, two conditions. One is that one must always attribute to and recognize in God the greatest nobility in essence, in virtues, and in action; the other condition is that the flowers not be contrary to one another, nor one be less than another. Without knowledge of these two conditions, one cannot have knowledge of the tree, of its virtues, or if its works.

"The second tree has forty-nine flowers, on which are written the

---

[8] See the miniature. Twenty-one because we have a combination of seven concepts taken two at a time, or

$$\binom{7}{2} = \frac{7 \cdot 6}{1 \cdot 2} = 21$$

The seven divine "virtues" are, of course, God's attributes, the dignities of Figure A (see the chart and following text in the introduction above, and "Llull's Thought," p. 79).

seven virtues of the first tree and the seven created virtues,[9] by means of which the blessed achieve eternal blessedness. This tree has, among others, two conditions. The first is that the created virtues be greater and nobler where they most strongly symbolize and demonstrate the uncreated virtues; the second condition is that the uncreated and created virtues not be contrary to one another.

"The third tree has forty-nine flowers, on which are written the seven virtues that are on the first tree, along with the seven vices, that is to say, the seven deadly sins by which the damned go to eternal fires. This tree has, among others, two conditions. The first is that the virtues of God not be concordant with the vices; the second is that everything which causes the virtues of God to be better represented to the human understanding by means of the vices should be affirmed, and that anything contrary to the above-mentioned greater representation, or which lessens the contrariness between the virtues of God and the sins of man, should be denied, excepting cases of conflict with the conditions of the other trees.

"The fourth tree has twenty-one flowers, on which are written the seven created virtues. This tree has, among others, two conditions. The first is that none of these virtues be contrary to another; the second is that whatever enhances them or, by their agency, causes man to have greater merit, must be true, and the contrary must be false, provided it not conflict with the conditions of the other trees.

"The fifth tree has forty-nine flowers on which are written the seven principal created virtues and the seven deadly sins. This tree has, among others, two conditions. The first is that the virtues and vices not be concordant with one another; the second is that the virtues most contrary to the vices be most lovable, and the vices most contrary to the virtues be most detestable.

"The above-mentioned ten conditions are themselves governed by two other conditions or principles. One is that all these conditions be directed toward a single goal; the other is that they not be contrary to this goal. And this goal is to love, know, fear, and serve God.[10]

---

[9] The three theological and four cardinal virtues, which can be combined with the seven "uncreated virtues" in $7^2 = 49$ ways, and similarly for the seven deadly sins of the next tree. As we have pointed out in the introduction, these virtues and vices constitute Figure V of the Art.

[10] For this goal, see "Llull's Thought," p. 54 above. Note that in later works Llull always refers to the "ten conditions of the *Book of the Gentile*," tacitly omitting these last two (as

"These conditions govern the flowers, which are principles and doctrine to rectify the error of those who have no knowledge of God nor of His works, nor even of their own beliefs. Through a knowledge of these trees, one can console the disconsolate and calm those in anguish. And by these trees one can subdue temptation and purify the soul of guilt and sin; and by the use of these trees—for someone who knows how to pick their fruit—a person can escape infinite pain and achieve everlasting peace."

When the lady had spoken these words to the three wise men, she took leave of them and went on her way; and the three wise men remained by the spring, beneath the five trees; and one of the wise men began to sigh and to say: "Ah! What a great good fortune it would be if, by means of these trees, we could all—every man on earth—be under one religion and belief, so that there would be no more rancor or ill will among men, who hate each other because of diversity and contrariness of beliefs and of sects! And just as there is only one God, Father, Creator, and Lord of everything that exists, so all peoples could unite and become one people, and that people be on the path to salvation, under one faith and one religion, giving glory and praise to our Lord God.

"Think, gentlemen," the wise man said to his companions, "of the harm that comes from men not belonging to a single sect, and of the good that would come from everyone being beneath one faith and one religion. This being the case, do you not think it would be a good idea for us to sit beneath these trees, beside this lovely fountain, and discuss what we believe, according to what the flowers and conditions of these trees signify? And since we cannot agree by means of authorities, let us try to come to some agreement by means of demonstrative and necessary reasons."

The other two agreed to what this wise man had said. And they sat down and began to study the flowers on the trees and to recall the conditions and the words the lady had spoken to them; and they decided to hold their discussion according to the manner the lady indicated to them.

Scarcely had they begun their discussion, however, when they saw coming toward them the Gentile who was wandering through

---

perhaps taken for granted). References, moreover, such as the somewhat surprising versicle 287 of the *Book of the Lover and the Beloved*, show the importance Llull attached to these conditions. His disciple le Myésier evidently agreed, for in the margin of the *Electorium* he wrote: "In these conditions of the trees lies the entire virtue of all of Ramon's Arts."

the forest. He had a long beard and long hair, and he came like a man exhausted, and he was thin and wan from the pain of his thoughts and the long journey he had made. His eyes streamed with tears, while ceaselessly his heart sighed and his mouth moaned. And because of the great anguish of his suffering, he was thirsty and needed to drink from the spring before he could talk to or greet the three wise men.

When the Gentile had drunk from the spring and had recovered his breath and spirit, he greeted the three wise men in his language and according to his custom. And the three wise men returned his greeting, saying they hoped that the God of glory, who was Father and Lord of all existing things, and who had created the whole world, and who would resuscitate the righteous and the wicked, would protect, console, and help him in his suffering.

When the Gentile heard how the three wise men greeted him, when he saw the five trees and read what was written on their flowers, and when he saw the peculiar bearing of the three wise men and their peculiar clothing, then he began to think things over and to wonder greatly at the words he had heard and at what he saw.

"Good friend," said one of the three wise men, "where have you come from and what is your name? You seem to be suffering and disconsolate over something. What is wrong, and why have you come to this place, and is there some way in which we can console and help you? Let us know what is on your mind."

The Gentile answered, saying he had come from distant lands, that he was a Gentile, that he had been wandering about this forest like a man out of his wits, and that chance had brought him to this place; and he recounted the pain and affliction which temptation[11] had brought him. "And since you have greeted me, invoking for me the help of God, who created the world and who will resuscitate men, I am filled with wonder at this greeting of yours, for I have never heard anyone speak of the God you mention, nor have I ever heard anyone speak of resurrection. And whoever could explain or prove the resurrection to me by convincing arguments would banish the pain and sorrow from my heart."

"What, my good friend!" said one of the wise men, "You do not believe in God nor have hope of resurrection?" "No, my lord,"

---

[11] "Temptation," which, although missing in Rosselló's text, is in all the best sources, should here be taken in the older sense of "test, (painful) trial."

replied the Gentile, "and if it is something you could explain in such a way that my spirit would have knowledge of the resurrection, please do it; for, as you surely know, my grievous sorrow comes from feeling the approach of death and believing that after death I will be nothing."

When the wise men heard and understood the Gentile's error and how he suffered because of that error, then charity and pity entered their hearts, and they decided they would prove to the Gentile that God existed and had in Him goodness, greatness, eternity, power, wisdom, love and perfection;[12] and they would prove these things by the flowers that were on the five trees, thus giving him knowledge of God and His virtues, and of resurrection, and thus gladdening his heart and putting him on the path to salvation.

One of the wise men said: "What method shall we use to prove these things? Perhaps it would be best to follow the method shown us by the Lady of Intelligence. But if we use all the flowers to prove these things, it will take too long. I therefore propose that we use only some of the flowers to investigate and prove God's existence, the existence in Him of the above-mentioned seven virtues, and the existence of the resurrection. One of you could begin by the first tree and use it in your proof; and the next get his proof from the second tree; and so on, in order, until we have, by the five trees, proved and demonstrated to the Gentile what he needs to know."

The other two wise men agreed to what the third had said, and one of the wise men began, saying: "Which of us will begin?" Each of them wanted to be polite and give the other the honor of beginning. But the Gentile, seeing them arguing among themselves and not starting, begged one of the wise men to begin, for he was most distressed at their delay in beginning something he so desired.[13]

---

[12] These are the dignities written on the flowers of the first tree. Although in this period there are normally sixteen (see the chart in the introduction), he has here reduced them to seven to facilitate binary combinations with the seven virtues and the seven vices. Note that the same seven dignities reappear in the *Principles of Theology*, a work, as I have said (n. 27 to the introduction above), closely related to the *Book of the Gentile*.

[13] Llull is purposely vague about which wise man is speaking when the beliefs common to the three religions are under discussion. It is precisely this common ground that is explored in the following Bk. I.

HERE BEGINS THE FIRST BOOK

THE FIRST TREE

1. *Goodness Greatness*[1]

"IT IS CLEAR to the human understanding that good and greatness accord with being;[2] for the greater the good, the more it accords with essence, or with virtue, or with both together. And evil and smallness, which are contrary to good and greatness, accord with nonbeing; for the greater the evil, the more it accords with lesser rather than with greater being. And if this were not the case, and the contrary were true, it would follow that everybody would naturally prefer nonbeing to being, and evil to good; and they would prefer lesser to greater, and lesser being to greater being. But this is not true, as reason demonstrates to the human understanding, and as bodily vision shows us in its representation of visible things.

"Sir," said the wise man to the Gentile, "you see that all the good which exists in plants, living things, and all other things of this world is limited and finite. Now, if God were naught, it would follow that no good would be in accord with infinite being, and that all existing good would be in accord with finite and limited being, and infinite being and nonbeing would be in accord with one another. Since, however, finite good accords with lesser being and infinite good with greater being (because infinity and greatness are in accord, as are finiteness and smallness); therefore it is revealed

---

[1] These "flowers" with their binary combinations of Lullian constants are a thinly disguised literary version of the "compartments" of the Art (see, for example, the *Ars demonstrativa*, Dist. 2, in *SW* I, 339ff, where for technical reasons the rectangular boxes had to be replaced by square brackets). This is why Llull writes them without the connecting "and" (*pace* the Latin versions and Rosselló). See also Bk. III, nn. 7 and 11 below.

[2] Notice how "it is clear to the human understanding" corresponds to the letter C of Figure S (see the chart in the introduction), how "good" and "greatness" constitute the first two components of Figure A, "accord with" to Figure T, and "being" to Figure X. Such correspondences continue, but from now on we will only point out those few that seem most significant.

and demonstrated that if finite goodness, which is lesser and in accord with nonbeing, is in being, how much more fitting, without any comparison, that there should exist an infinite good and that it be in being. And this good is, my dear friend, our Lord God, who is the sovereign good of all goodness, without whose being there would follow all the above-mentioned inconsistencies." [...]

6.   Love Perfection

"Love, perfection are in accord with being; and being and perfection are in accord with one another, as are nonbeing and defect. Now, if nonbeing and defect are in accord with being and with perfection in man and in the things of this world, how incomparably more fitting it would be for being and perfection to be in accord in something that had no nonbeing or defect. And if this were not the case, it would follow that being and perfection could be in accord in nothing without their contraries, nonbeing and defect, also being present. But this is impossible, and by this impossibility it is demonstrated to the human understanding that there exists a God in whom there is no nonbeing or defect, and in whom there is being and perfection; for in man and in everything else there is nonbeing, in that there was a time when they did not exist, and there is defect, in that they do not possess every perfection; yet they do have some perfection, in that they are in being, which being is perfection in comparison with nonbeing.

"If there existed no being in which love and perfection would be in accord without nonbeing and defect, love would naturally love defect as much as perfection, since without defect it could not have being or fulfillment. But this is not true, and therefore it is shown that there exists a God, in whom love and being and perfection are in accord without nonbeing and defect. And if love and perfection are in accord in a being which has privation, that is, nonbeing, and has defect, it is because of the influence, or rather, the abundance of God, which is in accord with being, perfection without any nonbeing or defect.[3]

---

[3] "Being" and "nonbeing" (with its synonym "privation"), along with "perfection" and "imperfection" (or "defect") constitute the most important subset of Figure X in this cycle of the Art (see the chart in the introduction).

"By the above-mentioned six flowers we have shown and proved God's existence, and by proving God's existence, we have proved in Him the existence of the above-mentioned flowers, without which God could not have existence. Now, since He exists, it necessarily follows that the flowers, that is to say, His virtues, exist. And, just as we have proved God's existence by the above-mentioned flowers, we could as well have proved it by the other flowers of the tree. But since we want to make this book as short as possible, and since we still have the Resurrection to prove, there is no need to exemplify God's existence by the other flowers of this tree. Instead, by five flowers of this tree we will prove the resurrection, which could as easily be proved by the other flowers of the tree. Insofar, however, as the essence of God is concerned, we do not mean to imply that the flowers have any diversity; it is only in relation to us and to our understanding that they present themselves as diverse, by the diversity of their actions."

7.   Goodness Eternity

"The goodness of God is eternal, and the eternity of God is the goodness of God. Now, since eternity is a much greater good than something that is not eternal, if God has created man's body to be everlasting, there is even greater goodness in the purpose (that is to say, the reason for which God created the human body) than would exist if the body had an end (that is to say, nonbeing), after which it did not exist. This being the case, if man's body rises up again and lasts forever after the Resurrection, God's goodness and eternity will be exhibited in greater nobility and in greater results. And since, according to the conditions of the trees, one should attribute greater nobility to God, therefore it necessarily follows, according to divine, eternal influence, that through that influence there come grace and blessing to the human body, by which it may achieve resurrection and be everlasting to the end of time." [...]

When the three wise men had proven to the Gentile, by the flowers of the trees, God's existence and the existence in Him of goodness, greatness, eternity, power, wisdom, love, perfection, and when they had made the Resurrection evident to him, and when the Gentile remembered and understood the reasonings exposed above, and when he looked at the trees and the flowers, then a divine radiance illuminated his understanding, which till then had been in darkness, and made his heart desire salvation. And by God's virtue, the Gentile spoke these words:

"Alas, sinful creature! You who for so long have received divine gifts in this worldly life from the Lord on high, who gave you being, whose goods you have eaten and drunk, who gave you your clothing, gave you children, and gave you whatever wealth you have, who has kept you alive and has honored you among people, you have never, for a single day or even for a single hour, thanked Him for all these things, nor have you obeyed His commandments. Ah, miserable wretch! How you have been deceived by ignorance, which so clouded the eyes of your soul that you did not recognize that Lord who is so honorable, so glorious, so worthy of honors!"

When the Gentile had spoken these words, he felt his soul unburdened of the torments and sorrow with which error and lack of faith had so long and grievously tormented him. Who could recount the joy and happiness the Gentile felt, or tell you of the blessing he bestowed on the three wise men?

The Gentile knelt down on the ground, raised his hands heavenward, as well as his eyes, which were filled with tears and weeping, and with fervent heart he worshipped, saying: "Blessed may You be, glorious God, Father, and mighty Lord of all that is! I give You thanks for having deigned to remember this sinful man, who was at the door of infinite, eternal condemnation. I worship You, O Lord; I bless Your name and ask Your forgiveness. In You I place my hope; from You I await blessing and grace. If ignorance made me not know You, may it please You, O Lord, that the knowledge You have now instilled in me make me love, honor, and serve You, and that from now on, for the rest of my days, my bodily and spiritual strength be employed in nothing save honoring and praising You and in desiring Your glory and blessing, and that in my heart there be nothing but You."

While the Gentile was worshipping our Lord God in this way, to his soul came remembrance of his land, of his father, of his mother, and of the lack of faith in which they had died; and he remembered all the people living in that land who were on the path to eternal fire without realizing it, and on which they found themselves for lack of grace. When the Gentile remembered these things, because of the compassion he felt for his father, his mother, his relatives, and all those who had died in his land and had lost the glory of God, he wept bitterly and said to the three wise men:

"Ah, wise men! You who have been blessed with the gift of grace, have you no pity for the many people who are in error and have no knowledge of God nor feel any gratitude toward God for the good they receive from Him? And you, whom God has honored so much more than others, why do you not go and honor God among people where God is dishonored, where nobody loves Him, nor knows Him, nor obeys Him, nor has hope in Him, nor fears His high dominion? For the sake of God, I pray you, gentlemen, go to that land and preach there, and indoctrinate me so that I may honor and serve God with all my power. And may it please you to teach me how, by the grace of God and by your doctrine, I may know and be able to lead to the path of salvation so many people who are on the path to eternal fire."

When the Gentile had spoken these words, each of the three wise men replied, saying the Gentile should convert to his respective religion and belief. "What!" cried the Gentile, "Are the three of you not of a single religion and belief?" "No," replied the wise men, "we differ as to belief and religion, for one of us is a Jew, the other a Christian, and the other a Saracen." "And which of you," asked the Gentile, "has the better religion, and which of these religions is true?" Each of the wise men answered, speaking one against the other, each praising his own belief and blaming the other for what he believed.

When the Gentile heard the three wise men arguing, and each saying that the other's belief constituted an error for which a person would lose the blessing of Heaven and go to infernal punishment, if formerly his heart had been full of ire and sorrow, now it was even more so, and he said: "Ah, gentlemen! How much happiness and hope you had given me, and how much sorrow you had banished from my heart! But now you have plunged me into much greater ire and grief than before, for then I had no fear of enduring infinite suffering after my death. But now I am sure that if I am not on the true path, every kind of punishment is waiting to torment my soul endlessly after I die. Ah, gentlemen, what stroke of fate is this which has lifted me out of the great error my soul was in, only to have it plunged back into even greater griefs?" Having said this, the Gentile could not help crying, nor can I describe to you how disconsolate he was.

For a long time the Gentile was disconsolate and his soul was belabored by oppressive thoughts; but in the end the Gentile begged the three wise men as humbly and reverently as he could that they debate before him and that each give his arguments as best as he could, so that he could see which of them was on the path to salvation. The wise men answered, saying that they would gladly debate in front of him, and that in fact, before he had arrived on the scene, they had already thought about debating, in order to investigate and find out which of them was on the true path and which in error.

One of the wise men said: "How shall we organize this debate we would like to have?" One of the other wise men replied: "The best way to organize it, and that by which we can best and most quickly declare the truth to this wise and noble Gentile who so sincerely asks us to show him the path to salvation, is to keep to the method the Lady of Intelligence showed us, and with the flowers we used to prove to this wise man God's existence, the existence of virtues in Him, and the existence of the Resurrection, each of us should try to prove the articles in which he believes, and because of which he thinks he is on the true path. And whoever can, according to his belief, make the articles in which he believes best accord with the flowers and with the conditions of the trees, will reveal and demonstrate that his belief is better than the others."

The other two wise men agreed with what this wise man had said. And since each wanted to honor the other, each hesitated to begin. But the Gentile asked which religion had come first, and the wise man said that of the Jews. And the Gentile therefore asked the Jew to be the first to begin.

Before beginning, the Jew asked the Gentile and his companions if they were going to raise objections to what he said; but upon the Gentile's suggestion, it was agreed among the three wise men that none would contradict the other while he was presenting his arguments, since contradiction brings ill will to the human heart, and ill will clouds the mind's ability to understand. The Gentile, however, requested that he alone be allowed to answer their arguments as he saw fit, the better to seek the truth about the true religion, which he so wanted to understand, and each of the wise men granted him his request.

HERE BEGINS THE SECOND BOOK

FIRST, the Jew prayed, saying, "In the name of the one, almighty God, in whom we place our hope of being delivered from our captivity." And when he had finished his prayer, he said that the articles in which he believed were eight, namely:

To believe in only one God.

The second article is to believe that God is the creator of all that is.

The third is to believe that God gave the Law to Moses.

The fourth is that God will send a Messiah who will free us from our captivity.

The fifth article concerns the Resurrection.

The sixth concerns the Day of Judgment, when God will judge the righteous and the wicked.

The seventh is to believe in heavenly glory.

The eighth is to believe in the existence of Hell.[1]

When the Jew had enumerated his articles, he then began with the first article.

Article 1.   ONE GOD

THE JEW said to the Gentile that there were many conclusive arguments by which he could prove the existence of only one God. "But among others, there are four arguments by which I want to prove it briefly, using the flowers of the trees; of which four arguments this is the first:

"As we can see, it is evident that the world is directed toward an

---

[1] I have been able to find no exact correspondence between this list of Jewish articles of faith and any historical list (see the entry in the *Encyclopaedia Judaica*). The best seems to be that between these (listed first) and the famous thirteen article of Maimonides (listed second), which is as follows: 1 = 2, 3 = 8, 4 = 12, 5 = 13, 6 = 11. Adding Maimonides' first article (on the existence of God) taken care of in Bk. I above, the score, although not bad, is not impressive.

end; and that everything nature does, it does with an end in view. And this direction and this course of nature signify and demonstrate the existence of only one God; for if there were many Gods, there would be many ends, and some men would naturally be disposed to love one God, and others to love another. And the same thing would happen with other creatures, for each creature would differentiate itself from the next in order to show that the God who created it was different from the other God who had not created it. And if each God had not ordained this in His creature, then His goodness, greatness, eternity, power, wisdom, will, would be imperfect; and if such were the case, it would be impossible for Him to be God. For just as it is not fitting for a creature to be creator, thus, and even less so, is it fitting for imperfection of goodness, greatness, etc., to be God, for to God befits all nobility, according to the conditions of the trees.

"The second argument is as follows: either the greatness of God is infinite in essence and in goodness, eternity, power, wisdom, love, perfection, or it is not. Now if there are two or three or more Gods, it is impossible for God's greatness to be infinite in essence and in the above-mentioned virtues; but if there is only one God, it is possible for God's greatness to be infinite in essence in all the above-mentioned virtues. And since possibility and being are in accord, as are impossibility and nonbeing, it is therefore shown that there is one God, whose essence is so great in goodness, eternity, power, wisdom, love, perfection, that no other essence or thing can limit or contain it, but rather it limits and contains all things within itself, and is essentially inside and outside all other things, for if it were not, it would be limited and finite."

Question. The Gentile said to the Jew: "According to the workings of nature, we know that the four elements are mixed in every body composed of them, and that in such a body each element exists essentially, virtually, and operatively.[2] Similarly there could be many Gods, each mixed among the others, and that the greatness of each be infinite in essence throughout all the virtues and throughout all places."

---

[2] Notice this kind of precursor of the theory of the correlatives, where "essentially" would correspond (see above, "Life," n. 83) to the noun ("goodness"), "virtually" to the first adjective ("bonificative"), and "operatively" to the verb ("bonifying"). For the last two, see the following note.

Solution. The Jew answered, saying: "It is true that in a compound body, each element is limited by the other, according to its own virtue, for the power of fire is limited by the power of water, which is contrary to it, and the power of water by that of fire, and the same happens with air and with earth. And just as one is limited by the other in virtue, so the operation[3] of one is limited by that of the other, since their workings are different and contrary. This is why each element wants to be simple, by itself and without the other elements, for if it could be without the others, it would be more in accordance with its own being and with its own virtue than it is when mixed with the others. And therefore it is shown that if there were many Gods, the power, goodness, etc., of each would be limited and bounded by the power, etc. of the other, and that it would be better for there to be one God who existed in His own essence, and in His power, etc., than for there to be all those other Gods; and He would be more in accord with being, and it would be more impossible for there to exist in Him envy, pride, imperfection, than if He were mixed with other Gods. And because the greatest nobility, and that by which God is most in accord with being, must be granted, according to the condition of the first tree, and because, as a result, faith, hope, charity, etc., can better be in accord with goodness, greatness, etc., and can be greater and more contrary to the vices, therefore it is demonstrated by these conditions that there must of necessity exist one God.

"The third argument is as follows: if there were one God in one place entirely by himself, and another God beyond that God in another place, and yet another God beyond that place, there would have to be an infinite God who bounded and included these Gods, and this one would more properly be God than the others. And if this were the case, it would follow that, above and beyond the lesser Gods, the greater God would be infinite, and at the same time He would be limited and bounded by the lesser Gods, according to the six directions inherent in anything placed in space, that is to say, up

---

[3] "Virtue" in the sense of "power, capacity, efficacy," corresponding to the correlative *potentia* (see the reference in the previous note), and "operation" in the sense of "performance, work, result, effect," corresponding to *actus* (ibid.). Both were basic terms of medieval medicine; in the *Principles of Medicine* Llull speaks of "the differing virtues and operations of herbs and medicines" (*SW* II, 1127–8). This explains their appearance here with elemental theory.

and down, right and left, and forward and backward.[4] And if this were true, it would follow that God would be a body, and if He were a body, He would be finite, for every body must be finite, if it is to be consistent with form, surface, and matter. Now since it is a contradiction for God to be both finite and infinite (the greater God would be bounded by the lesser Gods, and would be infinite beyond the lesser Gods), it is therefore shown that it is impossible for there to be more than one God, without whose unity and singularity it would not be possible for perfection of goodness, greatness, etc., to be in accord with Him."

Question. The Gentile said, "Perhaps there could be one God in one place and another God in another place, and thus many Gods, infinite in number[5] and finite in size."

Solution. The Jew replied: "Perfection of goodness, greatness, eternity, power, etc., are in accord with infinity of essence where there is perfection of goodness, greatness, etc., and are in disaccord with the limit of things bounded in space and multiplied in number, for with infinite number there cannot be perfection of goodness, greatness, etc., in each finite thing. For if there were, perfection of goodness, greatness, etc., would be as noble in a finite thing as in an infinite thing. This, however, is impossible, and by this impossibility it is shown that perfection of goodness, greatness, etc., is in accord with an essence infinite in goodness, greatness, etc., and is not in accord with many finite essences, even when they are joined together; for if it were, perfection would be the same in an infinite as in a finite thing, and that is impossible.

"The fourth argument is that hope can more fully develop by trusting in one God, Lord of all things, and charity can more fully develop by loving one God, infinite in goodness, greatness, etc., than they would if there were many Gods, of if there were one God divided into the two or three parts of which He was composed. And since that by which hope and charity are in accord with majority is in accord with truth, and their contrary with falsehood, according to the conditions of the trees, it is therefore shown that there exists only one God."

---

[4] If one divides each Cartesian coordinate of three-dimensional space into its positive and negative components, one gets these "six directions"; cf. *Ars brevis,* Part X, "Hundred Forms," no. 49.

[5] The original has *quantitat,* which, as Llull tells us in the *Taula d'esta Art* (ORL XVII, 396) can mean either "number" or "size, magnitude, dimension."

Question. "Sir," said the Gentile, "just as charity is better in accord with perfection the greater it is and can be in loving one God
infinite in goodness, greatness, etc., than it would be in loving one
or more Gods who were finite, so the will of a man who dislikes a
God who is evil and has infinite evil is more noble in its dislike than
the will which can dislike nothing more than finite and limited evil.
And since the more noble dislike should be granted, it is therefore
evident that there exists one evil, infinite God, who is the origin of
all evils and whom it is possible for man to dislike."

Solution. The Jew replied: "It is true, Sir, that with respect to
charity, created will would dislike more nobly if it disliked a God
whose evil was infinite rather than finite. But since the evil God
would be contrary to the good one, and the good God would not
have goodness, greatness, eternity, power, etc., if He did not destroy the evil God, therefore it is not right that all that by which the
will could dislike greater evil should exist, for created will cannot be
in accord with a nobility that would be contrary to the nobility of
the creator. And if the good God did not destroy the evil God, so
that created will could be improved, He would love his creature
more than Himself, which would be an imperfection in Him. And if
the good God could not destroy the evil God, they would be equal
in power, which is impossible; for if it were possible, being would
just as appropriately accord with infinite evil as with infinite good.
Since, however, good and being are in accord, as well as evil and
nonbeing, and since perfection accords with good and with being,
and is in disaccord with evil and with nonbeing, it is therefore
evident that it is impossible for infinite evil to exist; for if it did,
being and nonbeing would be equally in accord with eternity and
with infinity, and that is impossible."

After the Jew had proved to the Gentile that there was only one
God, he asked the Gentile if he felt satisfied with the proof he had
given him of God's unity by the above-mentioned four arguments,
or if he wanted him to pick more of the flowers of the trees, proving
God's unity with more arguments. But the Gentile replied that he
was quite satisfied with the proof, and if he had contradicted him, it
was only the better to seek the truth. He did, nevertheless, beg him
to explain what sort of a thing God was, and what He was in
Himself, for he very much wanted to know what God was.

"Sir," said the Jew, "by virtue of God and by the light of Divine
Grace, the human understanding arrives in this world at a knowl-

edge of what God is not, that is to say, we have good reasons for knowing that God is not a stone, nor a man, nor the sun, nor a star, nor any bodily thing, nor any spiritual thing which is finite or imperfect. We also know that God is good, great, eternal, powerful, etc., as was proved in the first book. And these things are sufficient for us to know while we are in this world. But what God is in Himself, no man can know, for no one can even know what his own soul is, so how can he know what God is. Nor is it necessary to know such a thing in this world, but in the next world it is known by those who are in glory; and if we knew it in this world, the next world would not be nobler than this one. Since, however, the next world must be nobler than this one, therefore has God ordained that man may not know in this world what he should know in the next."

Article 2.   CREATION

"IN ORDER to prove that God is creator, we will pick seven flowers—among the many we could pick—from the five trees, and by these it will be made manifest to the human understanding that God created the world; and by each of these flowers we will give a manifest demonstration."

1.   Goodness Eternity

"Eternity is a good thing, since good and being are in accord with eternity, and eternity and being with goodness. Now if eternity were a bad thing, nonbeing and goodness would be in accord against being and eternity; and if they were, all men, plants and animals would naturally wish not to exist, which is impossible, since everything that is likes being and dislikes nonbeing."

The Jew said to the Gentile: "If the world is not eternal and God did not create it, then the world must have received its beginning from itself or from something else. From itself it could not have received it, for nothing cannot begin something; for if it did, nothing would be something. And if the world had received its beginning from something else that was not God, and if that something had received its beginning from something else which had had a beginning, and so on to infinity, and if God had not been the beginning of any of these beginnings or things begun, it would follow that goodness would be more in accord with begun beginning than with eternity, which is impossible. By this impossibility it is shown that if the world had a beginning, it must have received it from eternal goodness, or from something else that had received it from eternal goodness. And since we have proved the existence of only one God, in whom there is eternal goodness, it is therefore made manifest that if the world had a beginning, it must have received it from God, or from something else that had received its beginning from God.

"If the world is eternal and not created, it is equal in duration to the eternity of God; but since the world is divisible into parts containing imperfection and evil, that is to say things which are limited in magnitude,[6] and which are corruptible, mortal, capable of suffering, and ignorant; and because these things are bad, in that they have imperfection of good, therefore the world is not so well in accord with goodness, as goodness, in which there is no division or evil, is in accord with an eternity in which there are no parts nor anything having beginning or end. It is therefore shown that the good there is in this world has a beginning; for if it did not have a beginning, it would be as much in accord with eternity as the goodness of God. And if created good has a beginning, how much more fitting that evil should have a beginning; for if evil were eternal without a beginning, eternity would not be in accord with goodness, in that it would be in accord with the contrary of good, and this is impossible; by which impossibility it is shown that the world is created and begun."

Question. The Gentile asked the Jew if God created evil.

Solution. The Jew replied that evil can be considered in two ways; one is evil of wrongdoing, the other is evil[7] of suffering. Now since evil of wrongdoing is contrary to good, it must therefore not have been created; and since evil of suffering is in accord with God's perfect justice in punishing sin, and with God's perfect wisdom in

---

[6] *Quantitat* in the original; see the previous note.

[7] The Romance *mal* (and Latin *malum*) has, as this passage makes clear, two meanings, one moral ("evil") and one physical or psychological ("hurt, harm"). Since English insists on distinguishing the two concepts, my translation of "evil" for both requires a bit of indulgence on the reader's part.

making evident the blessing of grace, evil of suffering must therefore have been created by the sovereign, eternal goodness. [...]

7. *Prudence Accidie*

"Prudence and accidie are contraries in that prudence is a virtue
and accidie a vice.[8] Now if the world were eternal and prudence
knew that it was, accidie would not be so contrary to prudence nor
to the virtues, which are in accord with prudence, as it would be if
the world were not eternal.[9] For accidie, insofar as it dislikes public
and private good, makes man negligent and lazy, and takes pleasure
in evil, is in accord with nonbeing, in that it desires that which is not
in accord with being and dislikes that which is in accord with being.
Thus if prudence knew that the world were eternal, it would know
that, if the world were not eternal, accidie would be more in accord
with nonbeing than with being; but this is something impossible to
know, since it is a contradiction. For if the world were eternal,
accidie, insofar as it would have an eternal subject, would be more
strongly in accord with being than if its subject, that is, the human
species, were not eternal; and insofar as the results of accidie are
contrary to being and in accord with nonbeing, its subject accords
better with nonbeing if the world was created than if it were eternal.
And seeing that, by the eternity of the world, there would be a
contradiction in what prudence would know, and prudence would
not be so contrary to accidie, therefore it is shown that the world is
not eternal, since contradictions cannot exist, and since that by
which prudence and accidie are most contrary should exist, according to the conditions of the fifth tree."

Question. "I am quite satisfied," said the Gentile, "with the demonstration and evidence by which you have proved to me that the
world was created. But pray tell me, what was God doing before
the world was created? For God is a nobler thing if He exists and acts
eternally, than if His works had a beginning."

---

[8] I use the older ecclesiastical term ("Li quars pechié de pereche, con apele en clerkois
accidie," as one Old French source puts it) because Llull himself always does, clearly distinguishing it from *peresa* ("indolence, sloth, laziness"), as in the *Thousand Proverbs*, ch. 45, no. 1:
"Accidie is indolence of the will that is negligent in loving God." His usual definition, such as
that in *Ars brevis*, Part IX, subject 9, no. 15, is even more markedly ethical.

[9] The negative, seemingly so essential for the meaning, is found only in the medieval Latin
and Spanish translations.

Solution. The Jew said: "The main reason why the Philosopher[10] tried to prove that the world was eternal was to honor the first cause, that is, God; of which first cause philosophers a long time ago acquired understanding, and they said that just as it was the cause and purpose of all things and was eternal, so the thing caused, that is, its effect, should be eternal; and this thing caused they said was the world. We, however, who believe that the world was created, honor God more and attribute greater honor to Him by saying that God has in Himself an eternal task in loving and understanding Himself, glorying in Himself, and understanding all things,[11] and by saying that this task is primary, and prior to the task God had and has in being the cause of the world, than the philosophers who knew nothing of the task God has in Himself and did not attribute to Him a task within Himself, but rather a task which is neither in Himself nor of Himself, that is, the world. And they said that this latter task was equal to Him in eternity. But since, according to the first condition of the first tree, one should attribute greater nobility to God, it is therefore demonstrated that the world was created by God, who is the first cause, and that the task He has in Himself, He had in Himself prior to the thing caused, that is to say, the world."

Question. The Gentile said to the Jew, "I find it impossible to understand how something can be created from nothing."

Solution. The Jew said: "It is in the nature of the human intellect to understand differently if a thing exists or not, and how that thing is made; and how, by the above-mentioned consistencies and inconsistencies, it is proved that God is creator. But the way in which God makes something out of nothing cannot be understood by intellect in the thing created. And do you know why? Because the intellect, when confronted with nothing, understands nothing; and since the intellect cannot understand how a thing is made out of something about which it understands nothing, that is why you cannot understand something about which you understanding nothing. But when it is a question of the perfect divine will, which has perfect power, perfect wisdom, you can understand how God can create

[10] The Spanish MS has "el filosofo Aristotil," thus dispelling any possible doubts that Llull is here using the usual medieval epithet for Aristotle. This preoccupation with refuting the Aristotelian doctrine of the eternity of the world was a constant throughout Llull's life, appearing in works from the *Lògica del Gatzel* and the *Book of Contemplation* to some written in the last years of his life.

[11] The medieval Latin translator has "all other extrinsic things."

something out of nothing, for His will can will it, His power can do it, and His wisdom knows how to do it.

"It is evident to your intellect that you have a soul and a body; but the way in which the soul is joined to the body you cannot understand. Now if your intellect fails to understand that which is in your own self, how much more reasonable it is for you to fail to understand something which is not in you. It is therefore sufficient for you to understand whether such a thing does or does not exist, and in this world there is no need for you to know how the thing was or was not created."

Question. The Gentile said to the Jew, "Neither the firmament, the paths of the heavenly bodies, nor their movements are corruptible, which shows they are eternal without a beginning."

Solution. "The firmament and the paths of the heavenly bodies, by being limited in magnitude, show that they were created; for eternity, just as it is in disaccord with a duration that has a beginning and an end, so it is in disaccord with a magnitude that is finite, limited, localized, and mobile. And thus it is with the firmament, which engenders the beginning and end of time, with which beginning and end eternity is in disaccord. Now the reason the firmament, the paths of the heavenly bodies, and their movement, are not corruptible, is that God created them incorruptible, in order to demonstrate His great power. For if God had not created incorruptible things, He would not demonstrate so forcibly His great power, which can create and annihilate incorruptible things. But since philosophers did not have a perfect understanding of divine power, knowledge, and will, nor of His perfection, and since they saw that the firmament and the paths of the heavenly bodies were incorruptible, they were therefore of the opinion that these things were eternal, without beginning and end, and for this reason they denied the Creation."

Article 3.   THE OLD LAW

"IN ORDER to prove that God gave the Law,[12] we must pick

---

[12] The additional "to Moses" of the medieval Latin translator (followed by *MOG* and Rosselló, who also changed the preceding title to "The Law God Gave to Moses"), appears in none of the Romance MSS. The lack of the name Moses is significant because what is being

flowers from the five trees by which we can prove it; which proof we will carry out as briefly as possible using seven flowers."

1. Goodness Greatness

"If God has given a law to His people with commandments as to what things a person should do to honor and obey God and to attain supreme happiness, and what things a person should not do in order to avoid God's malediction, then the greater is the goodness revealed in God and the greater the demonstration given of celestial glory and infernal punishment, than if God had given no law nor made commandments as to what man should do or should avoid doing.

"Just as doing good is in accord with being and doing evil is in accord with nonbeing, so a commandment is in accord with being and in disaccord with nonbeing. Now since a commandment to do good and to avoid evil is in accord with being and in disaccord with nonbeing, and being and good are in accord and nonbeing and evil are in accord, if God had not made a law in which he had commanded people to do good and avoid evil, God would have made a concordance of commandment and nonbeing, and of good and evil against commandment, being and good, insofar as commandment, would not exist. And if this were the case, it would follow that in God there would not be great goodness in power, wisdom, love, perfection; and since one must attribute great goodness to God, according to the conditions of the trees, it is therefore evident that God gave the Law to man.

"Celestial glory and infernal punishment are so great that commandments have to have been given to man, and this disposition has to have been made by God, in order that man could achieve everlasting life. Now if worldly things, which are small, are in accord with temporal commandment, how much more so are celestial and infernal things, which are great and without end. Thus if neither law nor commandments had been given by God's goodness, it would follow that God's great goodness would be more in accord with things of little use, and in disaccord with things of great use. And if this were the case, it would follow that a material cause

---

demonstrated here is not that God dictated a law to Moses, but the more general fact that, in addition to a natural law, there should exist an explicit divine law to direct men in their lives.

would be a final cause, and the final cause would be material, and what is lesser good would be greater good, and greater good would be lesser. And if this were the case, it would follow that God's great good would be less than any other good, and greater evil would be less than any other evil, which is impossible." [...]

6.   Temperance Gluttony

"Temperance and gluttony are contraries, and therefore temperance is in accord with obedience and gluttony with disobedience. Now if a Law of Grace is given, it follows that commandments are given against gluttony, which accords with nonbeing, in order to strengthen temperance, which accords with being. Thus if no Law of Grace were given, it would follow that the grace of God would be contrary to being and in accord with nonbeing; and if it were, this would mean that God and nonbeing would be in accord with gluttony against being and temperance, and this is impossible and against the conditions of the trees, and against this Art, by means of which the Law of Grace is made manifest."

The Jew said to the Gentile: "Using many other flowers, I could illustrate and make evident to you the Law of Grace which God gave to the Prophet Moses on Mount Sinai, in which law are written the Ten Commandments, along with many other commandments, and in which law the creation of the world and the origins of the Holy Fathers were revealed to Moses.[13] But since we have already given enough proofs that God gave a Law of Grace, and since I am afraid of wearying my companions with superfluous words, I don't want to go through all the flowers of the trees by which a Law of Grace is provable."

Question. "I am quite satisfied," said the Gentile to the Jew, "with what you have told me; but please tell me the truth: do Christians and Saracens both believe in the Law you mention?"

Solution. The Jew replied: "Christians and Saracens indeed believe that God gave the Law to Moses, and each believes that our Law is true. But because they believe other things that are contrary to our Law, therefore, and insofar as they believe these things contrary to our Law, they disbelieve our Law. Moreover, we and the

---

[13] "Holy Fathers" refers to the patriarchs Adam, Noah, Abraham, etc. For the "many other commandments" see Exodus 20ff.

Christians agree on the text of the Law, but we disagree in interpretation and commentaries, where we reach contrary conclusions.
Therefore, we cannot reach agreement based on authorities and
must seek necessary arguments by which we can agree. The Saracens agree with us partly over the text, and partly not; this is why
they say we have changed the text of the Law, and we say they use a
text contrary to ours."[14]

Article 4.   THE MESSIAH

THE JEW said to the Gentile: "We believe in the advent of a Messiah who will come to deliver the Jewish people from captivity, and
who will be a prophet and a messenger of God. Now, to prove the
coming of a Messiah, we must pick from the trees the flowers
necessary for this proof."

1.   Greatness Wisdom

"In God there is great wisdom, which has created and ordered all
existing things. And since the world is the work of God, it is only
proper that the world be ordered; for if it were not, the work
produced and created by God's great wisdom would not reveal
great wisdom in God, because the more perfect and better ordered
is the product, the better is represented the master who ordered it.

"We have proved that God gave the Law. Now if the Law God
gave had no subject in which it could exist and be ordered, then the
greatness of the wisdom that gave the Law would be less evident.
Thus, since we are in bondage to all peoples through the errors of
our first forefathers, and since, on account of this bondage of ours,
we cannot properly keep and carry out the Law God gave us, which
we would keep and could carry out in a more ordered manner—in
that order proper to it—in freedom, if we had such a thing, therefore God must necessarily send a Messiah to deliver us from our

---

[14] An excellent summary of the reasons for not basing interreligious disputes on authorities; see pp. 49 and 90 above. Accusations that the Biblical text was corrupt and incomplete,
and that Jews and Christians had misrepresented the revelations entrusted to them were
common in medieval Islam.

bondage, and to make us free, with kings and princes as we used to have. And if this were not the case, God's great wisdom would be contrary to the holy Law He gave us. And since it is impossible, and opposed to the conditions of the trees, for God to be contrary to his works, it is therefore evident that a Messiah must come."

2.   Goodness Charity

"God's goodness and the charity we feel towards God are in accord, for if they were in disaccord, it would follow that charity was not a virtue or that there was not perfect goodness in God, and each of these two inconsistencies is impossible. Now since, through our great charity towards God, we endure and have long endured this harsh captivity in which we are so insulted and scorned by the Christian and Saracen nations to which we belong and by which we are humiliated and tormented, and to whom we must pay tribute and redemption money every year; and all this hardship we willingly suffer and undergo so that we may love God the more and not leave the Law or the path He has marked out for us; it is therefore necessary that God's goodness, which is full of mercy and grace, be moved to compassion, and that it send us His messenger and deliver us from our captivity, in order that we may love, honor, and serve Him. Thus, if God's goodness did not help us and bring us succor amidst our hardships and tribulations—and all the more so since we could be free if we chose to abandon the Law by which we live— then it would mean that in God's goodness there was no perfection of greatness, power, love, which is impossible; and by this impossibility it is made evident to our charity and hope that God, by His great goodness, will send a Messiah who will deliver us from our captivity."

Question. The Gentile asked the Jew, "Have you been in this captivity of yours for a long time?"

Solution. The Jew replied, "We were in two previous captivities: one lasted seventy years and the other four hundred; but this one has lasted more than twelve hundred years.[15] As for the first two captiv-

---

[15] The "previous captivities" are those of Babylon and Egypt. As for the third, all sources for this passage give its duration as being MCCC or MCCCC years, which was puzzling since the Jewish exile traditionally dates from the fall of Jerusalem in A.D. 70. After finding almost identical passages in *Blaquerna*, ch. 84, and *Felix*, Bk. I, ch. 11, however, both of which have MCC, it became clear that all sources for this passage in the *Gentile* must stem from one with an excess of Cs.

ities, we knew why we were in them; but as for our present captivity we do not know why we are in it."

The Gentile said to the Jew, "Perhaps you are in a state of sin, and therefore contrary to God's goodness, and perhaps you do not realize you are in this state of sin and thus do not ask forgiveness of God's goodness, which is in accord with justice; by which justice He does not wish to free you until you have acknowledged your sin and asked forgiveness for it."[16] [...]

5.   Fortitude Pride

"In fortitude, humility is in accord with virtue and force;[17] and in pride, force is in accord with vice. And since pride and humility are contraries, therefore the force of humility is different and contrary to that of pride. And since virtue is in accord with being and vice with nonbeing, therefore the force that is in accord with humility vanquishes and dominates the force that is in accord with pride. And if this were not the case, it would follow that virtue would not be in accord with being, nor vice with nonbeing, or it would follow that force would be in accord with nonbeing and fragility[18] with being, which is impossible. And by this impossibility is revealed the force that exists with humility in the heart of Jews, which vanquishes and dominates the force that exists with pride in the hearts of Christians and Saracens. For no matter how many disgraces and torments of captivity they inflict on the Jewish people, they will not force them to give up or renounce the holy Law God gave Moses. This being the case, and since that by which fortitude is most contrary to the pride of Christians and Saracens (by which pride they hold us in captivity) should be in accord with truth, according to the conditions of the tree containing this flower of fortitude and pride, therefore God must send a Messiah who will utterly destroy the pride of the Christian and Saracen peoples who hold up captive, and who will make us lords, and them serfs and captives of ours."

Question. "Do you mean to tell me," said the Gentile to the Jew, "that if I, who am free, became a Jew I would be in the same

---

[16] Scholars have related the Gentile's somewhat surprising answer—in which suddenly he seems to be speaking for the Christian—to the reprobation of Israel in Romans 11.

[17] Perhaps "strength" would have been a better rendering of the Catalan *força* (omitted, incidentally, by *MOG* and Rosselló), but it would have disguised the connection with *fortitudo* so important in this section.

[18] *Fragilitat* is one of the Lullian contraries of "fortitude" or "force."

bondage as you? And I would be leaving my own error, only to become a serf through the sin which you say is yours, since it is that sin through which you are in captivity! That," said the Gentile, "does not seem to me to fit in with the dispositions which must have been ordained by divine wisdom, goodness, power, justice; for it would be sounder and better, in accord with the conditions of the trees, if a person who is sensually free with regard to his body and captive through error with regard to his soul could renounce his error and enter a state of bodily freedom, the better to observe the Law, and not change over from his own error to another's guilt and sin, than if he was in sin and therefore in captivity."

Article 5.   RESURRECTION

THE JEW said to the Gentile, "As for this article of Resurrection, there is no need to give another proof, for it was clearly enough proved in the first book." The Gentile replied,[19] "And well satisfied I am with that proof, and blessed be the five trees, along with their conditions and flowers, which have illuminated my soul to hope for Resurrection." "Yes," said the Jew, "but you should know that with regard to this article of Resurrection the Jews are divided into three opinions:

"The first opinion is that of some Jews who do not believe in the Resurrection. They give as their reason that since the body is of a corruptible nature, it cannot be returned to the same state it was in before death, and that, without eating and drinking, it could not maintain itself nor withstand the punishments of Hell, and that Paradise is not a fitting place for men to eat and drink, nor is it a place for physical bodies, which need something solid to support their weight. And for these reasons, along with many others, they deny and disbelieve the Resurrection. But I do not belong to this sect, for I believe in the Resurrection, and I am sure that the divine power, which has perfection in all things, can sustain a body in heaven, even though it is not a natural place for a body, just as the soul can exist here below in this world, which is a place for corporal

---

[19] This phrase, like the "said the Jew" at the beginning of the next sentence, is in none of the MSS save the Spanish one; but without it, one is asked to believe it is the Jew who is satisfied with the proof and glad to have found out about the Resurrection!

things. And just as God, through His virtue and His power, has made the soul incorruptible and immortal, so He will be able to preserve the body and make it be immortal without eating and drinking in whatever place He wishes, by way of demonstrating His power and His justice. And if God did not have the power to do this, the flowers of the first tree would lack perfection, and all the conditions of the trees would be destroyed.

"The second opinion is that of some Jews who believe that the Resurrection will take place after the end of the world,[20] and that after the Resurrection there will be peace throughout the world, and there will be only one sect, which will be that of the Jews; and they will have wives and children, and they will eat and drink, and they will commit no sin, and in that state they will remain for a long time. These Jews say and believe, however, that a time will come when all will die, and from then on there will be no Resurrection, and the souls of those who die thus will know glory, without their bodies resuscitating. This is an opinion held by many Jews, and one which I myself held before coming here and reading the flowers of the five trees, as explained in the first book.

"The third opinion is that of some Jews who believe in the Resurrection, and believe that we will all rise up from the dead after the end of the world, and the good will have eternal glory and the wicked will be punished for a certain time; and then, when God will have punished them for the sins they committed in this life, He will pardon them and give them glory for ever and ever. Some men, however, will remain in Hell for ever, but these are few in number and so guilty that they are not worthy of ever being pardoned. I am now of this opinion, and this is the opinion in which I want to remain, even though the Jews who share it are fewer than those who share the previously mentioned opinions."

The Gentile said: "I am amazed that you Jews can be divided and separated into different opinions over the above-mentioned article, which is so important. It seems to me, in fact, that your differences of opinion are due to either a lack of knowledge or a disdain for the next world."

"So great is our desire, Sir," said the Jews, "to regain the freedom

[20] Ths Latin translator rendered this phrase *post finem saeculi*, implying, as Rosselló suggested, that Llull does not mean the physical annihilation of the earth, which would make no sense in view of the following clause, but rather the end of our world or the world as we know it.

we once enjoyed in this world, and so great is our desire that the
Messiah come and deliver us from our captivity, that we hardly give
a thought to the next world. And this situation is made worse by the
fact that we are continually busy with our task of trying to live
among peoples who hold us in captivity, and to whom every year
we pay a very large tribute, without which they would not let us live
among them. And there is yet another impediment we suffer, in
that our language and alphabet is Hebrew, which is no longer used
as much as it once was and has become curtailed through lack of
knowledge. And for this reason we do not have as many books on
philosophical sciences and other subjects as we need. We have,
however, one science called *Talmud,* which is great, but whose
interpretation is so great and subtle a task that this impedes us from
having any knowledge of the next world; and above all, because of
this study, we incline toward the law, so that we can find fulfillment
in the things of this world." [...]

Article 7.   PARADISE

" O N E   C O U L D prove this article by all the flowers of the five trees;
but, for the sake of brevity, we will pick only six flowers to prove
the existence of Paradise." [...]

6.   *Prudence Accidie*

"Prudence, accidie are contraries, which contrariety is greater in
big things than in little ones; for the more prudence there is in
bigger things, the greater is virtue; and the greater the virtue, the
more contrary it is to vices. And the same thing happens with
accidie, for a person is more accidious against greater good than
against lesser. Now if Paradise exists, prudence can as a result be
more contrary to accidie and accidie to prudence, than if Paradise
does not exist. And because that by which prudence and accidie are
more contrary should exist, according to the conditions of the trees,
therefore Paradise is revealed in the greater contrariety existing
between prudence and accidie."

Question. The Gentile said to the Jew, "I feel quite satisfied with the proof you have given me concerning celestial bliss; but I would like you to tell me if, in that celestial glory you mention, a man will have a wife and will engender children, if he will eat, drink, and sleep there, and so for other aspects of this present life."

Solution. The Jew replied: "Paradise is not a place for all those things you mention, for in all of them there is imperfection, and all of them are given to man in this world so that he may live, and so that the human species not disappear from the earth. The truth of the matter is that Paradise is a place of perfection where man will achieve the fulfillment of all blessings by seeing God; by which sight he will achieve such fulfillment that he will need none of these temporal things."

Question. The Gentile replied, "If in Paradise a person neither eats nor drinks, it follows that in Hell there exists no hunger or thirst; and if there is none, what will be the punishment in Hell of those guilty before God of gluttony and drunkenness?"

Solution. The Jew replied, "In Hell the guilty must suffer hunger and thirst in order to demonstrate God's justice; but if in Paradise there were food to satisfy the glorified body, it would not be signified that the actual sight of God would suffice to give glory to the human body; and if it did not, God's goodness, greatness, and so on would lack perfection, which is impossible and contrary to the conditions of the trees."

Question. The Gentile said, "I would like to know if in Paradise a person will remember this world, and if people will recognize one another."

Solution. The Jew replied: "If in Paradise a person did not remember this world, he would not remember the merit a man has from doing good works; and if he did not remember this, he would not know God's justice. And if people did not recognize one another, then none could have glory in the glory of the others; and if they did not have this, divine will would be in accord with accidie, envy, imperfection, which is impossible." [...]

When the Jew had proved the above-mentioned articles, the Gentile let out a sigh of great sadness, saying: "Worthless wretch! And to think of the danger you were in for so long a time, and what endless suffering you would have had if you had died in your former state of error and darkness." After the Gentile had spoken these words, the Jew asked him if he was satisfied with the articles of his religion, which he had proved. He replied that he was quite satisfied, with the possible reservation of what he might hear from the other wise men. "But please tell me where Hell is, and what sort of punishment is suffered by those who are sent there."

The Jew replied: "On this question the Jewish people are divided into different opinions, for some believe that Hell is in this world in which we live, others say it is in the middle of the earth, and others say it is in the air; some say Hell is nothing else but not seeing God and realizing that one has lost the Glory and the sight of God; others say that Hell consists in having the body forever in fire, ice, snow, brimstone, and boiling water, and among devils, snakes, and serpents who ceaselessly torment it. And the punishment of the soul will be all the greater when it no longer desires to exist, but knows it will exist forever and its torments will never cease, and knows it has lost everlasting glory."

When the Jew had spoken these words, and many others that would take long to recount, the Jew said: "We have proved and demonstrated how the Jewish people have a true religion and are on the path of truth by the way we have made our articles accord with the flowers of the trees and with their conditions. For if our religion were not on the path to salvation, we could not have made the flowers and the conditions of the trees accord with the articles we believe, which accord we have demonstrated and signified, blessed be the Lord! And since the religions of the Christians and Saracens are contrary to ours, it is clear that they are in error, for everything contrary to the truth must be error. Therefore you, Gentile, will do a greater wrong than before if you leave the way of salvation and take the road by which sinners descend to everlasting fire and lose glory without end."

HERE BEGINS THE THIRD BOOK, WHICH TREATS OF THE CHRISTIAN RELIGION[1]

"WHICH OF YOU two will be the first to speak?" inquired the Gentile. The Jew replied: "According to what we decided, the Christian should speak first, since his religion preceded that of the Saracens." The Gentile therefore asked the Christian to begin to prove his religion, and the articles in which he believed. The Christian replied by asking the Saracen if he wanted him to begin as the Gentile had suggested, and the Saracen replied that he was in agreement.

The Christian knelt down and kissed the earth, and he raised his thoughts to God and his eyes and hands heavenward. Before his face he made the sign of the Cross, while saying, "In the name of the Father, the Son, and the Holy Ghost, one God in trinity, and trinity in unity." When the Christian had paid homage to the divine Unity and Trinity, he again made the sign of the cross, and in honor of Jesus Christ's humanity he said, "*Adoremus te, Christe, et benedicimus tibi, quia per crucem tuam redemisti mundum.*"[2]

When the Christian had finished his prayer, he said that the articles of his religion were fourteen in number, of which seven pertained to the divine nature of Jesus Christ, and seven to His human nature.[3] "Those pertaining to His divine nature are: One God, Father and Son and Holy Ghost, creator, re-creator,[4] glorifier.

---

[1] The original *lei* (or *lig*) can mean either "law," as in "The Old Law" of Bk. II, Art. 3, or "religion" as here.

[2] The Antiphone "We worship Thee, O Christ, and bless Thee, for by Thy cross Thou hast redeemed the world." Note the immediate emphasis on the dogmas of the Trinity and Incarnation; cf. n. 6 below.

[3] Llull wrote two important works devoted exclusively to the articles of faith, the *Liber de quattuordecim articulis catholicae fidei Romanae Ecclesiae sacrosanctae* and the *Apostrophe*, also called the *Liber de articulis fidei*, as well as dealing with them all or in part in many other works.

[4] For the concept of "re-creation," see n. 14 below.

Those pertaining to Jesus Christ's humanity are: conceived by the Holy Ghost, of Virgin born, crucified, descended into Hell, rose up again, ascended to Heaven, will come to judge the good and the wicked on the Day of Judgment."

Before beginning to prove his articles, the Christian said to the Gentile: "I would have you know, Gentile, that the articles of our faith are so sublime and so difficult to believe and understand that you will not be able to comprehend them unless you apply all the strength of your mind and soul to understanding the arguments by which I intend to prove the above-mentioned articles. For it often happens that one gives a sufficient proof of something, but since the person to whom the proof is directed cannot understand it, he thinks that no proof has been given of something that is in fact quite provable."

Article 1.   ONE GOD

"GOD IS ONE, and in one God we believe; and we say that this God is simple[5] and perfect, and is the consummation of all good; and in Him are all the flowers of the first tree. Thus all the nobility that the Jews and Saracens can attribute or ascribe to God's unity the Christians attribute and ascribe, and much more even than the Jews and Saracens can assign and attribute to Him. And this is because they do not believe in the Holy Trinity nor in the glorious Incarnation of the Son of God.[6] Now, as to the existence of one God, the Jew gave a perfectly adequate proof; if, however, you want me to prove it by many other arguments, I am prepared to do so."

The Gentile replied: "I am quite satisfied with the Jew's proof of the unity of God, so that you do not need to prove this first article,

---

[5] In the sense of "not composite or compound."

[6] It was these two dogmas that aroused strongest opposition among, or were most misunderstood by, Jews and Muslims, and proofs of which therefore formed the cornerstone of Llull's apologetics; see the "Life," §26–7 and n. 84, and "Llull's Thought," p. 49 above. In his *Liber de Trinitate et Incarnatione* written precisely on these two article of faith, he says, "Since Jews and Saracens are against the Holy Trinity and Incarnation, we have therefore written this book." He also wrote on the same subject a *Liber de secretis sacratissimae Trinitatis et Incarnationis*, the original Arabic version of which was apparently used as the basis for a dispute held in Fez in the presence of the king of Morocco in 1394 between the leading local doctors of Islam and the captain of the Christian militia of Morocco along with a cousin of the king of Portugal, all before a notary to attest to the proceedings.

since it is already proven. You can therefore begin to prove the other articles in which you believe."

Articles 2–4.   TRINITY

"In order to prove the existence of trinity in God, we first pick the flower of

1.   *Goodness Greatness*

from the first tree, by which we will prove, according to the conditions of the five trees, that God must necessarily exist in trinity. And by proving the Trinity, we will be proving three articles, namely, those of the Father, Son, and Holy Ghost, and we will be proving how these three articles are one essence, one God.

"God's goodness, greatness is either finite or infinite eternity, power, wisdom, love. Now if it is finite, it is contrary to perfection; if it is infinite, it is in accord with perfection. And since, according to the conditions of the trees, it is impossible for God's goodness, greatness to be contrary to perfection in eternity, power, wisdom, love, it is therefore demonstrated that God's goodness, greatness are infinite eternity, infinite power, infinite wisdom, love, perfection.

"It is clear that the greater the good, the more strongly it accords with eternity, power, wisdom, love; and the lesser the good, the closer it is to imperfection, which is contrary to perfection. Thus, if in God there exists one begetting good which is infinite goodness, greatness, eternity, power, wisdom, love, perfection, and which begets a good infinite in goodness, greatness, power, wisdom, love, perfection, and if from this begetting good and this begotten good there issues forth a good infinite in goodness, greatness, power, wisdom, love, perfection, then the flower[7] is greater in God than it would be if the above-mentioned things did not exist in God; for

---

[7] The Spanish and Latin sources (followed by Rosselló) add "of goodness, greatness," with the peculiarity that the Latin manuscript dating from Llull's stay in Paris places the two words inside a rectangular box, just as in the "compartments" of the Art (see Bk. I, n. 1 above).

each of the above-mentioned things is as good or as great by all the flowers of the tree as would be God's unity without the existence in it of trinity. And since, according to the conditions of the tree, one should grant God the greatest good, therefore the Trinity, by what we have said above, is demonstrable."

Question. The Gentile said to the Christian: "According to what you say, it follows that God's unity would be in a state of greater goodness if there were four or five or an infinite number of those good things you mentioned, than there would be with only three; for goodness, greatness accord better with the number four than with three, or with five than with four, or with an infinite rather than a finite number. This being the case, therefore, according to what you say, in God there should be an infinite number of good things—begetters, begotten, and issue."[8]

Solution. The Christian replied: "If in God there had been more than one begetter, one begotten and one issue, then each begetter would not be infinite in goodness, greatness, eternity, power, wisdom, love, perfection, for it would not be sufficient unto itself, as a begetter, to beget a thing sufficient so that an infinite goodness, greatness, power, wisdom, love, perfection could be begotten; nor would each begetter and each begotten be sufficient to bestow infinite goodness, greatness, etc. on an issue from both; nor would all the infinite number of begetters, begotten, or issue be sufficient to have perfection of goodness, greatness, eternity, power, etc., for infinite number cannot have perfection, since increase of infinite number and perfection are in disaccord. This being the case, there would, therefore, according to the perfection of the flowers, exist imperfection in God, and the flowers would be contrary to one another, if in God there were infinite begetters, begotten, and issue."

Question. The Gentile said, "An aggregate of four or five or a thousand can contain greater good than an aggregate of three; therefore, if there were three or four or a thousand good things in God, then God's goodness would be greater than if there were only three."

Solution. The Christian replied to the Gentile: "This problem can

---

[8] For "issue," the original has *proceyts*, which means literally "products," and refers, of course, to the procession of the Holy Ghost.

be solved by the same argument given above, for in God there cannot exist more than one begetter, one begotten, and one issue if each of these three is to have the property of being complete and perfect. And if there were more than three, none of the three would be perfect in itself, nor would it have complete goodness, greatness, eternity, etc. For just as it is not fitting for there to exist many Gods, and just as one God is sufficient for the possession of all the goodness, greatness, etc. of all of them together, and could even have more than all of them put together could have, so one begetter is sufficient for the possession of all the goodness, greatness, etc., which two or more begetters might have, and even of more than they could have; for if there existed two or more begetters, between them they could not have an infinity of goodness, greatness, eternity, power, etc., whereas one alone could have it. And the same would be the case with two or more begotten, and two or more issues."

Question. The Gentile said to the Christian, "The same must follow from God's unity; for if this unity is not sufficient in itself to be infinite in goodness, greatness, etc., without three distinct divine persons, then it contains within itself imperfection of goodness, greatness, etc."

Solution. The Christian replied: "That is not true, for if there existed no distinct personal properties in God, there would be in Him no activity by which, from infinite good in greatness, eternity, etc., would be engendered infinite good in greatness, eternity, etc. For if in God infinite good in greatness, eternity, etc. did not come from an infinite begetting good and an infinite begotten good, the flowers of the trees would not be in a condition of perfection, and the above-mentioned activity of God's unity would be defective, which activity is infinite in goodness, greatness, etc., and which activity, along with the three distinct persons, each having its own distinct property infinite in goodness, greatness, etc., constitutes the actual divine unity, which is a single essence and at the same time a trinity of persons. And since being and so glorious an activity as that just discussed are in accord, and lack of the above-mentioned activity and nonbeing are in accord; and since being in which there is activity for the good is in accord with greater nobility than being in which there is no activity; and since one should grant and attribute greater nobility to God's essence; therefore the fact that it necessarily follows that in God there is activity in trinity is made evident. For if there were not, there would exist contrariety among the flowers of the first tree, and this is impossible; by which impossibility the Trinity is demonstrable."[9]

2–4. *Power Wisdom, Power Love, Wisdom Love*

"In order to prove the Trinity, it will be best if I pick the above-mentioned three flowers at once from the first tree.

"It is clearly fitting, Gentile, for the sun to give light and for fire to give heat. And do you know why? Because the sun derives its brilliance from itself alone, as does fire with heat; thus if it were not fitting for the sun to give light nor the fire to give heat, the sun and fire would be in disaccord with the very things they are and derive from themselves, which is impossible. For if it were possible, each would be in accord with corruption and privation, by the inconsistency of each's usage within itself, which is impossible and against the rules of philosophy, of which you are called 'master'.[10]

"God, blessed may He be! is His own power, His own wisdom, and His own love. Now if, as we said above, it is fitting that use be made of the sun and fire, which are creatures, how much more fitting that use be made of the above-mentioned flowers, in order that God may make use of power, wisdom, and love in creatures. For if this were not the case, it would follow that the sun and fire would be more in accord with perfection of power than divine power, wisdom, love, which is impossible. By this impossibility is signified the fact that if the above-mentioned compartments, that is to say, the flowers,[11] can be used with creatures, how much more fitting that they be used with, and derive benefit from, themselves. And if this were not the case, it would follow that God would be

---

[9] This whole paragraph is based on the concept of *obra*, for which there is no satisfactory English equivalent. Sometimes I translate it as "works," and sometimes as "operation" (which is close to the *operatio* the medieval Latin translator invariably uses, as it is to the *operació* Llull occasionally employs as a synonym; cf. Bk. II, n. 3 above); then sometimes I translate it as "action," and sometimes, as here, "activity." For the important concept of the "activity" of the dignities, see "Llull's Thought," pp. 50–51 above, and for the use of this concept precisely in connection with the Trinity, see the "Life," n. 83.

[10] The degree entitling a man to teach in the university, a meaning that the two best MSS (O, F) emphasize by using the Latin form *magister* rather than the Old Catalan *maestre*, perhaps to distinguish it from the other meaning of "craftsman, artisan."

[11] More proof of the correspondence between the "flowers" of the *Gentile* and the "compartments" of the Art; see n. 7 above.

more in accord with activity outside Himself than activity within Himself, which is impossible. By this impossibility is signified the fact that God's power must of necessity empower, His wisdom make wise, and His love love,[12] and this in infinite goodness, greatness, eternity, power, wisdom, love, perfection; which necessity could not exist without distinction of personal properties, that is, properties distinct one from another and yet which together form a single divine essence, infinite in goodness, greatness, eternity, power, etc., and that that essence be three personal properties distinct by personal, essential, begetting generation, by personal, essential, begotten generation, and by personal, essential, proceeded procession, each of them containing all the flowers of the first tree, and being all together a single flower containing all the flowers of the trees.[13] This being the case, therefore, because of the above-mentioned necessity, the Holy Trinity after which we have been inquiring is signified and demonstrated." [...]

When the Christian had proved the existence of Trinity in God by means of the above-mentioned five trees, he said the following words: "Blessed be the Lord, by whose virtue we have knowledge of the glorious Trinity through the significance of the flowers and the conditions of the trees. Now if you, Gentile, do not feel satisfied with the demonstrations I have given you of the Holy Trinity of our Lord God, I will pick more flowers from the trees, by which your understanding might receive divine illumination and be elevated to having knowledge of God's Holy Trinity."

The Gentile replied: "There is no need for you to pick more flowers to prove the Trinity. But please tell me how these three

---

[12] A foretaste of the language of the correlatives (see the "Life," n. 83 above), but here only the verb of action is used. The translator is left with three possibilities: (1) to leave the word in the original Catalan and add an explanatory phrase, which is what the medieval Latin translator did, putting for the first two of these three verbs, "*poderejar*, hoc est potestatem facere," and "*savejar*, hoc est sapientiam operari"; (2) to use (or create) an equivalent neologism in his own language, which is what the *MOG* editors did here with "possificare" and "sapientificare," and what I did with "empower" (used in the older meaning of "to bestow power upon, make powerful"); (3) to use a circumlocution like my "make wise." Because of the close relation between the structural nature of Llull's thought and the technical vocabulary used to articulate it, I have preferred the second solution, only resorting to the last when the only available neologism is something as grating as "sapientize."

[13] F and S (followed by Rosselló) have "tree," which would seem more correct, but the plural is in the best MS, O, and in the Latin sources (the passage is missing in D and in the Spanish translation).

divine persons can be a single divine essence, without its being composed of these three persons."

The Christian said to the Gentile: "Composition can only exist with finite and limited things; therefore when it is a question of things infinite in goodness, greatness, eternity, etc., it cannot be. And if simplicity could not exist with reference to things infinite in goodness, greatness, eternity, etc., those things we refer to as infinite in goodness, greatness, eternity, etc., would be finite in goodness, greatness, eternity, power, etc. But since they are infinite, for this reason—that is to say, because of their infinity and infinite power—they can together constitute one simple, divine essence, without any composition."

Question. The Gentile said to the Christian, "Tell me why the Trinity which is in God consists of paternity, filiation, and procession, and not of some other thing which is neither Father, Son, nor Holy Ghost."

Solution. The Christian replied: "According to the conditions of the first tree, the greatest nobility a person can envisage should be attributed to God; now since, as we have already proved, there must be Trinity in God, we must acknowledge the Trinity in those virtues and properties by which God's trinity is most nobly exemplified and demonstrated to our intellect. Thus, since begetting, begotten and given (that is, proceeding from another) are closer in nature to one another than are other things not joined by generation or procession, therefore they must exist in God's unity and trinity, so that one divine person is closer to the other in virtue, in nature, and in goodness, greatness, etc., in order to be a single essence that is good, great, eternal, powerful, etc. And if this were not the case, it would follow that perfection would be contrary to goodness, greatness, etc., and this is impossible, by which impossibility it is shown that the Trinity in God must necessarily consist of Father, Son, and Holy Ghost."

Question. The Gentile said, "In nature, a father precedes the son, and therefore if in God there is a Father and Son, the Father must precede the Son."

Solution. The Christian replied: "There is a very great difference between created and uncreated nature. This is because eternity and perfection are in accord with uncreated nature, which is not the case with created nature. Therefore the generation and procession that exists in God is different from the generation and procession that exists in creatures. So, just as stone, being stone, cannot be man, thus the Son of God and the Holy Ghost, having perfection and eternity, cannot have a beginning or end; for if they did, they would not have perfection and eternity, which is without beginning or end. But since you have a beginning and end, therefore, by reason of a nature different from that of sovereign good, you can come after your father and you can precede your son in time."

Question. "Tell me, Christian, how the Father begets the Son."

Solution. The Christian replied: "Consider, Gentile, how a blade of grass is begotten from another, and how one man begets another, and you will see that, just as you have to take into consideration the difference in manner of begetting between grass or plants and animals, so you must take into consideration the difference in manner of begetting between that which the son of God received from the Father and that of creatures, for God's begetting is of a loftier and nobler kind than that of creatures. Thus, just as when you think of the begetting of creatures, you have to imagine the operation and properties of those creatures, so with the begetting the Son of God receives from the Father you must consider the flowers of the first tree, by which the begetting is exemplified. For since the divine Father loves and understands Himself as well as His own goodness, greatness, eternity, etc., He begets a Son like Himself in goodness, greatness, eternity, etc., and since He loves and understands that which is equal to Himself in goodness, greatness, eternity, etc., a Son is begotten who is equal to the Father in goodness, greatness, eternity, etc. And if the Father did not have such understanding, desire and will, He would be lacking in the flowers of the first tree, by which flowers the Father has the aforesaid knowledge, will, and power to beget the Son."

Question. The Gentile asked the Christian how the Holy Ghost proceeded from the Father and from the Son.

Solution. The Christian replied, saying: "This question can be answered by means of the solution to the preceding question, for the flowers of the first tree exemplify how it takes place and how it is different from the way one creature proceeds from another. For insofar as divine perfection accords with goodness, greatness, eternity, etc., and since the Father understands and loves Himself as well as the Son he begat, and the Son understands and loves the

Father as well as Himself, then from both there must proceed another person equal to them in goodness, greatness, eternity, etc., and this is the Holy Ghost about which you ask. And if from the understanding and love of the Father and Son, as well as from their goodness, greatness, eternity, power, perfection, there did not proceed another person equal to the Father and Son in goodness, greatness, eternity, etc., this would constitute a defect in the intellect and will of the Father and of the Son, which is impossible."

Question. The Gentile said, "Why does the Holy Ghost not proceed from just one person instead of from both of them?"

Solution. The Christian replied: "The more the Father as well as the Son are in accord with nobility, the less noble would be the Holy Ghost if it did not proceed from both persons. Thus, in order for the flowers of the tree to be more in accord with the Holy Ghost, it must proceed from the Father and from the Son."

Question. The Gentile said: "Why from the Holy Ghost does there not proceed another person equal to it in goodness, greatness, etc.? Or why does the Son not beget another person equal to Himself in goodness, greatness, etc.?"

Solution. The Christian replied: "Just as you feel yourself to be complete as a human being and with no deficiencies as a man, thus, and incomparably more so, the Father must realize that there is such perfection of goodness, greatness, etc. in Himself, in the Son, and in the Holy Ghost, that he has no desire to be Father to another Son nor to have another Holy Ghost proceed from him; for if He did, He would be desiring superfluity. And this same perfection is found in the Son and the Holy Ghost, and this is the reason for the preservation of perfection in the flowers of the tree, and in each of the persons. And if this were not the case, it would follow that neither in the persons nor in the flowers would there be perfection of goodness, greatness, etc. Hence, in the divine essence there must not be more than one paternity, one filiation, and one person of the Holy Ghost."

Question. The Gentile said, "Please tell me if from the Father, loving and understanding the Son, there proceeds the Holy Ghost, or if the Holy Ghost proceeds from the Son, who loves and understands the Father, or if the Father, understanding and loving the Holy Ghost, begets the Son."

Solution. The Christian replied: "The Son in His totality is begotten by the Father in His totality, and the Holy Ghost in its totality proceeds from the Father and Son each in His totality. And if this, as you inquire, were not the case, the above-mentioned totality would not accord with the flowers of the tree, and perfection would be contrary to the flowers, and this is impossible; because of which impossibility, as well as by the condition of the flowers, it is demonstrated that the totality is as you inquire."

Question. "Tell me, Christian, why is there a trinity of persons in God? And why would God not be complete without this trinity? Why would two persons not be enough for everything for which three persons are required?"

Solution. The Christian replied: "It is evident that there must be trinity in God, as we have already proved by the flowers of the trees. Moreover, we can add that being, in creatures, is more in accord with the numbers one and three than with any other number, since every creature exists as one substance and as the three individuals of which that substance is composed, just as a body that could not exist as a unit without length, breadth, and depth; and length, breadth, and depth that could not exist together without the body's being a unit. Thus, since the numbers of one and three are more befitting to creatures, it is therefore only fitting that God's being, which is more perfect than that of creatures, should be in accord with the numbers one and three. For if it were not, it would follow that being and number would accord better in creature than in God, which is impossible; by which impossibility it is demonstrated that God must be one essence which is in three persons, with no more nor less. For if this were not the case, there would be no concordance in the flowers of the first tree, nor would its conditions be respected."

Question. The Gentile asked if one of the persons in God could be nobler than the other, or if one could be lesser than the other; and he asked if each person was present in God of His own accord.

Solution. The Christian replied: "If one person were nobler than the other, then there would be imperfection in the one who was less noble. And if in God one person could be less than another, God's unity could be without trinity, but we have already proved that there must be trinity in God. And if in God each person were not present of His own accord, He would not be perfect in goodness, greatness, etc., but since each is in fact perfect in goodness, etc., therefore each is present of His own accord."

Question. The Gentile asked the Christian if the wise men accompanying him understood that he believed the above-mentioned Trinity to exist in God. And the Christian replied, saying: "The Jews and Saracens do not understand the Trinity in which we believe, and they think we believe in another trinity different from the one we really believe in, one that does not exist in God, and this is why we cannot agree with them, nor they with us. But if they understood the Trinity as we believe it to exist in God, the force of reason, and the concordance of the flowers of the first tree along with its conditions, would make them see the truth of the Holy Trinity of our Lord God." [...]

Article 6.   RE-CREATION[14]

1.   *Goodness Greatness*

The Christian said to the Gentile: "No good is to be found in nothing, for if some good were there, it would follow that nothing were something. Thus, if from nothing God causes some good to exist, then God's great goodness is made to seem greater through such an act than it would be if He made one good from another good. If God, however, united to Himself some good that came from another good, and caused this good to be one with His person, the result would be greater good in the good that would be one with Him and in the good from which that good came, than in the good which is created from nothing. And this is due to the nobility of the divine good, of the good coming from some other good and united to God, and of the good from which came the good united with the divine good. For the good which is created from nothing is only a single good with respect to creation; but God's good, the good united with the divine good (that is, Jesus Christ's humanity), and the good from which came Christ's humanity (that is, our Lady Saint Mary) are three goods, which is why there is greater good in

---

[14] In the strict etymological sense of "the action of creating again; a new creation," or in the sense of remaking that which had been undone (by Adam's fall). In the *Proverbs of Ramon*, ch. 37, no. 13, Llull says, "The first man sinned through pleasure, and Jesus Christ re-created the world through suffering."

this arrangement than in creating good from nothing. And if this were not a greater good, the goodness, greatness, eternity, and other flowers of God[15] would be contrary to perfection and majority, which is impossible; for if it were possible, minority and imperfection would be in accord with the flowers of the first tree, which is impossible.

"You have understood, Gentile, that, according to the conditions of the first tree, the greatest nobility a person can contemplate or understand should be attributed to God; for otherwise the flowers of the tree, contemplation and human understanding, would not be in accord with one another. To grant and recognize that God is the creator of everything that exists, is to recognize God's great goodness. And to say, think, and recognize that God wishes to be one with some created good is to recognize and love better God's good and the good united with Him, and in this way God's good is better exemplified in infinite greatness, eternity, power, etc. And since, according to the conditions of the tree, whatever makes God's great goodness more evident is affirmable, therefore re-creation is affirmable; which re-creation was brought about by the good God has in Himself and by the good united with Him, which good He took from another created good, which is our Lady Saint Mary.

"In nothing there is neither guilt nor sin; for if there were, nothing would be something. Thus to remove guilt or sin from some good, is a greater thing than creating something from nothing, since guilt and sin are things contrary to good and merit. Thus, if one must attribute creation to God, which is not such a good thing as removing guilt and sin from good, how much more one should attribute to God the re-creation of good where there was guilt and sin. And because in this task of re-creation there is greater good than in creation, it is therefore only right that for the carrying out of such a task there should exist more good than for creating good from nothing; which greater good is the union that takes place between created good and uncreated good, in order that created good, corrupted by guilt and sin, may be re-created and exalted by its union with uncreated good. Now since the greater and better task better signifies and demonstrates the great goodness of our Lord God than the lesser task, therefore in this greater demonstration of God's

[15] Llull has conflated "the flowers of the first tree" with "the dignities (virtues, or attributes) of God."

great goodness, re-creation is represented to the human understanding, which has knowledge of this greater significance; and this
re-creation is the union of the Son of our Lady Saint Mary, glorious
Virgin—may she and her virtue be blessed!—with the union[16] of
the Son of God. By which union, and by the suffering of Jesus
Christ's human nature, the world was re-created from original sin
which we had from the first man, that is, Adam, who disobeyed
God's command, as a result of which we are mortal, suffer hunger
and thirst, heat and cold, and ignorance, and have many other
defects we would not have if Adam had not sinned. And if the Son
of God had not become incarnate and had not died when He was a
man, we would all have gone to Hell's fires for ever and ever. But by
the sanctity of the union of the Son of God with Christ's human
nature, who are one person, and by the sanctity of the precious
blood Christ spilled to re-create the world, all those who believe in
re-creation are delivered from the power of the devil and are called
to glory without end."

2.   Power Charity

The Christian said to the Gentile: "It is clear that God created
creatures and their properties to exemplify His great power and
charity.[17] He therefore gave fire the property that it would, in burning wood, extend its size infinitely, as long as it were given an
infinite amount of wood and infinite space in which to burn, in
accordance with the place we are in. But since fire does not have
infinite material, it does not burn an infinite amount. Thus if fire,
which is a finite and limited creation, has this power and property,
and since it does not have this power and property from itself, but
rather as a gift from God, how much more power has God to place
infinite good in a creature, if the creature could receive it! And if this
were not the case, it would follow that God's will and power were
contraries, and that God had given greater power to fire than to
Himself, which is impossible.

---

[16] This perplexing "union . . . with the union" is in all the sources.

[17] A clear formulation of Llull's exemplarist doctrine (see above "Llull's Thought," p. 51
above). The verb here translated as "to exemplify" is *significar*, which is to be taken in the
literal etymological sense of "to be or act as a sign or symbol of"; see also *Ars brevis*, Part x,
no. 36.

"If God created a creature, made that creature be better than all others, and gave it greater power, wisdom, will than all other creatures, then the fact that God could make a creature infinite in power, wisdom, charity if the creature could receive it would be better exemplified than if God did not make such a creature. And since that by which God's power and charity is best shown to place infinite good in a creature, if the creature can receive it, must exist, therefore it is only fitting that God should have made a creature nobler in virtue and virtues than all other creatures. And because of the fact that this creature can be better than all other creatures, if it is joined to, so as to become one with, God's nature, it is therefore nearer to being infinite in virtue, if it could receive it,[18] than it would be if it were not joined to or united with God's power and charity. And since that by which God best demonstrates His power and charity must be granted, therefore, in this granting, which accords with being against its contrary, that is to say, negation, is manifested the re-creation we have been seeking.

"If created power and created charity exist in created man, and this man is one with the uncreated person, there can be greater concordance of power and love between uncreated power and uncreated charity on the one hand, and created power and created charity on the other, than there would be if the uncreated and the created person were not a single person. And since one must grant that by which the uncreated virtues and the created virtues are most in accord, as well as that by which it is most impossible for them to be contrary, therefore the uniting of the created person with the uncreated person can be manifested, by which manifestation re-creation can be represented." [...]

Article 7.   GLORIFICATION

[...]

5.   *Prudence Accidie*

"Prudence is choosing greater good and avoiding greater evil; and through accidie a person is negligent about choosing greater

---

[18] The Latin sources are more specific, having "infinity" instead of the last "it."

good and avoiding greater evil. Greater, however, is that accidie by which a person is more negligent in choosing greater rather than lesser good and in avoiding greater rather than lesser evil. Now this, for the reasons given above, being the case, God can be shown to be the glorifier; for if glory did not exist, the punishments of Hell would not exist, nor could one choose greater good or avoid greater evil so well, than is the case if heavenly glory and infernal punishment exist. And because, according to the conditions of this tree, that by which prudence, accidie are most contrary must exist, therefore in that which accords with being is demonstrated heavenly glory, without which whatever is not in accord with being would exist and whatever is in accord with being would not exist, and the conditions of this tree would be destroyed."

Question. The Gentile said to the Christian, "You have given me sufficient proof of the above-mentioned article; but could you please tell me how God will glorify the saints in Heaven."

Solution. The Christian replied: "The way in which God glorifies the saints is something too lofty for the human intellect to understand in this earthly existence; for if it could understand it, it would have as much glory in this world as those who are in glory in the next world. But I can explain something about what you ask by means of the following example. You know that it is characteristic of essence to be, of intellect to understand, and of will to love,[19] and so on for similar things. Now if with your mind's eye you saw the way your intellect accords with understanding and your will with loving, and if you saw how each of these things was distinct and different from the other, you would have a most agreeable pleasure in seeing these things. For to see a ship being made could give you greater pleasure than seeing a bench being made; and if you saw the sun and the moon and the stars being made, and the sky, sea, and earth, and everything there is in the world, it would give you greater pleasure than seeing just a ship being made. Thus, if you are in glory and see how the Father understands and loves Himself, and how, in understanding and loving Himself, the Son, and the Holy

---

[19] The first two pairs have the same roots in Catalan: *essència-ésser* (for which which see *Ars brevis*, Part x, "Hundred Forms," no. 2 and the corresponding note), and *enteniment-entendre* (invariably translated *intellectus-intelligere* in Latin). The last two pairs are, of course, from Figure S (see the chart in the introduction above).

Ghost, He begets the Son and has the Holy Ghost proceed from the Father and Son; and if you saw how the Son, in understanding and loving the Father, the Holy Ghost, and Himself, is begotten of the Father and has the Holy Ghost proceed from Him; and if you saw how the Holy Ghost proceeded from the Father and Son, loving and understanding the Father, the Son, and Himself; and if you saw the begetting and proceeding in God of infinite goodness, greatness, eternity, power, wisdom, love, perfection, and saw how all three persons are a single essence, infinite in goodness, greatness, eternity, etc., you can imagine what glory your soul would have—the very glory, in fact, you will have if you enter into the glory of Paradise.

"In glory you will see Jesus Christ's human nature be one with God the Son; and you will see how the Son of God took on human nature; and you will see how this divine and human nature constitutes a single person, and how God the Son and the humanity He took on understand and love one another; and you will see how this human nature is finer and nobler than any creature that exists or could exist; and you will see how Christ's humanity loves and honors our Lady Saint Mary; and you will see all the saints of glory honor Jesus Christ and our Lady Saint Mary; and you will see the ranks of angels and of archangels, and the ranks of martyrs, virgins, and confessors, all singing and giving glory and praise to God and to the human nature united with God. So, with this in mind, you can get some idea of the glory you will see if God calls you to His glory without end.

"In Paradise a person will neither eat, drink, nor lie with a woman. And since in this world the human body labors for the love of our Lord God, therefore, in order to reward the body in glory, you will see and hear the body of our Lord Jesus Christ united with God the Son. And when you think that your body and that of Jesus Christ are of one nature, and that His body was sacrificed to redeem you, the glory you will receive upon seeing that body so glorified is something about which you must not ask, for I could not describe it to you—nor could anyone describe the look of love He will give you."

After proving the above-mentioned article to the Gentile, the Christian said to him, "According to the way it was decided you would know which religion was better than the others, you can see by the above-mentioned glory that the Christian religion is worthier than the others, since the best and greatest glory is more in accord with the conditions of the trees than lesser glory, which is contrary to greater glory; which greater glory cannot be so well exemplified by the religion of the Jews or that of the Saracens as by that of the Christians." [...]

Article 9.   BORN OF VIRGIN

[...]

6.   *Justice Pride*

"Justice, pride are contraries. Now in our father, Adam, and in our mother, Eve, guilt and sin were born through pride. Thus, since pride and injustice are in accord against justice, humility, therefore, according to the conditions of the flowers, it was only fitting that justice, humility be in accord in the birth of a creature finer than any other, in order that in creatures there exist greater justice and humility than all the guilt and sin which was born in man through injustice, pride. And if this were not the case, the conditions of the flower would be destroyed, and in the flower of perfection, justice there would be contrariety, which would signify concordance in the flower of perfection, pride, which concordance is impossible; in which impossibility it is made evident that the Son of God was born with human nature, so that in human nature there would be born greater virtue of justice, humility."

Question. When the Christian had proved the above-mentioned article to the Gentile, the Gentile asked him: "Tell me, this woman you mention who gave birth to the Son of God, of what king was she a daughter? Or what sort of nobility can a woman have so that God would want to take on human nature in her and be born from her?"

Solution. The Christian replied: "It is true that our Lady was of the house of David, who was the noblest and most honored king the

Jews ever had; yet the father of our Lady Saint Mary was not a king, nor was her mother a queen; they were instead humble folk. And our Lady was a woman poor in earthly possessions, but in virtues she was richer and nobler than any other creature, with the exception of her Son. In fact, this woman was so poor that when she gave birth to the savior of the world, she had no house in which to do so, and she gave birth in a stable, which is a lowly house for animals. All this was to show the great humility of the Son of God, who is more contrary to pride than any other creature. For if the Son of God had wanted to be born of a queen, ruler of all the kingdoms in the world, He could easily have done so; but it would not have signified so great a concordance of humility, justice against injustice, pride."

Article 10.   CRUCIFIED

[...]

5.   *Hope Avarice*

"Avarice is contrary to hope, which is why poor people despair of rich, avaricious men and place their hope in generous, liberal men. Now if God became man, and that man died to save you and me and the others, think to yourself if there could be any better way to make you trust or hope in God, or make you more contrary to avarice. And since by the Incarnation of the Son of God and by the Passion of Jesus Christ you can have greater hope and can be more contrary to avarice, therefore in this greater hope and in this greater contrariety between hope and avarice is exemplified the Incarnation of the Son of God and the Passion of Jesus Christ.

"The Saracens claim that Jesus Christ did not die. And do you know why? Because they think they are rendering Him honor by saying that He did not die. But they do not understand the honor that is His in being the hope and consolation of every man, no matter how poor or guilty he may be, and for whom the hope would not be so real if He had not been God or died to save mankind."

Question. "I am astonished," said the Gentile, "that Jesus let Himself be killed, if He was as noble a person as you claim."

Solution. The Christian replied: "You hear and do not understand, and it is this hearing without understanding that gives rise to your astonishment, which would be dispelled by hearing and understanding. This being the case, try therefore to understand how in Jesus Christ's human nature and in His passion and death God demonstrates the perfection of the flowers of the first tree, as well as those of the second and fourth. And just as in a mirror your features are revealed, so in evil men and in those who are contrary to God are revealed the above-mentioned flowers by means of the flowers of the third and fifth tree, without which third and fifth trees they would not be made so evident to the human understanding." […]

When the Christian had proved his articles to the Gentile by means of the conditions and the flowers of the trees, he said: "You should know, Gentile, that the God of Glory—blessed may He be!—gave man memory to remember, reason to understand, and will to love God and His works. Thus, the greater the remembrance, intelligence, and love the soul has towards God, the nobler it is and the more it accords with the final cause for which it was made and created. This being the case, if you remember, understand, and love God better through what I have said to you in proving my articles, than through what the Jew has said or what the Saracen will say (because by their arguments you cannot remember, understand, or love God as profoundly as you can by what I have told you), therefore my religion is shown to be true. And since whatever nobility the Jews and Saracens can, according to their beliefs, attribute and ascribe to God, we can also attribute, and even more than they, insofar as we believe in the Trinity of God and in the Incarnation of the Son of God; and since, by what I have said, you can better make your memory, reason, and will accord with the flowers and the conditions of the trees, according to the disposition and the new manner of disputation given and shown us by the Lady of Intelligence, therefore you should believe my words and my arguments if you want to find supreme happiness in God's glory."

When the Christian had spoken these words, the Gentile answered him, saying: "I have heard your words and understood your arguments. But before I reply to these words, I want to hear what the Saracens believe and how they make their articles accord with the flowers and the conditions of the trees. I would therefore like the Saracen to tell me what he has to say."

HERE BEGINS THE FOURTH BOOK

W H E N   T H E Saracen[1] saw that the time and hour had come for him
to speak, he went to the spring and washed his hands, his face, his
ears, his nose, and his mouth; and afterwards he washed his feet and
other parts of his body, as a sign of original sin and cleanliness of
heart.[2] Afterwards he spread a cloth[3] on the ground and knelt three
times, touching his head to earth and kissing the ground; then,
raising his heart, his hands, and his eyes heavenward, he said: "In
the name of God the Merciful, the Mercifying, to whom all praise
be given, since He is Lord of the world;—Him I adore and in Him
I trust, for He leads us on the straight path of salvation."[4] And
the Saracen spoke many other words, as was the custom in his
prayers.

After finishing his prayer, the Saracen said to the Gentile that the
articles of his religion were twelve, namely: to believe in one God;
Creator; Mohammed is Prophet; the Koran is the law given by God;
the dead man, upon being buried, is asked by the angel if Mohammed is the messenger of God; all things will die, except God;

---

[1] This term, which originated as the late Latin and Greek name for the nomads of the
Syrian-Arabian desert, had by the Middle Ages come simply to mean "Muslim." In other
works, Llull uses derivatives of *sarraí*, such as *sarraïnitat* to mean "Islam," and even *sarraïnesc*
to refer to the Arabic language. The Spanish medieval translator, doubtless reflecting Castile's political and commercial orientation towards northwest Africa, invariably renders the
word as "moor."

[2] Regarding these ablutions made to achieve *ṭahāra* or purification, which constitutes a
necessary prelude to prayer, see the Koran, 5:6.

[3] A cloth of any kind spread on the ground can be used by a Muslim as a substitute for the
prayer rug or *sajjāda*.

[4] This invocation is a free version, perhaps written by Llull from memory, of the "Opening" (*Al-Fātiḥa*) of the Koran. Note that he translates *Allāh* as "God," which is often reserved
for the related *ilāh*, and it is interesting to see him dealing with the terms *raḥmān* and *raḥīm*,
both derived from the root *rḥm*, by means similar to those used with the correlatives,
rendering them as *misericordiós* and *misericordiejant*, which I have, in an attempt to retain this
structure, translated as "the Merciful, the Mercifying," rather than the more usual "the
Compassionate (or Beneficient), the Merciful."

Resurrection; Mohammed will be heeded on the Day of Judgment; we will give an accounting on the Day of Judgment; merits and faults will be weighed; all will pass along the path; the twelfth article is to believe in the existence of Paradise and Hell.[5]

Article 1.   TO BELIEVE IN THE EXISTENCE OF ONE GOD

WHILE THE Saracen was looking at the trees, in order to choose the flowers he would need to prove the existence of one God, the Gentile said to him: "You don't have to prove the existence of one God, because the Jew has already proved it quite adequately." But the Saracen replied that he wanted to prove that God was not divisible, not separated into parts, nor compound. "Rather, in every way He is one, without there existing in Him any trinity or plurality. For if there did, then He would have to be compound, and His goodness, greatness, eternity, power, wisdom, love, would have to be contrary to perfection; and since this is impossible, it is therefore evident that God does not exist in Trinity."

When the Saracen said this, the Christian wanted to reply, but the Gentile said it was not his turn to speak, and that he himself would answer the Saracen. The Gentile therefore said to the Saracen: "Surely you remember that I put that same question to the Christian.[6] Now, from what you say and from what I heard the Christian say, I realize that the Christian believes certain things concerning the Trinity of God, which are different from what you think he believes. It therefore seems to me that you cannot agree and live beneath the same faith and belief as the Christian. But let us leave this problem and continue with your articles, for there is no need to discuss this first article any further." [...]

---

[5] In Islam there is no fixed, agreed-upon list of articles of faith or *'aqā'id* (plural of *'aqīda*, "belief"). Llull's list, however, agrees quite well with those articles most generally accepted and which are based largely on those found in al-Ghazzali's *Ihyā 'ulūm al-din*. See the article on *'aqīda* in the new edition of the *Encyclopaedia of Islam*.

[6] See Bk. III, Arts. 2-4, pp. 123 and 126 above.

Article 3.   THAT MOHAMMED IS PROPHET

1.   Goodness Greatness

The Saracen said to the Gentile: "There was a time when all the inhabitants of Mecca and of the City of Yathrib,[7] where Mohammed was Prophet, were idolaters and had no knowledge of God, and were in the same error as you when you came here and had no knowledge of God. Now just as you needed consolation in your state of sorrow, so the above-mentioned people needed the help and enlightenment of faith. And since God's goodness is great, He had pity on those people who were going astray through ignorance, and He decided to enlighten them and give them knowledge of Himself and His glory. And that is why He sent Mohammed as Prophet, so that he could enlighten them and give them knowledge of God; which enlightenment and knowledge are in accord with God's great goodness, with which they could not accord if there had been no prophet. And since one good should accord with another, therefore, in God's good and in the good Mohammed did when he guided those who had strayed, lies the proof that Mohammed is the Prophet of God."

The Gentile replied, saying: "According to what you say, it would follow that God's perfection is not in accord with His great goodness, as of necessity should be the case, for in the country I come from there are just as many people going to perdition, without anyone giving them knowledge of God. And since God's goodness does not satisfy all needs, it is therefore contrary to greatness, with which it would be in accord if it could satisfy all needs. And if God's goodness is contrary to greatness, it cannot possibly accord with perfection; and this is contrary to the conditions of the trees."

The Saracen replied, saying: "It is clear that God gave man free will to do good and avoid evil. Now, if everyone were on the true path, those who are in fact on the true path would have nothing on which they could exercise their free will. God therefore allows some people to remain in error so that we, who are on the true path,

---

[7] This place-name, which appears as *Trip* in the Catalan and Latin sources, corresponds to the modern Medina, in Arabic *Madīnat al-Nabī,* "The Prophet's City," which explains Llull's use of the word "City" here and not before Mecca.

can, for the love of God, go preach to them, convert them, and bring them to the path of salvation, so that we, as a result, may be more glorious in God's glory."

2. Power Prudence

"It is customary for a king to practice on his subjects whatever customs he wants. Now since in man God has created prudence by which he can know God's great power, therefore, in order to demonstrate this great power, God has, at various times, sent prophets and transmitted customs to demonstrate that God has the power to make certain statutes at one time and others at other times. And this is why He sent the prophet Moses to give the law to the Jews, which law God saw fit to conserve until the coming of the prophet Jesus Christ, who was the spirit of God and was born of a woman who was holy and a virgin; and he gave the law to the Christians, which lasted until He sent Mohammed, who revealed to us the Koran, which is our law and the word of God. Now if God did not bring about these changes of customs and laws by different prophecies at different times, prudence would not be so enlightened in its knowledge of God's power. And since that by which prudence can know God's power must be in accord with being, therefore, in this being and in the concordance of God's power and of prudence, it is made clear that Mohammed was God's messenger."

The Gentile replied: "According to the flowers of the trees and their conditions, it follows that God did not send one prophet to oppose the other, nor for one to deny or disbelieve what the other had prophesied about God. Thus, since the Christian religion and yours are contrary to one another, it is impossible that both be God-given. And if they are, then the flowers of the first tree must be in accord with falsehood against truth, which is impossible. Furthermore, if the situation were as you claimed, it would follow that God should send another prophet who would refute what Mohammed has said, and then another one after that, and so on infinitely until the end of the world, and that is impossible and against God's wisdom, perfection. For any craftsman should love his work, so that by this love his work can achieve perfection, provided, of course, he has the necessary wisdom and power."

3.   *Wisdom Pride*

The Saracen said to the Gentile: "Mohammed was an uneducated man who could not read or write, and God revealed to him the Koran, which is a book of great wisdom and the most beautiful composition[8] there is or could be; for all the men in the world, or all the angels or devils, could not compose so beautiful a work as the Koran, which is our law. Now since those men whom wisdom has made proud and vainglorious customarily look down upon those who are less wise, therefore God wanted to enlighten Mohammed, who had such great wisdom that he was able to divulge the Koran, which is the word of God, without becoming proud, in order to destroy pride and vainglory by exemplifying the humility of God, who so wanted to exalt the wisdom and humility of Mohammed. And since Mohammed had greatness of wisdom and humility, in this greatness of wisdom and humility is signified the fact that Mohammed was a prophet."

4.   *Charity Justice*

"It is only fitting that one should revere and honor a man who has charity and justice. Now since Mohammed is honored in this world by so many people, it is only right that in him justice accord with God's charity; for if it did not, God would not allow him to be as honored as he is; and if He did, it would follow that injustice and honor would accord with charity against charity, dishonor and justice, and this is impossible; by which impossibility it is shown—by the honor with which God has so greatly honored Mohammed—that Mohammed is Prophet."

The Gentile replied to the Saracen: "According to what you say, it follows that Jesus Christ, who is so honored in this world, is God, and that His apostles and other martyrs, who are so honored in this world, died on the true path. For if God did not allow those who died in falsehood to be honored in this world, then what was said of Christ must be true; and if it were, then your religion would not be

---

[8] The original has literally "dictation," which is closer to the point the Saracen is trying to make about the method of elaboration of the Koran; but the more usual medieval meaning of this word is "composition."

true, nor would Mohammed be worthy of being honored or of being a prophet."

5. Hope Gluttony

The Saracen said to the Gentile: "According to what is recounted in the Koran, which is the word of God, in Paradise there will be many great blessings: there will be all kinds of food that will be most pleasing to eat; there will be beautiful clothes, beautiful palaces, and beautiful rooms; and there will be many beds with many beautiful women with whom one will experience agreeable bodily pleasures.[9] Now in order to destroy the gluttony, avarice, and lust of this world, God sent Mohammed so that people would place their hopes in the delights of Paradise and therefore not sin with the delights of this world. And since that by which hope and gluttony can be most contrary to one another must accord with being, and since hope and gluttony can be most contrary if there is the above-mentioned happiness in Paradise, therefore in this greater contrariety, according to the conditions of the tree from which we picked the above-mentioned flower, is signified the fact that Mohammed is Prophet."

The Gentile replied: "According to the conditions of the flowers, it follows that if one flower signifies the existence of a certain thing, then that flower must not be contrary to the other flowers, which signify the nonexistence of that thing. For if this were the case, the flowers could be contrary to one another, and that is impossible."

Article 4.   THE KORAN

1. Power Love

The Saracen said to the Gentile: "Mohammed was an uneducated man who could not read or write, and the Koran is the most beauti-

---

[9] Critics have pointed out that Llull makes much of the materialism and sensuality of Muslim ideas on Paradise, perhaps considering it one of the more vulnerable aspects of their creed. See Art. 12 below for a detailed presentation of the Muslim Paradise, which is described in many *sūras* of the Koran.

ful composition there is or could be. Now if it were not for God's will and action, Mohammed could not have written or composed such a beautiful composition nor put together such well-ordered words as those of the Koran. And since it is by God's power that the Koran is such a beautiful composition, and since it was transmitted by Mohammed who was illiterate and did not himself have the power to compose such beautiful words, therefore the Koran must be the word of God.

"Power and love are in accord in God, and since in the Koran there are so many blessings that God promises those who know His glory, therefore the Koran shows us God's great love for His people. And since no other religion promises men so many blessings as does the Koran, it is therefore evident that the Koran is more pleasing to God than any other law. And if this were not the case, it would follow that one could love God more if He promised lesser blessings rather than greater ones, which is impossible and against the conditions of the trees.

"If the Koran were not God-given, it would be contrary to the truth; and since truth has power over falsehood, and truth is pleasing to God and falsehood odious, and since the Koran cannot be refuted by the doctrines of the Christians nor by those of the Jews, it is therefore evidently God-given, in order to show the concordance existing between the power and will of God, which accord is based on the fact that the power can and the will wants what the Jews and Christians do not have the power to refute, even though they have the will to do so."

2.   Power Justice

"You should know, Gentile, that for both Christians and Jews the most honored and sought-after place in the world is a city called Jerusalem. In the beginning of the world, it was the principal city of the prophets. In that city Jesus Christ was crucified and killed, and there is His tomb, according to what the Christians believe. And this city the Saracens hold, have, and possess in spite of the Christians and Jews. And in that city the Koran is taught publicly, and no book or doctrine is so honored there as is the Koran. Now all of this bears witness to the power and justice of God, for since neither Christians nor Jews believe in the Koran, God punishes them in the most honored and sought-after place they have. It is therefore clear that the Koran is the word of God; for if it were not, it would follow that the power of God and justice would be contrary to the justice of the Christians and Jews, and this is impossible; by which impossibility it is made manifest that the Koran was transmitted and sustained by the power of God." [...]

Article 5. THE QUESTIONING OF THE DEAD MAN IN THE TOMB

THE SARACEN said to the Gentile: "We believe that when a man dies and is buried, two angels[10] ask him five things, namely: Who is God? From whom comes His law? What is His law? Is Mohammed His prophet? Is Mecca to the South?[11] And if God has given him the grace to reply that God is his creator, his law comes from God, his law is the Koran, and that Mohammed is the messenger of God, and if he grants that Mecca is to the south, then, until the Day of Judgment, he will lie happily and comfortably in his tomb, and he will see Paradise with the glory God promises the blessed, and he will see the infernal punishments he will have escaped. And if that man denies the above-mentioned things and does not know the answers he should give, then the tomb will be tightened around him and he will be in pain and sadness until the Day of Judgment, and he will see the infernal punishments awaiting him, and he will see the glory of Paradise which he has lost.

"The above is an account of what Saracens believe happens to men when they die. Now, to prove this article, we will first pick the flower of

1. Greatness Power

"So that God may prove the greatness of His power, in that by His power dead men can see the above-mentioned things from inside the tomb, He wants the above-mentioned questioning to

---

[10] Called Munkar and Nakīr.

[11] Instead of the "Who is God?" of the Catalan and Spanish sources, the Latin and French sources have "What is God?". Llull's use of the word "south" is puzzling; the Arabic term is *qibla*, which means the direction of prayer, i.e., towards Mecca, which from Spain would be more east than south. Was Llull here relying on some Middle Eastern source for his information?

take place. And since, without this questioning and vision, God's power would not be so demonstrable, and since that by which God's power is demonstrable accords with being, therefore in this greater demonstration and vision of power is the above-mentioned article shown to be true."

Question. The Gentile said: "How can a dead man see all these things, when his body is without a soul, and since a body without a soul cannot see nor understand nor speak nor answer?"

Solution. "Some of us believe that God returns the soul to the body; others believe that the soul remains between the body and the winding sheet. Therefore, by virtue of divine power and by the fact that the soul is still in the tomb, a man can answer and see all these things. And if God's power were not powerful enough for the dead man to do these things, it would follow that greatness and power were contraries in God, and this is impossible." [...]

Article 6.   DEATH

1.   *Power Perfection*

The Saracen said to the Gentile: "We believe that everything dies, except God; that is to say, men, angels, devils, and all living things. And this death will take place when the Angel Seraphim[12] sounds the trumpet and then himself dies. And nothing that has life will remain alive, with the sole exception of God. Now to prove this article, the above-mentioned flower is suitable; for if all living things die, then power, perfection will be better signified in God, for greater power and perfection exist in a thing that is not mortal than in one that is mortal, since mortality signifies imperfection, and immortality perfection. And because that by which God's power and perfection accord with greater nobility should be granted, according to the conditions of the tree, it is therefore shown that everything must and will die, with the sole exception of God.

Question. The Gentile said: "According to the way I understand

---

[12] Thus (here and in Art. 7 below) in all sources. The more usual Arabic name for the "Lord of the Trumpet," is *Isrāfīl* (which is why Rosselló changed the text to *Israphi*), but *Sarāfīn* (from the Hebrew *Serāfīm*) is an acceptable variant.

it, the conditions of the trees are so arranged that if greater nobility is shown to exist in God by one manner than by another, then one should assign less nobility to the contrary manner. Now if all things die, it is true that God's power and perfection will seem greater in terms of the use made of His perfect, immortal power. But since even angels and the souls of saints who deserve life rather than death would die, God's perfection would be against justice and against goodness, since death brings suffering and harm, which suffering and harm should not exist without guilt. Now since it is impossible for divine perfection to be against God's justice, goodness, it is therefore shown that what you say is not true."

Solution. The Saracen replied: "What you say would be true if God did not revive angels and souls again. But since they will all be alive again, and God will give them everlasting life, therefore God will be doing them no wrong in having them die, but rather He would be wronging Himself if in creatures He did not make use of His virtues so that they were seen in their greatest nobility and perfection."

Question. The Gentile said, "Death is the separation of body and soul. Now if angels have no body, how can they die?"

Solution. The Saracen replied, "Angels will die by become nothing, and this is what we mean when we say they will die."

The Gentile replied, "By making them become nothing, God would be contrary to that which accords with being, since the good angels, by the fact of serving God deserve to have being; and if they are naught, God's virtues accord with nonbeing against being, and that is impossible." [...]

Article 7.   RESURRECTION

WHILE THE Saracen was looking at the first tree, trying to choose a flower with which to prove the Resurrection, the Gentile remembered that in the first book the Resurrection had been proved quite satisfactorily, and he therefore said to the Saracen: "You don't have to prove the Resurrection, for it was already proved well enough in the first book. But do please tell me in what way you Saracens think you will arise from the dead."

The Saracen replied: "We believe that when all living things are dead, after forty days there will fall from the sky a rain as white as milk, and then men and beasts and birds and all other living creatures will germinate like grass. And the Angel Seraphim will sound the trumpet again, and the people will rise from the dead and shake the earth from their heads.

"Fire will come from the sky and the heat of the sun will be very great; and because of the great heat, people will lie down on the ground, which will be exceedingly white. And they will be bathed in sweat and their tongues will hang out, and it will seem to them that this day lasts fifty thousand years.[13] More angels than all the men living on earth will come down from the first heaven; and from the second there will come twice as many; and then from the third, and so on, from one heaven to the next each time doubling the number, until the seventh heaven, from which God, along with the angels from that heaven, will descend, saying, 'I would be unjust if on this day of Resurrection, any living creature escaped my taking revenge upon him for whatever injustice he had done.' This, Gentile, is the way we believe the Day of Judgment will be, and there are many other things I could tell you, but it would take too long to recount. Since in this discussion we have agreed to talk as briefly as possible, I have therefore told you concisely what our Prophet Mohammed says in the Koran, and what our wise men say in their commentaries upon our Law."

Article 8.   HOW MOHAMMED WILL BE HEEDED

THE SARACEN said to the Gentile: "We believe that Mohammed will pray to God on behalf of his people and will be heeded. Now, before I prove this article by means of the flowers of the trees, I want to tell you how we believe Mohammed will pray to God and be heeded.

"On the day that everyone will rise from the dead, God will gather them all together in one place, and they will be suffering greatly from the heat to which they will have been subjected and

---

[13] This is part of Islamic tradition, which states that the Day of Judgment will be as 50,000 years, yet for Allah it will be like the opening and closing of an eye.

from the sweat in which they will be bathed, for some will be in sweat up to their ankles, others up to their knees, others to their throat, others to their eyes, and yet others will be in sweat like frogs in water, and this will depend on how sinful each person has been.

"While these people are in pain and sweat, they will agree to go to Adam and entreat him to beg God to take them out of this pain, and to place in Paradise those who should be saved, and in Hell those who should be damned. But Adam will reply, 'I would be ashamed to beseech God, since I disobeyed Him when I ate of the fruit He had commanded me not to eat'; to which Adam will add, 'Go to Noah and have him pray for you.' They will go to Noah and beseech him as they did Adam. Noah will reply, 'I am not worthy of beseeching God nor of being heeded, for I forsook my people who perished on the day of the flood, and I would be ashamed to beseech God. But go to Abraham and ask him to pray for you.' They will then go to Abraham and tell him the same thing they told Noah. Abraham will reply, 'I am not worthy of beseeching God, for I lied twice: once when I told my father I had not broken the idols but that they had broken by themselves, and the other time when I said that my wife was my sister and not my wife. Thus, since I am not worthy of beseeching God nor of being heeded, I advise you to go to Moses and ask him to pray for you.' They will go to Moses and ask him to intercede for them. Moses will reply, 'I am not worthy of beseeching God nor of being heeded, for I killed a man and I commanded that all those who believed in the Golden Calf, making an idol out of it and worshiping it as if it were God, should die. So I advise you to go to Jesus Christ and ask him to intercede for you.' They will go to Jesus Christ and beseech him, but he will turn down their request, saying that he is not worthy to beseech God nor to be heeded, 'and I would be ashamed to beseech God on your behalf, since, without God's permission, people worshiped me and believed in me as if I were God.' And he will advise them to go to the holy Prophet Mohammed, so that he may pray for them. They will go to Mohammed, imploring him to beseech God to take them out of the pain in which they are, and to save whoever is to be saved and to condemn whoever is to be condemned. Mohammed will answer saying that he will gladly intercede for them; and at once, before God's throne, he will kneel down and bow to the ground, and he will beseech God to deliver them from their suffering, and to put in

Paradise whoever is to be saved and in Hell whoever is to be damned. While Mohammed will be beseeching God in this way, the voice of God will be heard in the sky, saying, 'Mohammed, today is no time to pray or to implore. Ask and it shall be given; beseech and it shall be granted.' Mohammed will then say that God should ask people for an accounting of their actions, so that whoever should go to Paradise may go there and whoever should go to Hell may go there. And God will reply that it will be done as Mohammed asks.

"This is one way, Gentile, that we believe Mohammed will beseech God and will be heeded. There is another way in which Mohammed will beseech God and be heeded: that is after God has passed judgment sending the good to Paradise and the wicked to Hell, and some sinners from among Mohammed's people will find themselves in Hell, then Mohammed will pray for those people, and God will take them from Hell because of Mohammed's prayers. And we believe in these two kinds of intercession, which of necessity must exist, as is signified by the conditions and flowers of the trees. And of this truth I offer the following proofs." [...]

2. Love Justice

The Saracen said to the Gentile: "We find that all the above-mentioned prophets, as we said before, committed sin after becoming prophets; on account of which sin they declined to beseech God, as we have recounted; but we do not find that Mohammed committed any sin after becoming a prophet. Thus, in order to demonstrate that God dearly loves justice and hates injustice, which is sin, Mohammed was honored over the other prophets in being heeded. And since this demonstration of the above flower would not be so complete without the above-mentioned article, therefore, according to the conditions of the trees, God wanted this article to accord with truth, in which concordance this article is provable." When the Saracen had finished these words, both the Jew and the Christian wanted to reply, but the Gentile did not permit it.

Question. The Gentile said, "Tell me, did Mohammed commit any sin before he became prophet?"

Solution. The Saracen replied, "The truth is that Mohammed sinned through ignorance before he became a prophet, in that he believed in idols, as was the practice in his country, and in which practice his father and mother, who were idolaters, had brought him up." [...]

Article 9.   TO GIVE AN ACCOUNTING

"YOU SHOULD know, Gentile, that God will ask for an accounting from all men, the good as well as the wicked, and we will all have to give an account of the good and evil we have done in this life. And God will punish a man who will wrongly have done injustice to his neighbor and yet have done some good, in such a way that the reward he should have had from the good he did will be given to the man he had wronged. And in the event that he has done no good, God will give him the punishment intended for sinners who had done some good; and this he will do to demonstrate His justice. And not only will God ask for an accounting from men, but also from the beasts and birds, and He will punish them for the wrongs they have done against one another. And after punishing them, He will command them to turn into earth; and they will all turn into earth, and from then on they will be nothing."

Question. The Gentile said, "What good will come from the resurrection of the beasts and the birds, or from the accounting they will give, if they will then become nothing, since they have no discernment and no knowledge of God's justice?"

Solution. The Saracen replied, saying, "The good that will come from the resurrection of beasts and irrational creatures lies in the fact that sinners will want to turn into nothing like irrational creatures, and instead they will have ire and suffering as a result of remaining in being."

Question. The Gentile said, "When will the balancing of the account be finished, with so many creatures having committed so many injustices one against the other?"

Solution. The Saracen replied: "According to our beliefs, the accounting will take no longer than it takes an egg to cook, and this will be as a demonstration of the greatness inherent in the power, wisdom, and perfection of God. Now that you have understood the way in which God will ask living creatures for an accounting, we should return to the procedure agreed upon for our discussion, and prove the above-mentioned article by the flowers of the trees." […]

Article 11. THE PATH TO PARADISE AND HELL

THE SARACEN said to the Gentile: "We believe that on the Day of Judgment there will be a path over which the blessed who shall be saved will pass. This path will take a thousand years to climb, a thousand to traverse, and a thousand to descend, and below it will be Hell, into which those unable to pass will fall. This path will be as narrow as a hair or the cutting edge of a sword; and some will pass over it as quickly as lightning, others like a horse galloping, others like a man running, and yet others like a child crawling, and everyone will travel along that path according to his merit; and if he does not deserve glory, he will fall from that bridge into Hell.[14] […]

5. Justice Pride

"Justice destroys pride, since pride tries to ascend through injustice. Thus, those proud people who will fall from the path that takes a thousand years to climb will fall from higher up through pride and injustice than they would if the path did not exist. And since that by which justice is most contrary to pride must be true, therefore the above-mentioned article must exist; for if it did not, it would follow that the flowers of the first tree would be contrary to that by which justice, pride were more contrary to one another, and that is impossible; by which impossibility it is demonstrated that the article is true."

Question. The Gentile said to the Saracen, "According to what you say, it follows that another path, longer and higher than the one you described, must exist, so that justice should be even more contrary to pride."

Solution. The Saracen replied: "What you say would be true if, by

---

[14] In Arabic this path is called *al-ṣirāṭ* or "the bridge." Llull's description of it as being as narrow as a hair or the cutting edge of a sword, as well as its passing over Hell, is indeed part of Muslim tradition. Its length, however, is often given as even greater, with some traditions maintaining that it is in seven sections, the last of which takes 640,000 years to cross.

another consideration, there did not result an inconsistency with the flowers of the first tree. But since, as far as we have heard, neither Christians, Jews, nor any other people believe in a path greater than the one in which we believe, it is therefore incongruous that the path you mention exist and be unknown; for if it did exist and were unknown, this would result in an inconsistency in the flowers of the first tree, which is impossible."

Question. "If what you say is true, tell me what those who crawl along the path will eat and drink, and where such a path would fit, for the whole world is not big enough for a path as long and as high as you describe."

Solution. The Saracen replied, saying: "According to the Koran and according to the Proverbs of Mohammed,[15] God will command the earth to expand so that everybody will fit on it on Judgment Day, and He will make the same commandment with respect to Paradise and Hell, so that those who enter them will find room. And this will better exemplify the greatness inherent in God's power and will, for as God commands, so shall it be. I therefore answer you, saying that the world will expand until the path will fit in it."

Question. "According to what you say, earth, Paradise, and Hell should be expanded infinitely and an infinite amount of people created, the better to manifest the greatness of God's power and will."

Solution. The Saracen replied, saying that nothing can be infinite, since nothing can be equal to God's greatness, which is infinite; and therefore everything God creates must be finite and in a quantity suitable to the thing created, according to the conditions of the trees.

Article 12.   PARADISE AND HELL

THE GENTILE said to the Saracen: "There is no need to prove Paradise or Hell, for they have already been proved quite satisfac-

---

[15] These are the Hadīth, narratives or traditions of the Prophet, embodying the *Sunna* ("the Way"), second in importance only to the Koran itself for Muslims.

torily. But I would like to know what you believe the glory of Paradise will be like."

The Saracen replied, saying, "We believe there are two ways in which we will enjoy the glory of Paradise; one is spiritual glory, and the other is physical glory. Spiritual glory is seeing God, and loving and contemplating God. This is the glory we will have in Paradise, according to what our Prophet Mohammed says in his Proverbs, where he states that those in Paradise will see God in the morning and in the evening, for if they lean out of any of the windows of the palaces in which they will be living, God will appear to them. And that vision will be so great a glory that no heart[16] can conceive it nor any mouth describe it.

"We will have physical glory through all the five bodily senses with which we served God in this present life. For if in Paradise we did not experience glory through our five senses, God would have neither perfect justice nor perfect goodness; by which imperfection physical glory is shown to exist in Paradise. So, in order that your soul may rejoice in the blessings you will receive in Paradise if you convert to our faith, I want to recount briefly the glory a person will experience in each of the bodily senses."

1.   Sight

"We believe that in Paradise a person will have beautiful palaces with beautiful rooms made of gold, silver, and precious stones, such as rubies, emeralds, sapphires, pearls, and other similar stones; and because of the way they are cut, and because of the stones themselves, which will be as large as big mountains, these palaces and these rooms will be very beautiful to behold.

"And in these palaces there will be many cloths of gold and silver and silk adorning the walls; and there will be many beds and mats and carpets of gold and silver and silk; and in these palaces there will also be many beautiful women and maidens,[17] all very nobly dressed and most agreeable to look upon.

---

[16] The heart used to be considered the seat of affective thought (as opposed to pure reasoning, with arguments, etc.), and indeed the medieval Latin translator rendered it as *mens* (cf. Epilogue, nn. 1-2).

[17] Thus in O; "young men" or "pages" in F; lacking in all other sources. Surely this is a reference to the "houris" (from the Arabic *ḥūrīya*, "virgin of paradise; nymph"). For these descriptions of Muslim Paradise, see n. 9 above.

"In the valleys and meadows there will be many springs and streams, and many trees bearing leaves, flowers, and fruit, and casting lovely shade. In fact, the beauty and grace of all these things will be such as to make them almost impossible to describe or recount.

"In Paradise we will see angels, who are a beautiful thing to see, and are very large and pleasing. And we will see the prophets and saints, and ranks of different people according to the way in which they will have served God in this world. And each person will be shining and resplendent, and very nobly dressed. Now this being the case, you can understand how great will be the glory of Paradise with all these things to be seen."

2. Hearing

"To hear the singing of angels, men, and women all praising and blessing God will, as you can well imagine, give great glory to all those who hear it, and all the more so considering how many will be singing these songs of sweetness, glory, and honor.

"In Paradise, if you succeed in entering, you will talk with your friends and companions about anything you wish, about everything you did in this world and about the glory you are experiencing; and those with whom you talk will talk to you similarly, and speaking and hearing such words will give a person great pleasure."

3. Smell

"I cannot find words to describe the glory which the blessed in Paradise will experience upon smelling the scents there; for in Paradise there will be scents of ambergris and musk, of leaves, flowers, and fruits in everything a person will eat or drink, dress in, or touch. And the breeze, which will be gentle and pleasant, will bring this scent, which will be so pleasant to smell that all the scents of this world will be as nothing compared to those of Paradise."

4. Taste

The Saracen said to the Gentile: "My dear friend, believe my words, hear and understand the blessings a person will have in

Paradise, and let it be these that you seek. For in Paradise there will be rivers of water and wine, of milk, butter and oil; and by the river banks and springs there will be many lovely trees, beneath whose shade a person will sit, eating and drinking whatever he wants; for if he wants to eat fruit from the trees, he can have some at once, and if it is meat or some other thing he desires, it will appear before him at once, prepared in whatever way he wishes. In fact, how could anyone possibly describe to you the flavor, the sweetness, and the pleasure a person will find in the food, in the drink, and in the above-mentioned things, and especially since in Paradise he will have much greater ability to eat and drink a lot than in this world! For just as the glory of Paradise is greater than the glory of this world, thus it is only right that in Paradise a person have greater power to eat and drink a great deal than in this present life."

5. *Touch*

"One derives happiness and pleasure in this world from handling, touching, and feeling, and therefore in Paradise one will have glory handling, feeling, and touching soft, smooth cloth, and lying on cushions and soft beds with sheets and bedspreads of silk.

"In order to give great bodily pleasure, in Paradise God has created for man many beautiful virgin maidens reserved for the blessed who will be saved, and in lying with whom men will have great pleasure, and who will never grow old, and whom a man will find intact every time he lies with them."

"In Paradise a man will lie with the same wives and women he had in his house in this world and with whom he had lain. And according as some men will be worthier of greater glory than others, they will have more maidens and more women—and more beautiful ones—in their beds than any other men.

"In order to increase the glory of Paradise and make it greater than the glory of this world, God will increase man's capacity to lie with women in Paradise; and for this reason men will lie much more with women in Paradise, so that they may have great glory.

"You should know, Gentile, that in Paradise men will have all the glories you have heard me describe. And in Paradise there will be many other glories I haven't told you about, glories that would take long to recount and which are so great I could not describe them to you."

Question. The Gentile said to the Saracen, "If things are as you say, then there must be filth in Paradise, for according to the natural order of things, from a man who eats and drinks and lies with women there must come forth filth and corruption, which filth is an ugly thing to see and touch and smell, and to talk about."

Solution. The Saracen replied: "What you say is true according to the world in which we live. But in the next world it will be just the opposite, as a result of divine influence and power, which can ordain and improve anything."

Question. The Gentile said to the Saracen: "As I understand it, the ultimate purpose for which man is made is to have glory in God; yet according to what you say, it would follow that man existed to have glory in the above-mentioned things. And if he did, the result would not be the purpose for which man was made; and if he did not, it would follow that in God wisdom would not accord with power, love, perfection, and this is impossible and against the conditions of the trees."

Solution. The Saracen replied, "Man was created principally to know and love God, and it follows that, according to God's justice, perfection, men should be recompensed with the above-mentioned happiness, without which men could not be recompensed."

Question. The Gentile said to the Saracen. "If God is just and gives many women to a just man in Paradise, and the juster the man has been, the more women he will have to lie with, so that his glory will be greater, it therefore follows that to a woman who is juster than a man and juster than another woman, God should give her many men to lie with in Paradise, so that she may have greater glory."

Solution. The Saracen replied, "God has honored man more than woman in this world, and therefore in the next world He wishes to do greater honor to him than to woman."[18]

Question. The Gentile said to the Saracen, "Pray tell me is it true that all you Saracens believe you will, in Paradise, have the sort of glory you just described to me?"

---

[18] If the Gentile's voice here can be taken as Llull's, this remarkable little exchange constitutes an interesting reflection of the differing attitude of the two cultures towards the role of women.

Solution. The Saracen replied, saying: "It is true that among us there are differing beliefs with respect to the glory of Paradise, for some believe it will be as I said, and this they take from a literal interpretation of the Koran, which is our law, of the Proverbs of Mohammed, and of commentators' glosses on the Koran and the Proverbs. But there are others among us who take this glory morally and interpret it spiritually, saying that Mohammed was speaking metaphorically to people who were backward and without understanding; and in order to inspire them with a love of God he recounted the above-mentioned glory. And therefore those who believe this say that in Paradise there will be no glory of eating or of lying with women, nor of the other things mentioned above. And these men are natural philosophers and great scholars, yet they are men who in some ways do not follow too well the dictates of our religion, and this is why we consider them as heretics, who have arrived at their heresy by studying logic and natural science. And therefore it has been established among us that no man dare teach logic or natural science publicly."[19]

When the Saracen had finished talking and had recounted everything required to prove his religion, he spoke the following words to the Gentile: "Now you have heard and understood my words, O Gentile, and the proofs I have given of the articles of our religion. And you have heard of the blessings of Paradise, which you will have everlastingly without end if you believe in our religion, which is God-given." And when the Saracen had spoken these words, he closed his book and finished speaking, and to the two wise men he made salutation according to his custom.

[19] Sala-Molins, *Choix*, p. 115, n. 35, says this was the opinion held by Avicenna, al-Ghazzali, and al-Farabi. Llull, however, seems also to be referring to al-Ghazzali's famous attack on the philosophers (and especially Avicenna and al-Farabi), whom he censured for relying too much on "logic and natural science," and mainly for rejecting the resurrection of the body.

EPILOGUE

THE END OF THIS BOOK

WHEN THE Gentile had heard all the arguments of the three wise men, he began to recount everything the Jew had said, and then everything the Christian had said, and similarly with what the Saracen had said. As a result, the three wise men were very pleased, for the Gentile had understood and retained their words; and together they said to the Gentile that it was clear they had not spoken to a man without heart[1] or ears. After recounting the above matter, the Gentile stood up and his understanding was illuminated by the path of salvation, and his heart began to love and to bring tears to his eyes, and he worshiped God saying these words:

Prayer

"Ah! Divine, infinite, sovereign good, which is origin and fulfillment of all good! To Your holy goodness, O Lord, I give reverence and honor; to it I attribute and give thanks for the great happiness I have received.

"Lord God, I adore and bless Your greatness, which is infinite in goodness, eternity, power, wisdom, love, perfection.

"Glory and praise be given to Your eternity, O Lord, for it is without beginning or end in goodness, greatness, power, wisdom, love, perfection.

"Lord God, that power You possess, which is infinite in Your goodness, greatness, eternity, wisdom, love, perfection, I worship and fear and honor above all other powers.

"Lovable God, who within Yourself have infinite wisdom in Your goodness, greatness, eternity, power, love, perfection, and in everything You have created, Your wisdom, O Lord, I love and worship with all my physical and spiritual strength.

"Your love, which is not an ordinary love, but a love above all

---

[1] Cf. Bk. IV, n. 16 above, and n. 2 below. Here the medieval Latin translator rendered it as *intellectus rationabilis*.

other loves, a love which is perfect in Your perfect goodness, greatness, eternity, power, wisdom—that love of Yours, O Lord, I worship and love, and to it, with all my will, with all the strength of my
intellect and will all that Your love has seen fit to give me, I give
everything, O Lord, to serve and honor and praise Your love every
day of my life.

"Divine perfection, You who are the light and cure of all imper-
fections, who are the hope of all sinners, and who are infinite
through all Your goodness, greatness, eternity, power, wisdom,
love, to You I turn and to You I ask forgiveness and grace and
counsel and help as to how to serve You and to recover, through
You, the days I lost through ignorance and wrongdoing."

After the Gentile, with sighs and tears and true contrition of
heart, had worshiped the flowers of the first tree, he beseeched and
asked God's grace and blessing to give him the flowers of the fourth
tree, saying these words:

"Ah, true faith, you who have taken so long in coming to enlighten my intelligence that my past days are lost and irrecuperable!
Ah faith, which is unknown in the land I come from, on account of
which ignorance so many men go to everlasting fires! Sweet faith,
you are welcome in my soul, for it has been enlightened through
you and in you, and you have banished from my mind the darkness
in which I have existed all my life. Pain, ire, despair, anguish,
tribulations, all these you have banished from my heart. To the God
of glory I give thanks for you, and I beg that, by His virtue, you
remain in me as long as I shall live, and that I serve you by recounting and spreading abroad your virtue and your fame and your
honor.

"Hope, my friend, where have you come from and where have
you been? Do you know the despair I have suffered for such a long
time? While despair tormented me so grievously, why did you not
come and help me against your enemy? Hope, you who are the
consolation of the disconsolate, the wealth and treasure of the poor,
you who strengthen the weak against the strong and cause the God
of Glory to be in the heart of those who desire and love Him, you
have entered my heart so strongly that from now on I shall no
longer fear your contrary who has so long been my mortal enemy.
In you, through you and with you I place my trust and hope in my

Lord's great power, that He fulfill my desire to honor and serve God, and make Him known among those who neither love nor know Him. I shall not despair of my poor power, knowledge, and will, nor shall I despair of my grievous and many sins, for you make me remember the great mercy of that Lord who can accomplish anything, can give any grace and can forgive any sin."

While the Gentile was saying these words, he frequently knelt down and kissed the ground, and raised his hands and eyes heavenward. He then conceived the desire, with the help of created charity, to worship and contemplate uncreated divine charity, worthy of all honor.

"Ah charity, lovable virtue! Whoever has and loves you is pleasing and lovable by that divine charity which eternally and infinitely loves whatever loves. Charity, you who give of yourself to everyone who will have you, and of whom they may take as much as they want, by what stroke of fortune were you willing to have me beneath your sway without my recalling, knowing, or loving you? Fortune, who has long been my enemy, has, by putting me in your hands, healed all my injuries; but since I am a poor sinner, and since you have made me so love God and my neighbor, how could I repay the great good I have received through you? Alas, wretched creature that I am! In what poverty and misery are all those who neither love nor know charity! And of what use to a man's heart are riches and blessings without charity? Sweet God, You who have enlightened and warmed me by the fire of charity, enlighten and warm with charity all those poor people lacking in charity who live in the land I come from, by which poverty they will be brought, through paths of darkness, to infinite, everlasting fire, where torments will not cease and where hope will be unable to hope for any alleviation.

"Do not let us forget justice in our prayer, for divine justice knows all my faults and can rightly punish me for all my failings. Whatever divine justice does with me, whether it punishes me and condemns me to everlasting torment, or pardons me to everlasting blessing, in every way I worship and bless God's justice. Let Him do with me what He will, for charity makes me love, fear, and worship God in His justice, which is always on the side of righteousness. And therefore, let my justice make me desire whatever God's justice would do with me.

"Prudence, you who are the light of salvation by which wise men go to the divine radiance that illuminates all those who love it, my understanding has long been in darkness because you were not part of it. But since you have now brought me such happiness, I beg you from now on not to let my soul be without you. And may it please the high, excellent, lofty, sovereign good that through you I may have knowledge and light from sovereign wisdom, which gives its light to you and to all other lights; and that through grace and the illumination of this sovereign light you may help me to give light and direction to so many men who are in a state or in times of darkness, ignorant of the path of salvation.

"Fortitude, who strengthens noble hearts so they do not succumb to wickedness or deceit, would you strengthen the weak heart of a lazy, fearful man so that he could suffer the hardships, dangers, and deaths necessary to give praise, glory, and blessing to the name of that Lord who is worthy of all honor and who wishes to be so honored that for the sake of serving Him no torments are feared? Could charity, justice, prudence, and you (together, perhaps, with hope) agree to come to my land and there do the same good I have received from God through you?

"Temperance, abstinence, patience, perseverance, and the other virtues, what are you doing? Do not sleep, for the vices that are your contraries are awake night and day, and they never cease their work of destruction in the hearts of people who are gluttonous, lustful, avaricious, accidious, proud, envious, and full of ire."

While the Gentile was speaking these words, he realized and saw that his eyes were not crying or shedding their usual tears. And in order that his heart bring to his eyes the water it once had—that which had bathed his eyes in tears—he wanted to recall in his heart the seven mortal sins, and he therefore said:

"Ah, how evil is the servitude of those who are serfs and captives of gluttony! For gluttony gives its servants continual torments; and it spares no one, neither rich nor poor; it brings death closer, and fattens our bodies, so that in a short time they become food for worms.

"Lust, you who not only soil the body, but also soil and deface the memory that recalls you, as well as the intellect that understands you and the will that desires you. And you are such a filthy thing that you are ugly and horrible to see and touch.

"Avarice, you who impoverish the rich and bring the poor beneath your sway, you who make men despair of God who alone can dispense every good, what do you do in this world to make the rich despise the poor and the poor hate the rich?

"Accidie, you who are a sign of damnation in those beneath your sway, and you who make men so indolent in praising and loving God (who is worthy of such praise and such great honor), when will you reward those whom you keep needy and poor, and why do you send them to Hell since they carry out so well your command not to love?

"Pride, if humility were naught, what would you be? And if humility raised you up instead of pulling you down, how great you would be! And just because you cannot be in glory, why do you prevent the humble from going there? For theirs is the glory you have lost and from which you have fallen.

"Envy, you who are sadness of soul, if you do not die while there is still time, when will you die? And if you are never satisfied envying what you do, why do you still desire it? And if you are always taking, when will you give? And if in so many things you employ deceit and treachery, is there nothing in which you are true and loyal?

"Ire, you who are darkness of thought and darkness of intellect and mortal will, contrary to charity, what are you doing among us, and why do you keep us from loving the honor of our Lord, who loves the honor of all His servants and scorns all those who follow you?"

While the Gentile was speaking these words, he realized and saw that his eyes were still not shedding tears, and he said: "Ah, miserable wretch, what is it that keeps your eyes from crying? For if you do not do so, when you can, for joy at the great happiness that came to you by chance (how, you do not know), and if you do not cry for your wrongs and for your sins while you have the chance, when will you cry, you worthless thing? And yet before this day you were crying, because you thought that after your death you would be nothing."

While the Gentile spoke these words, along with many others it would take too long to recount, his soul endeavored to recall, understand, and love divine virtue, which at last enabled his heart to bring tears to his eyes.

For a long time the Gentile cried sweetly and devoutly, saying: "Ah, God of virtue! How great is the difference between the tears I used to shed and those I am shedding now! For those tears tormented and afflicted the thought of my heart,[2] and these tears are so agreeable and pleasant, and they enliven my soul with such great happiness that I would want no better happiness in the whole world than to have my soul remain in this uninhabitable spot in a continual state of loving, and my eyes forever in tears. Yet I must go from land to land, and I must return to my own land, and I must spread word of God's honor among those who do not know God—that God through whom such good has come to me. To this end I must strive all the days of my life; and may it please you, Lord God, to let neither hunger, thirst, heat, cold, poverty, weariness, people's scorn, sickness, torments, nor being abandoned by one's lord, nor leaving one's wife, sons, daughters, friends, or worldly possessions, nor to be exiled nor to suffer cruel death, nor any other thing, banish from my heart the thought of your honor nor the praising of your glorious name.

"Lord God, You who give and forgive so many things, may it please You to forgive Your guilty sinner who asks Your forgiveness and who begs the blessed saints in glory to thank You for the good You have done me, for which I alone could not thank You sufficiently. In this hour, O Lord, forgive this sinner who gives You his soul and all his powers, so that he may go in Your path and perform those deeds by which You wish to be served by those beneath Your sway."

In this way the Gentile worshiped and blessed and thanked his Lord and his Creator. And so great was his endeavor to worship and praise God and to beg forgiveness for his faults, that the three wise men had great pity on him, and marveled at how nobly he prayed. And so great was the devotion they saw in the Gentile that in their souls their consciences made them uneasy and reminded them of the sins in which they had persevered; and all the more so when they realized that the Gentile, in so short a time, had conceived greater devotion in giving praise to God's name than they who had known of God for a long time.

How the Three Wise Men Took Leave of the Gentile

When the Gentile had finished his prayer, he went to the lovely spring and washed his hands and face, because of the tears he had

---

[2] See the previous note.

shed, and dried himself with a white cloth he carried, the one he had formerly used to wipe away his continual tears of sorrow. He then sat down next to the three wise men and said: "Through God's grace and blessing, I happened to meet you gentlemen here where God saw fit to remember me and take me as His servant. Blessed be the Lord, therefore, and blessed be this place, and may God bless you, and blessed be God for making you want to come here! And in this place, where I have received such good fortune, in the presence of you gentlemen, I want to select and choose that religion which, by the grace of God and by your words, seems to me to be true. And in that religion I want to be, and I want to work for the rest of my life to honor and proclaim it."

When the Gentile had spoken thus and stood up in order to kneel, and kneeling, proclaim the religion he preferred, he saw far away, coming through the forest, two gentiles who were from his land, whom he knew, and who were in the same error in which he had once been. And the Gentile therefore said to the three wise men that he wanted to await the arrival of these two Gentiles, so that he could proclaim the true religion in their presence. The three wise men then stood up and most agreeably and devoutly took leave of the Gentile. Many were the blessings the three wise men wished on the Gentile, and the Gentile on the three wise men; and their leave-taking and the end of their conversation was full of embraces, kisses, tears, and sighs. But before the three wise men left, the Gentile asked them in astonishment why they did not wait to hear which religion he would choose in preference to the others. The three wise men answered, saying that, in order for each to be free to choose his own religion, they preferred not knowing which religion he would choose. "And all the more so since this is a question we could discuss among ourselves to see, by force of reason and by means of our intellects, which religion it must be that you will choose. And if, in front of us, you state which religion it is that you prefer, then we would not have such a good subject of discussion nor such satisfaction in discovering the truth."[3] With these words,

---

[3] This extraordinary lack of desire on the part of the three wise men to hear the Gentile's opinion, leaving the entire book, as it were, up in the air, has been the subject of considerable comment. Surely, as one critic stated it, it is an ingenious device to hold back the solution of the religious problem, in order to leave the reader free to inquire and ask for himself, as stated at the end of the book, "what religion . . . the Gentile chose in order to find favor with God." At the same time, Llull—as we can see from references to the *Gentile* in other works—had no doubts that the protagonist would choose Christianity, whose spokesman's arguments he

the three wise men returned to the city from which they had come. But the Gentile, looking at the flowers of the five trees and recalling what he had decided, waited for the two gentiles who were coming.

What the Three Wise Men Said as They Returned

One of the three wise men said: "If the Gentile, who was so long in error, has conceived such great devotion and such great fervor in praising God, that he now states that in order to do so he would not hesitate to suffer any hardship or death, no matter how harsh it were, then how much greater should be our devotion and fervor in praising the name of God, considering how long we have known about Him, and all the more so since He has placed us under such obligation by the many blessings and honors He has given us and gives us every day. We should debate and see which of us is in truth and which in error. For just as we have one God, one Creator, one Lord, we should also have one faith, one religion, one sect, one manner of loving and honoring God, and we should love and help one another, and make it so that between us there be no difference or contrariety of faith or customs, which difference and contrariety cause us to be enemies with one another and to be at war, killing one another and falling captive to one another. And this war, death, and servitude prevent us from giving the praise, reverence, and honor we owe God every day of our life."[4]

When this wise man had finished, another began to speak, saying that people were so rooted in the faith in which they found themselves and in which they were raised by their parents and ancestors, that it was impossible to make them break away by preaching, by disputation, or by any other means man could devise. And this is why, as soon as one starts discussing with them, showing them the

---

had, of course, made more persuasive. In view of this unexpressed but foregone outcome, it might seem out of place to praise the ecumenical spirit of the work, as some critics have done, but they can on their side point to the Gentile's remarkably non-denominational prayer in the preceding section, and the plea for world unity in the following one (see the next note).

[4] One of Llull's clearest statements of his ideal of unity for the sake of peace, of a human unity that would reflect divine unity, doing away with "difference and contrariety" and leaving only "concordance." This was one of the aspects of Llull's teaching that most interested Nicholas of Cusa.

error of their ways, they immediately scorn everything one tells them, saying they want to live and die in the faith their parents and ancestors gave them.

The other wise man replied, saying: "It is in the nature of truth to be more strongly rooted in the mind than falsehood, since truth and being are in accord, as are falsehood and nonbeing. And therefore, if falsehood were strongly opposed by truth, continually and by many people, then truth would necessarily have to vanquish falsehood; and all the more so since falsehood never receives any help, great or small, from God, and truth is always helped by that divine virtue which is uncreated truth, which has created created truth for the purpose of destroying falsehood. But since men are lovers of temporal possessions, and lukewarm and of little devotion in loving God and their neighbor, they therefore care little about destroying falsehood and error; and they live in fear of dying and of suffering illness, hardship, and poverty, yet they do not want to give up their wealth, their possessions, their lands, or their relatives to save those who are in error, so they may go to everlasting glory and not undergo infinite suffering. And they should do this mainly in order to be counted among those who praise the name of God and proclaim His virtue, for God wants it to be proclaimed among all nations, and every day He waits to see how we will honor Him among those who dishonor, despise, and are ignorant of Him; and God wants us to do what we can to exalt His glorious name among us. For if we do what we can to praise God, how much more would God do as a result of having His name praised! For if He did not, it would be contrary to Himself and to His honor, which is impossible and against the conditions of the trees. But because we do not prepare ourselves to receive God's virtue and blessing, nor to be his valiant servants, who praise him, strengthened by stout hearts to face any hardship to exalt His honor, God therefore does not bestow on us that virtue which must be present in those who, through God's virtue, would destroy the error of people on the road to damnation who think they are on the road to salvation."

While the wise man was speaking these words and many others, the three of them arrived at the place where they had first met by the city gates; and there they took leave of one another most amiably and politely, and each asked forgiveness of the other for any disrespectful word he might have spoken against his religion. Each forgave the other,[5] and when they were about to part, one wise man said: "Do you think we have nothing to gain from what happened to us in the forest? Would you like to meet once a day, and, by the five trees and the ten conditions signified by their flowers, discuss according to the manner the Lady of Intelligence showed us, and have our discussions last until all three of us have only one faith, one religion, and until we can find some way to honor and serve one another, so that we can be in agreement? For war, turmoil, ill will, injury, and shame prevent men from agreeing on one belief."

Each of the three[6] wise men approved of what the wise man had said, and they decided on a time and place for their discussions, as well as how they should honor and serve one another, and how they should dispute; and that when they had agreed on and chosen one faith, they would go forth into the world giving glory and praise to the name of our Lord God. Each of the three wise men went home and remained faithful to his promise.

Here ends the *Book of the Gentile and the Three Wise Men*. Blessed be God, by whose help it was begun and finished, and in whose charge it is committed and placed, and for whose honor it is newly edited [and extracted from the *Brief Art of Finding Truth*, which most thoroughly investigates the cause and principles of all things in all fields of thought, in the liberal as well as the mechanical arts];[7] which book constitutes a doctrine and method for enlightening clouded minds and awakening the great who sleep, and for entering into union with and getting to know strangers and friends, by

[5] Many commentators have pointed out the exquisite courtesy with which the participants in this debate treat one another. That it was unusual in such disputes is perhaps less important than the fact that Llull is trying to set up a model of how such discussions should be carried out.

[6] Thus in all sources save F and the Latin texts (followed by Rosselló), which have the slightly more logical "two."

[7] The passage in square brackets appears only in the medieval Latin and Spanish translations, but since the former comes from Llull's immediate circle in Paris, and the latter is expressly translated from the Catalan and is in all other respects so close to the original, we can only assume that this passage was in that original, and for some reason was omitted from the archetype of three of the extant Catalan MSS (the fourth, D, which derives from the same archetype as the Spanish translation, is unfortunatly missing the entire last two paragraphs). The work referred to is the *Ars compendiosa inveniendi veritatem*, for which see the "Life," n. 52, and "Llull's Thought," p. 48 above.

asking what religion they think the Gentile chose in order to find favor with God.

May he who dictated and wrote this book, as well as he who reads and studies it, find favor in God's glory, and be kept in this world from those paths leading to infernal fires, on which those who incur God's ire find themselves.

THE BOOK OF THE
LOVER AND THE
BELOVED

Introduction

THE *Book of the Lover and the Beloved* is probably Llull's most popular work, judging from the number of editions and translations it has received, especially in modern times.[1] Although it has clearly been able to stand as an independent work,[2] it is in fact part of Llull's didactic romance, the *Book of Evast and Blaquerna*,[3] which relates the spiritual ascent of its hero, Blaquerna, who leaves family and home to become a hermit, then a monk, bishop, and finally pope, at which point he feels he can return to a life of contemplation, setting an example at each of these levels of the perfect Christian life.

In the explanation as to "How the hermit Blaquerna came to write the *Book of the Lover and the Beloved*," we learn that our hero was asked to write it upon the request of a visiting hermit, to enable him "to keep the other hermits in contemplation and devotion." After a long period of prayer and contemplation, Blaquerna decided to write "the *Book of the Lover and the Beloved*, in which the lover would be a faithful and devout Christian and the beloved would be God." It was therefore not intended as an apologetic work, directed toward the conversion of Muslims or Jews, but, like the didactic novel of which it is a part, as a work for the edification of other Christians.

Blaquerna then turned his thoughts to the manner in which he would compose the work, and remembered that, when he was pope, he had been told that the Muslims "had certain religious men, among whom the most highly considered were those called 'Sufis,' and that these men had words of love and brief examples which aroused great devotion in men. These are words which need exposition, and by their exposition the understanding rises up higher, and carries the will with it, increasing its devotion." Having decided to write the book in this way, Blaquerna then reflected on how he

---

[1] See the section entitled "Manuscripts, Editions, and Translations" at end of this introduction for more details.

[2] As it already did in Llull's time, in the Latin translation he included in a manuscript he sent to the Doge of Venice. See p. 185 below.

[3] Or simply *Blaquerna* as it is more usually known. This form of the name seems to have been the only one used in Llull's lifetime and for several decades after his death, when scribes began to write it "Blanquerna," perhaps because they felt it was more euphonic. For more details, see *SW* II, 690, n. 34.

himself meditated upon God and proceeded to write down his own experience in contemplation. He did this every day "bringing new reasoning to his prayers so that he could compose the *Book of the Lover and the Beloved* in many different manners, and that these would be brief." There would be as many versicles as days of the year, and each versicle could be the subject of an entire day of contemplation.[4]

Although no obvious external structure connects the versicles to one another, there is a strong feeling of unity to the work, because the parts relate to each other through their specific content and through the art of contemplation implicit within them.

The most important element in this art of contemplation is the triad of the Augustinian powers of the soul: memory, understanding, and will.[5] These are man's spiritual faculties, and he is master of them.[6] Through them, with his memory remembering, his intellect understanding, and his will loving God's attributes or dignities and their semblances in the world, man's soul can rise to a contemplation of the beloved.

The faculties are sometimes mentioned individually:

A question arose between the eyes and memory of the lover. His eyes claimed it was better to see the beloved than to remember him, but memory said that remembering brought tears to the eyes and made the heart burn with love. (v. 18)

Or they are grouped together:

The loves of the lover and beloved were bound with bonds of memory, understanding, and will, so that lover and beloved might not be parted. (v. 131)

They are also often referred to indirectly. Thoughts, remembrances, or love, or their opposites such as forgetfulness, or lack of love, occur frequently:

---

[4] See the end of this introduction for the problem of the number of versicles, which in all the early sources is nearer 357 than 365.

[5] R. Pring-Mill in his "Entorn de la unitat del «Libre d'amich e amat»," *Estudis Romànics* 10 (1962):33–61, reprinted in his *Estudis sobre Ramon Llull* (Barcelona/Montserrat, 1991), pp. 279–306, points out that these powers of the soul appear in seventy-nine versicles. Of the myriad studies of the *Book of the Lover and the Beloved* published over the years, this one is by far the most important; it quite revolutionized people's thinking about the work.

[6] In the *Art of Contemplation* which, in *Blaquerna*, comes immediately after the *Book of the Lover and the Beloved*, Llull says (Ch. 103): "A prince must not exercise his lordship without humility, therefore Blaquerna, who was prince and lord of his memory, understanding and will, humbled his possession. . . ."

The beloved tested his lover to see if his love was perfect, asking him what was the difference between the presence and absence of his beloved. The lover replied, "As ignorance and forgetfulness differ from knowledge and remembrance." (v. 7)

Another recurrent theme in the *Book of the Lover and the Beloved* is very much connected with Franciscan mysticism, which has been described as "the evangelical mysticism of the imitation of Christ."[7] Although a good number of versicles refer to the Trinity, many of the most moving relate specifically to the Incarnation and to Christ's passion:

With the tears of his eyes the lover told of the passion and sorrow his beloved had endured for his love. With sadness and heavy thoughts he wrote down the words he had spoken. And with mercy and hope he comforted himself. (v. 276)

The Franciscan ideal of poverty is also reflected in passages such as the following:

The lover went from door to door begging alms, to remember the beloved's love for his servants, and to practice humility, poverty, and patience, all of which are things pleasing to his beloved. (v. 274)

How mystical is this "evangelical mysticism of the imitation of Christ," and how mystical is Llull's *Book of the Lover and the Beloved*?

A little historical background may be helpful. Medieval mysticism,[8] was influenced by a Christian neo-Platonist, writing towards the end of the fifth century, known as the Pseudo-Dionysius.[9] In his theories about God he speaks of a negative and an affirmative approach. The negative approach, in his *Mystical Theology*, emphasizes the inadequacy of human concepts when applied to God, whereas the affirmative approach, exemplified in his *The Divine Names*, recognizes the reflection of the divine being in creation.[10] It was the *Mystical Theology* that was more influential, and its "chief theme is the ascent of the soul by the negative way, stripping aside first the senses and then all inward thoughts and reasonings until the soul passes into the 'darkness of unknowing,' wherein

---

[7] *Theologia Germanica*, ed. Joseph Bernhart (New York: Pantheon, 1949), p. 64.

[8] *Dictionnaire de Spiritualité* (Paris: Beauchesne, 1980), vol. 10, col. 1902, says mysticism in the modern sense of the term started in the sixteenth century. The medieval monks were contemplatives, rather than mystics.

[9] F. C. Copleston, *A History of Medieval Philosophy* (London, 1972), p. 50.

[10] Ibid., p. 51.

it is more and more enlightened by 'the ray of divine darkness' which is beyond all light and beyond all being."[11]

This negative way is traditional in ascetic and mystical teaching, much of it appearing in the sixteenth-century Spanish mystics, especially St. John of the Cross. A good medieval example can be found in the fourteenth-century English mystical work, *The Cloud of Unknowing*, whose unknown English author gives the following advice to someone about to enter a life of solitude and contemplative prayer:

. . . forget all the creatures that ever God made and the works of them, so that thy thought or thy desire be not directed or stretched to any of them. . . . At the first time when thou dost it, thou findest but a darkness and as it were a cloud of unknowing . . . this darkness and this cloud . . . hindereth thee so that thou mayest neither see him clearly by light of understanding in thy reason, nor feel him in sweetness of love in thy affection. . . . If ever thou shalt see him . . . it must always be in this cloud and in this darkness.[12]

Forget all the creatures that God ever made! What could be further from Llull, who says:

The lover was asked . . . "Who is your teacher?" He answered that it was the signs which created beings give of his beloved. (v. 57)

The positive tradition sees nature and the world as a book from which one can learn about God, or a mirror in which one can see his image.[13] Guillaume de Saint-Thierry, and other twelfth-century contemplatives, speak of "foi illuminée et non foi obscurcie."[14] As for a cloud of unknowing, only once in the *Book of the Lover and the Beloved* is there a mention of a cloud, and the contrast is dramatic. It is in the beautiful versicle which says:

Love lit up the cloud placed between the lover and the beloved, and made it as bright and shining as the moon by night, the morning star at dawn, the sun by day, and understanding in the will. And it is through this shining cloud that the lover and beloved speak to each other. (v. 123)

Love lights up the cloud between lover and beloved. It is a shining cloud, as shining as man's understanding in his will, and it is

---

[11] *Encyclopaedia Britannica* (1971 ed.), vol. 7, pp. 464–5.
[12] David Knowles, *The English Mystical Tradition* (London: Burns & Oates, 1961), p. 77.
[13] See "Llull's Thought," p. 51 above.
[14] *Dictionnaire de Spiritualité* (Paris: Beauchesne, 1980), vol. 10, col. 1906.

through it that lover and beloved can speak to each other. There is no darkness here.

Hand in hand with the need, in negative mysticism, to put aside all thoughts of the world, is an emphasis on the evil and sin prevalent in it. But for Llull, in a world that is posited as a divine creation, with God's attributes, such as goodness and greatness, actively and continually operating within it, literally constituting its reality, evil and sin are seen as nonexistent, that is to say, as lacking the reality imparted by the activity of God's attributes. This theory of evil as a privation is Neoplatonic in origin, and had a long history in medieval thought.[15] But the emphasis on sin, or obsession with it, is nonetheless very frequent.[16]

Another way in which the *Book of the Lover and the Beloved* can seem "unmystical" is that the goal of contemplation is not one of ecstatic union, involving total loss of self. This is so because for Llull, lover and beloved must remain different and separate entities, just as God's attributes are, in the created world, different and separate. Only in God can the many be one, can there be a distinction of three Persons in One, can the divine attributes be different, yet interchangeable and unified. The relational principle of "difference" in the created world involves multiplicity.

The principle of "difference" is joined by the term "middle"[17] to give us the triad of lover, love, and beloved. For it is in love that the lover and beloved are joined:

The beloved is far above love, and far below love is the lover. And love, which is in the middle, lowers the beloved to the lover and raises the lover to the beloved. (v. 258)[18]

---

[15] Copleston, *History,* p. 52.

[16] Saint Bernard, for instance, says, "Conceived in sin, we conceive sinners . . . born slaves, we conceive slaves"; cf. Étienne Gilson, *La théologie mystique de saint Bernard* (Paris: Vrin, 1947), p. 62. But the fourteenth-century English mystic Julian of Norwich, shared Llull's optimistic, positive approach to the mystical experience. As a young woman she had a series of visions, or "shewings" as she called them, of the crucified Christ (not unlike Llull), and the meaning of these visions were the subject of contemplation for the rest of her life. She worried about the existence of sin, which she never saw in her visions. "But Jesus answered . . . it behoved that there should be sin; but all shall be well, and all shall be well, and all manner of thing shall be well." See Knowles, *The English Mystical Tradition,* p. 131. The last part of the quote was used by T. S. Eliot at the end of his *Four Quartets.*

[17] These are terms from Llull's Art. The first is from the triad concordance-difference-contrariety, and the second from that of beginning-middle-end, both from Figure T (see the chart in the introduction to the *Gentile* above).

[18] In his *Tree of the Philosophy of Love,* ORL XVIII, 81 (and *OE* II, 29), Llull explains this further: "Middle and love are mixed together when, from the love of the lover and beloved

Even when the lover is overcome with love for his beloved, as in v. 235, it is in the sea of love that he perishes, not in direct union with the beloved. It is in the search for the beloved, along the perilous path "filled with worries, sighs, and tears and lit up by love" (v. 2) that the lover—with the help of his beloved—is able to join him in love.

Aside from the above-mentioned Franciscan and generally medieval-Christian aspects of Llull's mysticism, there has been an ongoing controversy among scholars regarding the relative importance of two other major influences on Llull—that of the Muslim mystics (the Sufis), and that of Troubadour poetry.[19] The controversy has been complicated by two facts, perhaps not always taken sufficiently into account. The first is the common fund of concepts shared by Sufis and Troubadours, partly because of common neo-Platonic influences, and partly because of a certain debt—one that has proved, it must be said, difficult to assess with any precision— of the latter to the former.[20] When scholars begin discussing specific themes, many of them, such as the paradoxes of love, love as a sickness, the lover's confusion when faced with the beloved, the prison of love, etc., turn out to be commonplaces of both Muslim mysticism and Western medieval love poetry. The second fact can only be described as a distaste on the part of some Romance scholars for taking seriously what Llull himself tells us in the prologue to the work—that he is following the manner of the Sufis, who "had words of love and brief examples which aroused great devotion in men."[21]

one love is forged, which brings the lover close to his beloved," and, from the same work, "Love is the cord that binds the lover to his beloved." L. Sala-Molins, in "Le refus de l'Identification dans la Mystique Lullienne," *Estudios Lulianos* 9 (1965):39–53, 181–92, explains that "If you must have a union (*une unité*), see it as existing in love, but do not look for it . . . in a compound of two persons" (p. 43). Sala-Molins speaks of Lullian mysticism as a "mysticism of difference." See also pp. 79–82 of the same author's *La philosophie de l'amour chez Raymond Lulle* (Paris, 1974), by far the best general work on Llull's mysticism.

[19] Both traditions were, of course, experienced by Llull during his lifetime: see pp. 9 and 16 of the "Life."

[20] Although James T. Monroe, in his *Hispano-Arabic Poetry: A Student Anthology* (Berkeley and Los Angeles: University of California Press, 1974), p. 20, clearly states that, "It was the application of this (Neoplatonic) philosophic superstructure to traditional Arabic love poetry that permitted Ibn Hazm to create a true doctrine of courtly love in al-Andalus two centuries before the poets of Provence."

[21] See p. 189 below. Critics have repeatedly said that no specific Sufi model has been found, when Llull in fact only states he is following a very general model, more than anything a manner of writing or conceiving mystic literature.

The truth would seem to be that, aside from the many themes common to both traditions, what can be more specifically ascribed to Llull's early troubadour training are some of the literary settings. These are particularly evident in the first thirty or so versicles, which emphasize nature: birds singing at dawn, the shade of a tree for the tired traveller, the spring, and so forth. We also find some feudal overtones, with the mention of noble lords and barons, serfs, and castles. Llull is here practicing a kind of *captatio benevolentiae*, in which his troubadour experience served him well.[22]

But as the versicles become progressively more abstract, Llull begins to rely less on the language and devices of courtly love, and more on his own rhetoric and "Arabic manner of speaking" with its insistent repetition of key words, its constant play of opposites, and its personification of abstract ideas.

However, the most striking Arabic influence on the *Book of the Lover and the Beloved* involves the masculinity of lover and beloved. This distinguishes Llull's prose versicles from both the nuptial imagery of the biblical Song of Songs and from the profane love poetry of the Troubadours.[23] This masculinity seems to be unique in Christian writing. St. John of the Cross, for instance, returns to nuptial imagery, with the human soul, the *amada*, being the bride of her beloved, the *amado*.

Apart from this, there seems to be a more general Arabic influence on Llull's mysticism. "Sufism was in its early stages . . . a personal relation between God and man, Creator and creature, Lord and slave."[24] Only later did it tend towards the ecstatic or pantheistic as in Ibn ʿArabī. Llull's mysticism was closer to that of al-Ghazzali, who in a sense returned to early Sufism in an attempt to reconcile mysticism with Islamic theology.[25] Llull could not have had a greater model for his purposes. Like Llull, al-Ghazzali rejected the idea of total mystic union with God. In his *Ihyā* he quotes an

---

[22] The standard study of this side of the question is Manuel de Montoliu, "Ramon Llull, trobador," *Homenatge a Antoni Rubió i Lluch 1, Estudis Universitaris Catalans* 21 (1936):363–98.

[23] Pring-Mill, "Entorn de la unitat", p. 57–8 (p. 302 of the reprint), feels that this masculinity is the work's principal debt to the Sufi tradition. It served in the human metaphor to distinguish this love from carnal love and was an inheritance from the Greeks. Pring-Mill contrasts the total lack of sensuality in the *Book of the Lover and Beloved* with the ever-present, although sublimated, sensuality of the poetry of courtly love.

[24] Annemarie Schimmel, *As through a Veil: Mystical Poetry in Islam* (New York: Columbia University Press, 1982), p. 15.

[25] We know Llull was well acquainted with al-Ghazzali; see p. 16 of the "Life" above.

early Sufi verse, which says, "I want union with him, and he wants separation from me. Therefore I give up what I want for that which he wants."[26] And similarly Llull says:

The lover's will left him, and gave itself to the beloved. But the beloved imprisoned it within the lover, so he would be loved and served by him. (v. 227)

To sum up, troubadour poetry was a literary inheritance, whereas the Arabic influence was a contemporary reality Llull felt he had to study and absorb for his proselytizing purposes, but which could then at times serve him for his Christian message as well.[27]

But as the reader is already aware, Llull, regardless of all these possible influences, is extremely *sui generis*, and quite unlike any other medieval thinker. There is, first and foremost, his Art, to which he makes explicit reference:

The lover was sent by his beloved as a messenger to Christian princes and unbelievers to show them the Art and principles by which they could know and love the beloved. (v. 143)

Llull's Art, in its first version, is ever-present in much of the *Book of the Lover and the Beloved*, mostly, as we said before, in terms of the powers of the soul (whose acts formed Figure S of the Art), but often represented by many of the figures at once.[28] Most important are God's attributes or dignities (from Figure A), which are mirrored in the world and are what the lover should be remembering, understanding, and loving. Then there are the relative principles (Figure T), the virtues and vices (Figure V), and occasionally the opposing principles of Figure X. Many versicles, some of which seem dry and difficult to understand, become more attractive when their building blocks are recognized as such, as in the following one:

---

[26] Schimmel, *As through a Veil*, p. 29. On the Islamic influences there are many interesting comparisons and observations in two works by M. Asín Palacios, *The Mystical Philosophy of Ibn Masarra and His Followers* (Leiden: E. J. Brill, 1978) and *El Islam cristianizado* (Madrid: Hiperíon, 1931), and in Américo Castro, *The Structure of Spanish History* (Princeton: Princeton University Press, 1954).

[27] Or to quote Hillgarth, *Ramon Lull*, p. 38: "In Llull's mystical writings the influence of the courtly Art of Love of the troubadours . . . and of Franciscan mysticism is blended with very strong Eastern influences. Lull's mysticism, like his philosophy, combines Eastern and Western influences in an original synthesis."

[28] The reader will follow the ensuing discussion more easily by consulting the chart on p. 79 of the introduction to the *Gentile*.

The lover extended and prolonged his thoughts on the greatness and everlasting nature of his beloved, and there found no beginning, nor middle,
nor end. The beloved asked, "What are you measuring, fool?" The lover
answered, "I am comparing the lesser with the greater, defect with fulfillment, and beginning with infinity, eternity, so that humility, patience,
charity, and hope can remain more strongly fixed in my memory." (v.
69)[29]

Does this mean that the *Book of the Lover and the Beloved* can be
appreciated only by those familiar with the Art? Such a notion is
patently untrue, given the fact that the work has enjoyed wide
popularity among a very large public. Llull's remarkable literary
and psychological gifts must certainly help explain such success. As
we have already seen, the *Book of the Lover and the Beloved* forms part
of a larger work, the didactic novel *Blaquerna*. It is the next-to-last
part, followed by the *Art of Contemplation*. Here, indeed, is a manual
for contemplation based on the Art, systematic and unmetaphori-
cal, whereas the *Book of the Lover and the Beloved* provides prose
verses that are themselves objects for contemplation, following the
Sufi manner, brief and affective, using every rhetorical means at
Llull's disposal,[30] from whatever sources he has available, and as
varied as they can be—"bringing new reasoning to his prayers so he
could compose the book in many different manners," as *Blaquerna*
says in the prologue.

There are indeed many different manners in the *Book of the Lover
and the Beloved*, and one great message—to know and love God.
There is a beauty to Llull's insistence on the equality of the intellect
and will in the search for his beloved.

So great was the love of the lover for his beloved that he believed everything he was told by him. And so greatly did he want to understand his
beloved that everything he heard about him he wanted to understand by
the light of reason.[31] Therefore the love of the lover lay between belief and
understanding. (v. 198)

---

[29] Greatness, eternity, humility, and patience are four of the sixteen attributes of God
(Figure A), beginning–middle–end and lesser–equal–greater are two triads from Figure T,
defect and fulfillment (synonyms of imperfection and perfection) are from Figure X, charity
and hope are from Figure V, and intellect and memory are two powers of the soul from Figure
S. Almost the entire vocabulary of this versicle derives from terms of the Art!

[30] One device, not apparent, of course, in translation, is internal rhyme, as in v. 6 "Dix
l'amic al amat, Tu qui umples el sol de resplan*dor*, umple mon *cor* d'*amor*. Respos l'amat, Sens
compliment d'*amor* no foren tos ulls en *plor*, ni tu vengut en est loch ver ton ama*dor*."

[31] Literally "for necessary reasons."

In the history of Western mysticism, there is nothing quite like this work, with its curious blend of Troubadour, Franciscan, and Islamic influences, mixed with Llull's own special outlook based on the Art, on the necessary equality of the powers of the soul, and on the concept of lover and beloved separate and yet joined through love. The result is a work of great subtlety, beauty, and originality.

Manuscripts, Editions, and Translations

The popularity of the *Book of the Lover and the Beloved* has been such that listing all its manuscripts, editions, and translations (which of course must include those of *Blaquerna*, of which it forms part) is a tedious task that would try the reader's patience with pages of bibliography. For more detailed information than that given here, check the lists in *SW* II, 1263–5 (brought up to date in *OS* II, 546–7), the far more detailed listings in Vol. IV, 106–24 of the *ENC* edition of *Blaquerna*, and above all in the forthcoming edition of the *Book of the Lover and the Beloved* that Albert Soler is preparing also for *ENC*.[32] Here we will only give a brief outline of the most important landmarks in this complicated tradition.

The original Catalan version of the work is preserved in three medieval manuscripts,[33] and in 1521 a curious "translation" of *Blaquerna* into the Valencian dialect of Catalan was published in that city by Joan Bonllavi. The best modern editions (also of the entire novel) are: (1) *ORL* IX, 1914, edited by Salvador Galmés; (2) *ENC*, 4 vols., 1935–54, also edited by Galmés, which contains (in vol. 3) the best text to date of the *Book of the Lover and the Beloved*; (3) *OE* I, 1957, which is basically a reprint of (1). The separate editions of the *Book of the Lover and the Beloved* worth mentioning are (4) that of M. Obrador (Palma, 1904), and (5) an earlier *ENC* edition dating from 1927, which precedes and is inferior to the later *ENC* edition of (2) above.

The French translation, done within Llull's circle in Paris, is preserved in five manuscripts,[34] the earliest of which was edited by A. Llinarès.[35] The Provençal translation, also probably stemming

---

[32] See n. 50 below for more information about this last work.

[33] One of all of *Blaquerna* (minus the beginning), and two of just the *Book of the Lover and Beloved*.

[34] Four of all of *Blaquerna*, and one of the *Book of the Lover and Beloved*.

[35] Raymond Lulle, *Livre d'Evast et de Blaquerne* (Paris, 1970).

from the same circle, is preserved in only one manuscript.[36] The Latin translation is preserved in seven manuscripts,[37] the earliest of which was sent, at the end of 1289 or the beginning of 1290, by Llull himself to the Doge of Venice,[38] and has recently received a critical edition.[39]

The relationship between these versions and the original is, as Albert Soler's recent researches have shown, quite surprising.[40] The French and Latin translations don't seem to have been done from the Catalan, but from the Provençal version, which was doubtless a language more familiar to scholars in Paris, where both were done. But the Renaissance edition of the *Book of the Lover and the Beloved* by Lefèvre d'Étaples (Paris, 1505), is apparently a new translation from Catalan into Latin,[41] and it was this Latin text on which the Renaissance Spanish translation was based.[42] The Spanish version published in Palma, 1749, however, was a new translation based on the Bonllavi edition of 1521, also using one of the medieval Catalan manuscripts existing in that city.[43] Yet another translation was done in our time by M. de Riquer.[44]

As for modern English translations, there have so far been three, all (more or less) by E. Allison Peers. The first was his *Book of the Lover and the Beloved* (London, 1923), but it was based on an earlier defective Catalan text;[45] that included in his translation of *Blanquerna* (London, 1926) is based on the *ORL* IX edition of the novel,

[36] From the first third of the fourteenth century, and of all of *Blaquerna*, but like the Catalan MS, missing the beginning. This means that the only medieval MSS which preserve the beginning of the novel are those in French.

[37] All containing only the *Book of the Lover and the Beloved*.

[38] See *SW* I, 313, for more information about this MS, which also contains the *Ars demonstrativa*.

[39] C. Lohr and F. Domínguez, "Raimundus Lullus, «Liber amici et amati»: Introduction and Critical Text," *Traditio* 44 (1988):325–372.

[40] In his *Edició crítica i estudi del "Llibre d'amic e amat" de Ramon Llull*, 2 vols., doctoral thesis for the University of Barcelona, 1991, and especially the *stemma codicum* in Vol. 1, p. 168.

[41] Perhaps because, like so many Renaissance scholars with medieval texts, he found the existing Latin version stylistically barbarous. For Lefèvre d'Étaples see "Lullism," p. 64 above.

[42] It exists in one MS in the Biblioteca Nacional of Madrid, was edited by G. M. Bertini in *Testi spagnoli del secolo XV* (Turin, 1950), and then reprinted in Ramon Llull, *Autobiografía y Libro del Amigo y del Amado*, ed. A. M. de Saavedra and M. Batllori (Barcelona, 1987). This last printing is occasionally referred to in the notes as the "old Spanish version."

[43] It appeared in two printings in the same year, one of all of *Blaquerna*, and one of only the *Book of the Lover and the Beloved*.

[44] *Libro de amigo y Amado* (Barcelona, 1950, reprinted 1985), with an introduction by Lola Badia.

[45] That listed above as (4) by M. Obrador (Palma, 1904).

and although textually preferable, is still defective, not only in its artificially antiquated language, but also in its idea of what Llull was trying to do;[46] finally, there is an edition by Kenneth Leech (London, 1946, 2d ed. 1978) which does an excellent job of modernizing Peers's language, but does not pretend to be a new translation and so cannot correct the original's errors.

Of the myriad translations of the *Book of the Lover and the Beloved* into modern French, the only one consulted has been that by G. Lévis Mano and J. Palau,[47] reproduced by Sala-Molins in his anthology with a few minor corrections and with some helpful notes.[48] It is excellent, as is the German translation with a long introduction by Erika Lorenz.[49]

For this translation we have had the good fortune to be able to consult the new critical edition being prepared by Albert Soler for *ENC*.[50] We have in general followed his readings, and have only given variants where they might be important (or interesting) for an understanding of Llull's text.

The one peculiar problem raised by the researches of Lohr, Domínguez, and Soler is that of the number of versicles. In the first place it has become clear that none of the medieval sources of the work number the versicles, in sharp contrast, for instance, to the *Book of Contemplation* written not too long before.[51] The practice of numbering versicles seems to have begun with Renaissance editors, who then found, doubtless to their horror, that the manuscripts they were using only had some 357. In order to justify the phrase about the book being divided "into as many verses as there are days in the year," they were forced either to break up longer versicles into two, or to add apocryphal ones of their own invention to get to 365 (or 366). The vagueness of our statement about "some 357" is

[46] See Pring-Mill's criticisms in the article cited in n. 5 above.

[47] *Le livre de l'ami et de l'aimé* (Paris, 1953).

[48] Sala-Molins, *Choix*, pp. 347–96.

[49] *Das Buch vom Freunde und vom Geliebten*, (Zurich and Munich, 1988).

[50] Which is basically that of the thesis cited in n. 40 above, with a updates and corrections as his research continues.

[51] Whose divisions and subdivisions are not only numbered in early MSS, but they are preceded first by elaborately laid-out tables of contents showing this organization, and then by a prologue explaining that the 366 chapters correspond to the days of the year, the five books to Christ's wounds, the forty distinctions to the days of Christ's fasting in the desert, etc.

due to the fact that the medieval sources not only disagree as to divisions between versicles, but the Latin and French versions, both of which probably passed through Llull's hands, lack respectively two and seven versicles that are in the Catalan version. So this number is merely an approximation to that circulating in the Middle Ages.

For the reader's convenience and ease of reference, however, we have retained the numbering of the classic *ENC* edition of *Blaquerna* (no. 2 above), warning the reader whenever we have followed it in separating two versicles joined in the medieval sources.[52]

---

[52] It should be pointed out that the 1927 *ENC* edition (no. 5 above) followed earlier editions in joining versicles 4 and 5, thereby making all subsequent numberings one less. This system was followed by the version in *OE* I (no. 3 above) and by Llinarès in his edition of the French text (see n. 35 above)

HOW THE HERMIT BLAQUERNA CAME TO WRITE THE *BOOK OF THE LOVER AND THE BELOVED*

I T H A P P E N E D O N E day that the hermit, who was in Rome, as we said before,[1] went to visit the other hermits and recluses living there, and found that they had many temptations regarding certain things because they did not know how to live in the manner best fitting their state. So he thought he would go to Blaquerna and ask him to make a book about the life of a hermit, so that through this book he would know how to keep the other hermits in contemplation and devotion. One day when Blaquerna was in prayer the hermit came to his cell and asked him to write the above-mentioned book. Blaquerna thought a long time about the manner in which he would make the book, and the matter he would put into it.

Thinking in this way he decided to give himself over to the worship and contemplation of God, so that in prayer God might show him the manner and matter to be used in the book. While Blaquerna was thus worshipping and weeping,[2] and when God had made his soul rise to the furthest limit of its strength in contemplation of him, Blaquerna felt himself overwhelmed by the great fervor and devotion he had, and he thought to himself that the force of love is overwhelming when the lover loves the beloved very intensely. Therefore Blaquerna decided to make a book, the *Book of*

---

[1] Two chapters before, Llull described urban hermits "living in the walls," presumably in cells hollowed out in the ruins.

[2] See n. 6 below.

the Lover and the Beloved, in which the lover would be a faithful and devout Christian and the beloved would be God.

While Blaquerna was thinking in this way, he remembered that once, when he was pope, a Saracen[3] had told him that the Saracens had certain religious men, among whom the most highly considered were those called "sufis," and that these men had words of love and brief examples which aroused great devotion in men. These are words which require exposition, and by their exposition the understanding rises up higher, and carries the will with it, increasing its devotion. Now when Blaquerna had heard this idea, he decided to make the book in the above-mentioned manner, and he told the hermit to return to Rome, and that in a short time he would send him, through the deacon, the *Book of the Lover and the Beloved*, and with this book he would be able to increase fervor and devotion in the hermits, whom he wished to inspire with a love of God.

PROLOGUE

BLAQUERNA WAS in prayer, and he thought about the manner in which he contemplated God and his virtues, and when he finished his prayers he wrote down the manner in which he had contemplated God. And he did this every day, bringing new reasoning to his prayers, so that he could compose *The Book of the Lover and the Beloved* in many different manners, and that these would be brief, so that in a short time the soul could reflect on many of them.

And with God's blessing, Blaquerna began the book, which he divided into as many verses as there are days in the year. And each verse suffices for an entire day of contemplation of God, according to the art of the *Book of Contemplation*.[4]

---

[3] See the *Book of the Gentile*, Bk. IV, n. 1, for an explanation of this term which for Llull's contemporaries simply meant "Muslim."

[4] The vast work written before the development of the Art (see p. 16 above); not to be confused with the *Art of Contemplation* which follows the *Book of the Lover and the Beloved* in *Blaquerna*.

HERE BEGIN THE MORAL METAPHORS[5]

1. The lover asked his beloved if there remained anything in him still to be loved. And the beloved answered that he still had to love that by which his own love could be increased.

2. The paths along which the lover seeks his beloved are long, perilous, filled with worries, sighs, and tears, and lit up by love.[6]

3. Many lovers gathered together to love one beloved who filled them with love. Each held as his own his beloved and his pleasant thoughts, which caused tribulations that were sweet to bear.

4. The lover wept, and said: "When will darkness leave the world, and the paths to hell cease to exist? When will water, which always flows downward, change its nature and flow upward? And when will the innocent outnumber the guilty?"

5. Ah! When will the lover boast of dying for his beloved? And when will the beloved see the lover languishing for love of him?[7]

6. The lover said to the beloved, "You who fill the sun with radiance, fill my heart with love." The beloved replied, "Without plenitude of love, your eyes would not be in tears, nor would you have come to this place to see the one who loves you."

7. The beloved tested his lover to see if his love was perfect, asking him what was the difference between the presence and absence of his beloved. The lover replied, "As ignorance and forgetfulness differ from knowledge and remembrance."

8. The beloved asked the lover, "Can you remember any way in which I have rewarded you for wanting to love me?" "Yes," he answered, "by making no distinction between the pains and pleasures you accord me."

9. "Tell me, lover," said the beloved, "will you still be patient if I double your suffering?" "Yes, as long as you also double my love."

---

[5] In addition to its usual meaning, "moral" in the Middle Ages could also mean "figurative, symbolic, requiring interpretation."

[6] For medieval mystics, tears were a gift of God; in the *Art of Contemplation*, ch. 107, Blaquerna states that "it is inappropriate to contemplate on a high level without weeping."

[7] Many printed sources, following the lead of one MS, which has the paragraph sign erased, join this versicle to the previous one.

10. The beloved asked the lover, "Do you know yet what love is?" He answered, "If I knew not what love was, would I know what suffering, sorrow and pain were?"[8]

11. The lover was asked, "Why do you not answer your beloved who is calling you?" He replied, "I brave great dangers in order to reach him, and I already speak to him in desiring his honors."

12. "Foolish lover, why do you destroy your body, spend all your money, abandon the delights of this world, and go about scorned by people?" He answered, "In order to honor the perfections of my beloved, who is unloved and dishonored by more men than honor and love him."

13. "Tell us, fool of love! What is better seen—the beloved in the lover, or the lover in the beloved? He answered, saying that the beloved can be recognized by love, and the lover by sighs and tears, pain and grief.

14. The lover was looking for someone who could tell his beloved of the hardships he underwent for love's sake, and of how he was dying. And he found his beloved, who was reading a book in which was written all the suffering love made him endure for his beloved, and all the pleasure he had from this love.

15. Our Lady brought her Son to the lover so he might kiss his feet,[9] and so that in his book he might write about the virtues of Our Lady.

16. "Tell us, O singing bird, have you put yourself in the care of my beloved so that he may protect you from lack of love, and increase your love?" The bird replied, "And who is it who makes me sing, if not the lord of love, for whom lack of love is a dishonor?"

17. Love has made its home between fear and hope, where it lives on its thoughts but dies from forgetfulnesses when its foundations are laid upon worldly pleasures.

18. A question arose between the eyes and memory of the lover. His eyes claimed it was better to see the beloved than to remember him, but

---

[8] Only Galmés's *ENC* edition (see no. 2 on p. 184 above) and Albert Soler's forthcoming edition have the question; all other editions and translations, instead of "would I," have "I would" (the Latin version here even adds a "therefore"). Since medieval scribes don't use question marks, one can only tell by meaning or syntax which is intended; in this case the question seems to agree better with Llull's concept of love.

[9] The original is in the singular, "his foot."

memory said that remembering brought tears to the eyes and made the heart burn with love.

19. The lover asked Understanding and Will which one was closer to his beloved. They both started running, and Understanding reached his beloved before Will.[10]

20. The lover and the beloved were at odds with each other. Another lover saw this and wept long and bitterly until he restored peace and concord between the beloved and the lover.

21. Sighs and Tears came to be judged by the beloved, and asked him by which of them he felt more deeply loved. The beloved judged that sighs were closer to love, and tears to the eyes.[11]

22. The lover came to drink from the fountain whose waters make those who do not love fall in love, and his suffering was doubled. The beloved then came to drink from the fountain so as to redouble the lover's love of him, and increase his suffering even more.

23. The lover was sick, and the beloved cared for him. He fed him from his merits, gave him to drink with love, put him to bed with patience, dressed him with humility, and gave him truth as his medicine.[12]

24. The lover was asked where his beloved was. He answered, "You can find him in a house nobler than all the nobility of creation, and you can find him in my love, my suffering, and my tears."

25. They said to the lover, "Where are you going?" "I come from my beloved." "Where do you come from?" "I go to my beloved." "When will you return?" "I will be with my beloved." "How long will you be with your beloved?"[13] "For as long as my thoughts remain on him."

---

[10] Although this versicle is a good example of the importance Llull attributes to the understanding, the fact is that the three faculties must work together for the soul to rise up in contemplation—none can reach the goal alone. In the *Tree of Science*, the same question is answered with a reference to the *Book of the Gentile*, whose protagonists argue purely intellectually. But then when the powers of the soul rose up towards God, the understanding, which had for that reason gone first, could no longer bear the heat of the sun, and asked the will, i.e., love, to take the lead.

[11] Because sighs come from the heart and are therefore more spiritual. See the note to v. 172.

[12] The phrase "and the beloved cared for him" has sometimes been translated as "and he thought of his beloved," but this is a misunderstanding of the double meaning of the verb in *e pensava'n l'amat*. As in many medieval Romance languages, the Catalan *pensar*, also meant "to care for, nurse."

[13] This last question is missing in many MSS.

26. The birds sang of the dawn, and the lover, who is the dawn, awoke. The birds ended their song, and the lover died in the dawn for his beloved.

27. The bird sang in the garden of the beloved. The lover came and said to the bird, "If we do not understand each other through language, let us understand each other through love, for through your song my beloved appears before my eyes."

28. The lover felt sleepy, for he had worked hard seeking his beloved. And as he was afraid he might forget him, he wept so as not to fall asleep and have his beloved absent from his memory.

29. The lover and the beloved met, and the lover said,[14] "You need not speak to me. Just signal to me with your eyes, which are like words to my heart, and I will give you whatever you ask of me."

30. The lover disobeyed his beloved, and the lover wept. The beloved came and died within the lover's cloak, so that the lover might regain what he had lost. And the gift he gave him was greater than that which he had lost.[15]

31. The beloved filled his lover with love, and had no pity on his suffering, so that he might be loved more greatly. And in his increased suffering the lover found pleasure and recovery.

32. The lover said, "My beloved's secrets torment me when I reveal them by my deeds, for my mouth keeps them secret and reveals them to no one."

33. The terms of love are: that the lover be long-suffering, patient, humble, God-fearing, diligent, trusting, and that he risk great dangers for the honor of his beloved. And the beloved pledges to be true, generous, compassionate, and just with his lover.

34. The lover sought true devotion over hills and plains, to see if his beloved was well-served, and he found none in any of these places. He then dug deeply into the earth to see if there he could find the complete devotion that was so lacking on earth.

35. "Tell me, O bird who sings of love to my beloved, why does he who has taken me as his servant torment me with love?" The bird an-

---

[14] Peers and Sala-Molins have "and the beloved said," which they got from *ORL* ix, 383.
[15] This versicle seems to refer to original sin and redemption.

swered, "If you did not suffer the pains of love, how else would you love your beloved?"

36. The lover followed the paths of his beloved absorbed in thought. He tripped and fell among the thorns, and it seemed to him that they were flowers and that he lay on a bed of love.

37. The lover was asked if he would exchange his beloved for another. He answered, "And what other is better or nobler than the sovereign good, eternal and infinite in greatness, power, wisdom, love, and perfection?"

38. Tearfully the lover sang songs of his beloved. He sang that love was quicker in the lover's heart than the brilliance of lightning to the eye, or thunder to the ear; that water had more vitality in tears than in the sea's waves, and that sighs were closer to love than was whiteness to snow.

39. The lover was asked why his beloved was glorious. He answered, "Because he is glory." They asked him why he was powerful. He answered, "Because he is power." "And why is he wise?" "Because he is wisdom." "And why is he lovable?" "Because he is love."

40. The lover arose early and went in search of his beloved. On the way he passed some people and asked if they had seen his beloved. They answered, "When did the eyes of your mind lose sight of your beloved?"[16] "Never," replied the lover, "for from the time I saw my beloved in my thoughts, he has never been absent from the eyes of my body, for all things visible reveal my beloved to me."

41. With eyes of thoughts and griefs, sighs, and weeping, the lover gazed upon his beloved. And with eyes of grace, justice, pity, mercy, and generosity, the beloved contemplated his lover. And a bird sang of the delights of the above sight.

42. The keys to the gates of love are gilded with cares, sighs, and tears. The cord that joins them is woven of conscience, contrition, devotion, and satisfaction. And the gates are guarded by justice and mercy.[17]

43. The lover knocked on the gate of his beloved with knocks of love and hope. The beloved heard the knocks of his lover with humility, pity,

---

[16] Indirect speech in the original.

[17] Justice and mercy (two of the divine dignities) represent God the Father, whereas in the next versicle it is Christ (with the virtues of humility, pity, patience, and charity) who opens the gates.

patience, and charity. The gates were opened by Deity and Humanity, and the lover went in to see his beloved.

44. Private and communal interest met and mingled, so that there could be friendship and benevolence between the lover and the beloved.

45. Two fires kindle the love of the lover. One is composed of desires, joys, and reflections, and the other of fear, suffering, weeping, and tears.

46. The lover desired solitude, and he left to be alone so that he would have the company of his beloved with whom he could be alone among people.

47. The lover sat alone in the shade of a handsome tree. Some men passed by and asked him why he was alone. The lover answered that it was only when he had seen and heard them that he had been alone, but before that he had been in the company of his beloved.

48. The lover and beloved spoke to each other with signs of love. With fear, weeping, thoughts, and tears, the lover recounted his suffering to his beloved.

49. The lover feared his beloved might fail him in his greatest need, so the beloved took away his love. There was then contrition and repentance in the lover's heart, and the beloved restored hope and charity to his heart, and tears and weeping to his eyes, so that love might return to the lover.

50. Between lover and beloved, nearness and farness are the same; for like the mixture of water and wine, the loves of lover and beloved mix together; like heat and light, their loves are linked together; and like essence and being they are in agreement and joined.[18]

51. The lover said to his beloved, "In you are both my suffering and my cure. The more you heal me, the greater my suffering, and the more I suffer, the more am I healed." The beloved replied, "Your love is a seal and an imprint, displaying my honors to all men."[19]

52. The lover saw himself captured and bound, wounded and killed, for love of his beloved. His tormentors asked him, "Where is your beloved

---

[18] This versicle has been interpreted as illustrating total union of lover and beloved, whereas they are in fact joined only in the middle ground of love. It is their loves that mingle as do water and wine, heat and light, essence and being.

[19] *Honraments* ("honors") is often used as a synonym for God's perfections, attributes, or dignities.

now?" He replied, "You can see him in the increase of my love, and in the strength it gives me to bear my torments."

53. The lover said to the beloved, "I have never fled from you, nor ceased to love you, since I first knew you. For I was always in you, and by you, and with you, wherever I went." The beloved replied, "Nor have I, since you started knowing and loving me, ever forgotten you, deceived you, or failed you."

54. The lover went through the city like a fool, singing of his beloved, and he was asked if he had lost his mind. He answered that his beloved had taken his will, and he had given him his understanding, so he had nothing left but his memory, with which he remembered his beloved.

55. The beloved said, "It would be a miracle against love if the lover were to fall asleep and forget his beloved." The lover replied, "And it would be a miracle against love if the beloved were not to wake the lover, since he had desired him."

56. The lover's heart rose up to the heights of the beloved, so he would not be prevented from loving in the abyss of this world. And when he reached his beloved, he contemplated him with tenderness and delight. The beloved then let him down to the world again, so he would contemplate him with tribulations and suffering.

57. The lover was asked, "What is your wealth?" He replied, "The poverty I bear for my beloved." "And what is your rest?" "The suffering I endure for love's sake." "And who is your doctor?" "The trust I have in my beloved." "And who is your teacher?" He answered that it was the signs which created beings give of his beloved.[20]

58. A bird was singing on a branch in leaf and flower, and the breeze stirred the leaves and bore with it the scent of the flowers. The lover asked the bird what the movement of the leaves and the scent of the flowers signified. The bird answered: "The stirring of the leaves signifies obedience, and the scent of the flowers suffering and sorrow."

59. The lover went on his way, desiring his beloved, when he met two friends who greeted and embraced and kissed each other with love and tears. And the lover fainted, so strongly did the two friends remind him of his beloved.

[20] See "Llull's Thought," p. 51 above.

60. The lover thought about death and was afraid, until he remembered his beloved. And he called out to those around him: "Ah, my friends, you must love, so as to fear neither dangers nor death in honoring my beloved."

61. The lover was asked where his love first began. He answered that it was with the perfections of his beloved, and that from that beginning he was led to love himself and his neighbor, and to reject[21] deception and sin.

62. "Tell us, fool, if your beloved ceased loving you, what would you do?" He answered: "I would love him still, so as not to die, for lack of love is death, and love is life."[22]

63. They asked the lover the meaning of perseverance. He said that perseverance meant both happiness and unhappiness for the lover who perseveres in loving, honoring and serving his beloved with fortitude, patience, and hope.

64. The lover asked his beloved to pay him for the time he had served him. The beloved added up the thoughts, tears, yearnings, trials, and dangers his lover had suffered for love of him. The beloved added eternal happiness to the account, and gave himself as payment to his lover.

65. The lover was asked the meaning of happiness. He replied that it was unhappiness borne for love.

66. "Tell us, fool, what is unhappiness?" "It is the memory of the dishonors done to my beloved who is worthy of all honors."[23]

67. The lover was gazing at a place where he had once seen his beloved, and he said, "O, place that recalls the beautiful ways of my beloved! Will you tell him that for his love I suffer hardship and sorrow?" The place answered, "When your beloved was here, he suffered greater hardship and sorrow than any other hardship and sorrow which love can give to its servants."

68. The lover said to his beloved, "You are all, and through all, and in

---

[21] See the following note.

[22] Indirect speech in the original. The verb *desamar* (translated as "reject" in the previous versicle), with its corresponding noun *desamor* (here translated as "lack of love"), corresponds to the letter H of Figure S (see the chart on p. 79) and is the opposite of "loving," but here "hating" would be too strong a translation.

[23] The best MSS join this versicle to the previous one.

all, and with all. I want all of you, so that I may have and be all of myself."
The beloved replied, "You cannot have all of me without your being all
mine." The lover said, "Have all of me, and I, all of you." The beloved
replied, "Then what will your son, your brother, and your father have?"
The lover replied, "You are all to such a degree that you can abound and be
all to whomever gives all of himself to you."

69. The lover extended and prolonged his thoughts on the greatness
and everlasting nature of his beloved, and there found no beginning, nor
middle, nor end. The beloved asked, "What are you measuring, fool?" The
lover answered, "I am comparing the lesser with the greater, defect with
fulfillment, and beginning with infinity, eternity, so that humility, patience, charity, and hope can remain more strongly fixed in my
memory."[24]

70. The paths of love are both long and short, for love is clear, pure,
untainted and true, subtle yet simple, strong, diligent, and bright,
abounding in new thoughts and old memories.

71. The lover was asked, "What are the fruits of love?"[25] He answered,
"Joys, reflections, yearnings and sighs, worries, hardships, dangers, torments, and griefs. Without such fruits love's servants cannot be touched
by her."

72. Many people were with the lover, who complained about his beloved for not increasing his love, and about love for making him suffer
hardships and sorrows. The beloved excused himself, saying that the hardships and sorrows for which he blamed love were in truth an increase of
love.

73. "Tell us, fool, why do you not speak, and what makes you so
confused and perplexed?" He answered, "The beauties of my beloved, and
the likeness of the joys and sorrows brought to me by love."[26]

74. "Tell us, fool, which existed first, your heart, or love?" He answered that his heart and love came into being at the same time, for if they
had not, the heart would not have been made for love, nor love made for
reflection.

---

[24] See p. 183 of the introduction for a commentary on this versicle.
[25] Indirect speech in the original.
[26] This and the previous two versicles on the concurrence of pain and pleasure in love have
clear parallels in Islamic mysticism, as well as in troubadour verse.

75. They asked the fool where his love first began, whether with the secrets of his beloved, or with his revealing them to the people. He answered that love, when it is perfect, makes no such distinctions. Secretly the lover keeps secret his beloved's secrets, and secretly he also reveals them, and with revealing them keeps them secret still.

76. The secrets of love, when unrevealed, cause pain and suffering. The revelation of love brings fervor and fear. Thus the lover must suffer in either case.

77. Love called his lovers and told them to ask for whatever gifts they found most pleasing and desirable. And they asked love to clothe and adorn them in his own manner, so as to be the more pleasing to the beloved.

78. The lover cried out to the people, saying that love commanded them to love when awake or asleep, when walking or sitting, when speaking or when silent, when buying or selling, laughing or crying, in gain or in loss, in joy or in sorrow. In whatever they might do they must love, for this was love's commandment.

79. "Tell us, fool, when did love first come to you?" He answered, "When it enriched and filled my heart with thoughts, desires, sighs, and suffering, and filled my eyes with tears and weeping." "What did love bring you?" "The beautiful features, honors and worth of my beloved." "How did they come to you?" "Through memory and understanding." "What did you receive them with?" "With charity and hope." "How are you keeping them?" "With justice, prudence, fortitude, and temperance."

80. The beloved sang, and said that little did the lover know of love if he was ashamed of praising his beloved, or afraid of honoring him in those places where he was most dishonored. And little did he know of love if he was impatient with unhappiness. And he who despaired of his beloved allowed of no concordance between love and hope.

81. The lover sent letters to his beloved, asking if there were another lover who could help him endure the great pains he suffered for his love. And the beloved wrote back and told his lover there was no way that he could fail or wrong him.

82. The beloved was asked about the love of his lover. He answered that it was a mixture of joy and sorrow, of courage and of fear.

83. The lover was asked about the love of the beloved. He answered that his beloved's love was the influence[27] of infinite goodness, eternity, power, wisdom, charity, and perfection, which is the influence that the beloved has on the lover.[28]

84. "Tell us, fool, what do you mean by a marvel?" He answered, "To love things absent more than things present, and to love visible, corruptible things more than invisible, incorruptible ones."

85. The lover went in search of his beloved, and came upon a man who was dying without love. And he said it was a great shame for a man to have to die any sort of death without love. So he asked the dying man, "Tell me, why are you dying without love?" And he answered, "Because it is without love that I have lived."

86. The lover asked his beloved which was greater, love or loving. The beloved answered that in created beings love was the tree and loving the fruit, and the trials and suffering were the flowers and leaves, but that in God love and loving were one and the same thing, without any trials or suffering.

87. An excess of thoughts caused the lover suffering and sorrow, and he begged his beloved to send him a book describing his features, in the hope that this would provide some help. The beloved sent the book to his lover, and the lover's trials and suffering were doubled.

88. The lover was sick with love, and a doctor came to see him. The doctor increased his suffering and his thoughts, and then the lover was healed.

89. Love and the lover drew apart, and yet were both joyful in the beloved. The beloved appeared before them. The lover wept, and love vanished as the lover fainted. But the beloved revived his lover by reminding him of his features.

90. The lover said to the beloved, "Many are the paths by which you come to my heart, and reveal yourself to my eyes, and my words name you by many names, but the love by which you both mortify and give life to me is one, and one alone."[29]

---

[27] Here in the etymological sense of "inflowing."
[28] The best manuscripts combine this versicle with the previous one.
[29] Indirect speech in the original.

91. The beloved revealed himself to his lover clothed in new crimson robes. He held out his arms so he could embrace him, he lowered his head so he could kiss him, and he remained on high so he could always be found.[30]

92. The beloved left his lover, and the lover sought him with memory and understanding, so that he could love him. The lover found his beloved, and asked him where he had been. He answered, "In the absence of your memory, and in the ignorance of your understanding."

93. "Tell us, fool, are you ashamed when people see you weeping for your beloved?" He answered that shame without sin was a defect of love not knowing how to love.

94. The beloved planted yearnings, sighs, virtues, and love in the lover's heart. The lover watered the seeds with weeping and with tears.

95. The beloved planted trials, tribulations, and suffering in the lover's body. The lover healed his body with hope, devotion, patience, and consolations.[31]

96. On a great feast-day the beloved held court for a group of honorable barons, offering a great banquet and many gifts. The lover came to this court and the beloved said to him, "Who asked you to come to my court?" The lover replied, "Necessity and love impelled me to come so I could behold your beauty and bearing."[32]

97. The lover was asked to whom he belonged. He answered, "To love." "What are you made of?" "Of love." "Who gave birth to you?" "Love." "Where were you born?" "In love." "Who brought you up?" "Love." "How do you live?" "By love." "What is your name?" "Love." "Where do you come from?" "From love." "Where are you going?" "To love." "Where are you now?" "In love." "Have you anything other than love?" "Yes, I have faults and wrongs against my beloved." "Is there pardon in your beloved?" The lover said that in his beloved were mercy and justice, and that he therefore lived between fear and hope.[33]

---

[30] The "crimson robes" refer to the blood of the crucified Christ.

[31] The best MSS join this to the previous versicle.

[32] *Tes fayçons e tos capteniments*; the phrase is a commonplace of Provençal love poetry. In v. 89 above, *fayçons* was translated as "features."

[33] "Justice," one of God's attributes, refers mainly to that of the Last Judgment and hence it is paired with "fear," while the other attribute, "mercy," is paired with "hope."

98. The beloved left the lover, and the lover sought him in his thoughts and asked people about him in the language of love.

99. The lover found his beloved, who was held in contempt by people, and he told him what great wrong was being done to his honor. The beloved answered that his dishonor was due to a lack of fervent and devoted lovers. The lover wept, and his sorrows were increased. But the beloved consoled him by revealing his beauties to him.[34]

100. The light of the beloved's room lit up that of the lover, dispelling its darkness and filling it with joys, sorrows, and thoughts. And the lover chased all things from his room to provide space for his beloved.

101. The lover was asked what sign his beloved placed on his banner. He answered, "That of a dead man." He was asked why he chose such a sign. He answered, "Because he was a man who died on the cross, and because all those who boast of being his lovers should follow in his steps."

102. The beloved came to stay at the lover's lodgings, and the steward demanded payment from him. But the lover said that his beloved was to be lodged without charge.

103. Memory and Will joined together and climbed the mountain to the beloved, so that Understanding might be exalted and love greatly increased in loving the beloved.

104. Sighs and tears are daily messengers between the lover and the beloved, so that between them there may be pleasure, companionship, friendship, and goodwill.

105. The lover longed for his beloved, so he sent him his thoughts, that they might return from his beloved with the happiness which had been his for so long.

106. The beloved rewarded his lover with tears, sighs, griefs, thoughts, and sorrows, and the lover served his beloved for this reward.[35]

107. The lover begged his beloved to give him bounty, peace, and

---

[34] The best MSS join this versicle to the previous one.

[35] *Pensaments*, here translated as "thoughts," is a word much repeated in the *Book of the Lover and the Beloved*. It does not refer to thoughts in a purely intellectual sense, but rather those accompanied by emotion, usually of sorrow, such as those concerning Christ's suffering, the lack of honor paid to God by the ungrateful, etc.

honor in this world, and the beloved revealed his features to the lover's memory and understanding, and gave himself as object to his will.

108. The lover was asked what he thought honor was. He replied that it was understanding and loving his beloved. He was then asked what dishonor was. He replied that it was forgetting and ceasing to love his beloved.

109. "Love tormented me until I told him you were present in my torments. Love then lessened my suffering, and you, as a reward, increased love, which doubled my torments."

110. "On the path of love I met with another lover who was silent. Pale and thin, suffering and weeping, he reproached love, and made accusations against him. Love excused himself with loyalty, hope, patience, devotion, fortitude, temperance, and happiness. I therefore reproached the lover for crying out against love when love had given him such wonderful gifts."

111. The lover sang, and said, "O, what great unhappiness is love! O, what great happiness is loving my beloved, who loves his lovers with infinite, eternal love, perfect and complete in every way."

112. The lover was walking in a foreign land, where he thought he would find his beloved, when he was attacked on the road by two lions. The lover feared death, for he wanted to live in order to serve his beloved. He sent his memory to his beloved, so that love would be with him during his passage, and help him withstand death. While the lover was remembering his beloved, the lions came up to him humbly and licked the tears from his weeping eyes, and kissed his hands and feet. And the lover continued in peace in search of his beloved.[36]

113. The lover wandered over mountains and valleys, but could find no place to escape from the prison in which love held captive his body, his thoughts, and all his desires and joys.

114. While the lover was wandering in this troubled way, he came upon a hermit asleep near a lovely spring. The lover awakened the hermit, and asked him if he had seen his beloved in his dreams. The hermit answered

---

[36] This miracle—the only one Llull recounts in the *Book of the Lover and the Beloved*—reminds one of the Sufi "charismas" and of the legends about St. Francis recounted in the *Fioretti*.

that his thoughts were held captive in love's prison equally whether he was awake or asleep. The lover was very pleased to have found a fellow-prisoner, and they both wept, for the beloved had few such lovers.[37]

115. There is nothing in the beloved that does not cause the lover anxiety and sorrow. And there is nothing in the lover over which the beloved has no dominion, and in which he does not rejoice. Therefore the love of the beloved consists of action, and the love of the lover, of suffering and passion.

116. A bird was singing on a branch, saying "I will give a new thought to the lover, who will give me two."[38] The bird gave the new thought to the lover, and the lover gave two to the bird to lessen his torments. But the lover felt his pains of love increase.

117. The lover and the beloved met, and their greetings, embraces, kisses, weeping, and tears bore witness to their meeting. The beloved asked the lover how he was, and the lover felt confused in the presence of his beloved.[39]

118. The lover and the beloved quarreled, and their loves made peace between them. And the question arose: which love gave most of itself?

119. The lover loved all those who feared his beloved, and feared all those who did not fear him. It was therefore a question as to which was greater in the lover, love or fear.

120. The lover strove to follow his beloved, and he came to a path with a fierce lion who killed anyone passing by indolently and without devotion.[40]

121. The lover said, "He who does not fear my beloved should fear all things. But he who does fear my beloved should be bold and daring in all things."

122. The lover was asked what he meant by "occasion." He answered that occasion was the chance to experience pleasure in penance, understanding in conscience, hope in patience, health in abstinence, consolation

---

[37] All the medieval sources except one join this versicle to the preceding one.

[38] Indirect speech in the original.

[39] As Erica Lorenz points out, this "confusion" is a Sufi motif, one of the stages in the mystic ascent.

[40] Cf. 1 Kings 13:24 and 1 Peter 5:8.

in remembrance, love in diligence, loyalty in shame, riches in poverty, peace in obedience, and strife in malevolence.[41]

123. Love lit up the cloud placed between the lover and the beloved, and made it as bright and shining as the moon by night, the morning star at dawn, the sun by day, and understanding in the will. And it is through this shining cloud that the lover and beloved speak to each other.[42]

124. The lover was asked, "What is the greatest darkness?" He answered, "The absence of my beloved." "And what is the brightest light?" He answered, "The presence of my beloved."[43]

125. The stamp of the beloved is on the lover, who for love's sake suffers tribulations, sighs, tears, and troubled thoughts, and is held in contempt by the people.

126. The lover wrote the following words, "Let my beloved be joyful, for to him I send my thoughts, for him my eyes do weep, and without the pains of love I can neither live, nor feel, nor see, nor hear, nor smell."

127. "Ah, Understanding and Will! Bark and awaken the large dogs who are asleep, forgetting my beloved. Weep, O eyes! Sigh, O heart! And Memory—remember the dishonor of my beloved at the hands of those he so honored."[44]

128. "The enmity between the people and my beloved increases. My beloved promises gifts and rewards, and threatens with justice and wisdom, but memory and will scorn his promises and threats."

129. The beloved drew near to the lover to comfort and console him for the suffering he endured and for the tears he shed. And the nearer the beloved came, the more the lover suffered and wept out of pity for the dishonor done to his beloved.

130. With pen of love, water of tears, and on paper of suffering, the lover wrote letters to his beloved, telling him that devotion was late in

[41] "Occasion" is defined in the *Proverbs of Ramon*, ch. 165, no. 2, as "the instrument of cause and effect." It is therefore equivalent to "ground," "circumstance," or "opportunity."
[42] See the discussion of this versicle on p. 178 of the introduction above.
[43] Indirect speech in original.
[44] One critic suggests that the dogs who should be watching their Christian flock are the pope, the kings, and by extension the whole church hierarchy. This might also be a reference to the Dominicans, who, in a medieval pun became the *Domini canes*, "the dogs of the Lord," whose task it was to guard the Christian flock against the wolves of heresy.

coming, that love was dying, and that sin and error were ever increasing his enemies.

131. The loves of the lover and beloved were bound with bonds of memory, understanding, and will, so that lover and beloved might not be parted. And the cord which bound them together was woven of thoughts and yearnings, sighs and tears.

132. The lover lay in a bed of love. His sheets were made of joys, his coverlet of sorrows, and his pillow of tears. And the question was whether the cloth of the pillow was the same as that of the sheets, or as that of the coverlet.[45]

133. The beloved dressed his lover in a tunic, vest, and cape. He made him a hat of love, a shirt of thoughts, stockings of tribulations, and a garland of tears.

134. The beloved begged his lover not to forget him. The lover said he could not forget him since he could not be without knowledge of him.

135. The beloved asked to be praised and defended in the places where men most feared to praise him. The lover asked to be provided with sufficient love, and the beloved answered that for love of him he had become incarnate and had died on the cross.[46]

136. The lover asked his dear beloved to show him how he could make him known, loved, and praised by the people. The beloved filled his lover with devotion, patience, charity, tribulations, thoughts, and tears. And boldness to praise his beloved came into the lover's heart. In his mouth were praises of his beloved, and in his will contempt for the reproaches of the people who judge falsely.

137. The lover spoke to the people in these words: "He who truly remembers my beloved, in this remembering forgets all else. And he who forgets all else in remembering his beloved, him my beloved defends in all ways, and to him he gives a part of all things."

138. The lover was asked what gave birth to love, what it lived on, and

---

[45] That is to say, were they tears of joy or of sorrow? Castro, *The Structure of Spanish History*, pp. 310–11 says that in neither Saint Augustine nor Saint Bernard is there anything comparable to Llull's style—so similar here to that of the Sufis—which infuses the most commonplace reality (sheets, coverlets, pillows) with poetic and symbolic intention. The following versicle continues in the same vein.

[46] All the medieval sources join this versicle to the previous one, even though they don't seem to belong together.

why it died. He answered that love was born of remembering, lived on understanding, and died through forgetting.

139. The lover forgot all that existed below the sovereign sky, so that his understanding might rise up higher towards an understanding of the beloved, whom his will desired to contemplate and make known.

140. The lover went into battle to honor his beloved, and he took with him faith, hope, charity, justice, prudence, fortitude, and temperance, to enable him to defeat the enemies of his beloved. And the lover would have been defeated, had his beloved not helped him to make known his perfections.

141. The lover desired to pass on to the final goal of his love for the beloved, but other goals blocked his passage.[47] Therefore his longing thoughts and desires caused the lover sadness and grief.

142. The perfections of his beloved filled the lover with pride and joy, but too many thoughts and reflections caused him suffering. And the question arose—which did he feel more strongly, the joys or the sorrows?

143. The lover was sent by his beloved as a messenger to Christian princes and unbelievers to show them the Art and principles by which they could know and love the beloved.[48]

144. If you see a lover dressed in fine clothes, honored for his haughtiness, fat with food and sleep, know that in that man you see damnation and torments. But if you see a poorly dressed lover, scorned by men, pale and thin from fasting and keeping vigil, know that in him you see salvation and everlasting blessedness.

145. The lover complained and his heart cried out from the heat of love within him. The lover died; the beloved wept for him, and gave him the comfort of patience, hope, and reward.[49]

146. The lover wept for what he had lost, and no one could comfort him, for his losses could not be regained.

[47] As Sala-Molins points out in his anthology, Llull is here playing on the double meaning of "passage"—the normal one and that into the next life. This refers to Llull's original goal of death through martyrdom, and the other goals man has in serving his beloved on earth, making for a conflict.

[48] See the introduction, p. 182 above.

[49] The Old Spanish translation has "eternal reward," which is undoubtedly what Llull meant here.

147. God created the night for the lover to keep vigil and reflect upon the perfections of his beloved, and the lover thought it had been created so that those wearied by love could rest and sleep.

148. Men mocked and reproached the lover because he acted like a fool for love's sake. The lover felt contempt for their mockery, and reproached them in turn for not loving his beloved.

149. The lover said, "I am dressed in coarse cloth,[50] but love clothes my heart with happy thoughts and my body with tears, griefs, and suffering."

150. The beloved sang, and said, "I have directed those who praise me to praise my worth, but the enemies of my honors torment them and scorn them. So I have sent my lover to weep and lament my dishonor, and his laments and tears are born of my love."

151. The lover swore to the beloved that for love of him he loved and endured hardships and suffering, and he begged the beloved to love him and have compassion on his hardships. The beloved swore that it was the nature and property of his love to love all those who loved him, and to pity those who endured hardships for love's sake. And the lover was made happy and consoled by the nature and essential property of his beloved.

152. The beloved forbade his lover to speak, and the lover found comfort in the contemplation of his beloved.

153. The lover wept so bitterly and cried out so loudly to his beloved that the beloved descended from the supreme heights of heaven and came to earth to weep, grieve, and die for love's sake, and to teach men to love, know, and praise his perfections.

154. The lover blamed Christians for not placing the name of his beloved, Jesus Christ, at the beginning of their letters, so as to honor him as the Saracens honor Mohammed—who was a deceiver—whose name they place at the beginning of their letters.[51]

155. The lover met a squire walking pensively, and he was thin, pale, and poorly dressed. He greeted the lover and said, "May God guide you to find your beloved." The lover asked him how he had recognized him. The

---

[50] The wording is remarkably similar to a passage in the "Life;" see p. 14 above and n. 38 for the Franciscan significance of *de panno vili*. Notice also that the Sufis originally got their name from their garments of coarse wool (*sūf*).

[51] Llull carried out this Islamic practice by beginning each of his works with an invocation praising God.

squire replied, "Some of love's secrets reveal others, and that is why lovers can recognize each other."[52]

156. The perfections, honors, and good works of the beloved are the riches and treasures of the lover. And the treasures of the beloved are the thoughts, desires, torments, tears, and suffering which the lover endures for the honor and love of his beloved.

157. Great companies and hosts of loving spirits have gathered together, and they carry a banner of love with the image and sign of their beloved upon it. And they will not admit to their company anyone lacking in love, for fear that their beloved be dishonored.

158. Those who play the fool in order to amass money move the lover to become a fool of love.[53] And the shame the lover feels at going about as a fool among men serves to make them esteem and love him. The question is, which of the two actions provides a greater occasion for love?

159. Love sank the lover into sorrow through too much reflection. The beloved sang, and the lover rejoiced when he heard him. The question is, which of the two proved a greater occasion for an increase of love in the lover?

160. The secrets of the beloved are revealed in the secrets of the lover, and the secrets of the lover are revealed in the secrets of the beloved. And the question is, which of these two secrets is the greater occasion for revelation?

161. The fool was asked by what signs his beloved was known. He answered and said it was by mercy and pity, which were essentially and immutably in his will.

162. Because of his own special love of the beloved, the lover loved the common good more than the special good, so that his beloved might be commonly known, praised, and desired.[54]

163. Love and Lack-of-love met in a garden where the lover and beloved were talking in secret. Love asked Lack-of-love with what intention he had come to that place. Lack-of-love answered that it was so the lover might

---

[52] Indirect speech in the original.

[53] Llull frequently opposes minstrels or jongleurs who "play the fool" for money, and the *joculator Dei* ("minstrel of God") or "fool of love." He devotes pages to the subject in the *Book of Contemplation* (ch. 118) and *Felix* (*SW* II, 885–6 and 901); see also v. 281 below.

[54] "Special" in the sense of "private," and "common" in that of "general."

cease to love, and the beloved be dishonored. The beloved and lover were very displeased by Lack-of-love's words, and they increased Love so it could conquer and destroy Lack-of-love.[55]

164. "Tell us, fool, where do you feel your will to be stronger, in loving or in hating?" He replied, "In loving, for I have only hated in order to love."[56]

165. "Tell us, lover, what do you understand better, truth or false-hood?" He answered that he understood truth better. "Why?" "Because I understand falsehood only so I may better understand truth."

166. The lover perceived that he was loved by his beloved, and he asked him if his love and mercy were one and the same thing. The beloved admitted that in his essence there was no distinction between his love and his mercy. The lover then asked him why his love tormented him so, and why his mercy did not cure him of his pains. The beloved answered that it was his mercy that gave him the pains, so that through them he might more perfectly honor his love.

167. The lover wanted to go to a foreign land to honor his beloved, and he wanted to disguise himself so as not to be captured on the way. But he could not hide the tears in his eyes, nor his pale and drawn face, nor the laments, thoughts, sighs, sorrow, and suffering of his heart. As a result, he was captured on his journey and delivered for torture by his beloved's enemies.

168. The lover was imprisoned in the prison of love. Thoughts, desires, and memories held and bound him so he would not escape his beloved.[57] His longings tormented him. Patience and hope consoled him. The lover almost died, but the beloved revealed himself to him, and the lover revived.

169. The lover met his beloved, and wept upon recognizing him. The beloved reproached him for not having wept before recognizing him, and asked, "How did you know me, if not through your tears?" The lover

---

[55] "Lack-of-love" here translates *desamor*, for which see the note to v. 62.

[56] Here "hate" translates *aïrar*, which is always stronger than the *desamar* of the previous note. A similar thought was expressed by Julian of Norwich: "True love teacheth us that we should hate sin only for love." This is a good example of the positive mysticism discussed in introduction above.

[57] Peers mistranslates this as "flee to his beloved."

answered, "Through memory, understanding and will, which were greatly increased as soon as you appeared to my bodily eyes."[58]

170. The beloved asked the lover the meaning of love. He replied that it was the presence of the words and features of the beloved in the sighing heart of another lover,[59] and faintness from weeping and desire in the heart of the lover.

171. "Love is the fervent mingling of boldness and fear. It is desiring the beloved as the final purpose of one's will. Love is that which kills the lover when he hears someone sing of the beauties of his beloved. And love is that which contains my death, and in which my will dwells every day of my life."[60]

172. Devotion and yearning sent thoughts by means of messengers to the lover's heart to bring tears to his eyes, for his eyes had wept for a long time and wanted to weep no more.[61]

173. The lover said, "You who love,[62] if you need fire, come and light your lanterns at my heart. If you need water, come to my eyes that are streaming with tears. And if you need thoughts of love, come and gather them from my reflections."

174. One day it happened that the lover was meditating on the great love he felt for his beloved, and on the great hardships and dangers into which this love had long led him, and he reflected that his rewards would surely be great. But while thinking in this way, he remembered that his beloved had already paid him well by kindling in him a love of his presence, and by giving him the pains of love.

175. The lover wiped away from his face and eyes the tears he had shed for love's sake, so as not to reveal the suffering his beloved had caused him. The beloved asked him why he hid these signs of love from other lovers, since he had given them to him so others might come to love and honor his worth.

---

[58] Indirect speech in the original.

[59] Llull usually introduces the word *amador* instead of *amic* when speaking of other lovers, normally in the plural. There seems to be no other clear distinction between the two terms.

[60] All the MSS except one join this versicle to the previous one.

[61] See n. 6 above. A propos of thoughts coming to the heart, in his scientific mode, Llull located the intellect in the brain, but in his literary writings affective thoughts came and went from the heart.

[62] *Amadors*, for which see the note to v. 170 above.

176. "Tell us, you who go about as a fool for love's sake, how much longer will you be a serf, forced to weep and to suffer hardships and pains?" He answered, "Until such time as my beloved separates my soul from my body."[63]

177. "Tell us, fool, do you have money?" He replied, "I have a beloved." "Do you have towns, castles, cities, counties, or duchies?" He answered, "I have love, thoughts, tears, desires, hardships, and suffering, which are better than empires or kingdoms."

178. The lover was asked how he recognized the sentence of his beloved. He answered that it was in the equality of joys and suffering, on the basis of which the beloved judged his lovers.

179. "Tell us, fool, who knows more of love, he who has joy from it, or he who has pains and suffering?" He answered, saying that one could have no knowledge of love from either without the other.

180. The lover was asked why he did not defend himself when people accused him of sins and false crimes. He answered that it was his beloved, falsely accused by men, whom he had to defend, whereas man, subject to deceit and error, was hardly worthy of any defense.

181. "Tell us, fool, why do you defend love when it so tries and torments your body and your heart?" He answered, "Because it increases my merits and my happiness."

182. The lover complained about his beloved for making love torment him so terribly. And the beloved defended himself by increasing his lover's hardships and dangers, thoughts, weeping, and tears.

183. "Tell us, O fool, why do you defend the guilty?" He answered, "So as not to be like the accusers who accuse the innocent along with the guilty."[64]

184. The beloved raised the lover's understanding up to a knowledge of his great heights, so that he would direct his memory towards remember-

[63] The motif of the lover as serf or slave of the beloved is a commonplace of both Sufi and troubadour literature.

[64] Llull's love of opposites: accusers of the innocent vs. defenders of the guilty. He points out the error of the one by stating its opposite but equivalent.

ing his faults, and his will towards rejecting them and rising up to love the perfections of his beloved.

185. The lover sang of his beloved, saying he bore him such good will that the things he hated for love of him gave him more pleasure and happiness than the things he loved without the love of his beloved.

186. The lover was passing through a large city, and he asked if there was someone with whom he could speak as he desired about his beloved. And he was shown a poor man who was weeping for love's sake, and who was seeking a companion with whom to speak about love.

187. The lover was thoughtful and perplexed, wondering how his suffering could have its origin in the nobilities of his beloved, who contains within himself such great bliss.[65]

188. The lover's thoughts wavered between the forgetting of his torments and the remembrance of his joys. For the joys of love drive out the memory of sorrow, and the torments of love recall the happiness which love brings.

189. The lover was asked if it was possible for his beloved to take away his love. He answered that it was not, so long as his memory remembered and his understanding understood the nobilities of his beloved.

190. "Tell us, fool! What can be best compared and found most similar?" He answered "The lover and the beloved." They asked him why. He answered "Because of the love which exists between them."[66]

191. The beloved was asked if he had ever felt pity. He answered that had he not felt pity he would never have had his lover love him, nor would he have tormented him with sighs, tears, hardships, and suffering.

192. The lover was walking in a large forest seeking his beloved. There he came upon Truth and Falsehood, who were arguing about his beloved. Truth was praising him and Falsehood reproaching him. The lover therefore called to Love to come to the aid of Truth.

193. Temptation came to the lover in order to deprive him of his be-

[65] "Nobilities" (like the "honors" of v. 51) is a frequent synonym in the *Book of the Lover and the Beloved* for the divine virtues or dignities.
[66] Indirect speech in the original.

loved, and to make memory reawaken and recover the beloved's presence, remembering him more strongly than ever, so that his understanding might rise up even higher to understand him, and his will to love him.

194. On a certain day the lover forgot his beloved, and on another day he remembered that he had forgotten him. On the day he remembered that he had forgotten him the lover was both in pain and sorrow because of his forgetting, and in glory and bliss because of his remembering.

195. So intensely did the lover desire praises and honors for his beloved that he doubted he could remember them enough. And so intensely did he hate the dishonors done to his beloved that he doubted that he hated them enough. The lover was therefore confused between his love and his fear of the beloved.

196. The lover was dying of joy and living through pain. And the joys and torments came together and united to become one and the same in the lover's will. And so the lover was both living and dying at the same time.

197. The lover wanted to ignore and forget his beloved for just one hour, so as to have some rest from his pains. But since forgetfulness and ignorance caused him such suffering he chose to have patience and lifted up his understanding and memory for contemplation of his beloved.

198. So great was the love of the lover for his beloved that he believed everything he was told by him. And so greatly did he want to understand his beloved that everything he heard about him he wanted to understand by the light of reason.[67] Therefore the love of the lover lay between belief and understanding.

199. The lover was asked what thing was furthest from his heart. "Lack of love," he replied. "And for what reason?" "Because what is closest to my heart is love, which is the opposite of lack of love."[68]

200. "Tell us, fool, are you ever envious?" He replied, "Yes, whenever I forget the generosity and riches of my beloved."

201. "Tell us, lover, have you riches?" He replied, "Yes, I have love." "Have you poverty?" "Yes, I have love." "How is that?" "I am poor because love is no greater, and does not fill more lovers with love so as to honor the virtues of my beloved."

---

[67] Literally, "for necessary reasons."
[68] Indirect speech in the original.

202. "Tell us, lover, where is your power?" He replied, "In the power of my beloved." "With what do you struggle against your enemies?" "With the strength of my beloved." "In what do you find comfort?" "In the eternal treasures of my beloved."

203. "Tell us, fool! What do you love more, the mercy of your beloved, or his justice?" He answered that it was so right for him to love and fear justice that he could have no desire in his will to love anything more than the justice of his beloved.[69]

204. Faults and merits waged a battle in the lover's conscience and will. Justice and memory increased the remorse in his conscience, and mercy and hope increased happiness in the beloved's will. Therefore merits conquered faults and wrongs in the penitence of the lover.

205. The lover affirmed that all was perfection in his beloved, and denied the existence of any imperfection in him. And the question arose as to which was stronger, the affirmation or the negation.

206. There was an eclipse in the heavens and darkness over all the earth. This made the lover recall that for a long time sin had caused his beloved to be absent from his will. Because of this absence, darkness had banished the light of his understanding, and this is the light by which the beloved reveals himself to his lovers.

207. Love came to the lover, and the lover asked him what he wanted. Love said he had come to nurture and direct him in such a way that when the moment of his death came he would be able to conquer his mortal enemies.

208. Love fell ill when the lover forgot his beloved. And the lover fell ill because, with an excess of remembering, his beloved sent him hardships, anxiety, and suffering.

209. The lover came upon a man who was dying without love. The lover wept for the dishonor caused the beloved by the death of this man without love, and he asked the man why he was dying without love. He answered that it was because no one had ever given him knowledge of love, nor taught him how to be a lover. Therefore the lover sighed and wept, and said, "Ah, devotion! When will you be greater, so that blame may be lesser, and my beloved then have fervent and ardent followers and lovers who would not hesitate to praise his honors."

[69] For "justice" and "mercy" in this and the next versicle, see the note to v. 97.

210. The lover tempted love, to see if it could remain in his heart without the memory of his beloved, and his heart ceased thinking and his eyes ceased weeping, and love was destroyed. The lover was left confused, and went about asking people if they had seen love.[70]

211. Love, loving, lover, and beloved are in such great accord in the beloved that they are one actuality in essence. And the lover and beloved are different but concordant, with no contrariety or difference of essence. The beloved is therefore lovable in a greater measure than any other object of love.

212. "Tell us, fool, why do you have such great love?" He replied, "Because the journey in search of my beloved is long and perilous. I must seek him carrying a great burden, and must travel very fast. And I could not accomplish these things without great love."

213. The lover kept vigil, fasted, wept, gave alms, and traveled to far-off lands, so that the will of the beloved might be moved to inspire his subjects with the desire to love and honor his perfections.

214. If the love of the lover does not suffice to move the beloved to pity and pardon, the love of the beloved suffices to give his creatures grace and blessing.

215. "Tell us, fool! How can you be most like your beloved?" He replied, "By understanding and loving with all my power the traits of my beloved."

216. The lover was asked if his beloved was lacking in anything, and he answered, "Yes, in lovers and praisers to honor his worth."

217. The beloved wounded his lover's heart with rods of love, to make him love the tree from which he had gathered the rods with which to strike his lovers. For this was the tree on which he had suffered death, pain, and dishonor, so that he might restore love to those lovers whom he had lost.

218. The lover met his beloved, and saw that he was very noble and powerful, and worthy of all honor. And he told him that he wondered at how little people knew, loved, and honored him, when he was so deserv-

---

[70] For "heart" see the note to v. 172 above. As Sala-Molins points out in *La Philosophie de l'amour* (see n. 18 to the introduction above), pp. 263–5, the lover is both slave and free; he can break the triad of beloved-love-lover at will, as he does in this versicle, tempting love by removing the memory of the beloved.

ing. The beloved answered, saying he had been sorely disappointed, for he had created man in order to be known, loved, and honored, and that out of a thousand men, no more than a hundred feared and loved him, and of that hundred, ninety feared him lest he give them eternal punishment, and ten loved him hoping to be granted glory; and there was hardly anyone who loved him for his goodness and nobility. When the lover heard these words, he wept bitterly for the dishonor done to his beloved, and said, "Beloved, you who have given so much to man, and have honored him so greatly, why has man so forgotten you?"[71]

219. The lover was praising his beloved, saying that he had transcended "where," for he was there where the "where" could not be reached. Therefore, when the lover was asked where his beloved was, he replied: "He *is*," but one knows not where. However, he did know that his beloved was in his remembrance.[72]

220. The beloved, with his honors, bought a slave subject to cares, suffering, sighs, and tears. He asked him what he ate and drank. He answered, "Whatever you wish." He asked him how he was clothed. He answered, "However you wish." The beloved then asked, "Have you no will of your own?" He answered, "A serf and subject has no other will than that of obeying his lord and beloved."[73]

221. The beloved asked his lover if he possessed patience. He answered that all things pleased him, so he had no need for patience, and that he who was not lord of his will could not be impatient.

222. Love gave himself to whomever desired him, and since he did not give himself to many nor inspire lovers with fervent love, which he could have done, the lover cried out against him, and accused him before his beloved. But love defended himself, saying he would not go against free will, for he wanted his lovers to have great merit and great glory.[74]

223. There was great strife and discord between the lover and love, for the lover was weary of the pains he endured for love's sake. They argued over whether love or the lover was to blame, and decided to go to the

[71] The Muslim woman saint, Rabi'a, is said to have walked around with brushwood in one hand and a watering can in the other, to burn Paradise and put out the fires of Hell, so people would love God disinterestedly.

[72] Castro, *The Structure of Spanish History*, p. 312, quotes al-Hallaj (858–922): "Thou occupiest the boundary of nearness and farness, and the *where* knows not where thou art."

[73] Original in indirect speech.

[74] After the previous two versicles describing the lover as slave to the beloved, Llull feels it important to remind his readers of free will.

beloved to be judged. He punished the lover with pain and longing, and rewarded him with an increase of love.[75]

224. A question was raised as to whether love was closer to thought or to patience. The lover solved the problem by saying that love was engendered by thought, but nourished by patience.

225. The lover's neighbors are the beautiful ways of the beloved, and the neighbors of the beloved are his lover's thoughts, tears, and the pains he endures for love's sake.

226. The will of the lover wanted to rise up high to greatly love his beloved, so it ordered the lover's understanding to rise up with all its might, and understanding ordered memory to do the same. And all three rose up to contemplate the beloved in his perfections.[76]

227. The lover's will left him, and gave itself to the beloved. But the beloved imprisoned it within the lover, so he would be loved and served by him.[77]

228. The lover said, "My beloved must not think that I have left him to love another, for all my being has been disposed by love towards loving one beloved alone." The beloved answered and said, "Let not my lover think that I am loved and served by him alone, for I have many lovers who love me more strongly and lastingly than does his love."

229. The lover said to his beloved, "O, my beloved, you have nourished my eyes and accustomed them to seeing your perfections, and my ears to hearing of them. And so my heart is accustomed to thoughts that have brought tears to my eyes and suffering to my body." The beloved answered the lover, saying that without such customs and nourishment his name would not be inscribed in the book of those going to eternal blessedness, and would not be removed from the book of the eternally damned.

230. The noble traits of the beloved are gathered together in the lover's heart, increasing his thoughts and torments. Were the beloved to increase the thoughts of his honors in the lover's heart, the lover would surely perish and die.

231. The beloved came to dwell in the hostel of his lover. His lover

---

[75] This versicle, in the form of a dispute between two people resolved by a third, is similar to that of the Provençal *tensó*.

[76] See the note to v. 19 above.

[77] See p. 182 of the introduction above.

made him a bed of thoughts, and sighs and tears were his servants. And the beloved paid for his stay with remembrances.[78]

232. Love mixed pains and pleasures in the thoughts of the lover. The pleasures cried out against this mixture, and accused love before the beloved. But when the beloved separated the pleasures from the torments love gives its lovers, the pleasures vanished.

233. The signs of love made by the lover to his beloved are, in the beginning, tears, in the middle, tribulations, and at the end, death. And it is by these signs that the lover preaches to those who love his beloved.[79]

234. The lover left so as to be alone, and his heart was accompanied by thoughts, his eyes by tears, and his body by fasting and afflictions. But when the lover returned to the company of men all of the above things abandoned him, and he remained alone among the people.

235. Love is a great sea troubled by wind and waves, without port or shore. The lover perishes in the sea, and, in his peril, his torments perish and the work of his fulfillment begins.

236. "Tell us, fool, what is love?" He replied, "Love is the concordance of theory and practice towards a given end, to which the fulfillment of the lover's will is impelled, the end being to make people honor and serve his beloved. And the question is, does this end really accord with the will of the lover who desires to be with his beloved?"[80]

237. The lover was asked who his beloved was. He replied that it was he who made him love, desire, suffer, sigh, weep, be mocked, and die.

238. The beloved was asked who his lover was. He replied that it was he who feared nothing in order to honor and praise his perfections, and who gave up all things in order to obey his commandments and counsels.[81]

239. "Tell us, fool, which burden is heavier and harder to bear, the suffering of love, or the suffering from lack of love?" He replied, "You must ask those who do penance out of love for their beloved, and those who do penance out of fear of the pains of hell."

240. The lover fell asleep, and love died, for it had nothing on which to

[78] The hostel, as heart or soul of the lover, is a motif common to both Christian and Muslim mysticism.
[79] The triad of "beginning," "middle," and "end" from Figure T (see the chart on p. 79).
[80] See v. 227 and p. 182 of the introduction above.
[81] The Latin sources join this versicle to the previous one.

live. The lover awoke, and love revived through the thoughts the lover sent his beloved.

241. The lover said that infused knowledge came from will, devotion, and prayer, and acquired knowledge came from study and understanding. And the question therefore is, which of the two comes to the lover first, which does he find more pleasing, and which is the greater in him.[82]

242. "Tell us, fool, where do your needs come from?" He replied, "From thoughts, and from desire, worship, suffering, and perseverance." "And where do all these things come from?" He replied, "From love." "And where does love come from?" "From my beloved." "And where does your beloved come from?" "My beloved comes from himself alone."

243. "Tell us, fool, do you want to be free of all things?" He answered, "Yes, except of my beloved." "Do you want to be a prisoner?" He answered, "Yes, of thoughts and sighs, of trials, perils, exiles, and tears, so that I may serve my beloved, who created me to praise his great worth."

244. Love tormented the lover, and he wept and complained of this torment. His beloved called to him to come to him and be healed. The nearer the lover came to his beloved, the greater were love's torments, for greater was the love he felt. But because he felt more joy the more he loved, the more effectively did the beloved heal him of his suffering.

245. Love was ill. The lover treated him with patience, perseverance, obedience, and hope, and love was cured. The lover fell ill, and the beloved healed him with the memory of his virtues and honors.

246. "Tell us, fool, what is solitude?" He answered, "It is the solace and companionship of the lover and beloved." "And what are solace and companionship?" He answered, "Solitude in the heart of the lover who remembers nothing but his beloved."

247. The lover was asked the question, "Where is there greater danger, in enduring the pains of love, or in happiness?" The lover conferred with his beloved and then said that the dangers of unhappiness came from impatience, while those of happiness came from ingratitude.

---

[82] In Ch. 63 of *Blaquerna*, Llull tells us that "the hermit was . . . contemplating God and our Lady, and an abundance of great devotion raised his understanding to greater intelligence through infused knowledge than the understanding of many monks who have acquired knowledge, but through failure of devotion cannot have knowledge of the divine essence or its operation."

248. The beloved set love free, and allowed men to take as much of him as they wanted. Yet love could hardly find anyone to take him into his heart. Therefore the lover wept, saddened by the dishonor paid to love in this world by false lovers and ungrateful men.

249. Love killed all that was in the heart of his true lover, to make room for himself to live. And the lover would have died, had he not had the memory of his beloved.

250. There were two thoughts in the lover. One was a constant thought about the essence and virtues of his beloved, while the other was a thought about the beloved's works. And a question arose as to which thought was more luminous and more pleasing to the beloved and to the lover.

251. The greatness of his love caused the lover to die. The beloved buried him in his land, where the lover was raised up again. And the question is, from whom did he receive the greater gift?[83]

252. The beloved kept misfortunes, dangers, griefs, dishonors, and distractions in his prison, so they would not hinder the lover from praising his honors and from filling with love those who held him in contempt.

253. One day the lover was in the presence of many men whom his beloved had in this world too greatly honored, for they dishonored him in their thoughts. These men had contempt for his beloved and mocked his servants. The lover wept, tore out his hair, struck at his face, and tore his clothes, crying out loudly, "Has a greater sin ever been committed than that of holding my beloved in contempt?"

254. "Tell us, fool, do you want to die?" He answered, "Yes, to the pleasures of this world and the thoughts of those wretches who forget and dishonor my beloved. I want to be neither understood nor desired in their thoughts, since my beloved is absent from them."

255. "If you, fool, tell the truth, you will be wounded by men, and mocked, blamed, tortured, and killed." He replied, "According to those words, it follows that if I speak falsely, I will be praised, loved, served, and honored by men, and rejected by lovers of my beloved."

256. False flatterers were once speaking ill of the lover in the presence of

---

[83] The medieval French text and some modern translators add, "From love or from the beloved?"

his beloved. The lover was patient and the beloved showed his justice, wisdom, and power. And the lover preferred being blamed and reproached than being like any of the false accusers.[84]

257. The beloved planted a variety of seeds in the lover's heart, from which one plant sprouted, put forth leaves, flowered, and ripened into a single fruit. The question is, can this single fruit give rise to a variety of seeds?

258. The beloved is far above love, and far below love is the lover. And love, which is in the middle, lowers the beloved to the lover and raises the lover to the beloved. This lowering and raising are the beginning and the life of that love by which the lover suffers and the beloved is served.[85]

259. To the right of love is the beloved, and the lover is to the left. Therefore the lover cannot reach his beloved without passing through love.

260. And in front of love is the beloved, and behind the beloved is the lover. Therefore the lover cannot reach love unless his thoughts and desires have first passed through the beloved.[86]

261. The beloved made for his lover two beloveds similar to himself in honor and in worth. And the lover loved all three equally, although love is one only, as a sign of the essential unity of the one in three beloveds.

262. The beloved dressed himself in the cloth in which his lover was dressed, so that he would be his companion in eternal glory. The lover therefore always wanted to wear crimson robes, so that the cloth would be more like his beloved's.[87]

263. "Tell us, fool, what did your beloved do before the world existed?" He answered, "It was appropriate that he be, by virtue of his various eternal, personal, and infinite properties, wherein are contained lover and beloved."

264. The lover was saddened and wept when he saw unbelievers losing his beloved through ignorance. And he rejoiced in the justice of his beloved, who tormented those who knew him and were disobedient. This is

---

[84] *Falses loadors* ("false flatterers") were a stock element of Provençal poetry (where they were called *lauzengiers*).

[85] See the discussion of this versicle in the introduction, p. 179 above.

[86] All medieval sources (except one) unite this versicle to the previous one.

[87] See the note to v. 91 above.

why he was asked which was greater, his sadness or his joy, and whether his happiness upon seeing his beloved honored was greater than his sorrow upon seeing him dishonored.

265. The lover contemplated his beloved in the greatest difference and concordance of virtues and in the greatest contrariety of virtues and vices, and in being and perfection, which accord with one another more strongly, without any imperfection and nonbeing, than with said imperfection and non-being.[88]

266. The lover saw the secrets of his beloved in diversity and concordance, which revealed to him the plurality and unity of his beloved, through a greater congruity of essence without contrariety.

267. They said to the lover that if decay—which is contrary to being, in that it is contrary to generation (which is contrary to nonbeing)—was eternally decaying the decayed, it would be impossible for nonbeing or end to accord with decay or the decayed. By these words the lover saw eternal generation in his beloved.[89]

268. If that which increases the love of the lover for his beloved were false, then that which diminishes his love for him would be true. And if this were so, it would follow that there would be a lack of majority and truth in the beloved, and a concordance of falsehood and minority.

269. The lover was praising his beloved, saying that if in his beloved there is the greatest possibility of perfection and the greatest impossibility of imperfection, it follows that his beloved must be simple, pure actuality in essence and in operation. And as the lover was thus praising his beloved, the trinity of his beloved was revealed to him.[90]

270. The lover found greater concordance between the numbers one and three than between any other numbers, because every bodily form passed from nonbeing to being by the above numbers. The lover therefore

---

[88] See p. 182 of the introduction for a commentary on the terms of the Art used here (a use which continues in the next few versicles).

[89] "Generation" and "decay" (*corrupció*) were, for medieval science (following Aristotle), contrary processes characteristic of the sublunar world. These accord respectively with "being" and "nonbeing" from Figure X (see the chart on p. 79). Llull is here saying that this process of decay must be finite, for if it continued eternally, it would never bring things to an end, i.e. to nonbeing, with which it must accord. The lover then thinks of the complete opposite of temporal decay, which is the eternal generation within God of the Son by the Father. Versicles 265–72 are all in praise of divine perfections.

[90] "Operation" here refers to God's activity *ad intra*, which for Llull is necessarily Trinitarian.

contemplated the unity and trinity of his beloved in this greater concordance of number.

271. The lover praised his beloved's power, wisdom, and will, which[91] had created all things with the exception of sin. And yet sin would not have existed without the power, wisdom, and will of his beloved. But neither the power nor wisdom nor will of his beloved was an occasion of sin.

272. The lover praised and loved his beloved for having created him and given him all things. And he praised and loved him for having wanted to take his likeness and his nature. And on this subject one could ask, which praise and love should be considered more perfect?

273. Love tested the lover's wisdom and asked him whether the beloved showed him greater love by taking his nature or by re-creating it. The lover was confused, but then replied that the re-creation was necessary to avoid unhappiness, and the Incarnation to bestow happiness. And from this reply arose another question: "Which was the greater love?"[92]

274. The lover went from door to door begging alms, to remember the beloved's love for his servants, and to practice humility, poverty, and patience, all of which are things pleasing to his beloved.

275. They asked the lover to pardon them for love of his beloved, and the lover not only pardoned them, but gave them himself and his possessions.

276. With the tears of his eyes the lover told of the passion and sorrow his beloved had endured for his love. With sadness and heavy thoughts he wrote down the words he had spoken. And with mercy and hope he comforted himself.

277. Love and the beloved came to see the lover as he slept. The beloved called to his lover and love awakened him. And the lover obeyed love and answered his beloved.[93]

278. The beloved nurtured his lover so he would love. Love taught him to risk dangers, and Patience instructed him in how to bear afflictions for love of him to whom he had offered himself as a servant.

---

[91] The Latin, French, and Spanish sources have "who" with the following verb in the singular.

[92] For Llull's use of the term "re-creation" for "redemption," see the *Gentile*, Bk. III, n. 14.

[93] Again the dialogue between lover and beloved is made possible through the middle term of love.

279. The beloved asked people if they had seen his lover, and they asked him to describe his qualities. The beloved said that his lover was brave and fearful, rich and poor, cheerful and sad, thoughtful and ever-suffering for the sake of his love.

280. And the lover was asked whether he would sell his desire. He answered that he had sold it to his beloved for a price so high that it could buy the entire world.

281. "Preach, you fool, and tell people about your beloved! Weep and fast!" So the lover renounced the world and went with love in search of his beloved, and he praised him in those places in which he was dishonored.

282. The lover built and fashioned a beautiful town where his beloved could stay. He fashioned it with love, thoughts, laments, tears, and suffering. He adorned it with pleasures, hope, and devotion, and he fitted it out with faith, justice, prudence, fortitude, and temperance.

283. The lover drank of love at the spring of his beloved. There the beloved washed the feet of his lover, who had often forgotten and disdained his honors, because the world is in an evil state.[94]

284. "Tell us, fool, what is sin?" He replied, "It is intention turned around and directed against the final intention and reason for which my beloved created all things."

285. The lover saw that the world was created, in that eternity accords more with his beloved, who is infinite essence in greatness and in all perfection, than with the world, which is finite in quantity. The lover therefore saw, in the justice of his beloved, that his eternity must have existed prior to finite time and quantity.[95]

286. The lover defended his beloved against those who claim the world is eternal, saying that the justice of his beloved would not be perfect if he did not restore to each soul its own body, and for this there would not be enough place nor primordial matter.[96] Nor would the world be ordered toward a single end if it were eternal, and without this end his beloved's wisdom and will would lack perfection.

---

[94] The original Catalan for "because" could also be interpreted as "therefore." Either could make sense.

[95] The Creation in time vs. the eternity of the world taught by Aristotle was a problem for all three religions in the Middle Ages (cf. *Gentile*, Bk. II, n. 10).

[96] See the *Gentile*, *SW* I, 161, where this question is treated at greater length.

287. "Tell us, fool, how do you know that the Catholic faith is the true one and the beliefs of the Jews or Saracens are in falsehood and error?" He answered, "From the ten conditions of the *Book of the Gentile and the Three Wise Men*."[97]

288. "Tell us, fool, where does wisdom begin?" He answered, "With faith and devotion, which are a ladder by which the understanding rises to understand the secrets of my beloved." "And faith and devotion, where do they begin?" He replied, "With my beloved, who illumines faith and kindles devotion."

289. The lover was asked what was greater, possibility or impossibility. He answered that possibility was greater in created beings and impossibility in his beloved, since possibility and power[98] are in accord, as are impossibility and actuality.

290. Tell us, fool, which is greater, difference or concordance? He answered that, apart from his beloved, difference was greater in plurality and concordance in unity, but that in his beloved they were equal in plurality and in unity.

291. "Tell us, lover, what is worth?" He replied that it was the opposite of worldly worth, which is desired by false and vain lovers who want to have worth, while being unworthy and at the same time persecuting worth.

292. "Tell us, fool, have you ever met someone bereft of reason?" He answered that he had once seen a bishop who had many goblets on his table, and many plates and serving dishes of silver, and in his bedroom many garments and a large bed, and chests full of money. But there were few poor people at the door of his palace.[99]

293. "Fool, do you know what baseness is?" He replied, "Base thoughts." "And what is loyalty?" "Fear of my beloved, born of charity and a sense of shame, which fears the blame of people." "And what is honor?" He answered, "To think about my beloved, and to desire and praise his honors."

294. The trials and tribulations which the lover endured for the sake of love unsettled him and made him impatient. The beloved reproached him

---

[97] See the *Gentile*, Prologue, n. 10 above.
[98] Here "power" means "potentiality," as opposed to the pure actuality of the beloved.
[99] That is, waiting for alms.

with his perfections and promises, saying that he who was affected either by troubles or happiness knew little of love. The lover felt contrite and wept, and begged his beloved to restore his love.

295. "Tell us, fool, what is love?" He answered that love is that which puts free men into bondage and gives liberty to those in bonds. And the question is, which is closer to love, liberty or bondage?

296. The beloved called to his lover, who answered him, saying: "What is it you wish, beloved, you who are the eyes of my eyes, thought of my thoughts, fulfilling of my fulfillment, love of my loves, and even the beginning of my beginnings?"[100]

297. "O, my beloved," said the lover, "to you I go and in you I go, for you call me. I go to contemplate contemplation in contemplation with contemplation of your contemplation. I am in your virtue, and I come with your virtue, which is the source of my virtue. I greet you with your greeting, which is my greeting in your greeting, from which I hope for eternal greeting[101] in the blessing of your blessing, in which I am blessed in my blessing."

298. "You are high, O beloved, in your heights, to which you exalt my will, exalted in your exaltation with your height. And this, in my re-membrance, exalts my understanding, exalted in your exaltation to an understanding of your perfections, so that the will may then have exalted loving and memory have great remembrance."

299. "Beloved, you are the glory of my glory, and with your glory and in your glory, you give glory to my glory, which has glory from your glory. By this glory of yours I find glory equally in the pains and sufferings I endure for the honor of your glory, and the joys and thoughts that come to me from your glory."

300. "Beloved, in the prison of love you hold me enamored with your love, which has enamored me of your love, by your love and in your love. For you are nothing but love, in which you keep me alone, with the company of your love and your perfections. For you alone are in me alone,

---

[100] This is first of five similar versicles, characterized by an unusually insistent repetition of words. This, plus their strongly conceptual style, made Obrador in his edition of 1904, followed by Peers in his first translation, omit them as inauthentic.

[101] Llull is playing on the etymology of Catalan *salutació* ("greeting"), which comes from *salut* ("health, salvation"), which is in fact what the Latin text has for this last appearance of the word.

who am alone with my thoughts, since your aloneness—alone in perfection—has alone made me praise and honor its worth, without fear of those who are ungrateful, and do not have you alone in their love."

301. "Beloved, you are the solace of all solace, for in you my thoughts find solace with your solace, which is the solace and comfort of my griefs and tribulations caused by your solace, when you do not solace the ignorant with your solace, and do not increase the love of those who know your solace so they may more strongly honor your honors."[102]

302. The lover complained to his lord about his beloved, and to his beloved about his lord. The lord and beloved said, "Who is it that makes a division between us, when we are but one?" The lover answered, saying that it was pity from the lord, and tribulations on account of the beloved.[103]

303. The lover almost drowned in the great sea of love, but he trusted in his beloved, who came to his aid with cares, tribulations, tears, and weeping, sighs, and grief. For the sea was one of love, and of honoring his honors.

304. The lover rejoiced because his beloved *was*.[104] For from his being all other being was derived, and through it sustained and constrained and bound to honor and serve the being of his beloved, who cannot be condemned or destroyed or diminished, nor made lesser or greater, by any other being.

305. "Beloved, in your greatness you make great my desires, my thoughts, and my trials. For you are so great that everything that has remembrance, understanding, and pleasure from you is great, and your greatness makes small all things contrary to your perfections and commandments."

306. "My beloved eternally begins and has begun and will begin, and he eternally does not begin nor has begun nor will begin. And in my beloved

---

[102] Both *solatz* in Provençal (it was a catchword of Troubadour poetry) and *solaç* in medieval Catalan had two meanings: "pleasure, company, happiness," and "comfort, solace." Here the second meaning is clearly intended, but in other versicles Llull uses it in the first sense.

[103] The lord and the beloved here seem to refer to the first and second Divine Persons.

[104] Latin has *est esse*, "is being." There is the famous passage in *Exodus* (3:14–15) where God says to Moses, "I am who am," and orders him to tell the children of Israel that he was sent by "He who is." The Old French translation omits this versicle.

these beginnings are not contradictory, because he is eternal and has within himself unity and trinity."

307. "My beloved is one, and in his unity my thoughts and my love unite in one will. And the unity of my beloved suffices for all unities and all pluralities. And the plurality which is in my beloved suffices for all unities and pluralities."

308. "The good of my beloved is supreme good, and he is the good of my good. For my beloved is good without any other good, since if he were not so, my good would come from another supreme good. And since it does not, may all my good in this life be spent in honoring the supreme good, for this is as it should be."

309. "When you, beloved, know I am sinful, you become merciful and forgiving. And because what you know within yourself is better than I am,[105] I know that in you is forgiveness and love, for you have made me feel contrition and pain and the wish to suffer death in praise of your worth."

310. "Your power, beloved, can save me through your goodness, mercy, and pardon; and it can condemn me through your justice and the fault of my sins. May your power fulfill your will in me, for all is fulfillment, whether it brings salvation or damnation."

311. "Beloved, truth visits my contrite heart and draws water from my eyes whenever my will loves it. And since your truth is sovereign, it raises up my will so that it may honor your perfections, and lowers it so that it may cease to love my faults."

312. "Nothing was ever true without my beloved being in it, and that in which my beloved is not is false, and that in which my beloved will not be will be false. It therefore necessarily follows that everything that will be, was, or is, is true if my beloved is in it; and that whoever is in truth without my beloved being in it, is in fact in error, without this involving any contradiction."

313. The beloved created and the lover destroyed. The beloved judged and the lover wept. The beloved re-created glory for the lover. The be-

---

[105] The Catalan original has simply "than me"; the medieval Latin translation has "than that which I know in myself."

loved finished his work and the lover remained forever in the company of his beloved.[106]

314. Along the paths of vegetation, sensation, imagination, understanding and will, the lover went seeking his beloved. Along these paths he met with dangers and sorrows for his beloved's sake, so that his understanding and will would be raised up to his beloved, who wants his lovers to understand and love him greatly.[107]

315. The lover moves towards being through the perfection of his beloved, and moves towards nonbeing through his own imperfection. It is therefore a question as to which of the two movements has greater natural power over the lover.

316. "You have placed me, beloved, between my evil and your good. On your part may there be pity, mercy, patience, humility, pardon, help, and restoration. On my part, may there be contrition, perseverance, and remembrance—with sighs, weeping, and tears—of your holy passion."

317. "O beloved, you who make me love, if you do not help me, why did you ever create me? Why did you endure such suffering or undergo such a grievous passion for me? Since you have so helped me to rise, help me, beloved, to descend to the memory and hatred of my offenses and faults, so that my thoughts may the better rise to desire, honor, and praise your worth."

318. "You have made my will free to love your perfections or to scorn your worth, so that your love may be increased within it."

319. "With this liberty, beloved, you have placed my will in danger. Beloved, in this danger, remember your lover who with his free will chooses servitude in order to praise your perfections and increase the suffering and tears of his body."[108]

320. "Beloved, no fault or sin in your lover ever came from you, nor

---

[106] The first line is one of the few references in this work to Adam's fall.

[107] This is the versicle Pring-Mill analyzes in depth in his study mentioned in the introduction above (see n. 5 there). He rightly criticizes Peers for translating the opening as "By verdant paths of feeling," and thereby not understanding that Llull is here referring to the physical levels of being in man (see *Ars brevis*, Part IX, Subjects 5–7), which, added to the spiritual faculties of understanding and will, act as paths leading up to the beloved.

[108] All the medieval MSS except one join this versicle to the previous one, a joining seemingly confirmed by the "this" in the first sentence.

any perfection except through your grace and pardon. Since the lover then possesses you so, do not forget him in his tribulations and perils."

321. "Beloved, who in one name are named both man and God! By that name, Jesus Christ, my will desires you as man and God.[109] And if you, beloved, have so honored your undeserving lover that he names you thus and desires you to be so named, why do you not honor so many ignorant men who have not been as knowingly guilty towards your name as your lover has been?"

322. The lover wept and spoke to his beloved in the following words: "Beloved, you were never sparing or ungenerous with your lover in giving him being, in re-creating him, or in granting him many creatures to serve him. How is it then, beloved, that you who are sovereign generosity[110] have been so ungenerous to your lover with tears, thoughts, longings, wisdom, and love, with which to honor your honors? Your lover therefore asks you, beloved, for a long life so as to receive from you many of the above-mentioned gifts."

323. "Beloved, if you help just men against their mortal enemies, help increase my thoughts in desiring your honors. And if you help unjust men to become just again, then help your lover that he may sacrifice his will to your worship, and his body through the path of martyrdom as a testimony of love."

324. "In my beloved there is no difference between humility, humble, and humbled, for it is all humility in pure actuality. Therefore the lover reproaches pride, who wants to raise up to the heights of his beloved those whom in his humility he has so honored in this world, and whom pride has clothed in hypocrisy, vainglory, and vanity."

325. Humility has humbled the beloved before the lover through contrition and also through devotion. And the question is, in which of these two ways did the beloved humble himself more before the lover?

326. The beloved, because of his perfection, had mercy on his lover, but he also had mercy on him because of his lover's needs. And the question arose: which of these two reasons moved the beloved more strongly to forgive his lover's sins?

---

[109] "My will desires you" disguises the similar roots of *te vol ma volentat*.

[110] The original has *libertat*, which usually meant "liberty, freedom," but which, as here, could also mean "(moral) generosity, liberality."

327. "Our Lady and the angels and saints in heaven prayed to my beloved. And when I remembered the error in which the world lies through ingratitude, I also remembered the great justice of my beloved and the great ingratitude of his enemies."[111]

328. The lover raised up the powers of his soul, mounting the ladder of humanity, to glory in the divine nature. And by the divine nature he lowered the powers of his soul to glory in the human nature of his beloved.

329. The narrower the paths leading the lover to his beloved, the broader is his love; and the narrower his love, the broader are the paths. Thus in all ways, for the sake of his beloved, the lover receives love, pain, suffering, joys, and consolations.

330. Love issues from love, and thoughts from sorrows, and tears from the heart's sighs;[112] and love leads to love, and thoughts to tears, and sorrows to sighs. And the beloved watches his lover who bears all these tribulations for his love.

331. The desires and memories of the lover held vigil and went on journeys and pilgrimages to the perfections of his beloved. They brought back his traits and filled the lover's understanding with splendor, by which his will greatly increased in love.

332. With his imagination the lover painted and formed the traits of his beloved in bodily things, and with his understanding he made them shine in spiritual things, and with his will he worshipped them in all creatures.[113]

333. The lover purchased a day of tears with another day of thoughts, and he sold a day of love for another of tribulations, and both his love and his thoughts were increased.

334. The lover was in a foreign land and forgot his beloved, and he longed for his lord, his wife, his children, and his friends. But he returned to the memory of his beloved, so that he might be comforted and so that his exile might cause him neither longing nor sorrow.

---

[111] For the last word, one ms has *amichs*, "friends," a reading followed by many modern editions, but all medieval sources have *enemichs*, which would seem to be the correct reading.

[112] This follows the Latin sources; instead of "the heart's sighs," the Catalan and other Romance sources have "the heart's sorrows." The repetition of "sorrows" seems to be a mistake.

[113] The imaginative faculty is the highest level of man's physical makeup, one which he shares with animals. See *Ars brevis*, Part IX, Subject 5.

335. The lover heard words of his beloved, through which his under-standing beheld him, for his will took pleasure in what was heard and his memory remembered the virtues of his beloved and his promises.

336. The lover heard evil spoken of his beloved, and in this evil-speaking his understanding perceived the justice and patience of his be-loved, for justice punished the evil-speakers and patience awaited their contrition and repentance. And the question is, in which of the two did the lover believe more strongly?

337. The lover was sick and made out a will with the advice of his beloved. He left faults and sins to contrition and penance, and worldly joys to contempt. He bequeathed tears to his eyes, sighs and love to his heart, the traits of his beloved to his understanding, and to his memory the passion his beloved had endured for love's sake. And to his own mission he left the conversion of the infidels, who through ignorance are doomed to perdition.

338. The scent of flowers made the lover recall the stench of the miserly rich, of the lascivious, and of the ungrateful proud. The taste of sweet things recalled to him the bitterness of temporal possessions and of our entry into and exit from this world. The experience of earthly pleasures made him understand how brief is our passage on earth and how the delights that are here so pleasurable are the occasion of everlasting torments.

339. The lover suffered hunger, thirst, cold and heat, poverty, naked-ness, sickness, and tribulations, and would have perished had he not re-membered his beloved who healed him with hope and remembrance, with the renunciation of this world, and with contempt for the reproach of others.

340. The lover's bed lay between trials and joy. In joy he lay down to sleep and in trials he awoke. The question is, to which of the two was the bed of the lover closer?

341. The lover lay down to sleep in anger, for he feared people's blame, but he awoke in patience when he remembered the praises of his beloved. The question is, before whom did he feel greater shame, before his beloved or before the people?[114]

---

[114] "Anger, ire" and "patience" are opposites in Llull. See *Ars brevis*, Part IX, Subject 9, nos. 9 and 17.

342. The lover thought about death and was frightened, until he remembered the city of his beloved, the city to which death and love are the gates and entrance.

343. The lover complained to his beloved of temptations that constantly came to trouble his thoughts. And the beloved answered that temptations served as an occasion for man to have recourse to memory, so as to remember God and to love his noble qualities.

344. The lover lost a jewel he greatly prized, and could not be consoled until his beloved asked him which was the more valuable for him, the jewel he had possessed or the patience he had in the works of his beloved.

345. The lover fell asleep reflecting upon the hardships and obstacles he met with in serving his beloved, and he feared that, because of these obstacles, his works would perish. But the beloved sent him consciousness which awakened him to his merits and to the powers of his beloved.[115]

346. The lover had to make a long journey over paths that were rough and hard, and the time came for him to set out and carry the heavy burden that love makes its lovers bear. The lover therefore unburdened his soul of the thoughts and pleasures of this world, so his body could more easily carry its burden and the soul follow these paths in company of his beloved.

347. One day, some people spoke badly of his beloved in front of the lover, without the lover answering or defending him. Who then was more to blame, the men who spoke badly of the beloved, or the lover who was silent and did not defend him?

348. In contemplating his beloved, the lover's understanding was sharpened, and his will was filled with love. The question is, which of the two sharpened his memory more in remembering his beloved?[116]

349. With Fervor and Fear the lover set out on his journey to honor his beloved. Fervor carried him along, and Fear preserved him. While he was thus on his way, he came upon Sighs and Tears, who brought him greetings from his beloved. The question is, through which of the four did the lover find greatest comfort in his beloved?

---

[115] Llull is here referring to his own works (and merits).

[116] "Sharpened" is *asubtil·lava* in the original, coming from the same root as "subtlety," which for Llull was equivalent to "acuteness, perspicacity, cleverness, ingenuity." Cf. v. 363 below.

350. The lover gazed upon himself so he could be a mirror in which to behold his beloved. And he gazed upon his beloved so he could be a mirror in which he could have knowledge of himself. And the question is, to which of the two mirrors was his understanding closer?

351. Theology, Philosophy, Medicine, and Law met the lover, who asked them if they had seen his beloved. Theology wept, Philosophy doubted, Medicine and Law rejoiced. The question is, what did each of the four reactions signify to the lover in search of his beloved?

352. Full of tears and anguish, the lover went in search of his beloved along paths of the senses and ways of the mind. And the question is, which of the two roads did he take first while searching for his beloved, and on which did the beloved reveal himself to the lover most clearly?[117]

353. On the day of judgment the beloved will ask men to place on one side what he had given them in this world, and on the other what each of them had given to the world, so it may be seen how sincerely they have loved him, and which of the two gifts is nobler and greater.

354. The lover's will loved itself, and his understanding asked it if it were more like the beloved in loving itself or in loving the beloved, considering that the beloved loves himself more greatly than anything else. The question therefore is, how could the will answer the understanding most truly?

355. "Tell us, fool, what is the greatest and noblest love to be found in a creature?" He answered, "That which is one with the creator." "Why?" "Because there is no way the creator can make a creature nobler."[118]

356. One day the lover was praying, and he could feel no tears coming to his eyes; and so that he might weep, he turned his thoughts to money, women, children, food, and vanity, and his understanding found that any one of the above had more people serving it than had his beloved. And at this thought his eyes filled with tears, and his soul was in sadness and pain.

357. The lover was walking lost in thought about his beloved, when he met a large group of people who asked him for news. The lover, who was finding pleasure in his beloved, refused to answer them, saying that for fear of losing the closeness to his beloved he preferred not replying to their words.

[117] See the note to v. 314.
[118] This versicle answers the question of the one before.

358. The lover was enveloped in love both inwardly and outwardly, and he went in search of his beloved. Love said to him, "Lover, where are you going?" He answered, "I am going to my beloved, so that you may grow greater."

359. "Tell us, fool, what is religion?" He answered, "Purity of thought, and a longing for death to honor my beloved, and renunciation of the world so there may be no obstacle to contemplating him and telling the truth about his perfections."

360. "Tell us, fool, what are trials, laments, sighs, tears, tribulations, and perils in the lover?" He answered, "Pleasure for the beloved." "Why?" "Because through them he is more greatly loved, and the lover more greatly rewarded."

361. The lover was asked in whom love was greater, in the lover who was alive or in the lover who was dying. He answered, "In the lover who is dying." "Why?" "Because love cannot be greater than in a lover who dies for love, but it can still be greater in one who lives for love."

362. Two lovers met. One of them revealed[119] his beloved, and the other understood him. The question arose as to which of the two was nearer his beloved, and by the answer to this the lover had knowledge of the demonstration of the Trinity.

363. "Tell us, fool, why do you speak with such subtlety?" He answered, "To provide an opportunity for the understanding to rise up to the perfections of my beloved, and so that more men may honor, love, and serve him."

364. The lover became drunk on the wine of memory, understanding, and love of the beloved. The beloved watered that wine with the weeping and tears of his lover.[120]

365. Love heated and inflamed the lover with the memory of his beloved. And the beloved cooled his ardor with weeping, tears, forgetfulness of the delights of this world, and renunciation of vain honors. And love grew as the lover remembered for whom he suffered pains and tribula-

---

[119] *Mostrava* in the original, which normally means "showed, revealed," but which in Llull can also mean "explained," "taught," and even "demonstrated." The obscurity of meaning in this versicle makes it difficult to know which translation to choose.

[120] Thus in all medieval sources save one; this last, followed by all subsequent editions, has "with his weeping and with the tears of his lover."

tions, and for whom the men of the this world suffered hardships and persecution.[121]

366. "Tell us, fool, what is this world?" He answered, "It is the prison of lovers who serve my beloved." "And who imprisons them?" He answered, "Conscience, love, fear, renunciation, contrition, and the company of wicked people. And it is hardship without reward, and is therefore punishment."

Since Blaquerna had to write a book about the *Art of Contemplation*, he decided to end the *Book of the Lover and the Beloved*, which is now finished to the glory and praise of Our Lord God.

[121] Notice how here and in the previous versicle the beloved does not want ecstasy and loss of control in his lover: he waters the wine and cools his ardor.

THE BOOK OF THE
BEASTS

Introduction

BOTH THE *Book of the Lover and the Beloved* and the *Book of the Beasts* form seemingly disparate parts of longer didactic novels, *Blaquerna* in the first instance, and *Felix* or the *Book of Wonders* in the second. As such both have achieved a certain status as independent works.[1] Moreover, neither one of these shorter works can be understood without reference to the ladder-like structure of the longer works in which they are embedded. But here the resemblances end. *Blaquerna* is a utopian novel, in which the rungs of the ladder present the various stages of a model Christian life. *Felix,* on the other hand, is a work of social and spiritual criticism, in which the protagonist's father sends him out to "travel through the world and wonder why men no longer love and know God" the way they used to "in the time of the Apostles and Martyrs."[2] The world through which he travels gives him *exempla* for studying the medieval ladder of being: God, Angels, Heaven, Elements, Plants, Metals (or Minerals), Beasts, Man, Paradise, Hell.[3] And it is precisely in the seventh book, the *Book of the Beasts* that the social criticism becomes most acid, but in order to do this Llull has created a curious anomaly in the general structure of the longer work.

Instead of the treatise on animals we might have expected after those on Elements, Plants, and Minerals, the *Book of the Beasts* consists of a series of animal fables, with no narrator or teacher as in the other books, and in which Felix himself disappears from view. Moreover, it is the only work in which Llull used identifiable preexisting material to any notable degree. And the nature of this material is interesting: with the exception of the name and character of the main protagonist, taken from the French *Roman de Renart,*[4] it is all

---

[1] The *Book of the Beasts* only in modern times, in contrast to the *Book of the Lover and the Beloved* which was from Llull's lifetime sometimes treated as an independent work (see the introduction to that work, n. 2).

[2] Prologue to the longer work, *SW* II, 659.

[3] In the order of creation, i.e., God who first created the Angels and Heaven, and then the sublunary world starting with the elements and working up to Man and his destiny in the next world.

[4] Cf. n. 5 to the text.

of oriental origin. There is one story from the *Seven Wise Masters* (also called the *Book of Sindbad* or *Sendebar*),[5] one from the *Thousand and One Nights*,[6] and no fewer than ten from the Arabic *Kalila and Dimna* which stems ultimately from the Indian *Panchatantra*.[7] Even the one autobiographical bit seems to refer to Llull's unfortunate relations with the Moslem slave who taught him Arabic.[8]

Most extraordinary, perhaps, is the psychological and narrative unity Llull imposes on this material. The reader, accustomed to the loosely connected string of *exempla* of the first six books of *Felix,* begins the chain of animal fables of the *Book of the Beasts* in the same frame of mind. His surprise comes when he begins to see more and more pieces of the narrative fitting into place and realizes that he is experiencing a different literary world, one with a plot that builds and sweeps the reader along to a truly dramatic ending.

The modern reader's tendency to think of animal fables as a branch of children's literature or as elegant court *amusettes* leads to another surprise. As Dame Reynard's machinations become more and more appalling and her power greater and greater, the reader sees how penetrating and realistic are Llull's observations of the nastier side of palace politics; the surprise comes from confronting a kind of medieval predecessor to George Orwell's *Animal Farm*. The realization that this is indeed a political tract is confirmed by the Epilogue: "Here ends the *Book of the Beasts,* which Felix brought to a king so that he might learn, from the things done by the beasts, how a king should reign, and how to keep himself from evil counsel and from treacherous men."

All scholars have agreed, chiefly because of the place and date of composition of *Felix,* that the king in question must be Philip IV the Fair of France, who at that time was young (around twenty), still inexperienced (some three years of reign), and whom Llull perhaps felt he had a certain freedom to advise (since Philip was the nephew

[5] Cf. n. 14 to the text.

[6] Cf. n. 37 to the text.

[7] Cf. nn. 13, 15, 17–20, 22, 25, 33, 38 to the text. See also nn. 16, 43 for other stories possibly stemming from this source. See n. 13 for more information. For more detailed information on all these sources see the corresponding notes in *SW* II, where the reader will also find references to E. J. Neugaard, "The Sources of the Folk Tales in Ramon Llull's *Llibre de les bèsties,*" *Journal of American Folklore* 84 (1971), and from there, the corresponding numbers in Stith Thompson, *Motif-Index of Folk-Literature* (Bloomington, Indiana, 1955–7).

[8] Cf. n. 12 to the text.

of Llull's patron, James II of Majorca).[9] But no adequate historical counterpart to Dame Reynard has been suggested. All the more notorious "evil councilors" of Philip's reign, such as Pierre Flote, Guillaume de Nogaret, and Enguerren de Marigni, came into prominence some ten years later.

There is surprising agreement among scholars as to the place and date of composition of *Felix*. The opening sentence of the Prologue, "In a foreign land there was once a man who was sad and melancholy," coupled with the account in Book VIII, Chapter 89, of a man coming to Paris to ask King and University to support his missionary work based on the *Ars demonstrativa,* has led most scholars to agree that the work was written in Paris during Llull's first stay there in 1287–9.[10]

Manuscripts, Editions, and Translations

THE POPULARITY of *Felix* is attested by the fact that the original Catalan version is preserved in twelve manuscripts, seven from the Middle Ages, and five from the sixteenth through eighteenth centuries. Moreover, we also possess medieval translations into French, Spanish, and Italian.[11] For this edition I have only consulted five early Catalan manuscripts, which, with the letters used to identify them, are:

14th C. **V** = Vatican lat. 9443   **L** = London, B.M. add.
         A = Palma, Soc. Arq. Lul. 6   16428

15th C. **B** = Palma, Soc. Arq. Lul. 7 **S** = Munich, Staatsbibl. 595
                                              hisp. 51

The two columns correspond to two families of manuscripts, and

---

[9] For Llull's relations with Philip the Fair, see the "Life," nn. 66 and 92.

[10] The only subject of debate has been a possible earlier date for the *Book of the Beasts*, which has been cleverly laid to rest by an article also interesting for its suggestion of possible Islamic models for the work: J. Dagenais, "New Considerations on the Date and Composition of Llull's *Libre de bèsties*," *Actes del Segon Col·loqui d'Estudis Catalans a Nord-Amèrica, Yale, 1979* (Montserrat, 1982), 131–9.

[11] The French translation is preserved in a single beautiful fifteenth-century manuscript that, curiously enough, also contains the *Roman des sept sages*, on which Llull drew for the *Book of the Beasts*. The Spanish translation is also preserved in a single fifteenth-century manuscript, this one in the Escorial. The Spanish version published in 2 vols., Palma, 1750, seems to be a new translation from MSS **A** and **B** (see the list below). It was apparently this text

previous editions, including the best one of Salvador Galmés,[12] only consulted A and B from the first family. I have therefore compared the readings of these two manuscripts with L and S of the second family, and used V as a further control on the first family. I have given in the notes whatever variants I felt the reader or scholar should have at his disposal.

Since the publication of the original English edition of *Felix* from which this version of the *Book of the Beasts* is extracted, the above-mentioned comparisons have given rise to a new Catalan text, which the reader can consult in Vol. II of *OS*.

Other editions and translations that have appeared in the inter-vening years include a good Spanish translation of *Felix* by the poet Pere Gimferrer, which appeared in *Ramon Llull: Obra escogida* (Madrid, 1981). As for the *Book of the Beasts*,[13] there have appeared three more Catalan editions, as well as new translations into En-glish, French, Italian, and Japanese. They are respectively:

Catalan editions:

Llull, Ramon. *Llibre de les bèsties: Llibre d'Amic e Amat,* ed. Manuel Llanas, Història de la Literatura Catalana 27 (Barcelona: Edicions 62/Orbis, 1984).

Llull, Ramon. *El llibre de les bèsties,* ed. Jordi Rubió and Armand Llinarès (Barcelona: Edicions 62, 1985; 4th ed. 1988).

Llull, Ramon. *Llibre de les bèsties,* ed. Agnès Bosch (Barcelona: Diputació de Barcelona i Diari de Barcelona, 1989).

Translations:

"The Book of the Beasts," trans. David Rosenthal, *Catalan Review* Vol. 4 (1990): 409–50.

---

that was copied in another eighteenth-century MS now in Palma, and reprinted in the *Obras literarias* (Madrid, 1948). The Italian translation is preserved in four fifteenth-century MSS and one from the seventeenth century. None of these medieval translations have been edited, or even compared with the original Catalan text.

[12] *ENC,* 4 vols., 1931–4. This superseded the earlier edition (also of all of *Felix*) of Rosselló in the *Biblioteca Catalana* (1872–1904), reproduced in *Obras de Ramón Lull* III (Palma, 1903), and again, for some mysterious reason (the far superior Galmés edition had already been circulating for almost a quarter of a century), in *OE* I.

[13] As implied in n. 1 above, there are no separate medieval manuscripts, but, by the time of the publication of the bibliographical chart in *SW* II, 657, there had appeared thirteen modern editions in five languages.

Raymond Lulle: Le Livre des bêtes, trans. Patrick Gifreu (Paris: Chiendent, 1985; 2d ed., Paris: La Différence, 1991).

Raimundo Lullo, Il libro delle bestie, trans. Loretta Frattale, "Narciso di Novecento" 23 (Palermo, 1987).

Mihara, Y., "Fabulario Medieval Catalan," *Journal of Osaka University Foreign Studies* 44 (1979): 37–52.

HERE BEGINS THE SEVENTH BOOK, WHICH TREATS OF BEASTS

WHEN FELIX had taken leave of the philosopher, he went off through a valley full of trees and springs. As he was leaving the valley, he met two men, poorly dressed, with long beards and long hair. Felix greeted them, and they greeted him.

"Dear sirs," Felix said, "where do you come from? To what order do you belong? For from your clothes, it would appear that you belong to some order."

"Sir," said the two men, "we come from far away lands, and have just passed through a plain near here. In that plain is a great gathering of wild beasts who are about to elect a king. We belong to the Order of the Apostles,[1] and our clothes and poverty are a reflection of the Apostles' condition while they lived in this world."

Felix was in great wonder at how these two men had undertaken[2] so high an order as that of the Apostles, and he said: "The Order of the Apostles is sovereign over all other orders. And whoever is in the Order of the Apostles should not fear death, and should go forth to show the path of salvation to unbelievers who are in error. And he should spread the doctrine of the holy life, by example and by

[1] The Apostolici or Apostolic Brethren was a sect founded about 1260 by a certain Gerard Segarelli of Parma. Their exalted Franciscanism tinged with the apocalyptic ideas of Joachim da Fiore brought them into conflict with the Church, which tried to call them to order in 1286. They refused, and were therefore branded as heretics. In 1290 persecution began, in 1294 four followers were burned, and in 1300 Segarelli himself died at the stake. Seven years later the remainder of the sect was rounded up, its new leader burned, and its teaching more or less effectively stopped. Llull's praise for them here and in *Blaquerna*, ch. 76, together with his condemnation of them later on in *Felix* (Bk. VIII, ch. 56), would seem to indicate that he thought the idea a splendid one, which they had botched by their excesses. Note too that *Felix* was written between the call to order of 1286 and the first persecutions of 1294.

[2] Thus, *emparat*, in all sources save A (followed by Galmés), which has *empetrat* ("obtained by entreaty").

preaching, to Christians who are in sin. Never should any man in the Order of the Apostles cease preaching[3] and doing good works to the best of his ability." These and many other things Felix told the two men who said they belonged to the Order of the Apostles.

"Sir," said the two men, "we are not worthy of leading so sublime a life as that of the Apostles; but we try to imitate their way of life, which we do through our clothes and our poverty, and through our wanderings through the world, from one land to another. We have hopes that God will send men of holy life who will belong to the Order of the Apostles and who will know sciences and languages in order to be able to preach and convert unbelievers with the help of God, and to set Christians a good example by their way of life and by their holy words. And so that God be moved to pity, and so that Christians shall desire the coming of such men, we try to imitate the Apostles."

Felix was very pleased with what the two men told him, and together with them he wept a long time, saying: "Ah, Lord God Jesus Christ! Where is the holy fervor and devotion there once was among the Apostles, who for the sake of loving and knowing You, never hesitated to suffer hardship or death? Fair Lord God, may it please You to bring about a time in which is realized the holy life symbolized by the life of these men."

After these words, Felix commended the holy men to God, and went to the place where the beasts were about to elect a king.

37.   THE ELECTION OF THE KING

IN A LOVELY plain through which ran a lovely stream, many beasts were gathered together to elect a king. The majority agreed that the lion should be king; but the ox was very much opposed to this choice, and he said: "Gentlemen, a king's nobility must be accompanied by beauty of person; he must be at the same time large and humble, and he must do no harm to others. The lion is not a large beast, nor one that lives on grass, but rather one that eats other

---

[3] MS A (followed by the printed sources) has *pregar* ("beseeching, praying"), but all the other MSS consulted have *preycar* ("preaching"), which, in the context, seems more apt.

beasts.[4] The lion has a speech and voice that make us all tremble with fear when he roars. So if you take my advice, you will elect the horse as king; for the horse is a large beast, and handsome and humble; the horse is a nimble beast, not proud in his ways, and does not eat meat."

The red deer, the roe deer, the sheep, and all the other plant-eating animals were very pleased with what the ox had said, but Dame Reynard[5] stepped forward to speak before them all, saying: "Sirs, when God created the world, He did not do so with the intention that man should be known and loved, but rather that He Himself should be known and loved by man; and according to this intention, God willed that man should be served by beasts, and man lives on meat and plants alike. You should therefore pay no attention to what the ox says, since he dislikes the lion for being meat-eating; instead you should follow the rules and dispositions God has given and placed over creatures."

The ox and his friends, however, argued against Dame Reynard's words, the ox saying that from the fact of his wanting the grass-eating horse to be king, it would seem that he and his friends had no ulterior motive in the matter of the election; for if they did, they would not want a creature like the horse, who eats the same grass they eat, to be king. Nor should they believe Dame Reynard with respect to the election of a king, for she is interested in having the lion be king more because she lives on the leftovers from what the lion hunts and leaves uneaten, than because of the lion's nobility.

There was so much discussion on one side and the other that the

---

[4] The eighteenth-century Spanish translator has an ingenuous and oversimplified, but not uninteresting explanation of these categories: "In this treatise, the meat-eating animals represent the nobles, and those that eat grass, the common people. The lion represents the king, the leopard the man of honor, the lynx the flatterer, the fox the man of cunning, the snake the prudent man, and so on." To which he adds the suprising (in view of the fact that he had just finished translating the previous chapter of *Felix*, in which Llull pokes terrible fun at alchemy): "N.B. In addition to the above, this treatise includes everything concerning the transformation of metals, if one knows how to interpret it properly."

[5] *Na Renart* in the original—the only animal in Llull's fable given a proper name (and a title). The original Germanic name of Reginhard (from which modern Reinhart) for the fox in a series of animal fables spread to France, where the *Roman de Renart* became so famous that the proper name displaced the older French word (*goupil*) for the animal. Even in Catalan it came to be used for the fox, but apparently not till after Llull's time, for one of the fourteenth-century MSS of *Felix* (MS L) has the more usual *guineu* written above one of the first appearances of the name *Na Renart* to explain what animal was being discussed.

entire court was thrown into confusion, and the election held up. Then the bear, the leopard, and the lynx,[6] each of whom had hopes of being elected king, said that the court should be put off until it had been decided which animal was worthiest of being king.

Dame Reynard realized that the bear, the leopard, and the lynx were putting off the election because each had hopes of being king, and she said in everyone's presence:

"An election was once being held in a cathedral church, and in the chapter there was disagreement over the election of a bishop; for some canons wanted the sacristan of the church to be bishop, since he was a man of wisdom, culture, and virtue. The archdeacon, however, wanted to be elected bishop, and the same was true of the precentor,[7] both of whom opposed the election of the sacristan, and permitted the election of an ordinary canon who was handsome but ignorant, and moreover of weak character and very lascivious. The entire chapter was in great wonder at the attitude of the archdeacon and precentor. In the chapter there was a canon who then said: 'If the lion is king, and the bear, the lynx, and the leopard disagree with his election, there will forever be ill will toward the king; and if the horse is king, and the lion commits some wrong against the king, how will the horse get his revenge, if he is not as strong as the lion?' "[8]

After hearing Dame Reynard's example, the bear, the lynx, and the leopard were very afraid of the lion; so they consented to the election and desired him to be king. Because of the pressure brought by the bear and the other meat-eating animals, and in spite of the plant-eating beasts, the lion was elected king, whereupon he gave all meat-eating animals permission to eat and live off the grass-eating animals.

One day the king held a meeting to decide on the constitution of his court. The meeting between the king and the barons lasted all

[6] *Onça* in the original, which, like the French *once* and the English *ounce*, in the Middle Ages referred to the European lynx. I have avoided the homonym since nowadays in English (as in French) the word is only used to refer to the snow leopard of central Asia.

[7] *Cabiscol* in Catalan, like the English "precentor," refers to the person who directs the singing of a church choir. Scholars have pointed out Llull's curious habit of having the animals occasionally give examples concerning human beings.

[8] A curious instance of the characters in a story within a frame story referring to the characters in the frame story.

that day, almost until nightfall, with none of them having eaten or drunk a thing. When the meeting was over, the lion and his companions were hungry, and he asked the wolf and Dame Reynard what there was to eat. They replied that it was late to procure food, but nearby there was a calf, son of the ox, and a colt, son of the horse, on whom they could dine plentifully. The lion had the calf and the colt brought to him, and he and his friends dined on them. The ox was very angry over the death of his son, as was the horse. Together they went to man to place themselves at his service, so that he might revenge the wrong their lord had done them. When the ox and the horse presented themselves before man to serve him, the man mounted the horse and set the ox to plowing.

One day it came to pass that the horse and the ox met, and each asked the other about his situation. The horse said that he was very overworked in the service of his master, for every day he was ridden and made to gallop up hill and down hill, and was in harness day and night. The horse desired greatly to be free of this servitude to his master, and he would have willingly once again undergone submission to the lion. But because of the fact that the lion ate meat, and because the horse had received some votes in the election of king, he was afraid to return to the land where the lion reigned, and preferred to suffer beneath the dominion of man, who does not eat horseflesh, rather than be in the company of the lion, who does.

After the horse had told him about his situation, the ox replied that he too was very overworked, every day, from plowing, and that his master would not let him eat the wheat grown on the land he plowed, but instead, when he was finished with his plowing and exhausted from it, he was sent to graze on the grass the sheep and goats had been eating while he was out plowing. The ox complained bitterly about his master, and the horse consoled him as best he could.

While the ox and the horse were conversing in this way, a butcher came to see if the ox was fat, for the ox's master had offered him up for sale. The ox said to the horse that his master wanted to sell him to be killed and given to man to eat. The horse said this was a poor reward for the service he had rendered. For a long time the horse and the ox wept, and the horse advised the ox to flee and return to his native land; for it was better to be in danger of death, but in peace among one's own kind, than in danger of death,[9] and suffering under an ungrateful master.

38. THE KING'S COUNCIL

WHEN THE LION had been elected king, he made a fine speech before all his people, saying: "Sirs, it is your will that I be king. Now you all must know that the position of king is a very dangerous one, and very difficult. It is dangerous because often, on account of a king's sins, God sends down hunger, sickness, death, and wars, just as He does for the sins of a people. And this is why it is dangerous for a king to rule, and why his reign is also dangerous for his people. And since it is very difficult for a king to govern himself and his subjects, I therefore beg all of you gathered here together to give me councilors to help and counsel me in such a way that both I and my people may be saved. And I pray that the councilors you give me be wise, loyal, and such as are worthy of being councilors and in the company of a king."

All the barons and others of the assembly were pleased with what the king had said, and they all thought themselves fortunate with his election. It was agreed that the bear, the leopard, the lynx, the snake, and the wolf would be councilors of the king. All of them swore in presence of the court that they would give the king loyal counsel to the best of their abilities.

Dame Reynard, however, was unhappy at not having been elected king's councilor, and before the assembly she said the following words: "According to the Gospel, Jesus Christ, who is king of heaven and earth, preferred, in this world, the friendship and company of simple and humble men, which is why he chose the Apostles from among simple, poor people in order that He might exalt them through their virtue, thus increasing their humility. Subject to the approval of all present, it would seem to me that the king should have in his council simple, humble beasts, so that they should have pride neither of power nor of lineage, nor want to be equals of the

---

[9] Thus in all sources save A (followed by Galmés), which lacks, "but in peace . . . of death."

king, but rather give an example of hope and humility to the simpler beasts who live off grass."

The elephant, the wild boar, the goat, the sheep, and the other animals who lived off grass agreed with what Dame Reynard had said. And they all advised the king to take Dame Reynard, who spoke well and had great wisdom, into his council. And Dame Reynard gave her advice, saying that it would be a good idea if the elephant, the wild boar, the goat, and the sheep also formed part of the king's council.

The bear, the leopard, and the lynx were quite worried when they heard that Dame Reynard was in the king's council, for they were very afraid that with her cleverness of speech and her craftiness she might cause them to incur the king's anger, and all the more so since Dame Reynard had been more in favor of the king's election than any other animal.

"My lord," said the leopard to the king, "in your court there is the rooster, who is handsome and who is wise, and who is lord over many hens; moreover at dawn he sings very clearly and beautifully; in short, it would seem to me much more advisable to have him in your council than Dame Reynard."

The elephant agreed that it would be a good idea to have the rooster on the king's council, to give him an example as to how to rule the queen and make her submissive to him, and to wake him at dawn so he could pray to God;[10] and he added that Dame Reynard would make a good king's councilor, because she was a wise beast and had knowledge of many things.

The leopard said that in a king's council there should not be two persons who by nature bear ill will toward each other, since such ill will could upset the king's council. Dame Reynard also spoke, saying that in a king's council the beasts should be handsome and large, like the elephant, the wild boar, the goat, the sheep, and the red deer, since beauty of person is fitting for those in the king's presence.

It was the king's wish that Dame Reynard and her companions be members of his court and his council, and thus it was done, but the leopard spoke secretly to the king as follows:

---

[10] Thus in L S; all other sources have, "and to wake him at dawn and (to) pray to God," giving the less likely situation of its being the rooster who prays to God.

"My lord, there was once a count at war with a king; and since the count was not as powerful as the king, he had to exercise craft in his war with the king. What he did was to give large gifts in secret to the king's secretary, so that the latter would tell him of all the stratagems the king was going to employ against him. And thus the king's secretary prevented the royal power from bringing this war with the count to a successful conclusion."

After the leopard had finished speaking, and the lion had understood the example, he said that the rooster should belong to his court and Dame Reynard not, so that she would not tell the elephant and the other beasts who ate grass about the stratagems of the king and his companions who ate meat.[11]

39. OF THE TREASON DAME REYNARD ATTEMPTED AGAINST THE KING

DAME REYNARD and her companions were most displeased at not being on the king's council; and from that moment on Dame Reynard began to harbor treason in her heart, and to desire the death of the king. She therefore said to the elephant:

"From now on there will be great enmity between the animals who eat meat and those who eat grass; for the king and his councilors eat meat, and you have no animal of your kind on his council to uphold your rights."

The elephant answered that he had hopes that the snake and the rooster would be able to defend their rights in the king's court, since they were animals who did not live on meat.

Dame Reynard answered, saying that in a certain land there was once a Christian who had a Saracen whom he trusted very much, and whom he did many favors; the Saracen however, being against him because of his religion, was unable to bear him any good will, but rather was continually thinking how he could kill him.[12] "And this is why you should realize, Sir Elephant," Dame Reynard said,

---

[11] The last three words are lacking in A B, and hence in Galmés's edition.
[12] Undoubtedly a reference to the slave from whom Llull learned Arabic (cf. the "Life," § 11–13 above).

"that the snake and the rooster are of a lineage so different from yours and that of your companions that, although they eat no meat, you should not trust them, but rather realize that they will consent to anything that will harm you and all your companions."

The elephant was very worried by what Dame Reynard had told him, and for a long time he considered the harm that could come to him and his companions from the choice they had made of king and councilors. While the elephant was thinking over these matters, Dame Reynard told him he should have no fear of the king and his friends, for if he wanted to be king she would see to it that he would be king. But the elephant worried that Dame Reynard might betray him, since she should by nature prefer animals who lived on meat to those who lived on grass. And he said to Dame Reynard:

"In a certain land it came to pass that a kite was carrying off a mouse, and a hermit prayed to God that the mouse fall in his lap. As a result of the holy man's prayers, God caused the mouse to fall into the lap of the hermit, who then prayed God to turn it into a beautiful maiden. God heeded the hermit's prayers and turned the mouse into a beautiful maiden."

"Dear child," said the hermit, "do you want the sun as your husband?"

"No, sir, for clouds rob the sun of its brilliance."

The hermit then asked her if she wanted the moon as her husband, and she said the moon did not produce its own light, but rather received it from the sun.

"Dear child, do you want a cloud as your husband?"

She replied she did not, for the wind led the clouds wherever it desired. Yet she did not want the wind as her husband, because the mountains impeded its movement; nor did she want the mountains, because mice made tunnels in them; nor did she want a man for a husband, since men killed mice. So in the end the maiden begged the hermit to turn her back into a mouse, as she was before, and to give her a fine mouse for a husband.[13]

When Dame Reynard had heard this example, she realized that

---

[13] This is the first of the fables of oriental origin in the *Book of the Beasts*. It comes from a collection Llull drew on extensively in this work, and which began its history in India as the *Panchatantra* ("Five Cases of Wisdom"). From there it passed (with additions along the way) through Persian into Arabic, where it was called *Kalila and Dimna*. It entered Europe by two routes: the first was through a Hebrew translation, which was put into Latin in the thirteenth century by John of Capua as the *Directorium humanae vitae*; the second was by means of a

the elephant was suspicious of her, and was afraid he would denounce her. She would gladly have asked the wild boar to be king, just as she had asked the elephant, but in order that her scheming not be discovered, she wanted at all costs to have the elephant made king. She therefore said:

"In a certain land it came to pass that a knight had a handsome son by his wife. But she died, and the knight took a second wife who disliked the boy whom her husband loved so much. When this boy was twenty years old, the woman thought up a way to have her husband banish his son from their house, by telling the husband that the son had proposed making love to her. The knight so loved his wife that he immediately believed everything she told him, and he drove his son from the house, commanding him nevermore to appear in his presence. The young man was very angry with his father for driving him from his house and withdrawing his favor for no reason at all."[14]

The elephant was partially consoled by Dame Reynard's example, and he had hopes that he would become king as she had said. He asked her how she would manage to have the king die and himself elected king, since the present king was physically so powerful and had such a wise council, and since Dame Reynard was such a small animal and so weak.

Dame Reynard replied with the following example: "In a certain land it came to pass that all the animals agreed to hand over one animal to the lion every day, so that he would not make them suffer with his hunting, and the lion accepted the bargain. Every day these animals drew lots, and the one to whom the lot fell went to the lion

---

Spanish version commissioned by Alfonso X of Castile, which in turn was translated into Latin at the beginning of the fourteenth century by Raymond of Béziers (who curiously enough, was among the forty Masters and Bachelors of Arts and Medicine who approved Llull's lectures on the *Ars brevis* in Paris in 1310; cf. the "Life," n. 117 above, and *ROL* v, 139). We don't know which of these several versions Llull used. This particular tale was used by la Fontaine in *Fables*, IX, 7.

[14] This story comes from another collection of oriental origin called *The Seven Wise Masters*, the *Book of Sindbad* (or *Sindibad*), or just *Sendebar*, the early history of which is obscure. It entered Europe, however, in two forms: one as the French *Roman des sept sages de Rome* (included, as we mentioned before, in the same MS containing the medieval French translation of *Felix*; see the introduction, n. 11 above), from which descends a version in Catalan verse, and several Spanish versions of the fifteenth and sixteenth centuries; the second was the Spanish *Libro de los engaños* translated at the command of Don Enrique, the brother of Alfonso X, in 1253. Again we don't know which version Llull used, but the tale told here is the frame story of *The Seven Wise Masters*.

and was eaten by him. One day it happened that the lot fell to a hare, who put off going to the lion till midday, for she was afraid of dying. The lion was very angry over the hare's procrastination, for he was very hungry, so he asked the hare why she had taken such a long time. The hare excused herself, saying that nearby there was a lion who claimed to be king of the land and who had almost captured her. The lion was very angry, for he believed the hare's story, and told her to take him to this lion. The hare went first and the lion followed. They came to a large body of water that was part of a reservoir surrounded on all sides by a high wall. When the hare was over the water and her image and that of the lion appeared in the water, she said to the lion, 'Do you see, sir, the lion in the water who wants to eat a hare?' The lion thought his image was another lion, and he jumped in the water in order to fight with it. The lion drowned, and the hare, with her wits alone, succeeded in killing the lion."[15]

After hearing this example, the elephant answered Dame Reynard by means of another one: "A king had two pages who attended to his person. One day it happened that the king was sitting on his throne before a great throng of noble barons and knights. One of these pages was next to him, and saw a flea on the white samite robe the king was wearing. This page asked the king's permission to draw near and pick off the flea that was on his cloak; the page picked off the flea, which the king then wanted to see. The king showed it to all his knights, and said what a great wonder it was that so tiny a beast dared approach a king. He ordered that the page be given a hundred bezants. The other page was jealous of his companion, and the next day he put a louse on the king's cloak, and he spoke to the king as his companion had. The page gave the louse to the king, and the king drew back in horror, saying that the page deserved to die for not keeping his clothes free of lice; and he had him given a hundred lashes."[16]

Dame Reynard realized that the elephant was afraid of being king, and she was in great wonder at the amount of fear so great a creature could harbor. She said to the elephant: "It is said that the

---

[15] Another tale from *Kalila and Dimna*.

[16] Some scholars have claimed this story is an adaptation of the fable of the Louse and the Flea from *Kalila and Dimna*, but aside from these two parasites, the stories have little in common.

serpent, along with Dame Eve, who was one woman only, brought down God's anger on Adam and on all his descendants. So if the serpent along with Eve managed to do such harm, it may well happen that I, with my wisdom and cleverness, can manage to have the king incur the wrath of his people."

From the moment Dame Reynard had recounted the example of Eve, the elephant began to think of betraying the king; and he told Dame Reynard that he would willingly be king once she had had the present king done away with. Dame Reynard told the elephant that she would see to it that the king died, and the elephant promised that he would give her great gifts and honors if she could arrange for him to become king.

40.   HOW DAME REYNARD BECAME ROYAL DOORKEEPER

IN THE KINGS court it was ordained that the cat would be royal chamberlain and the dog would be doorkeeper. The cat was made chamberlain so he would eat the mice who were destroying hangings, and because of his similarity to the king. The dog was made doorkeeper so that, with his ability to hear things from afar, he could bark and let the king know when people were coming.

While the cat and the dog were carrying out their duties, Dame Reynard went off to find the ox and the horse, who had left the royal court. On her way she met the ox, who was returning to the king's court. It was in a lovely plain that Dame Reynard and the ox met. Each greeted the other in friendly fashion, and the ox told Dame Reynard about what had happened to him, how he had gone to man a free being, how man had held him for a long time in servitude, and how finally he had almost sold him to a butcher who wanted to kill him.

Dame Reynard on her side told the ox about the situation at court, as recounted above.

"Sir Ox," Dame Reynard said, "what do you intend to do?"

The ox replied that he was returning to the royal court, to flee from man, who had wanted to sell him for slaughter.

Dame Reynard then spoke to the ox in the following words: "In a certain kingdom there was a king of evil habits who was also badly counseled. As a result of the malice of king and council, the whole kingdom suffered hardships and incurred the wrath of God, for the harm the king and his council did to the people of that kingdom was inestimable. In fact, it lasted so long that the people of the country could stand it no longer; and because of the evil life and bad example of the king and his council, the people came to desire the death of both king and council."

The ox understood, from what Dame Reynard said, that the king and his council were wicked, and he hesitated as to whether he should return and be subjected to an evil government. So he said to Dame Reynard:

"In a certain city there was once a bishop who did things very contrary to his office, and as a result of the bishop's wickedness and dishonesty and of the bad example he set his chapter and the people of that city much harm was done and much good lost, good that would have been done had the bishop been the person he should have been, according to the rule and doctrine Jesus Christ gave his Apostles and their followers. One day it came to pass that the bishop did a great wrong, and then went off to say mass. One canon was in such horror at the wrong the bishop had committed that he left the city and went to live with shepherds in the woods, saying that he preferred being with shepherds who guarded their flocks against wolves than with a shepherd who killed his sheep and gave them to the wolves."

After recounting this example, the ox said to Dame Reynard that he would leave the country altogether rather than put himself at the discretion of a king and council who governed so wickedly.

"Sir Ox," said Dame Reynard, "have you heard about the question the hermit put to the king?"

"No," said the ox, "What question was that?"

Dame Reynard said there was once a holy hermit living on a high mountain. This hermit led a saintly life, and every day he heard many complaints about the king of that land, who was a sinful man and one who ruled badly; and the people spoke very badly of him to the holy man. The hermit was very annoyed at the king's evil attitude, and he vowed that he would try to change it for the better. The good man came down from his hermitage and came to a beautiful city where the king was staying. "My lord," the good man said to the king, "which do you think is more pleasing to God in this world: the hermit's life or the life of a king who rules his people well?" The king thought about the question for a long time before he answered; then finally he said that the life of a king devoted to good works is grounds for greater good than a hermit's life. "My lord," said the hermit, "I am very pleased with your answer, according to which it is clear that a wicked king does greater harm than the good a hermit can do in his hermitage. And this is why I came down from my hermitage to see you, and I intend to stay with you until you and your reign are in a better condition, and to speak words of God to you so that you will have knowledge and fear of God." The hermit stayed for a long time in the king's court speaking good words of God, by which the king changed his ways, and brought his entire kingdom under a good government.

After recounting this example, Dame Reynard said to the ox: "Sir Ox, you are a beast similar to the hermit, and if you want, I will counsel you so that you may induce the king—my lord and yours—to take on a better attitude, from which action of yours there will follow much good."

The ox promised Dame Reynard that he would do all the good things he could to bring the king and his subjects into a better situation. Dame Reynard therefore advised the ox to go to a lovely meadow near where the king and his barons were staying, and to eat and rest, so that he would be handsome to look at and in strong voice for bellowing. "And as soon as you feel yourself well and strong again, Sir Ox, you must bellow as loud as you can, three times by day, and three times by night, and in the meantime I will have discussed your situation with the king."

The ox followed Dame Reynard's advice, while she returned to the royal court. When the ox had rested a great deal and was strong again, he began to bellow mightily. And when Dame Reynard heard him bellowing, she went before the king and stood there while the ox bellowed. So afraid was the king of the ox's bellowing that he could not contain himself nor keep himself from trembling. And he was ashamed in front of his barons, afraid that they would think he was a coward. While the lion was in this state of fear, and none of his barons had as yet noticed his fear, Dame Reynard drew near; and the rooster crowed and the dog barked when she drew near the king. The king was pleased to have Dame Reynard nearby, and he asked her if she knew what sort of an animal was producing that noise, because from the sound of it, it seemed to him that it must be a large and powerful beast.[17]

"Sir," said Dame Reynard, "in a certain valley there was a minstrel who had hung his tambourine on a tree, and the wind made it move and bump into the branches of the tree. And because of this bumping against the tree, such a sound issued from the tambourine that it made the whole valley resound. Now in that valley there was a monkey who heard the sound and went over to the tambourine; and he thought that because the sound was so great the tambourine must be full of butter or something of that sort that would be good to eat. So the monkey tore a hole in the tambourine, and found it was completely empty.[18] In the same way, my lord," Dame Reynard said to the lion, "you may be sure that the sound you hear comes from an animal that is empty inside, and doesn't have the strength one would imagine from the voice alone. So be strong and of good courage, for it is not seemly for a king to be afraid, and even less so to be afraid of something unknown."

While Dame Reynard was saying this to the king, the ox cried out and bellowed very loudly; so much so that he caused the king's entire surroundings to reverberate, and the lion and his friends to tremble. The king could not help showing his fear, and he said that if the animal's strength were in proportion to its voice, some evil would come to that place. The ox bellowed once again, and the lion and all the members of his council were afraid; but Dame Reynard showed no fear at all, maintaining instead her cheerfulness in front of the king and his council. The king and all the others were in great wonder at Dame Reynard's lack of fear, and the king said to her:

"Reynard," said the king, "how can it be that you are not afraid of so powerful and strange a voice? As you can see, I, who am so strong, and the bear, the leopard, and many other beasts stronger than you, are afraid of this voice."

Dame Reynard answered the king, saying:

"A crow used to make its nest in a rock, and every year a large snake would come and eat the fledglings. The crow was very angry at the snake that ate its fledglings, but he did not dare fight it, since

---

[17] Another tale from *Kalila and Dimna*.

[18] Even though the characters are different (no minstrel, and a fox instead of a monkey), the story is the same as one in *Kalila and Dimna*.

he was not strong enough to be able to defeat it by force of arms. The crow realized he would have to employ some ruse, since his strength was inadequate. It came to pass one day that a princess was playing with her companions in an orchard, and she had placed her diadem of gold, silver, and precious stones on the branch of a tree. The crow took the diadem and flew about with it for a long time until many men were following him to see where he would put down the diadem, which the princess especially loved, and over whose loss she was crying bitterly. The crow put it down near the snake, and when the men came to retrieve the diadem they saw the snake and killed it. Thus did the crow, through art and cunning, make use of others against the snake.[19] And in the same way, my lord," Dame Reynard said to the lion, "such is my art and cunning, that if it came to pass that I could not vanquish by force of arms this animal who has so loud and terrifying a voice, I would use art and cunning to make an end of him."

After Dame Reynard had recounted her example, the snake, who was one of the king's councilors, recounted this one:

"In a certain pond there was a heron who for a long time had been accustomed to fish there. The heron grew old, and on account of his age he often lost his prey, so he thought up a way to make use of art and cunning, which method turned out to be the cause of his death."

The lion told the snake to explain how the heron had caused his own death.

"My lord king," said the snake, "one day the heron stood sadly on the banks of the pond until nightfall, without even trying to fish, A crab wondered at the heron who wasn't fishing the way he usually did, and he asked the heron what was worrying him. The heron wept and said he felt very sorry for the fish in the pond with whom he had lived such a long time, and felt very unhappy over their death and misery; for two fishermen, now fishing in another pond, intended to come to this one when they had finished fishing there. 'These fishermen are masters in the art of fishing, and such is their cunning that no fish will be able to escape them, and they will catch all the fish in this pond.'

"When the crab heard these words, he was very afraid, and he

---

[19] Another tale from *Kalila and Dimna*.

told it to the fishes in the pond. All the fish got together and came before the heron, asking him to counsel them. 'There is only one piece of advice I can give you,' said the heron, 'and that is to let me carry you one by one to a pond about a league away from here, one so full of reeds and mud that the fishermen will not be able to harm you.' The fish agreed, and every day the heron took as many fish as he wanted, and pretended he was carrying them to another pond, when in fact he would land on a mountain and eat the fish he was carrying, and then go back for more. This the heron did for a long time, being able to live without the work of fishing.

"One day it came to pass that the crab asked the heron to take it to the other pond. The heron stuck out its neck and the crab grabbed onto it with both its claws. While the heron was flying with the crab hanging on to its neck, the crab was surprised not to see the pond to which the heron was taking it. When the heron drew near to the place where he normally ate the fish, the crab saw the bones of fish the heron had eaten, and he realized the trick the heron had been playing. The crab said to himself, 'While there's still time, you'd better get your revenge on this traitor who intends to eat you.' So the crab squeezed the heron's neck so tight that he broke it, and the heron fell to the ground dead. And the crab returned to his friends and told them about the treason the heron had been practicing on them, which treason was the cause of the heron's death."[20]

"Sir," said Dame Reynard, "when God drove Adam from Paradise, He cursed the serpent who had counseled Eve to eat the fruit that God had forbidden to Adam, and from then all serpents have been horrible to look upon and poisonous; and from this serpent have come all the evils of the world. And this is why a wise man caused a snake to be driven from a king's council, although the king loved the snake dearly."

The lion asked Dame Reynard to recount this example.

"Sir," said Dame Reynard, "a certain king had heard talk about a holy man of very great wisdom, and he sent for him. The holy man came to the king, and the king begged him to stay with him to counsel him in the government of his kingdom and to reprove him for his vices, if he found him indulging in any. The holy man stayed

---

[20] Even though in some versions the animals are replaced by a cormorant and a crayfish, substantially the same story appears in *Kalila and Dimna*, where it is also associated with the previous story about the crow and the snake.

with the king so that he could advise him how to do good works and to avoid evil.

"One day the king held a council concerning an important event that had happened in his kingdom. Near the king was a large serpent whose counsel the king valued above that of the others. When the holy man saw the serpent he asked what a king stood for in this world, and the king replied: 'Kings were established in this world in the image of God, that is to say, that a king must uphold justice on earth and govern the people God has put beneath his care.' 'Sir,' said the wise man, 'what animal was most contrary to God when He created the world?' And the king replied that it was the serpent. 'My lord king,' said the wise man, 'according to your answer, you should kill the serpent: and you commit a great sin by having it in your court. For if, as king, you represent the image of God, you should hate everything God hates, and more so that which God most hates.' Because of what the holy man said, the king killed the serpent, without the serpent's being able to use any art or ruse to prevent his own death."[21]

After Dame Reynard had recounted this example, the ox cried out and bellowed so loud that he made the entire palace tremble, and the lion and all the others were terrified. So Dame Reynard said to the king that if he wanted, she would go to the beast from whom issued so strange a voice, and she would see if she could bring it to the king and have it become part of his court. The lion and all the others were glad that Dame Reynard was willing to go to the beast who was bellowing.

Dame Reynard then begged the king to promise that, if she was lucky and was able to bring this animal back to his court, it would be safe and sound there, and that no one would harm it nor commit any villany against it. And the lion, before his entire council, granted Dame Reynard everything she asked of him.

Dame Reynard went to the meadow where the ox was resting, and when the ox saw her he was very pleased at her arrival. They greeted each other warmly, and Dame Reynard told the ox everything that had happened since she had left him.

"My dear friend," said Dame Reynard, "go before the king, act

---

[21] Neugaard (see n. 7 to the introduction) says this "example" appears in several Semitic and Indian collections.

humble, and make the gestures of somebody who is very wise. I will say that you have felt great contrition for having so long escaped the king's dominion, and then, in front of everybody, you must ask the king to pardon you for having gone to live with man and having put yourself beneath another's dominion. My dear friend," said Dame Reynard, "you must speak before the king and his court in such a way that the king and his entire council are pleased with your words and gestures. And tell the king about the affairs of men, and counsel the king to make friends with the king of men."

The ox and Dame Reynard went to the royal court. When the king and his barons saw the ox and Dame Reynard approaching, the king and everybody else recognized the ox, and they all felt very stupid at how afraid they had been of the ox; and the king was in great wonder as to how the ox could have so loud and terrifying a voice.

The ox went up to his lord and made the proper reverence for a king, and the king asked him about his present situation. The ox recounted everything that had happened to him while he was in the service of man. The king told the ox he was astonished at how his voice had changed, and the ox said he had cried out in fear and contrition, because he felt guilty towards the king and his court for having left them so long for another's dominion. And since fear and contrition made his heart tremble, this had altered his voice, as a sign of fear, terror, and dread, because it issued from a body containing a fearful and penitent heart.

The ox begged forgiveness of the king, and the king forgave him in front of his entire court. The king asked the ox about the affairs of the king of men, and the ox replied that the snake had spoken the truth when he said that the most evil and false animal in the world is man. The lion asked the ox to tell him why the snake said that man is the most evil and false animal in the world.

"My lord king," said the ox, "it once happened that a bear, a crow, a man, and a snake fell into a deep pit. A holy man who was a hermit was passing by that place; he looked into the pit and he saw the four of them inside, unable to climb out. They all begged the holy man to help them out of the pit, and each promised him a good reward. He pulled the bear out of the pit, then the crow and the snake; but when he was about to pull out the man, the snake told him not to do it, because if he did he would receive an unpleasant reward for his services. The hermit refused to believe the snake's advice, and he pulled the man from the pit.

"The bear brought the holy man a beehive full of honeycombs. When the hermit had eaten his fill of honeycombs, he went off to the city to preach. As he entered the city, the crow brought him a lovely diadem belonging to a princess, from whose head he had taken it. The hermit took the diadem with great pleasure, for it was worth a great deal. Through that city went a man crying out and announcing that whoever had the diadem should return it to the princess, and he would be given a large reward; and if someone had the diadem hidden and was found out, he would be severely punished. The good hermit came to a street where there was the man he had helped out of the pit, who happened to be a silversmith. The holy man secretly entrusted the silversmith with the diadem, and the silversmith took it to court, with accusations against the holy man, who was then taken, beaten, and imprisoned.

"The snake whom the holy man had pulled out of the pit went to the princess while she was sleeping and bit her on the hand. The princess cried out and wept, and her hand became very swollen. The king was very upset at his daughter's illness, with her hand swollen and poisoned, and he had it announced throughout the city that he would give large gifts to whoever could cure his daughter. The snake came while the king was sleeping and whispered in his ear that in the prison of his court there was a captive who had an herb with which he could cure his daughter. The snake himself had given this herb to the good man and explained to him how he should put it on the princess's hand, and how he should ask the king to bring the silversmith to justice since he had given him such an ill reward. Everything was done as the snake had arranged, and the holy man was released from prison, and the silversmith was brought to justice."[22]

The lion along with his entire council were very pleased with the example the ox had related against man, and he asked the ox if he thought he should be afraid of the king of men. And the ox replied that it was dangerous to be on bad terms with the king of men,

---

[22] *Kalila and Dimna* has an almost identical story, except that the animals are a badger (or tiger), a monkey, and a snake.

because from a man who was evil, powerful, and clever no animal could defend itself.

The king thought over carefully what the ox had said, and Dame Reynard realized that the lion was afraid of the king of men, so she said to him:

"My lord, the proudest animal, and the one with greater avarice than any other, is man. And therefore, if you and your council approve of the idea, it might be wise to send messengers with gifts to the king of men, messengers who on your behalf would tell him of your good will toward him and give him your presents; and in his heart the king would conceive a love for you and your people."

The king and all his council thought Dame Reynard's suggestion a good one, all except for the rooster, who was against it, saying:

"In a certain land Strength and Cunning were disputing before a king. Strength said that she had a natural dominion over Cunning, and Cunning said it was the other way around. The king wanted to know which should have dominion over the other, and he arranged for them to fight, in which fight Cunning conquered and overcame Strength. And this is why, my lord king," said the rooster, "if you enter into friendship with the king of men, and send him messengers, and he sends you his messengers, those messengers will have knowledge with respect to your person and your barons, so that no stratagem or art will suffice to defend you against the king of men, who fights with art and stratagem, vanquishing all those who fight by strength alone, without art and cunning."

On the other hand, Dame Reynard maintained that God does what He does by power, with no art or cunning, and hence it is natural that those who fight with weapons similar to God's must be more powerful in battle than those who fight with weapons dissimilar to God's.[23]

The lion was very pleased with what Dame Reynard had said, and he wanted at all costs to send presents and messengers to the king of men. The king asked which messengers he should send to the king of men, and what sort of presents. Dame Reynard said that the ox should counsel him, since he knew about the ways of men, and what sort of things pleased them most. The king asked the ox to

---

[23] "Than those who . . . to God's" is missing in MS A, and hence in Galmés's edition.

counsel him as to the messengers and presents he wanted to send to the king of men, whereupon the ox said:

"My lord king," said the ox, "it is normal for kings of men to send messengers from among their council and even from among the noblest members of their council. Now it would seem to me that the noblest councilors you have are the lynx and the leopard. On the other hand, the cat resembles you, and the king would be very pleased if you sent him the cat and the dog as presents: the cat because of his resemblance to you, and the dog for hunting, because men are very fond of hunting."

The lion did exactly as the ox had recommended, and he sent the lynx and the leopard as messengers, and the dog and cat as presents. And when the messengers had left the court, the king made the ox his chamberlain and Dame Reynard was given the post the dog had held.

41. CONCERNING THE MESSENGERS THE LION SENT TO THE KING OF MEN

THE LION instructed the leopard and the lynx as to how they should carry out their duties as messengers, saying: "The master's wisdom is reflected in messengers who are wise, speak well, give good counsel, and are good diplomats. And the master's nobility is reflected in messengers who spend money honorably, who are well dressed, and whose retinue is well-mannered and well-equipped; and the messengers and their retinue must be free of avarice, as well as of gluttony,[24] lust, pride, ire, or any other vice. All these things and many others are required of a noble prince's messengers, so that his mission may find favor with the king and court to whom the messengers are being sent."

When the lion had instructed his messengers as to how they should address the king and how they should behave, the messengers left his court and traveled through many different lands. They

---

[24] Thus, *gula*, in V and the medieval French translation; A, followed by Galmés, has *nulla* ("none, no"); S and B (and hence earlier editions) omit the word.

journeyed on until finally they arrived at a city where the king was holding a great assembly. At the entrance to that city there were prostitutes who, in the presence of the messengers, were sinning with men. The messengers were astonished at what they saw, and the leopard said to his companion:

"A burgher was married to a woman he loved very much. This man rented lodgings near his own house to a prostitute. The burgher's wife often saw dissolute men visiting the prostitute, and she was overcome with a desire to indulge in the sin of lust. For a long time she lived in the sin of lust, until one day her husband found her sinning with a man. The burgher was furious at his wife's transgression, to which she replied:

"'It once came to pass that two wild goats[25] were fighting in a meadow, and as a result of the violent blows they gave one another, blood flowed from their foreheads. It fell on the thick grass where they were fighting, and a fox saw the blood and licked it up. Now the fox happened to be in the way of one of their charges, and he was wounded on both flanks. So great was the blow that the fox died of it; and before dying he admitted that he had been the occasion of his own death.'"

"Sir Leopard," said the dog, "it is a great wonder how men who believe in God can have so little conscience as to allow these prostitutes to sin in the presence of people entering and leaving the city. It would seem that the lord of this city as well as its inhabitants were given to lust, and practice lust as shamelessly as dogs."

With these words they entered the city and arrived at an inn; afterwards the leopard and the lynx went to the king with the presents they had brought. But they had to wait many days before they could speak to the king, for the king was accustomed to keep people waiting a long time, as a sign of his nobility, which was so dear to him. One day it happened that the messengers had waited all day at the king's door without being able to talk to him; and they were very angry with the king and irritated at having to be in his court. Then a man who had been wronged, and who had also been

---

[25] The two oldest MSS, V and A (followed by Galmés) have *bous* ("oxen, bulls"); but since all the other sources have *bocs* ("goats"), and since the story in *Kalila and Dimna* from which it is taken also has "goats," I have decided to keep the latter. According to Neugaard (see n. 7 to the introduction) the frame story about the adulterous woman is also from *Kalila and Dimna*.

waiting at the court for a long time without being able to speak to the king, said in front of the messengers:

"God, who is king of heaven and earth and all that is, is humble; for whenever a person wants to see Him or speak to Him, he may do so and explain his needs. This king has no doorkeepers to whom one has to give money, nor councilors who for money will commit any villainy or fraud. He believes no one's flatteries, nor does He name provosts, judges, bailiffs, or attorneys who are proud, arrogant, avaricious, lustful, and iniquitous. Blessed be such a king, and blessed be all those who love, know, honor, and serve Him!"

By what this man said, the messengers realized that the king was an unjust man, and the lynx said to the leopard:

"Once there was a king who wanted to give his daughter in marriage to another king, and he secretly sent a knight to that king's country to find out what sort of person he was. This knight asked peasants and other people about the king, and everyone spoke badly of him. One day the knight happened to meet two minstrels who had just come from the court where the king had given them money and clothes. The knight asked the minstrels what the king was like, and they told him that the king was generous, that he liked to hunt, and that he loved the company of women; and they praised the king in many other ways. By these praises, and by the way the common people blamed the king, the knight understood that the king was evil and of base customs.[26] The knight told his lord what he had heard about the king, and the king no longer wanted to marry his daughter to that king, for his conscience would not allow him to marry his daughter to a man of such bad customs."

The two messengers entered into the king's presence and gave him the gifts the lion had sent, and they also gave him a letter from their lord, with the following message:

"In a certain province there was once a king with many honorable barons, who were men of great power. In order to make these barons fear him, and in order to have peace and justice in his land, the king tried to be on the best of terms with the emperor. This emperor loved the king very much, because of the favors he did him

---

[26] To this criticism of the usual ideal of the troubadour patron, Llull opposes the *joculator Dei* or "minstrel of God," for which see n. 28 below.

and because of his good ways; and the king's barons, for fear of the emperor,[27] did not dare disobey their lord in whatever he commanded them; and thus they were submissive and the king had peace in his land."

When the king heard the letter the lion had sent him and had accepted the presents, he gave the cat to a draper who was standing next to him, and he gave the dog to a knight who liked to hunt. The messengers were very displeased at the king's giving the cat to the draper, who was not a man of honor, considering that the lion had sent the cat because of his resemblance to himself.

When the messengers had returned to their inn after talking to the king for a long time about the mission on which they had been sent, the dog appeared and said he was very unhappy with the king's having given him to that knight, who intended to use him to hunt against the lion's humbler subjects; and his conscience troubled him at doing something against his former lord.

The king invited the two messengers to a great court he was holding that day. The king and queen, accompanied by many knights and ladies, dined in a beautiful hall, and the messengers dined in the king's presence. While the king and queen were dining, minstrels went up and down the hall singing and playing instruments, and the songs they sang were contrary to good manners. These minstrels praised what should have blamed, and blamed what should have been praised. And the king, the queen and all the others laughed, and took pleasure in what the minstrels did.

While the king and all the others were enjoying what the minstrels did and said, a man, poorly dressed and with a long beard, entered the banquet hall, and, in the presence of the king, of the queen, and of everybody else, said:[28]

"Let neither the king nor queen forget, nor their barons, nor any others, great or small, who eat in this hall, that God created all the things which are on the king's table, and on those of the others; that He made them varied and delectable to eat; and He caused them to be brought from faraway lands so that they might be at the service

---

[27] Thus in all sources except A and B (followed by Galmés), which omit "king's" and "for fear," leaving "and the barons of the emperor"!

[28] This appearance of a Llull-like character in a palace banquet is very reminiscent of an earlier episode of *Felix* (Bk. v, ch. 30; see *SW* II, 758). For this character as an antiminstrel or *joculator Dei*, see the *Book of the Lover and the Beloved*, versicles 158 and 281.

of man, and so that man might serve God. Let neither the king nor
the queen think that God will forget the improprieties committed in
this hall, in which God is dishonored, for there is no one here to
reprove what is reprovable, nor to praise what is praiseworthy, nor
to thank God for the honor which, in this world, He has bestowed
on the king, the queen, and all the others."

After the good man had said these words, a wise squire knelt
before the king and begged him to give him the duty in his court of
praising what was praiseworthy and blaming what was blameworthy. The king, however, would not grant the squire his request, for
fear that the squire would blame him for the wrongs he was wont to
commit, wrongs in which he took great pleasure and which he
wanted to continue doing until the end of his days, when he intended to make due penance for his sins.

While the squire was asking the king to give him this duty and the
king was saying no, the provost of the city entered into the king's
presence, bringing with him a man who had very wrongfully killed
a knight. The king ordered the man who had killed the knight to be
hung, but the man said:

"My lord king, it is God's custom to pardon a person who begs
Him for mercy; and of you, who are God's lieutenant on earth, I ask
pardon, and you should grant it, since God Himself pardons."

And the king replied, saying: "God is just and merciful. He does
justice if He pardons a man who has not knowingly committed a
wrong—who has erred by accident or by chance and then repents
and asks for pardon, in which case God's mercy pardons him.
God's justice, however, would not accord with mercy, if mercy
pardoned a person who intended to sin in the hope of subsequently
asking for pardon. And since you intended to kill the knight, at the
same time hoping I would pardon you, that is why you are not
worthy of being pardoned."

The messengers realized that these words of the king went
against what the squire had said, in that the king had not wanted to
give him the duty he had requested.[29]

When the king and all the others had finished eating and had left

---

[29] This confusing paragraph is partly clarified by the eighteenth-century Spanish translation, which has, "By these words, spoken by the king himself, the messengers realized that
the king had acted against himself in having denied the squire the duty he had requested," to
which the translator adds a tag of his own, "since by [these words] he was worthy of praise."

the hall, the messengers returned to their inn, and one remarked to
the other how great was the nobility of that court, and how great the
king's power in terms of people and wealth—if only he were wise
and God-fearing.

When they arrived at their lodgings, they found the innkeeper in
tears, overcome with grief. "Sir innkeeper," they said, "why are
you weeping? What is wrong?"

"Sir messengers," replied the innkeeper, "in this city the king has
held a great parliament for which he had many people come from
faraway lands. The king's expenses have been great, and as a result
he has ordered a tax to be raised in the city, one that will cost me a
thousand sous, which I will have to borrow from the Jews."

"Sir innkeeper," said the messengers, "has the king no treasury?"

The innkeeper replied that the king did not have a treasury, but
borrowed from his subjects, and raised taxes whenever he held
courts, which was twice a year. He was thus ruining his subjects
who were forced to spend great sums for these courts, and he was
impoverishing his entire land as a result of the way he spent money.

"Dear friend," said the lynx, "what good comes from these
courts the king holds every year?"

The innkeeper answered that no good at all came from them, but
rather great harm, for they impoverished the people who then, as a
result of their poverty, were deceitful and committed wrongs, causing the king to be angry with his subjects. For he gave away and
spent so much in these courts he held, that his income did not
suffice, and he ended up taking from some and giving to others.
And when people imagined that the king had some news to give, or
some important matter to discuss, and he said nothing, then they all
went away angry, and laughed at the king and spoke of him
scornfully.

When the messengers had learned such words about the king,
they felt scorn for him and all the people of his country, and the
leopard said to the innkeeper: "Great harm has come to this country
as a result of not having a ruler of good habits who maintains justice
and peace."

"Sir," said the innkeeper, "no man can reckon the harm done by
an evil sovereign: part of it comes from the evil he does, and the rest
from the good he could do, but does not do. And thus an evil
sovereign causes harm in two different ways, as I have just ex-

plained. This king to whom you have been sent is a person who places too much trust in his council, and this council is contemptible and evil, and made up of men of base extraction. And each member of this council thinks he could be a better king than the king himself, and between them they lay waste to his kingdom; and the king does not care, nor does he worry about anything but hunting, enjoying himself, living in lust, and indulging his vanities."

The following morning the messengers returned to the palace, but they could not enter to speak to the king until they had bribed the doorkeepers. When the messengers were before the king, he honored the leopard more than the lynx, in that he looked at him more favorably and had him sit nearer to him. The lynx was jealous of this, and angry with the king; for the lynx felt he should be honored as much or more so than the leopard.

While the king was with the messengers, there arrived eight notables sent by four cities, to complain about the royal officials in those cities, who were wicked and sinful men, and were ruining the land. The eight notables begged the king, in the name of all the inhabitants of the cities, to give them good officials; and the king sent them on to his council, which he said would take care of the matter. But when the eight notables went before the king's council and explained their case, the council reproved them sharply, for on that council sat friends of the officials in the four cities, on whose advice they did their evil work and who shared in their ill-gained profits. So these eight notables returned without having settled anything with the king.

"My lord king," said the leopard, "what message do you have for our king?" The king told the leopard to convey his greetings to the king, and to ask him to send him a handsome bear and a wolf, for he had a very powerful boar, which he wanted to pit against as powerful a bear as he could find, and he had a mastiff he wanted to pit against the fiercest wolf in the lion's court.

Both messengers took leave of the king, and went away discontented, for he had kept them a long time without giving them anything and without sending any presents to their lord and king, but instead giving them the impression of wanting to subjugate their lord the lion.

On the way back to their country, they ran into the eight notables who were returning very angry and dissatisfied with the king and his council. As the messengers traveled with the notables they commented on the king's words, those of his council, and of his attitude. All of them spoke ill of the king and his council, and the leopard asked the notables: "Sirs," said the leopard, "do you think the king is responsible for the harm resulting from his evil rule?"

One of the eight notables replied, saying: "In a certain city there was an honorable burgher who was very rich; and when he died he left everything he had to his son. This son was sought after by many people. Some wanted to arrange a marriage for him, others begged him to enter a religious order. This young man, however, wanted to sell all his possessions and build a hospice and a bridge. The hospice was to provide lodging for pilgrims returning from the Holy Land,[30] and the bridge was for pilgrims to use so they would not risk drowning in the river, for that river was at the entrance to the city, and many people had drowned in it on their way to or from Jerusalem. When the burgher's son had completed the hospice and the bridge, one night, when he was sleeping, he dreamed that for all the good ensuing from the hospice and the bridge he would find merit before God."

By these words, the leopard realized that the king would suffer punishments in Hell equal to the harm continually caused by the bad customs his wicked council spread throughout the land, and he said that the punishment awaiting king and council was beyond reckoning. And he then said to himself that he preferred being an irrational beast, even though he would not exist after death, to being a king of men who would bear the burden of guilt for the great harm done by bad government.

The messengers and notables parted company and said goodbye to one another in a friendly fashion. The leopard told the notables that they should trust in God to bring them soon a good ruler with a good council and good officials, and not to despair of God's help; for God does not allow wicked princes to live long, in order that they not work the evil they could if they did live a long time.

When at first the lion had sent off his messengers and presents to the king of men, Dame Reynard, who was doorkeeper, told him that the leopard's wife was the most beautiful animal in the whole

---

[30] In the Middle Ages a *hospital* (as Llull calls it) was an institution, usually charitable, for the reception of the poor, the sick, and above all, pilgrims and travelers (hence the Knights Hospitalers).

world. So much did Dame Reynard praise the leopard's wife to the king, that he fell in love with her and took her as his wife, in spite of queen and council, which council was very afraid of Dame Reynard, when they saw how she had persuaded the king to commit such a wrong against his own good wife and against the leopard, who was his loyal servant.

"My dear friend," the ox said to Dame Reynard, "I am very afraid that the leopard might kill you, when he finds out you have persuaded the king to violate his wife."

Dame Reynard replied: "It once happened that a lady-in-waiting did something treacherous against the queen she was serving; this lady-in-waiting, however, was very intimate with the king, because of which intimacy the queen was afraid of the lady-in-waiting, and for fear of the king she did not dare get her revenge on the lady-in-waiting."

When the messengers had returned and given an account of their mission, the leopard went to his house where he expected to find his wife, whom he loved very much. The weasel and all the other members of the leopard's household were very sad when they saw their master; and they told the leopard of the dishonor the king had done him when he had violated his wife. The leopard's anger against the king was alarming to see, and he asked the weasel if his wife had been angry or pleased with the king when he took her into his service.

"Sir," said the weasel, "your wife was very angry at the king's advances, and she cried for a long time, and bemoaned having to leave you, whom she loved above all else."

The leopard's anger grew even greater at the thought of his wife's being forced to enter the king's service; for if she had liked the idea, he would not have been so displeased. So while the leopard was in this state of anger he began thinking about how he could avenge himself upon the lion who had so betrayed him.

42. CONCERNING THE BATTLE BETWEEN THE LEOPARD AND THE LYNX

THE LEOPARD arrived at the court of the king, and Dame Reynard, who saw him coming, said secretly to the king: "My lord, as a result of your affair with the leopard's wife, I have incurred the leopard's wrath. So, unless you honor me in front of the leopard, that is, do me the honor of letting me be closer to you than anyone else, I think the leopard will kill me." From that moment on, the lion made Dame Reynard a member of his council, and kept her near him so the leopard would not dare to wound or kill her. And on Dame Reynard's advice, he gave the post of doorkeeper to the peacock, who had an excellent sense of smell.

All of the king's council and all of the barons there were displeased by the honor the king accorded Dame Reynard, and more than any of them, the leopard was displeased, because he had been informed that Dame Reynard was responsible for his wife's marriage to the king.

The leopard went up to the king, and in the presence of many other honored barons, he accused the king of treason, saying that he had treacherously taken his wife, and if there was any baron who wanted to exonerate the king of treason, he would do battle with him, and make him say that the king was a traitor. The leopard then confirmed his intention to do battle by giving the king his gage.

The king, upon being accused of treason before all his subjects, was very angry with the leopard, and he felt very ashamed at having been called a traitor in front of his subjects. The king therefore said to his barons: "Which of you wants to do battle with the leopard, who as accused me of treason?" All the barons were silent, until Dame Reynard spoke up, saying:

"Treason is a thing most disagreeable to God, and it is a great dishonor for all a king's subjects to have their lord accused of treason. Therefore, just as the leopard does his lord great dishonor, for the sake of which he is willing to risk death, so great honor will come to any baron who defends the king from this charge, and whoever does battle to save the king's honor will receive a large reward from the king."

Because of the king's great dishonor at being accused of treason, and because the lynx hated the leopard ever since the king of men had honored his fellow messenger more than himself, the lynx agreed to do battle and defend the king from the charge of treason. Yet his conscience bothered him, for he knew the king had done something wrong and deceitful against the leopard, who had served him loyally all his life.

The leopard and the lynx entered the lists, and everyone said, "Now we will see which will win, truth or falsehood." The rooster then asked the snake which he thought should win, and the snake said: "Trial by combat was instituted so that truth might confound and destroy falsehood; and since God is truth, any person who upholds falsehood fights against both God and truth."[31]

These words, which the snake spoke secretly to the rooster, were overheard by the leopard and the lynx. The leopard found them very consoling, but they gave the lynx pangs of conscience and worry, and he became afraid that the king's sins would be the cause of his dishonor and death.

The battle between the leopard and the lynx lasted all day long till the hour of complin;[32] and the lynx defended himself stoutly against the leopard, whom he would have conquered and killed, had not his conscience restrained him; while for the leopard, truth and anger against the king gave him strength and revived him whenever he felt himself flagging. So strong, in fact, was the leopard, through the hope he placed in right being on his side, that he felt nothing could conquer him. At last he overcame the lynx and made him say, before the entire court, that the king was deceitful and traitorous. The king felt confounded and ashamed by the combat. The leopard killed the lynx, and everyone was ashamed of their lord's dishonor.

The king felt such shame and confusion in front of his subjects, and he was so angry with the leopard who had brought him such dishonor, that he could not contain himself, and in front of everybody he killed the leopard, who was so exhausted he could not defend himself. Everybody present in the square was angry at the crime the king had committed, and all desired to be beneath the dominion of another king, for it is a dangerous thing for a people to be subject to a king who is unjust, resentful, and traitorous.

All that night the king was very irate and angry. The next morning he called a meeting of his council, and asked them to advise him concerning the message from the king of men, in which he asked to be sent a bear and a wolf.

"My lord," said the serpent, who was the wisest councilor the

[31] This was the idea behind the medieval institution of the judicial duel or trial by battle.
[32] The last of the canonical hours, either combined with vespers (at sunset) or said afterwards.

king had, "there are many bears and wolves in your country—from whom you can easily choose whatever ones you think it would be best to send."

Dame Reynard, however, spoke up and said that the king of men was the noblest and most powerful king on earth. "And this is why, my lord, you must send the wisest and strongest bear and wolf you have, for if you don't, you might find yourself blamed and even in danger.'"

The king asked Dame Reynard which were the wisest and strongest bear and wolf in his kingdom, and Dame Reynard replied, saying that since there was a bear and a wolf on his council, it would seem only logical that each was wiser and stronger than any other bear or wolf in his kingdom.

The king approved of the idea of sending the bear and wolf who were members of his council, and neither the bear nor the wolf tried to get out of going, for both prided their honor and feared that, if they tried to get out of it, they might be accused of cowardice. Dame Reynard then said to the king that since he was sending the king of men the noblest personages in his whole country, it was only right that he also send the wisest messengers in his court to bring the bear and wolf as presents. The king also approved this idea, and told the snake to act as ambassador.

Before leaving the court on his mission, the snake said: "It once happened that, in a lovely meadow, a wolf came across some animal's entrails, in which a fisherman had hidden a hook in order to catch the wolf if he ate the entrails. The wolf, seeing these entrails, did not want to touch them, saying to himself, 'These entrails weren't put in this meadow without some intention of causing trouble and danger."

After sinning and killing the leopard, the lion no longer had the same subtlety or cleverness of mind as he had had before, and he did not understand what the snake's words signified; so he asked the snake to explain these words, since he did not understand them. The snake said that ever since the ox and Dame Reynard had been admitted to his court, it had not had a moment without trouble and suffering; and thus the honor the lion had done the ox and Dame Reynard had been the occasion of trouble and suffering to the king and his court.

When the ox heard the snake accuse him in front of the king, he apologized to the king, in the presence of his court, saying that he was not really guilty of anything, nor could he imagine ever doing anything bad against the king or his court, since the king had seen fit to honor him. And since he was an animal that kings found good to eat, and the king did not want to eat him, he therefore felt especially obliged to keep and maintain all the king's honor. The ox apologized in all ways, and explained how Dame Reynard had advised him to bellow three times during the night and three times during the day, and then to come to court to do good work for the king.

The ox apologized to the king in such a manner that Dame Reynard was displeased, and in her heart conceived ill will toward the ox. One day it came to pass that it had snowed a great deal and been very cold, and the lion and the other members of the court had nothing to eat and were very hungry. The lion asked Dame Reynard if she could think of anything they could eat. Dame Reynard said she did not know, but she would go talk to the peacock and find out if he smelled any animal nearby that the king and his companions could eat.

When the peacock saw Dame Reynard coming a great dread came over him, for he was very afraid of her. She told him that if the king asked him if he smelled any edible animal nearby he should reply that he smelled no animal the king should eat, but he smelled that the ox's breath stank and that he was sure to die soon of illness. Because he feared Dame Reynard and because the ox ate the grain that the peacock was meant to eat, the peacock acquiesced in the matter of the ox's death, and told the lion what Dame Reynard had instructed him to say.

After the lion had asked the peacock what he could eat and the peacock had replied that he did not know, but that he was sure that according to what one could smell from the ox's foul, rotting breath, he did not have long to live, the lion was eager to eat the ox; but he felt pangs of conscience about killing him, since the king had promised him loyalty, and since the ox had served him for a long time and trusted him.

When Dame Reynard saw the king hesitating about eating the ox, she drew near the king and asked him why he did not eat the ox, since the ox would probably die soon from sickness, according to the peacock, and all the more so since it was God's will that a king satisfy his needs by means of his subjects whenever the occasion called for it.

The lion answered Dame Reynard, saying that for nothing in the world would he break the vow he had made the ox. "My lord," said Dame Reynard, "would you eat the ox if I got him to tell you to eat him and if he released you from the vow you made him?" And the lion told her that he would.

Dame Reynard then went to a crow who was very hungry and said to him: "The lion is very hungry, and I am trying to get him to kill the ox, who is very fat and who will provide food for all of them, considering how large he is. And if the lion says in front of you that he is hungry, you must offer yourself to him, and say that he should eat you. But he won't eat you, for I will make excuses to him, and he never departs from my advice, for he does everything I suggest. And if I offer myself for the king to eat me, you must say that I am not good to eat—that my flesh is unhealthy."

After indoctrinating the crow, Dame Reynard went to the ox and told him that the king wanted to eat him, since the peacock had said that the smell of his breath indicated that he was soon to die. The ox was very afraid and said that what the peasant said to the knight was true.

"And what was it that he said?" asked Dame Reynard; to which the ox replied:

"A rich peasant desired honor, and he married his daughter to a knight who coveted the peasant's wealth. Honor attracted wealth, yet wealth did not have enough power in the peasant to bring him honor; but the knight's honor attracted to itself the peasant's wealth, with the result that the peasant ended up poor and without honor, and the knight rich and honored. The peasant then said to the knight that in friendship between a peasant and a knight lay poverty and suffering for the peasant, and honor for the knight. And in the same way," added the ox, "in friendship between an ox and a lion, lies death for the ox and satiety for the lion."

Dame Reynard, however, reassured the ox that the lion had promised him fidelity and would not betray him; and she advised the ox to offer himself to the lion to eat if it were necessary. The lion would then be grateful to him, and because of his gratitude and indebtedness, he would not harm him. "And what's more, I will help you and make sure that the lion does you no villainy or wrong."

When Dame Reynard had arranged all these things, she went to the lion with the ox and the crow, and the crow introduced himself to the lion, saying he had heard the lion was hungry, and offering himself to be eaten. Dame Reynard replied and made excuses for the crow, saying that his flesh was not fit for a king to eat. She then said that the king should eat her, since she had nothing else to offer him except her own body; but the crow told the lion that Dame Reynard's flesh was unhealthy to eat.

Then, with similar words, the ox offered himself, saying the lion should eat him, since he was large and fat, and had flesh that was good to eat. So the lion killed the ox, and the king, Dame Reynard, and the crow dined off the ox until they had had their fill.[33]

When the ox was dead, the lion asked the rooster who should be his chamberlain. The rooster wanted to speak first, but Dame Reynard gave him an angry look, which made him think it might be wiser to be quiet until she had spoken. Dame Reynard then spoke to the king saying that the rabbit was a humble beast of pleasant appearance, who would do well in the post once held by the cat and the ox. The lion asked the rooster if he agreed with Dame Reynard's suggestion,[34] and the rooster did not dare oppose Dame Reynard's counsel, since he was very afraid of her; he therefore gave the king the same advice she had given. So the lion made the rabbit chamberlain, and Dame Reynard had great power in the court, for the rooster, the peacock, and the rabbit feared her, and the lion believed everything she said.

One day it came to pass that the king had to attend to an important matter that had taken place in his kingdom, so he took counsel with the rooster and with Dame Reynard. The rooster said that he alone, without the help of others, did not feel up to counseling the king concerning such important affairs, and he advised the king to increase his council, for it did a king no honor to reduce his council, which is what had happened with the disappearance of the snake, the leopard, the lynx, and the wolf. The king thought it a good idea

---

[33] This story is from *Kalila and Dimna*, except that there it is the crow who sets up the treachery, with a wolf and jackal as companions, and a camel as the animal finally eaten.

[34] This last clause ("if he agreed . . .") is missing in A and B, and therefore in Galmés's edition.

to name more councilors, and indeed would have done so if Dame Reynard had not said:

"In a certain land there lived a man upon whom God had bestowed so much knowledge that he understood everything the beasts and birds said. But God had given this knowledge to this man on one condition—that he not tell a thing he heard and understood the beasts and birds saying to anyone, for the day he did, he would die.

"Now this man had a garden in which an ox drew water from a noria, and a donkey brought the manure needed for the garden. One evening it came to pass that the ox was exhausted,[35] and the donkey told him not to eat his oats that evening, so that the next day he would not be put to work turning the noria, and would be allowed to rest. The ox took the donkey's advice, and that evening did not eat his oats. The gardener thought the ox was ill and put the donkey in his place to turn the noria. All that day the donkey labored hard at the noria. When night came on he went to the stable where he found the ox lying down and resting. The donkey burst out crying in front of the ox and said, 'Our master has decided to sell you to a butcher, since he thinks you are ill; it might therefore be best for you to go back to your job and not look ill if you don't want him to kill you.'

"The donkey said this to the ox so that he himself would not be put back to turning the noria, which was harder work than his usual task of bringing manure. The ox was afraid of dying, and that night he ate his oats and made it appear as if he were cured.

"Now the master of the ox and the donkey understood what they had said to one another, and it caused him to laugh in front of his wife. The wife wanted to know what it was that made him laugh, but he refused to tell her, since he was afraid of dying as a result of explaining that he could understand the beasts and birds. The wife begged her husband over and over again to tell her what he had laughed at, but he still refused to tell her.[36] The wife then announced that she would not eat or drink, and would even allow herself to die, if he did not tell her. All that day and that night the wicked woman fasted, refusing to eat or drink. The husband, who

---

[35] Thus, *hujat*, in some sources, followed by earlier editions; other sources, followed by Galmés, have the less likely *anujat* ("annoyed").

[36] "Since he was afraid . . . refused to tell her" is missing in A and hence in Galmés's edition, but it is in all other sources.

loved her very much, finally said he would tell her, and he made out his will. After making out his will, he was about to tell her what had made him laugh, when he heard what the dog said to the rooster and what the rooster replied to the dog."

"And what was that?" the lion asked Dame Reynard.

Dame Reynard told the lion that while the man was making out his will, the rooster crowed and the dog reproved him for crowing, since his master was about to die. The rooster was in great wonder at the dog's reproof, but the dog told him how their master was about to die, and even wished to die, so that his wife might live. The rooster replied that it was just as well that he died, since he was a contemptible man who did not know how to control a woman. The rooster then called ten hens, brought them together in one place and did with them whatever he wanted, which he did to console the dog for the death of his master. So they consoled each other over the death of their master, and the rooster crowed and the dog was happy.

"My friend," the dog said to the rooster, "if you had as foolish a wife as my master and it came to pass that she brought you to death's door, as has happened in this case, what would you do?"

The rooster replied that if he was in his master's place, he would cut five rods from the pomegranate tree in his garden, and he would beat his wife until he had broken the rods and made her eat and drink; either that, or he would let her die of hunger and thirst.

After overhearing this conversation between the dog and the rooster, the man got out of bed and did what the rooster suggested; and the wife, after being beaten, ate and drank, and did everything her husband desired.[37]

After Dame Reynard recounted the above example, she said that the rooster was so wise that he could give counsel on any subject, and therefore the king didn't need to increase his council; all the more so since with many councilors there is too great a disparity of varying purposes, opinions, and desires, which often cause royal councils to be thrown into confusion.

When Dame Reynard had finished speaking, the rooster said: "There was once a parrot sitting in a tree next to a crow, and beneath the tree was a monkey who was putting kindling over a glowworm, thinking it was fire, and blowing on the kindling in the hope that it

---

[37] This story is from the prologue of the *Thousand and One Nights*.

would burn so he could warm himself. The parrot called out to the monkey, telling him that it was not fire but a glowworm. The crow said he should not try to criticize or instruct someone unwilling to receive advice or correction. The parrot repeated many times to the monkey that what he thought was fire was in fact a glowworm and not fire; and each time the crow reproved him for tying to straighten out something that was naturally crooked. Finally the parrot came down from the tree and approached the monkey to try to make him understand what he was saying; and he came so near that the monkey grabbed him and killed him."[38]

When the rooster had recounted this example, the king got the idea that it was meant to refer to him, and he gave the rooster a savage look, full of ill will. Dame Reynard then took the rooster, killed him, and ate him before the king.

When Dame Reynard was left sole councilor of the king, and the rabbit was royal chamberlain and the peacock doorkeeper, she was completely happy, and did with the king whatever she wanted. And while she was in this happy state, she remembered the treason she had conceived against the king when she had told the elephant that she would see to it that the lion died and that he would be king. Dame Reynard would gladly have remained in her present situation, but she was afraid the elephant might betray her; and she therefore decided to look into the matter of bringing about the death of the king, so as to carry out her part of the bargain with the elephant.

43.   DAME REYNARD'S DEATH

IN NOT FORGETTING to look into the matter of the king's death, Dame Reynard did forget the honor the king had done her, setting her above all the other barons of his court. One day Dame Reynard told the elephant that the time had come for the king to die; and all the more so since everything was so well prepared by there being no other councilor in the court besides Dame Reynard herself. The elephant thought about the matter for a long time, and his conscience bothered him for agreeing to the death of the king. On the

---

[38] Llull used this story from *Kalila and Dimna* earlier in *Blaquerna*, ch. 52, and later in the *Tree of Science* (OE I, 813).

other hand he was afraid that if he disobeyed Dame Reynard she would denounce him and plot his own death.

At the end his conscience did not allow him to consent to the king's death, and the elephant decided not to go along with Dame Reynard. Furthermore he was afraid that if he became king, Dame Reynard would betray him as she was betraying the present king. So the elephant preferred to be in danger of death rather than betray his natural lord.

While thinking about this, the elephant said to himself that in the same way that Dame Reynard intended to use cunning to have the king killed, he would use cunning to have the king kill Dame Reynard. "For if in Dame Reynard's body there is enough room for treason, guile, and cunning, how much more room," said the elephant, "there must be in my body, which is so large, for loyalty, wisdom, and cunning."

"Sir Elephant," said Dame Reynard, "what are you thinking about? And why are you not anxious to become king before the snake, who is so wise and cunning, returns from his mission?"

It then occurred to the elephant to wait for the snake before doing anything against Dame Reynard, so the snake could help him get the king to kill her. But when Dame Reynard saw that the elephant seemed to be losing interest in her plans, she was afraid of the snake's return and of the elephant denouncing her; and she therefore told the elephant to hurry up, for if he did not,[39] she would take care of matters in ways he had never imagined.

The elephant was very afraid of Dame Reynard's cunning, and so he asked her what position she wanted to have if he became king. Dame Reynard replied that she wanted to have the same position with respect to him as she had had with the present king, that is to say, sole councilor, with the rabbit as chamberlain and the peacock as doorkeeper. After Dame Reynard had stated the position she wanted to hold with the elephant, he asked her how the king's death would be arranged, and she told him her plan for killing the king, saying:

"Between the boar and the king there is ill will,[40] for the boar

[39] V and A, followed by the printed sources, omit the "not," making the rest of the sentence, I suppose, a promise instead of a threat.

[40] Thus in L V S and the French medieval translation. The later correcting hand in A has, "Between the boar and the king I will create discord and ill will," the reading followed in earlier editions. B has, "You should know that the boar is very proud." The uncorrected text of A omits the phrase altogether, which was the solution adopted by Galmés.

thinks himself the equal of the king in presence and in strength. And I will tell the boar to be on guard against the king, who wants to kill him; and I will tell the king to be on guard against the boar, who wants to be king. And when the boar is dead and the king exhausted from his fight with the boar, then you, Sir Elephant," said Dame Reynard, "will easily be able to kill the king and become king yourself."

Following her example, the elephant then decided to deceive Dame Reynard, and he said to her: "A promise without witnesses is worthless, and I therefore think," said the elephant, "that you, Dame Reynard, should have witnesses to the promise you want me to make you: namely, that you be my only councilor, that the rabbit be my chamberlain and the peacock be my doorkeeper. For without witnesses, if I went back on my promise, you could not prove it, and then maybe when I was king I would not feel so obliged to honor you as I do now when I am not king and you are the king's councilor."

Dame Reynard thought a long time about the elephant's suggestion, and she was afraid of the witnesses denouncing her for treason. When the elephant saw that Dame Reynard was worried, he told her that the best witnesses she could have were the rabbit and the peacock, for they were afraid of her and would be delighted to be his officials, and hence there was no cause for fearing that they might betray any of their secrets.

Dame Reynard accepted the elephant's advice, and in the presence of the rabbit and the peacock he made a solemn promise to Dame Reynard, and the rabbit and the peacock promised secrecy to the elephant and Dame Reynard.

Afterwards, the elephant advised Dame Reynard first to tell the boar that the king wanted to kill him, and then to tell the king. Dame Reynard therefore went off to talk first to the boar, and while she was doing so, the elephant spoke to the king, telling him all that he and Dame Reynard had planned to do; and he asked the king to forgive him for the treason he had conceived against him, saying how much he repented, and how he preferred to be a loyal subject than a traitorous king.

"How can I be sure," said the lion, "that you are telling the truth?" The elephant said he could tell by the fact that Dame Reynard had arranged matters so that she was the only animal on his council, and that the rabbit, who feared her by nature, as well as the peacock, were made members of his household. "And I can, my lord king, give you another certain proof, in that Dame Reynard has gone off to the boar to tell him you want to kill him, and she will then come and tell you the same, that is, that the boar wants to kill you, and she will counsel you to treat the boar haughtily, so that the boar will believe what Dame Reynard told him is true."

The elephant then told the king that the rabbit and the peacock had agreed to his death. The king was in great wonder at how Dame Reynard, whom he had honored so much, could conceive such treachery and offense against him, and he said:

"I remember hearing my father tell how my grandfather, who was king of a great country, wanted to humiliate the barons to whom great honor was due, and to exalt the viler beasts, to whom honor was not befitting; and among these beasts was the monkey, to whom he did great honor. Now this monkey, because of his resemblance to man, began wanting to be king, and instead of honor, he planned treason against my grandfather."

"My lord," said the elephant, "not much wine can fit in a small goblet, nor can great honor or great loyalty be present in someone of vile origin; therefore it would be good if you slew Dame Reynard, and had a good council, and were free once again in your own domains, and that you not cause the nobility that God gave you, in your person and your office, to be subjected to a wicked person."

After this, the elephant went to the boar, with whom Dame Reynard had just spoken, saying that he knew what she had told him, and then the elephant proceeded to repeat exactly what she had said to him.[41] The boar wondered how it was the elephant knew it, and the elephant told him the whole story.

While these two were talking, Dame Reynard went to the lion and told him the boar wanted to kill him, and then the lion knew that Dame Reynard was trying to betray him. So he called for a great gathering of barons, among whom were the elephant, the boar,[42] Dame Reynard, along with the rabbit and the peacock. In front of everybody the lion asked the rabbit and the peacock to tell him the truth about the testimony they had promised to bring

---

[41] This last clause (from "and then the elephant . . .") is missing in A and hence in Galmés's edition, but it is in all other sources.

[42] "The boar" is missing in A and hence in Galmés's edition.

Dame Reynard after his death. The rabbit and the peacock were very afraid, but even greater was Dame Reynard's fear, and she said to the king:

"My lord king, in order to test your barons to see if they were good and loyal, I told the elephant what I told him, and I said the same to the boar. As for the rabbit and the peacock, I tell you that I never spoke to them about what the elephant said against me." And then Dame Reynard trusted that neither the rabbit nor the peacock, who were so afraid of her, would dare accuse her to the king nor reveal anything.

After Dame Reynard had spoken, the king gave the rabbit and the peacock a terrible look, and he let out a huge roar, so that the nature of his high dominion might have greater power in the conscience of the rabbit and the peacock than their fear of Dame Reynard. After letting out this great roar, he angrily told the rabbit and the peacock to tell him the truth; and they, no longer able to restrain themselves, told the king the truth, whereupon the king killed Dame Reynard with his own hand. [43]

After Dame Reynard was dead, the court returned to its former good estate. The king appointed the elephant, the boar, and other honored barons to his council, and he cast out the rabbit and the peacock.

Here ends the *Book of the Beasts,* which Felix brought to a king so that he might learn, from the things done by the beasts, how a king should reign, and how to keep himself from evil counsel and from treacherous men. [44]

---

[43] Scholars have pointed out interesting parallels between the death of the fox here and that of Dimna in *Kalila and Dimna.*

[44] Scholars agree that the king in question must have been Philip the Fair of France, for whom see the introduction, p. 242 above.

ARS BREVIS

Introduction

THE *Ars brevis,* historically Llull's single most influential work, was the culmination of a long process of adaptation in response to criticisms concerning the complications and difficulties of earlier versions of the Art.

As the *Contemporary Life* implies, Llull's first teaching experience at the University of Paris in 1288–9 must have been disheartening.[1] One can easily imagine what today might be called the "culture shock" of his coming to this, the greatest center of Western learning in the Middle Ages. As in any structured academic or intellectual world, Paris had its fashions as to topics discussed, modes of discussing them, and the vocabulary used. All of these were far removed from the question Llull wanted to discuss: the conversion of infidels, by means of a method—the Art—which resembled nothing anybody had seen before, and employing a vocabulary that must often have seemed bizarre.[2]

Llull, however, was not easily discouraged. Converting the infidels was the task to which he had dedicated his life; the instrument for doing so, the Art, was for him God-given; and the vocabulary was essential to his purpose. So there was no question of abandoning them; all he could do was to try to persuade the Parisian schoolmen of the importance of his missionary aims,[3] in the process use the bizarre vocabulary more sparingly, and modify the Art itself so that it would not *look* so alarming. And, of course, what made it look alarming was the number and complication of the figures, as well as the letter symbolism.[4]

Towards the beginning of 1290 in Montpellier, therefore, Llull set

---

[1] See the "Life," § 19.

[2] See n. 67 to the above-mentioned section of the "Life" for the specific nature of these difficulties.

[3] Llull rightly felt that it was important for the achievement of his goals to get the backing of the French court and the University of Paris as representing the political and intellectual centers of Europe.

[4] Even the faithful disciple, le Myésier, complained to his master about "the confusion caused by the meanings of the alphabet of the *Ars demonstrativa* and its sixteen figures, which confound the mind." This is the end of the upper speech coming from le Myésier's mouth in the miniature of Plate VII.

about writing the *Ars inventiva veritatis,* beginning a new phase of the Art that was to culminate in the *Ars generalis ultima* of 1305–8 and its abridged version, the *Ars brevis* of 1308.[5] In this process several important changes were made in the Art. First, the figures were reduced from twelve to four. This simplification involved a jettisoning of principles that had been fundamental to the previous quaternary phase of the Art, such as Figure S and the Elemental Figure.[6] The former had been a touchstone for almost all its discourse, and the latter a foundation for much of its analogical method. In fact, the only figures left are A and T.[7]

The next major change was a reduction of the Alphabet from twenty-three to nine letters.[8] At the same time, Figures A and T, since they were now represented directly in the Alphabet, were reduced to nine components each. This involved a loss of seven dignities of Figure A, and two of the triangles of Figure T.[9] Moreover, Llull now made explicit something only implied in earlier versions of the Art: that is, multiple significates for each letter. This would have been confusing had it not been for a concomitant change that probably did more than anything to defuse the complaints of Llull's critics. From now on the letters of the Alphabet were not to be used in the text itself; they were kept merely for convenience in the combinatorial manipulation of the figures and for an occasional reference to a given Rule or Question. Gone, therefore, was the algebraic look of the Llullian discourse.[10]

So far I have dwelt almost exclusively on losses; the gains came from unexpected quarters. The first was in the form of definitions (of the eighteen principles from Figures A and T, of the Virtues and

[5] For the *Ars inventiva veritatis* see again § 19 of the "Life" above. For the ternary phase of the Art see "Llull's Thought," p. 48 above.

[6] In addition to the seven figures represented by the letters A S T V X Y Z of the chart on p. 79, the *Ars demonstrativa* also had a Demonstrative Figure, an Elemental Figure and three figures of Theology, Philosophy, and Law. See the charts following p. 318 in *SW* I for these figures, and p. 320 n. 1 for the number sixteen sometimes given for this version of the Art.

[7] With the Demonstrative Figure (see the previous note) resurfacing, transformed into the new Third and Fourth Figures.

[8] See the miniature from the *Breviculum* in Pl. VII above.

[9] Looking at the chart on p. 79, the dignities lost were simply the last seven under the letter A. Also, the first and last triads were jettisoned of Figure T, although the last triad (affirmation–doubt–denial) resurfaces in Question B of Part IV here.

[10] Llull himself says in the Prologue to the *Ars inventiva veritatis* (*MOG* v, 1), "In this Art we will necessarily have to use letters in place of terms in the figures, but not in the discourse [*non autem in processu*]; for otherwise no inquiry or invention could be carried out with the last two figures of this Art."

Vices, of the Hundred Forms, etc.). But here again we find our-selves confronted with something completely original on Llull's part. Instead of the usual Aristotelian definition based on genus and difference, we have one based, as Llull puts it, "in terms of a power and its specific act," and therefore on the dynamism of each being, and ultimately on its correlative structure. Llull explains that appar-ent tautologies such as "Man is a manifying animal," or "Man is that being whose function is to manify" are preferable because "by means of such a definition a person can have cognition of the subject and its specific act, whereas by means of the other one cannot, but only of its parts."[11]

The second gain was one that would probably bring Llull his greatest fame in succeeding centuries, and this was what was known as his "Ars combinatoria." Here he worked out devices for combining mechanically various components of the Art, devices such as the half-matrix of the Third Figure and the rotating wheels of the Fourth Figure of Part II, as well as the "Table" of Part v below. But this was only a subset of a vaster system of "mixture," in which other components were systematically, although not always so me-chanically, combined, or in which one set of components was used to investigate another. In order to do this, all the components had to be systematized, including a *scala naturae* or ladder of being (the Nine Subjects of Part IX) and a method for investigating it (the Rules or Questions of Part IV). To this he added specific instructions for manipulating the combinatory mechanism and the mixtures: the Evacuation of the Third Figure, the Multiplication of the Fourth Figure, and the mixture of Principles and Rules (constituting Parts VI–VIII). Finally we have several sections on the application of all these structures, which include not only Parts XII–XIII on "Habitua-tion" and on the "Method for Teaching this Art," but, more impor-tantly, that curious Lullian conceptual dictionary of the Hundred Forms (Part x).[12]

This brief introduction will perhaps give some idea of how much the Art had by now become not only a structure in itself, but also one in which the relation of its own inner parts was structured, as

---

[11] For definitions of the eighteen principles, see Part III, and n. 1 there, and for Llull's defense of this method (including the sources of the above quotes), see Part XI, nn. 4 and 8.

[12] For the often complicated prehistory of these various parts of the *Ars brevis*, see the notes at the beginning of the various chapters of the work.

well as its relation to subject (the user) and object (the world)—an extraordinary network of systems systematizing systems. This regimentation of the process of the Art, and hence of our process of thought and its application to the world about us, represents the first attempt in Western thought to create not only an *Ars combinatoria,* but also a total method for "finding the truth." These two programs intrigued succeeding generations down to Leibniz, and the former earned Llull the title of discovering the germ, however remote and primitive, of modern computer science.

This systematization and mechanization was accompanied by another major change: the abandonment of analogical methods. This meant, first of all, in relation to the Art of the quaternary period, the replacement of a large sprawling structure, whose parts were loosely (and often only analogically) interrelated, by a far more compact structure, whose parts are much more tightly and explicitly (and of course, mechanically) interrelated.

Secondly, it meant the replacement of analogy as a mode of reasoning by Llull's own version of traditional logic. The reader will not have gone far into the work before he finds himself immersed in propositions with their subject and predicate, in syllogisms, and in the problem of finding the middle term. But in spite of using many of the same molds and terms, Llull's logic has little to do with the formal logic of Aristotle,[13] but is rather a realistic, ontological logic. Indeed, just five years before, Llull had written the *Logica nova,* in which he explains the subject *in terms of* the Art (which is, of course, what makes it *nova*). Now he turns around and uses that logic as a fundamental element of the Art. As a result the Art now becomes a method for "finding" all the possible propositions and syllogisms on any given subject and for verifying their truth or falsehood.

Thirdly, it involved the replacement of analogy by inclusion. Instead of the former reliance on "simile, example, and metaphor,"[14] we now find Llull reassuring us that "everything which exists is

---

[13] And even less to do with the semantic logic of Llull's contemporaries, with their studies of *appellatio* and *suppositio* to try to systematize the contextual, semantic use of terms. Cf. Mark D. Johnston, *The Spiritual Logic of Ramon Llull* (Oxford: Oxford University Press, 1987).

[14] Cf. the *Ars demonstrativa* (*SW* I, 333 and n. 39), as well as *Principles of Medicine*, Dist. x, "Which treats of Metaphor" (*SW* II, 1199ff).

implicit in" such and such a figure, that "whatever exists is reducible to the above-mentioned principles," how this Art is general and universal, and how by its use the reader or practitioner can make his thought general and universal.[15] Where before he offered a looser, more open-ended method of comparison, he is now giving a much tighter and more systematized method of invention, of "finding" the right place within the structure to locate the answer to a question.[16]

As a result of this last change, the Art is now more explicit, and hence, in spite of its extraordinary intricacy, more straightforward in its application. It is therefore easier to assimilate and use. The above-mentioned open-endedness of the earlier Art, where many aspects of its use were left up to the reader's initiative, where there was considerable fluidity in the application of similes, examples, and metaphors, and where even many of Llull's more fully explained answers were only a shorthand or outline of all the structures being referred to, is replaced by a technique where the reader is led much more carefully by the hand and told much more explicitly how and where to find his solutions. As a result, it *looks* easier, and *is* easier, to understand and apply.

Manuscripts, Editions, and Translations

All these new aspects probably played their part in the great success of the *Ars brevis* (as well as of its companion piece, the *Ars generalis ultima*). In the most immediate sense, it brought Llull the recognition he had sought so long: in February of 1310, during his fourth and last visit to Paris, forty masters and bachelors in arts and medicine signed a document attesting to the fact that they had heard and approved of his lectures on the *Ars brevis*.[17] The defeat of twenty years earlier was now clearly reversed. Not long after Llull's death, his disciple Thomas le Myésier included a slightly altered "anthologized" version of the work in the *Breviculum,* the only work of

[15] See, for example, Part II, every section of which contains some statement to this effect.
[16] This does not mean, of course, that earlier phases of the Art had *no* pretensions to generality, or that *all* use of analogy was banned from later formulations of the Art. The change was one of basis and emphasis. The universality of this version of the Art, however, was one of the things that most impressed Renaissance Lullists; see for example Agrippa von Nettesheim's remarks quoted in "Lullism," n. 24 above.
[17] See the "Life," § 42 and n. 117 there.

Llull's to appear in its entirety in that magnificent manuscript destined for the queen of France.[18]

In subsequent centuries, no other work of Llull's was so often copied or commented. We possess, in fact, sixty-one manuscripts of the *Ars brevis*.[19] During the Renaissance and Baroque period, it was Llull's most famous work; of the twenty-five editions in which it was printed prior to the 1980s, all but four appeared between 1481 and 1669.[20] Moreover, either the *Ars brevis,* or the version of the Art represented by it together with the *Ars generalis ultima,* was commented on by Agrippa von Nettesheim, Giordano Bruno, and Johann Heinrich Alsted. It was these works and commentaries that made up the greater part of Zetzner's anthology. In fact, Zetzner began his anthology with the *Ars brevis,* so for many seventeenth-century readers it provided their first contact with Ramon Lull, as was certainly the case with the young Leibniz.[21]

After that, interest in the work—as in all of Llull's works—waned. In the more than three centuries between 1669 and 1984 one finds only four editions.[22] Since then, aside from new translations into Catalan, English, and French,[23] there have been two editions: of the Catalan text in Vol. I of *OS,* and a monumental edition of the Latin text in *ROL* XII. It was this last text I was able to use for my original translation (which is that reproduced here) thanks to a typescript which its editor, Alois Madre of the Raimundus–Lullus–Institute of Freiburg, very kindly sent me before it was published. This I compared with printed editions which had historical importance, which were interesting in themselves, or which I thought the modern reader might have occasion to consult.[24]

---

[18] For the *Breviculum,* see "Lullism," p. 61 above.

[19] Fifty-seven Latin MSS (listed in *ROL* XII, 188–90), plus two Catalan and two French MSS.

[20] See the list of the Latin editions in *ROL* XII, 181–2. In addition to a French translation published in 1632, see the four editions listed in n. 22 below.

[21] For Agrippa, Bruno, Alsted, and Zetzner, see "Lullism," pp. 65–68 above.

[22] Two editions were published in Palma in the same year of 1744, a French translation in 1901, and a Catalan adaptation in 1934.

[23] The Catalan translation appeared in *Ramon Llull, Antologia filosòfica,* ed. M. Batllori (Barcelona, 1984); the English translation in *SW* I; and the French version in *Raymond Lulle, L'Art bref,* ed. A. Llinarès, (Paris, 1991).

[24] This meant the Zetzner editions (for which see "Lullism," pp. 67–68 above); the Palma (1669) edition with commentaries by Frances Marçal (reprinted Frankfurt, 1970); and the two Palma (1744) editions mentioned in n. 22 above.

GOD, WITH THE HELP of Your grace, wisdom, and love, here begins the *Ars brevis*, which is a replica of the General Art, that is, of the work beginning "God, with the help of Your supreme perfection, here begins the *Ars generalis ultima*."

PROLOGUE

WE HAVE WRITTEN this *Ars brevis* so that the *Ars magna* may be more easily understood. For once the former is understood, the latter, along with the other Arts, can be easily understood and learned.

The subject of this Art is the answering of all questions, assuming that one can identify them by name.[1]

This book is divided into thirteen parts, just like the *Ars magna*.[2]

The first part concerns the Alphabet. The second, the Figures. The third, the Definitions. The fourth, the Rules. The fifth, the Table. The sixth, the Evacuation of the Third Figure. The seventh, the Multiplication of the Fourth Figure. The eighth, the Mixture of Principles and Rules. The ninth, the Nine Subjects. The tenth, Application. The eleventh, Questions. The twelfth, Habituation. The thirteenth, the way the Art should be taught.

And now we will begin by discussing the first part.

---

[1] That is to say, assuming that one knows under which of the ten general questions (see Part IV below) any particular question should be classified. The point is made more clearly in the corresponding passage of the *Proemium* of the *Ars generalis ultima*.

[2] These "parts" correspond exactly, which greatly facilitates crossconsultation. Note that throughout the *Ars brevis* Llull almost always refers to the *Ars generalis ultima* as the *Ars magna*.

PART I, WHICH TREATS OF THE ALPHABET OF THIS ART

W E H A V E employed an alphabet in this Art so that it can be used to make figures, as well as to mix principles and rules for the purpose of investigating the truth. For, as a result of any one letter having many meanings, the intellect becomes more general in its reception of the things signified, as well as in acquiring knowledge. And this alphabet must be learned by heart, for otherwise the artist will not be able to make proper use of this Art.

THE ALPHABET[1]

B   signifies goodness, difference, whether?, God, justice, and avarice.

C   signifies greatness, concordance, what? angel, prudence, and gluttony.

D   signifies eternity or duration,[2] contrariety, of what?, heaven, fortitude, and lust.

E   signifies power, beginning, why?, man, temperance, and pride.

F   signifies wisdom, middle, how much?, imaginative, faith, and accidie.

G   signifies will, end, of what kind?, sensitive, hope, and envy.

H   signifies virtue, majority, when?, vegetative, charity, and ire.

---

[1] To see the changes between this Alphabet and that of the quaternary phase, compare the chart here with that on p. 79.

[2] Some of the MSS and all of the printed sources consulted have just "duration." These two concepts are interchangeable in this slot of Figure A, which does not mean that they are synonymous, except as an attribute of God.

I   signifies truth, equality, where?, elementative, patience, and
     lying.
K   signifies glory, minority, how and with what?, instrumenta-
     tive, pity, and inconstancy.

TABLE 3. THE ALPHABET OF THE *ARS BREVIS*

	Fig. A	Fig. T	Questions and Rules†	Subjects	Virtues	Vices
B	goodness	difference	whether?	God	justice	avarice
C	greatness	concordance	what?	angel	prudence	gluttony
D	eternity*	contrariety	of what?	heaven	fortitude	lust
E	power	beginning	why?	man	temperance	pride
F	wisdom	middle	how much?	imaginative	faith	accidie
G	will	end	of what kind?	sensitive	hope	envy
H	virtue	majority	when?	vegetative	charity	ire
I	truth	equality	where?	elementative	patience	lying
K	glory	minority	how? and with what?	instrumentative	pity	inconstancy

* or duration

†See Part IV, n. 1, for the original Latin terms and their relationship to the equivalent "rules."

PART II, WHICH TREATS OF THE FOUR FIGURES

1. THE FIRST FIGURE, DENOTED BY A

THIS PART is divided into four sections, one for each of the four figures. The First Figure is that of A, and it contains nine principles, to wit, goodness, greatness, etc., and nine letters, to wit, B, C, D,

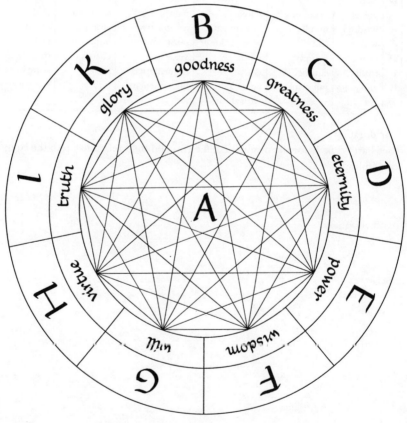

The First Figure.

E, etc. This figure is circular to show that any subject can become a predicate and vice versa, as when one says, "goodness is great," "greatness is good," and so on. In this figure, moreover, the artist seeks the natural conjunction between subject and predicate,[1] as well as their relative disposition and proportion, so that he can find the middle term and thus reach a conclusion.

Each principle, taken by itself, is completely general, as when one says "goodness" or "greatness." However, as soon as one principle is applied to[2] another, then it is subordinate, as when we say "great goodness." And when some principle is applied to a singular thing, then it is completely particular, as when we say "Peter's goodness is great." And thus the intellect has a ladder for ascending and descending; as, for instance, descending from a completely general principle to one neither completely general nor completely particular, and from a principle neither completely general nor completely particular to one that is completely particular.[3] And in a similar fashion one can discuss the ascent of this ladder.

Everything that exists is implicit in the principles of this figure, for everything is either good or great, etc., as God and angels, which are good, great, etc. Therefore, whatever exists is reducible to the above-mentioned principles.

2.   THE SECOND FIGURE, DENOTED BY T

THE SECOND FIGURE goes under the name of T, and it contains three triangles, each of which is general and all-embracing.

1. The first triangle consists of difference, concordance and contrariety, and it comprises everything which exists, according to its category. For everything which exists is either in difference, concordance or contrariety, and outside of these principles nothing can be found.

One must know, moreover, that each angle of this triangle has three species. For there is a difference between sensual and sensual,

---

[1] Note how this phrase is identical with what is defined as the activity of a logician in Part X, "Hundred Forms," no. 87 below, and how it is couched in terms identical with the new definition of "conjunctive middle" of Figure T, sec. 2 below.

[2] *Contrahitur* could also be translated as "joined or combined with," at the same time carrying with it the idea of "contraction." Llull elsewhere opposes *contracció* to "abstraction."

[3] Many of the printed sources omitted part of this sentence.

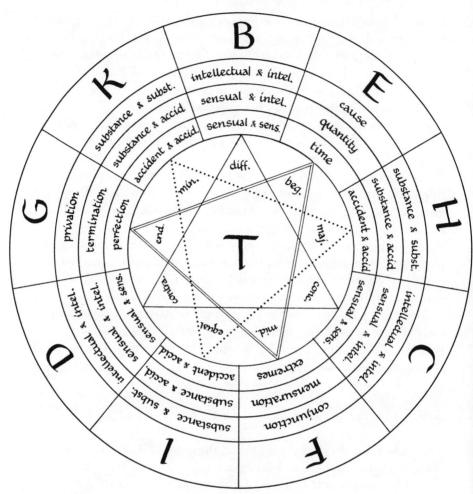

The Second Figure.

as for instance between a stone and a tree. There is also a difference between the sensual and the intellectual, as for instance between body and soul. And there is furthermore a difference between intellectual and intellectual, as between soul and God, between the soul and an angel, [4] between one angel and another, or between God and an angel. And the same can be said for concordance and contrariety, each in its own way. And this difference existing in each angle of this

---

[4] "Between the soul and an angel" is missing in the early printed sources consulted.

triangle is the ladder by which the intellect ascends and descends, so that it can find the natural middle term between subject and predicate, with which middle term it can reach a conclusion. And the same is true for the ladder of concordance and contrariety, each in its own way.

2. The second triangle consists of beginning, middle, and end, and it comprises everything that exists. For everything that exists is either in beginning, middle, or end, and outside of these principles nothing can be found.

The word "cause" written in the angle of "beginning" stands for the efficient, material, formal, and final cause. The words "quantity" and "time" refer to the other predicaments, and to those things that can be reduced to them.[5]

The angle of "middle" contains three species of middle. First there is the conjunctive middle, which exists between subject and predicate, as when we say, "man is an animal." For between man and animal there are middle terms, such as their life and body, without which man would not be an animal. Then there is the middle of mensuration, which refers to the act existing between the doer and the doable, like loving between the lover and the lovable. And then there is the middle between extremes, like a line between two points. And this angle of "middle" acts as a general ladder with respect to the intellect.

The angle of "end" also contains three species. The first is the end of privation, which refers to a privative state[6] and to those things that are in the past.[7] The second species is the end of termination, which refers to the extremities, like the two points that terminate a line, or like the lover and beloved in relation to loving. The third species is the end of perfection, which refers to ultimate purpose, like man, who exists to multiply his species, and to understand, love, and remember God, and so forth. This angle also acts as a general ladder with respect to the intellect.

3. The third triangle is made up of majority, equality, and minority, and it is general and all-embracing in its way. For whatever exists is either in majority, equality, or minority. Majority has three

---

[5] The "predicaments" are the Aristotelian categories, for which see Part x, n. 13 below.

[6] Thus *habitum privativum* in the MSS, and not *habitum privatum* as in most of the early printed sources.

[7] The early printed texts and a few of the MSS add, "like death which ends life."

species. The first is when there exists majority between substance and substance, as, for instance, the substance of heaven, which is greater than the substance of fire. The second species is when there exists majority between substance and accident, like a substance that is greater than its quantity; for substance exists of itself, which is something no accident does. The third species is when there exists majority between accident and accident, like understanding, which is greater than seeing, and seeing than running.[8] And what we have said about majority applies equally to minority, since they are correlative to one another.

The angle of equality has three species. The first is when things are substantially equal, like Peter and Martin, who are equal in substance. The second species is when substance and accident are regarded as equal to one another, such as substance and its quantity. The third species is when there is equality between accident and accident, like understanding and loving, which are equal in their object. And this angle is a ladder by which the intellect can ascend and descend, as was said of the other triangles. And when the intellect ascends to general objects, then it itself becomes general; and when it descends to particulars, then it itself becomes particular.

The Figure T serves the First Figure, for through difference one can distinguish between goodness and goodness, between goodness and greatness,[9] etc. And by joining this figure to the first, the intellect acquires knowledge. And because this figure is general, therefore the intellect becomes general.

3.   THE THIRD FIGURE

THE THIRD FIGURE is a composite of the first and second; for the letter B that appears in it stands for the B that is in both the first and second figures; and similarly for the other letters.

---

[8] Thus in the early printed sources and some of the MSS; other MSS, instead of *currere* ("running"), have *credere* ("believing").

[9] Thus in most sources; the Zetzner editions, however, have "greatness and greatness" for this pair.

The Third Figure.

BC	CD	DE	EF	FG	GH	HI	IK
BD	CE	DF	EG	FH	GI	HK	
BE	CF	DG	EH	FI	GK		
BF	CG	DH	EI	FK			
BG	CH	DI	EK				
BH	CI	DK					
BI	CK						
BK							

This one consists of 36 compartments,[10] as can be seen in the illustration. Each compartment has many different meanings as a result of the two letters it contains. Thus the compartment of B C has many different meanings as a result of B C, and similarly the compartment of B D has many different meanings as a result of B D, and so on.[11] And this should be clear from the alphabet we gave above.

Each compartment contains two letters, and these represent subject and predicate, between which the artist seeks the middle term that will join them, like goodness and greatness that are joined through concordance, and similarly for other terms. With this middle term the artist tries to reach a conclusion and state a proposition.

This figure is meant to show that any principle can be attributed to any of the others: thus to B we can attribute C, D, etc., and to C we can attribute B, D, etc., as can be seen from the illustration. This is so that the intellect may know each principle in terms of all the others, and be enabled to deduce many arguments from a single proposition.

[10] Combination without repetition of nine elements taken two at a time, hence

$$\binom{9}{2} = \frac{9 \cdot 8}{1 \cdot 2} = 36.$$

[11] In the *Lectura super Artem inventivam et Tabulam generalem* (*MOG* v, 402 = Int. v, 44) Llull is more explicit: "Each compartment has six meanings, like the compartment of B C, which signifies Goodness, Greatness, Difference, Concordance, First and Second Rule, and like the compartment of B D, which signifies Goodness, Duration, Difference, Contrariety, First and Third Rule, and so on for the others," which is followed by a detailed interpretation of each compartment.

To give an example with "goodness," we make it into a subject and use the other principles as predicates, giving:

	goodness is different
goodness is great	goodness is concordant
goodness is enduring	goodness is contrary
goodness is powerful	goodness is beginning
goodness is knowable	goodness is mediating
goodness is lovable	goodness is ending
goodness is virtuous	goodness is magnifying
goodness is true	goodness is equalizing
goodness is glorious	goodness is lessening

What we have said of goodness can be applied equally well to the other principles, each in its own way.

This figure is very general, and by using it the intellect is made very general in acquiring knowledge.

It is a condition of this figure that one compartment not be contrary to another, but that they be concordant in their conclusion. Thus the compartment of B C should not be contrary to that of B D, and so on for the others.[12] With such a condition, the intellect is conditioned to the acquisition of knowledge.

4.   THE FOURTH FIGURE

THE FOURTH FIGURE has three circles, the outermost of which is fixed and the two inside ones of which are mobile, as appears in the illustration. The middle circle revolves on top of the outer fixed circle, so that, for instance, C can be put opposite B. The innermost circle revolves on the middle circle, so that, for instance, D can be put opposite C. And in this way 9 compartments are formed at a time, one being B C D, another C D E, and so on. After that, E of the smaller circle can be put opposite C of the middle one, with which another 9 compartments are formed. When all the letters of the smallest circle have been brought opposite B on the largest circle and C on the middle circle, then C is the middle term between B and

---

[12] The Zetzner editions leave out "should not be contrary to that of B D."

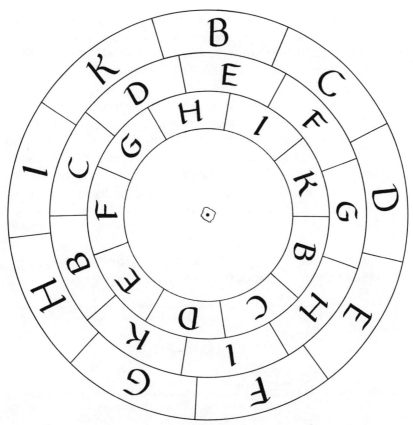

The Fourth Figure.

D, since B and D are related to one another through the meanings of C. And the same is true of the other compartments. And thus by means of these compartments, one may seek out necessary conclusions and find them.

After that, we can bring all the letters opposite the B of the largest circle and D of the middle circle, and so on for all the letters of the middle and smallest circle, by rotating them, with the B of the largest circle remaining immobile, until we arrive at a position with B on the largest circle, I on the middle one, and K on the innermost; and this will make a total of 252 compartments.[13]

---

13 Llull is saying that with the outer wheel remaining fixed, we can place opposite the B on

This figure is more general than the third, because in each compartment of this figure there are three letters, whereas in each compartment of the Third Figure there are only two. Thus the intellect is rendered more general as a result of the Fourth Figure than as a result of the Third.[14]

The condition of the Fourth Figure is that the intellect must apply to a proposition those letters that are most applicable to it. And once the compartment has been formed from three letters, it must grasp the meanings of the letters, keeping in mind the agreement between subject and predicate and avoiding disagreement. And with this condition, the intellect can acquire knowledge by means of the Fourth Figure, and can form many arguments toward a single conclusion.

So much for the four figures, which the artist must learn by heart, for without them he cannot use or practice this Art.

---

that wheel all the possible two-letter permutations of the remaining eight letters of his alphabet, which gives

$$\binom{8}{2} = \frac{8 \cdot 7}{1 \cdot 2} = 28$$

usable portions of the two inner wheels (i.e., without repetitions of letters). Now since in any one position we can read off nine compartments between the linked-up spokes, as it were, this gives us a total of $28 \times 9 = 252$ compartments. This does, however, involve repetitions; in fact, each compartment is repeated three times, since, B C D = C D B (which appears when C K are lined up under B) = D B C (which appears when I K are lined up under B). For Llull's combinatorial purposes here, however, this is unimportant. In the table in Part V he has eliminated the superflous combinations, giving $252 \div 3 = 84$ columns (see n. 3 there).

[14] Marçal (see introduction, n. 24 above) in his commentary on this passage quotes the statement from Llull's Art amativa that "the entire Art is contained in this Fourth Figure."

PART III, WHICH TREATS OF DEFINITIONS OF THE PRINCIPLES

IN THIS ART, the principles thereof are defined, so that they may be known by said definitions, and so that one may use them, affirming or denying in such a way that the definitions remain unimpaired. With such conditions, the intellect acquires knowledge, discovers middle terms, and dispels ignorance, which is its enemy.

1. Goodness is that thing by reason of which good does good.[1]

2. Greatness is that by reason of which goodness, duration, etc. are great.[2]

3. Eternity or duration[3] is that by reason of which goodness, etc. endure.

4. Power is that by reason of which goodness, etc. can exist and act.

5. Wisdom is that by reason of which the wise man understands.

6. Will is that by reason of which goodness, greatness, etc. are lovable or desirable.[4]

7. Virtue is the origin of the union of goodness, greatness, and the other principles.[5]

---

[1] The early printed sources, along with two MSS, add "and thus good is being and evil is nonbeing," for which see "Llull's Thought," p. 53 above. These definitions of the eighteen principles appear in every work of the Art from the *Ars inventiva veritatis* on, as well as the *Tree of Science*, sometimes with extensive commentaries. For the unusual nature of these definitions, see the introduction, p. 297 above. Llull was aware of the reactions these definitions aroused; at the end of this section in the *Ars generalis ultima*, with uncharacteristic anger, he rails against "those who, with dog's teeth and a serpent's tongue scorn and slander these principles of mine and their definitions. The Art, however, requires one principle to assist another." This is a reference to the "mixtures" (in this case of one dignity defined in terms of the others) so essential to the Art. For a defense of the dynamic nature of the thing defined (and hence of its correlative structure), see Part XI, n. 4 below.

[2] A few MSS and all the early printed sources add, "and it encompasses all the farthest reaches of being."

[3] The early printed sources and three MSS omit "eternity or" (cf. Part I, n. 2 above).

[4] The printed sources omit "lovable or."

[5] Note the curious linking of "virtue" and "unity," ever present in these Lullian definitions.

8. Truth is that which is true concerning goodness, greatness, etc.

9. Glory is that bliss in which goodness, greatness, etc. come to rest.

10. Difference is that by reason of which goodness, etc. are clearly distinguishable from one another.

11. Concordance is that by reason of which goodness, etc. accord in one or in several things.

12. Contrariety is the mutual opposition of certain things as a result of different goals.

13. Beginning is that which is found in everything where there is any question of priority.

14. Middle is the subject through which end influences beginning, and beginning reinfluences end, and thus it participates in the nature of both.

15. End is that in which beginning comes to rest.

16. Majority is the image of the immensity of goodness, greatness, etc.

17. Equality is the subject in which the end of concordance, goodness, etc. comes to rest.

18. Minority is the thing close to nothingness.

So much for definitions of the principles, which must be learned by heart; for without knowing these definitions, the Art is unteachable.

PART IV, WHICH TREATS OF RULES

THE RULES of this Art consist of ten general questions, to which all other possible questions can be reduced. They are the following

B. Whether a thing is.
C. What is it?
D. Of what is it?
E. Why is it?
F. How much is it?
G. Of what kind is it?
H. When is it?
I. Where is it?
K-1. How is it?
K-2. With what is it?[1]

Each of these questions is divisible into various species.

B. "Whether" has three species, to wit, dubitative, affirmative and negative, so that, from the outset, the intellect assumes either side to be possible, and does not bind itself to believing, which is not as natural to it as is understanding. And thus it must take that side with which it has the greatest understanding, which side must be that of truth.[2]

C. "What?" has four species:

1. The first is definitional, as when one asks, What is the intellect? To which one must reply that it is that power whose function it is to understand.

2. The second species is when one asks, What does the intel-

---

[1] These ten Rules or Questions first appeared in the *Taula general* of 1293–4, and were reproduced almost verbatim in the *Arbre de filosofia desiderat* of 1294. From then on no work of the Art is without them, and they play an important role in the *Logica nova*. So the reader can get an idea of the original terminology, the list of rules with their corresponding questions in the *Ars generalis ultima* is as follows: B. *possiblitas—utrum?*; C. *quidditas—quid?*; D. *materialitas—de quo?*; E. *formalitas—quare?*; F. *quantitas—quantum?*; G. *qualitas—qualis?*; H. *tempus—quando?*; I. *locus—ubi?*; K-1. *modalitas—quomodo?*; K-2. *instrumentalitas—cum quo?* Note that in order to accommodate ten rules to a nine-letter alphabet, Llull had to put two rules in the last slot. It is curious to observe that Giordano Bruno in his *De lampade combinatoria lulliana* (Zetzner, Strasbourg, 1617, p. 705), refers to these ten questions as the "syncategoremata" of the Art, in opposition to the "categoremata" of Figures A and T. Marçal in his edition of the *Ars brevis* (see introduction, n. 24 above) has an interesting *scholium* on the double nature of these questions (referring to the unknown or doubtful) and rules (referring to methods or argumentation or teaching).

[2] The three "species" of this question correspond to the lost black triangle of Figure T (cf. Introduction, n. 9 above).

lect have coessentially in itself?[3] To which one must reply that it has its correlatives, that is to say, intellective, intelligible, and understanding,[4] without which it could not exist, and would, moreover, be idle and lack nature, purpose, and repose.

3. The third species is when one asks, What is the intellect in something other than itself? To which one must reply that it is good when understanding in goodness, great when understanding in greatness, etc.; and grammatical in grammar, logical in logic, rhetorical in rhetoric, etc.

4. The fourth species is when one asks, What does a thing have in another thing? As when one asks, What does the intellect have in another thing? To which one must reply, In knowledge understanding and in faith belief.

D. The rule "Of what?" has three species:

1. The first is the original meaning, as when one says, Of what is the intellect? To which one must reply, Of itself, since it is not naturally derived from some other general thing.

2. The second species is when one inquires specifically, What is a thing composed of? As when one asks, What is the intellect composed of? To which one must reply that it is composed of its own specific matter and form, with which it achieves specific understanding.[5]

3. The third species is when one asks, Whose is a thing? As when one asks, Whose is the intellect? To which one must reply that it is man's, as a part belongs to the whole, and a horse to its master.

E. The fourth rule[6] has two species, to wit, formal and final.

1. The formal aspect is when one asks, Why does a thing exist? As when one asks, Why does the intellect exist? To

---

[3] The *Ars generalis ultima* has "essentially and naturally" instead of "coessentially."

[4] *Intellectivum, intelligibile et intelligere*; see the "Life," n. 83, for this correlative doctrine.

[5] The different version of this last sentence in the *Ars generalis ultima* helps to explain Llull's meaning: "To which one must reply that it is composed of its own essential principles, that is to say, its intellective, intelligible and understanding. And similarly with man who is made up of his body and his soul, with a nail which is of iron, and so on."

[6] The early printed souces add "of why?" The two species are further clarified in the *Taula general* (ORL xvi, 341), where Llull says they involve asking respectively "why things exist, and why they do what they do." In the corresponding section of the *Ars generalis ultima* he says one is *per existentiam* and the other *per agentiam*.

which one must reply that it is because of its specific matter and form, with which it has a specific understanding and with which it acts in accordance with its own species.

2. The second species is with respect to end, as when one asks, Why does the intellect exist? To which one must reply, So that objects may be intelligible, or, So that one may have knowledge of things.

F. The fifth rule asks about quantity, and has two species:[7]

1. The first is what one inquires about continuous quantity, as when one says, How much intellect is there? To which one must reply that there is as much as there can be through spiritual quantity, and this quantity has nothing to do with points or lines.

2. The second species is when one inquires about discrete quantity, as when one says, How much intellect is there? To which one must reply that there is as much as the amount of its correlatives, by which[8] it is diffused and sustained, that is to say, the intellective, intelligible, and understanding, with which it operates theoretically and practically, with respect to the general and the particular.

G. The sixth rule concerns quality, and it has two species:

1. The first is when one asks, What is the characteristic and primary quality of intellect? To which one must reply, The intelligibility with which it is clothed. Extrinsic understanding is a secondary and more distant property, with which the intellect understands a man, a lion, etc. It is of this that the intrinsic and substantial understanding of the intellect is clothed, and similarly for what is extrinsically intelligible.

2. The second species is when one inquires about appropriated quality, as[9] when one asks, What is an appropriated quality of the intellect? To which one must reply, Believing, doubting, or supposing. For these acts are not those of the intellect proper, but of the understanding.

---

[7] "Quantity" and the following "quality" reappear in Part x, "Hundred Forms," nos. 16–17.

[8] The early printed sources and many MSS have "in which."

[9] "When one inquires about appropriated quality, as" is missing in the early printed sources consulted.

H. The seventh rule inquires about time, and it has fifteen species signified by the rules of C, D, K, as is pointed out in the *Ars magna*.[10] But since this Art is brief, we must discuss this rule in few words, as when we ask, In what way does the intellect exist in time, if it is not made up of points and lines? To which one must reply that the intellect exists in time because it had a beginning and because it consists of temporal succession, by means of the motion of the body to which it is attached.[11]

I. The eighth rule inquires about place, and it has fifteen species signified by the rules of C, D, K, as is pointed out in the *Ars magna*.[12] Thus when one asks, Where is the intellect, one can answer briefly that it is in the subject in which it is, like a part in the whole, not however confined but rather diffused in it, for the essence of intellect has nothing to do with point, line, or surface.

K contains two rules, namely of modality and instrumentality.

K-1. The modal rule has four species, as when one asks (1) How does the intellect exist?[13] (2) How does one part exist in another?[14] (3) How do the parts exist in the whole, and the whole in its parts? and (4) How does it transmit its likeness outside itself? To which one must reply that subjectively it exists in the manner already determined through the above-mentioned species. Objectively,[15] it understands by finding the middle term existing between subject and predicate designated by the figures, and by multiplying alien species abstracted from sense and imagination, which are characterized and understood in its own intellectual faculty.

K-2. The second rule of K has four species, as when one asks, (1)

[10] See the corresponding section of the *Ars generalis ultima*, as well as the *Logica nova* (see *Raimundus Lullus: Die neue Logik - Logica nova*, ed. C. Lohr [Hamburg, 1985] pp. 34–5), where Llull explains that these species correspond to the 4 of the second rule (C), the 3 of the third (D), the 4 of the ninth (K-1), and the 4 of the tenth (K-2). For example, the questions based on C he formulates as, "When is the intellect?" "When does the intellect exist coessentially in itself?" etc.; those based on D as, "What is time composed of?" etc.; and so on for the other two rules. He admits, however, that "it is very difficult for the intellect to understand time" by means of these fifteen species.

[11] This example is from the ninth rule [K-1]; cf. the corresponding part of the *Ars generalis ultima*.

[12] See the references under n. 10 above. The distribution is presumably the same here.

[13] *Quomodo est intellectus?* Literally, "How is the intellect?" The *Ars generalis ultima* phrases it as, "How does a thing exist in itself?" In the version of the *Ars brevis* appearing in the *Breviculum* (fol. 35r), as well as in the Questions of the *Logica nova* (cf. the reference in n. 10 above, pp. 36–7), it appears as, "How does a part exist as a part?"

[14] Literally, "How is a part in a part?"

[15] The "objectively" is missing in the early printed sources and in many MSS.

With what does the intellect exist? (2) With what does one part exist
in another? (3) With what do the parts exist in the whole, and the
whole in its parts? and (4) With what does it transmit its likeness
outside itself?[16] To which one must reply that it exists with its
correlatives, without which it can neither exist nor understand.
And it understands with alien species, from which it fashions an
instrument for understanding.

So much for the rules with which the intellect solves questions,
which it does by reducing them by means of rules; by keeping in
mind what a rule and its species means subjectively; by reducing a
question by means of principles and rules; by having the intellect
discard whatever question is dubious as a result of applying the
definitions of principles; by choosing and by understanding intel-
ligibly the affirmative or negative side of the question; and this so
that the intellect be removed from doubt.

[16] Note the exact parallel between these four species and those of the first rule of K.

PART V, WHICH TREATS
OF THE TABLE[1]

THIS TABLE is the subject in which the intellect becomes universal, because by said table it understands and abstracts many particulars on all matters, with the principles surveying the particulars objectively, and the rules subjectively.[2] And this it does by applying to each question twenty arguments to explain said question, one argument being extracted from each compartment of a given column.

The table, as one can see, has 7 columns, in which the 84 columns of the *Ars magna* are implicit. In this table T means that the letters which come before it belong to the First Figure, and those after it to the Second Figure.[3]

By means of this table the intellect is ascendant and descendant. It

---

[1] The *tabula* (Cat. *taula*), which is derived directly from the Fourth Figure (cf. n. 3 below), first appeared in the *Taula general* of 1293–4. In its full form it only reappeared in the *Ars compendiosa* of 1299 and in the *Ars generalis ultima*; the abbreviated form only appears in the *Ars brevis*.

[2] For the earlier *intelligit*, "understands," many MSS have *colligit*, "gathers, brings together." The phrase "and the rules subjectively" is missing in the Zetzner editions.

[3] As Llull says here, this table is an abbreviation or sample of the larger one in the *Ars generalis ultima*. The latter is engendered by the machinery of the Fourth Figure, but omitting the repetitions, which gives us

$$\binom{9}{3} = \frac{9 \cdot 8 \cdot 7}{1 \cdot 2 \cdot 3} = 84$$

compartments (cf. Part II, n. 13). For these compartments, see Giordano Bruno, *De lulliano specierum scrutinio* (Zetzner, Strasbourg, 1617), pp. 670–1, and Agrippa von Nettesheim, *In Artem brevem*, pp. 841–9. Llull then takes each of them and sets it at the head of a column containing further variations achieved by distinguishing the letters referring to Figure A from those referring to Figure T. If for the sake of our calculations we do this by using uppercase for the former and lowercase for the latter, instead of merely separating them by the letter T as Llull does, it will become clear that the first column, for instance, consists of all the permutations of the six letters B C D b c d taken three at a time, or

$$\binom{6}{3} = \frac{6 \cdot 5 \cdot 4}{1 \cdot 2 \cdot 3} = 20,$$

giving us the number of triads in each column. We thus have a total of 1,680 compartments. Now for the *Ars brevis*, Llull takes just 7 of the 84 columns of the larger table. He chooses them by taking the first of the 28 starting with B, the first of the 21 starting with C, etc., ending with the one starting with H (cf. the passages cited from Bruno and Agrippa; the former says that the *Ars brevis* uses the first element of each "domus").

is ascendant when it ascends to things that are prior and more general, and descendant when it descends to things that are posterior and particular. And in addition it is connective, since it can connect columns, as, for instance, the column of B C D with that of C D E, and so on.

The Table

B C D	C D E	D E F	E F G	F G H	G H I	H I K
B C T B	C D T C	D E T D	E F T E	F G T F	G H T G	H I T H
B C T C	C D T D	D E T E	E F T F	F G T G	G H T H	H I T I
B C T D	C D T E	D E T F	E F T G	F G T H	G H T I	H I T K
B D T B	C E T C	D F T D	E G T E	F H T F	G I T G	H K T H
B D T C	C E T D	D F T E	E G T F	F H T G	G I T H	H K T I
B D T D	C E T E	D F T F	E G T G	F H T H	G I T I	H K T K
B T B C	C T C D	D T D E	E T E F	F T F G	G T G H	H T H I
B T B D	C T C E	D T D F	E T E G	F T F H	G T G I	H T H K
B T C D	C T D E	D T E F	E T F G	F T G H	G T H I	H T I K
C D T B	D E T C	E F T D	F G T E	G H T F	H I T G	I K T H
C D T C	D E T D	E F T E	F G T F	G H T G	H I T H	I K T I
C D T D	D E T E	E F T F	F G T G	G H T H	H I T I	I K T K
C T B C	D T C D	E T D E	F T E F	G T F G	H T G H	I T H I
C T B D	D T C E	E T D F	F T E G	G T F H	H T G I	I T H K
C T C D	D T D E	E T E F	F T F G	G T G H	H T H I	I T I K
D T B C	E T C D	F T D E	G T E F	H T F G	I T G H	K T H I
D T B D	E T C E	F T D F	G T E G	H T F H	I T G I	K T H K
D T C D	E T D E	F T E F	G T F G	H T G H	I T H I	K T I K
T B C D	T C D E	T D E F	T E F G	T F G H	T G H I	T H I K

PART VI, WHICH TREATS OF THE EVACUATION OF THE THIRD FIGURE[1]

THE INTELLECT evacuates the compartments of the Third Figure by extracting from them as much as it can, taking from each compartment those things that the letters signify, so as to apply the things signified to the proposition, and it thus becomes applicative, investigative, and inventive. We will give an example of this in one compartment, and the others are to be dealt with in similar fashion.

From the compartment of B C the intellect draws forth 12 propositions by saying:

goodness is great	difference is good
goodness is different	difference is great
goodness is concordant	difference is concordant
greatness is good	concordance is good
greatness is different	concordance is great
greatness is concordant	concordance is different[2]

And having formed these 12 propositions by changing subject into predicate and conversely, the compartment is evacuated of these propositions.

Then it is evacuated of 12 middle terms. And they are called middle terms because they are placed between subject and predicate, with which they accord in genus or species. And with these middle terms, the intellect can become disputative and determinative. Thus, for instance, one can say, Everything which is magnified

---

[1] The techniques in this and the next part made their first hesitant appearance in the *Lectura Artis quae intitulatur Brevis practica Tabulae generalis* of 1306(?). In the *Ars brevis* and *Ars generalis ultima* we have the first and only time they appear in their fully developed form.

[2] The compartment of B C implies those of B B, C C, and C B, and this for the two different meanings of each letter. We therefore have four concepts, each of which can be combined with three others, or 4 × 3 = 12.

by greatness is great; goodness is magnified by greatness; therefore goodness is great, and so on for the others.[3]

After performing this evacuation, the intellect evacuates the same compartment by means of 24 questions, since two questions are implicit in each proposition. Thus one has:

goodness is great:
  Whether goodness is great.
  What is great goodness?
goodness is different:
  Whether goodness is different.
  What is different goodness?
goodness is concordant:
  Whether goodness is concordant.
  What is concordant goodness?
greatness is good:
  Whether greatness is good.
  What is good greatness?

greatness is different:
  Whether greatness is different.
  What is different greatness?
greatness is concordant:
  Whether greatness is concordant.
  What is concordant greatness?

difference is good:
  Whether difference is good.
  What is good difference?
difference is great:
  Whether difference is great.
  What is great difference?

difference is concordant:
  Whether difference is concordant.
  What is concordant difference?
concordance is good:
  Whether concordance is good.
  What is good concordance?
concordance is great:
  Whether concordance is great.
  What is great concordance?
concordance is different:
  Whether concordance is different.
  What is different concordance?

Once this evacuation of questions has been carried out, the intellect then evacuates the compartment with the definitions of goodness and greatness, and with the three species of difference and concordance that appear in the Second Figure. Then it evacuates the compartment with the three species of Rule B and with the four

---

[3] This last sentence is missing in the Zetzner editions.

species of Rule C. Having carried out this evacuation, the intellect solves the aforementioned questions in said evacuation, by observing the conditions of the compartment, affirming, or denying. And thus the intellect banishes doubts from the compartment, remaining in it calmly and positively. Moreover it now knows itself to be completely general and artful, and clothed in great knowledge.[4]

---

[4] The *Ars generalis ultima*, whose text—with the exception of the larger table—has up to this point been very similar to that of the *Ars brevis*, now continues with examples of questions and answers from each of the thirty-six compartments of the Third Figure.

PART VII, WHICH TREATS OF THE MULTIPLICATION OF THE FOURTH FIGURE[1]

THE MULTIPLICATION of the Fourth Figure consists of the following, namely, that the first compartment B C D in the Fourth Figure or in the Table means that B has one condition with C and another with D; and C has one condition with B and another with D; and D has one condition with B and another with C.[2] And therefore in this compartment there are six conditions with which the intellect is conditioned and disposed to investigating, finding, arguing, proving, and determining.[3]

After these six conditions, the intellect acquires another six, by turning the smallest circle, putting its E where its D was, opposite the C on the middle circle. And then, since the compartment has been changed, so have its conditions. And thus the intellect now has twelve[4] conditions; and similarly for the other compartments, by multiplying columns and turning them.

---

[1] Cf. Part VI, n. 1.

[2] This curious use of the word "condition" is defined in the *Taula d'esta Art* (*ORL* xvii, 392) as being "the mixture of principles, with some being conditioned in others according to their definitions and properties, like goodness which is conditioned to being great by reason of greatness, and to being enduring by reason of eternity, and it is great and enduring in accordance with its own condition, that is to say, that its greatness and duration be good; and the same is true of 'condition' with respect to the other principles.

[3] In the Zetzner editions this paragraph is followed by a figure exhibiting the six conditions:

in which one reads the relationships from left to right, with the figure right-side-up for 1, 2, and 4, and upside-down for 3, 5, and 6.

[4] The Zetzner editions have fifteen, but since we are adding the six conditions of B C E to the six of B C D, this is surely an error. The peculiar phrase at the end of the sentence would

The conditions that the intellect multiplies in this way are difficult to enumerate. For from each compartment the intellect can
evacuate 30 propositions and 90 questions, just as from the compartment B C of the Third Figure we derived 12 propositions and 24
questions.[5] And as a result the intellect realizes it has become completely general and artful, over and above another intellect ignorant
of this Art, who would reduce it to a multitude of inconsistencies
and impossibilities. The sophist will thus not be able to stand up to
such an intellect as that of the artist of this Art, who uses primary
and natural conditions, as opposed to the sophist, who uses conditions that are secondary and unnatural, as is explained in the *Ars
magna*.[6]

---

seem simply to indicate a continuation of the process of rotating the wheels and deriving the
six conditions from each resultant compartment.

[5] Since each letter stands for two principles, in the compartment of B C D we therefore
have six principles, any one of which can form propositions with the remaining five, giving
thirty propositions, to each of which we can apply three questions, giving a total of ninety.
This is merely a ternary version of the binary mechanism of Part VI.

[6] The equivalent Part VII of the *Ars generalis ultima*, divided into five sections which
correspond only roughly to the five dispositions of the intellect given at the end of the first
paragraph, constitutes a small treatise on Lullian logic. After presenting (1) different ways of
multiplying the Fourth Figure (along with the Table), he goes on to (2) use the ternary
configurations to find the middle term between two concepts, leading him naturally into the
syllogistic, with which (3) he investigates (*De modo probandi*) the three types of demonstration
(see Part XI, n. 6 below); then he discusses (4) the fourteen fallacies mentioned in the *Logica
nova*, and ends with (5) a section on how the Art can be used to acquire other sciences such as
Theology, Philosophy, etc. With this equipment the artist will acquire superiority over the
"sophist" or logician; see the further comparison from the *Ars generalis ultima* quoted in Part
x, n. 40 below.

PART VIII, WHICH TREATS OF THE MIXTURE OF PRINCIPLES AND RULES[1]

IN THIS PART the intellect mixes one principle with another, examining each principle, with its definition, by means of the others, and examining each principle by means of all the species of the rules.[2] By means of such an examination the intellect becomes acquainted with each principle, and every time it mixes said principle differently, it will find out something new about it. Who in fact could enumerate all the means the intellect discovers for drawing conclusions, with the intellect evacuating this mixture as it did the compartment of B C discussed earlier?

This mixing is the center and foundation for the finding of all sorts of propositions, questions, middle terms,[3] conditions, solutions, and even objections. But we will desist from giving examples of this to the discerning mind, for the sake of brevity, and since this type of mixing is explained and exemplified in the *Ars magna*.[4]

Furthermore, this mixture is subject and refuge for the artist of this Art, so that he may find it in whatever he wants. For if he needs to find out something that has to do with goodness, he has only to examine said goodness by means of all the principles and rules, and from it he will find whatever he wants to understand. And what we have said about goodness applies equally to the other principles.

---

[1] This mixing of principles and rules first appears in embryonic form in the *Investigatio generalium mixtionum secundum Artem generalem* of 1298 (printed in *ROL* XVII), and then in its fully developed form in the *Liber de praedicatione* of 1304 (printed in *ROL* III–IV).

[2] The middle part of this sentence is missing in the early printed sources.

[3] In place of the *media* of all the other sources, the Zetzner editions have *materiae*, "matters."

[4] And this at great length, in two sections of the *Ars generalis ultima*. The first has eighteen chapters, each devoted to one principle of the Art and its mixture with the other seventeen principles. The second section similarly has eighteen chapters, each devoted to one principle of the Art, but here each principle is mixed with all the species of the ten rules. In this second section, under Rule C ("What?"), each of these principles is defined again.

This mixture is conditioned and disposed according as one thing is different from another. For if one examines divine goodness by means of the principles and rules, this examination requires other definitions and rules than does an examination of the goodness of an angel; and the examination of the goodness of angel, another than the goodness of man; and the goodness of man another than the examination of the goodness of a lion, and so on.

PART IX, WHICH TREATS OF THE NINE SUBJECTS

IN THIS ART we have put nine subjects, those indicated in the Alphabet. They include everything that exists, for outside of them there is nothing.[1]

The first subject is God, denoted by the letter B.

The second subject is angel, denoted by the letter C.

The third subject is heaven, denoted by the letter D.

The fourth subject is man, denoted by the letter E.

The fifth subject is imagination, denoted by the letter F.

The sixth subject is the sensitive, denoted by the letter G.

The seventh subject is the vegetative, denoted by the letter H.

The eighth subject is the elementative, denoted by the letter I.

The ninth subject is instrumentality, denoted by the letter K.

Since in the *Ars magna* each subject is deduced by means of principles and rules, we will therefore not investigate them here, since we want to make this *Art* shorter than that one, and since said deduction is implicit in this *Art*. For this reason we will desist from presenting this matter to the discerning mind, which should be content with the example given in the Third Figure, where we apply all the principles to "goodness," as well as all the rules of this Art to "intellect."

In dealing with these subjects, we must keep in mind four conditions. By these the intellect will be conditioned to examine the aforementioned subjects in a conditioned way, by means of the principles and rules, according as each subject is conditioned by its nature and essence. For divine goodness has one condition in God; angelical goodness another in an angel; and so on for the rest. And the same is true for the rules.[2]

---

[1] The idea of a *scala naturae*, or a ladder of being, is present in many works of Llull, but it is not incorporated into the structure and Alphabet of the Art until the *Liber de praedicatione* of 1304 (*ROL* III, 144–53). In the *Ars generalis ultima* each subject is treated much more extensively and systematically.

[2] This last sentence is missing from the printed texts.

The first condition is as follows, namely, that each subject must have a definition differentiating it from any other subject. And if any inquiry is to be made into said subject, the answer must be formulated in such a way, by affirming or denying, that the definitions of the principles accord with that of the subject; and the same is true for the rules, without any injury being done to either principles or rules.

The second condition is that in a judgment or in practice the difference between subjects be preserved. Thus divine goodness is different from the goodness of an angel by infinity and eternity, since such goodness is the reason why God does infinite and eternal good, whereas the goodness of an angel is finite and newly created.

The third condition is that the concordance between one subject and another not be destroyed, as for instance, the concordance existing between God and angel, for they are concordant in their spirituality. And the same could be said of the other subjects.

The fourth condition is that, insofar as one subject is nobler and loftier, one should assign it loftier and nobler principles and rules than to another, as in the case of God, who is a loftier and nobler subject than angel, and angel than man, and so on.

1. THE FIRST SUBJECT, WHICH IS GOD, EXAMINED BY MEANS OF THE PRINCIPLES

GOD CAN BE examined by means of the principles and rules, for God is good, great, etc. Many definitions can be given of Him, if one wanted to do things extensively. But we will only give one: God is that being who needs nothing outside Himself, because in Him exist all perfections. With this definition, God is different from any other being, for all other beings need something outside themselves.

In God there is no contrariety or minority, for they are principles having to do with privation and defect. Nevertheless, in God there is majority with respect to other beings; and there is equality, since He has equal principles, such as goodness, greatness, etc., as well as equal acts and relations.

In God there is difference of correlatives, without which said correlatives could not exist at all; nor without them could God exercise His infinite and eternal intrinsic action; moreover, without them his dignities[3] would be idle, which is completely impossible.

In God there is concordance, so that with it He may be infinitely and eternally far from contrariety, and so that His correlatives may accord infinitely and eternally in a single essence and nature. And this is what can be said about His dignities.

In God there is no quantity, no time, nor any accident. The reason is that His substance is separated from and stripped of all accident, because it is infinite and eternal. And with God being conditioned by the four above-mentioned conditions, the intellect understands that it is conditioned to understand God and those things which can be said about Him by means of the principles and rules appropriate to God, and it also knows and understands that if an angel has natural power in itself, and so on for the others, so much more should God, since He is a higher subject, as is clear through the relationship of lesser to greater.

2.   THE SECOND SUBJECT, WHICH IS ANGEL

ANGEL CAN BE derived by means of principles and rules. Indeed, it has natural goodness, greatness, duration, etc. And it is defined thus: an angel is a spirit not joined to a body.

It has no natural contrariety, for it is incorruptible. In it there is the matter of -able, that is to say, of bonifiable, magnifiable, etc., as is indicated by the second species of D.[4]

In an angel there is majority, for it is more similar to God than is man, since it contains higher principles and rules than man. As a result, the intellect realizes that, if man cannot make use of his senses without the corresponding organs, it does not follow from this that an angel is similarly incapacitated, for an angel is of a superior nature. As a result, the intellect realizes that angels can talk

---

[3] Here referred to as *rationes* (Cat. *rahons*); cf. "Llull's Thought," p. 50 above.

[4] That is, Rule D.2 of Part IV. From here on, single letters are to be taken as referring to these Rules.

to one another and act upon us without any organs, and they can travel from one place to another without any means of locomotion, and so on, as is clear to the intellect upon examining the rules.

In an angel there is difference, for its intellect, will, and memory are different from one another. There is equality of understanding, loving, and remembering in an angel, by reason of the supreme object, that is, God, who is equally intelligible, lovable, and memorable. In an angel there is minority, since it has been created from nothing.

3.   THE THIRD SUBJECT, WHICH IS HEAVEN[5]

HEAVEN HAS natural goodness, greatness, duration, etc., and it is defined as follows: Heaven is the first mobile substance.

There is no contrariety in it, for it is not composed of contrary principles. It has natural instinct and natural appetite, and therefore movement, without which it could not possess a nature, instinct, and appetite.

Nevertheless, it has a beginning, for it acts as an efficient cause in things below it; moreover, this beginning is made up of its own specific form and matter, so that it may act in accordance with its species. Its movement constitutes its own end and resting place.

Heaven is in its place, like a body within its surface. Moreover, it exists in time, for it was created. It is also in time in the way that an efficient cause is related to its effect. And so on for its other accidents, each in its own way.

4.   THE FOURTH SUBJECT, WHICH IS MAN

MAN IS COMPOSED of soul and body, and is therefore derivable by means of the principles and rules in two ways, that is to say, in a spiritual and a corporeal way. And he is defined thus: man is a

---

[5] Under this heading Llull usually discusses astronomy, for which see Part x, "Hundred Forms," no. 83 below.

manifying animal.[6] All the principles and rules exist twice in man, because of his double nature, that is, the spiritual and corporeal parts of which he is composed. And thus he is more general than any other created being, as a result of which one can say without doubt that man constitutes the largest portion of the world.

5.   THE FIFTH SUBJECT, WHICH IS THE IMAGINATIVE FACULTY[7]

T H E R E A R E specific principles and rules in the imaginative faculty for the purpose of imagining imaginable things, just as there are in a lodestone for the purpose of attracting iron. And it is defined thus: the imaginative is that power whose function it is to imagine. And it is thus deduced by means of the principles and rules proper to the imaginative faculty. The intellect has great knowledge of it, as well as of those things that accord with it.

The imaginative faculty extracts species from the things sensed with the individual senses; and this it does with its correlatives, as indicated in the second species of Rule C. With goodness it makes these species good, and with greatness it magnifies them, as when it imagines a great mountain of gold. With minority it lessens them, as when it imagines an indivisible point. The imaginative faculty has instinct, just as the lower animals have the will to live, and a goat the instinct to avoid a wolf. The imaginative faculty has an appetite to imagine the imaginable, so that, by imagining it, it may come to rest.

When the individual senses apprehend sensible things, as when the eyes see something colored, they impede the imaginative faculty, which then cannot carry out its act, since it cannot imagine any

---

[6] *Homo est animal* (the Zetzner editions add *rationale*) *homificans*. See Part XI, § 2, Question 3 below, for a defense of this definition (see also p. 295 in the introduction above).

[7] In the philosophical vocabulary of the Middle Ages, *imaginatio* had nothing to do with its modern connotations (as when we say a person has "imagination"), but, closer to its etymology, referred to the faculty of perceiving images when the objects of perception are no longer present to the senses. Note Llull's definition in the *Taula d'esta Art* (*ORL* XVII, 394): "The imaginative (faculty) is the power by which man imagines imaginable things, like a person who, with his imagination, imagines figures that he has seen, or lands where he has been, and so on." See also Part X, "Hundred Forms," no. 31 below.

imaginable thing outside itself until the eyes are closed, at which point the imaginative faculty carries out its act, or can carry it out.

The person seeing apprehends the colored object better by seeing than by imagining, for something sensed is closer to the particular sense. The imaginative faculty, however, apprehends the imaginable object through the intermediary of sense. The imaginative faculty is thus not as general a power in sensed things as is the sensitive faculty, as can be seen from the sense of touch, with which a man holding a stone can, at one and the same time, feel several different things, such as the weight, coldness, roughness, and hardness of the stone; the imaginative faculty, however, cannot do this, except successively. And the same is true of other such things. And this, for the sake of brevity, is enough.

6.   THE SIXTH SUBJECT, WHICH IS THE SENSITIVE FACULTY

THE PRINCIPLES and rules exist in the sensitive faculty in a specific way, for it has one power through sight, another through hearing, etc.; and this is especially so with the properties of instinct and appetite. And it is defined thus: the sensitive is that power whose function it is to sense. The sensitive faculty causes things to be sensed with its specific principles and rules. It is general through the common sense, particular through the individual senses. Through the common sense it has common correlatives; through the individual senses it has individual correlatives.[8] The radical life of the sensitive faculty comes from vegetable life, with which it is connected, and in which it is planted, as is the vegetative in the elementative. The sensitive faculty uses all the senses to sense objects, as when it uses sight to sense something colored, and hearing

---

[8] In the Middle Ages "common sense" did not mean what it means now. As the *Oxford English Dictionary* says, it was "an 'internal' sense which was regarded as the common bond or centre of the five senses, in which the various impressions received were reduced to the unity of a common consciousness." The correlative business means that each individual sense had its correlative unfolding (sight, for example, into *visitivum*, *visibile*, and *videre*), all six of which could then be joined vertically, as it were, into a common *sensitivum*, *sensibile*, and *sentire*. For the sixth sense, see the following note.

to sense a voice, using the *affatus* to give it a name. For without *affatus* the hearing cannot properly sense the voice, and therefore the intellect knows that the *affatus* is a sense.[9]

7.   THE SEVENTH SUBJECT, WHICH IS THE VEGETATIVE[10]

IN THE VEGETATIVE there are specific principles and rules with which plants act according to the species they belong to. For a pepper, a rose, a lily, each acts according to its species. The principles of the vegetative are denser than those of the sensitive, just as the principles of the sensitive are denser than those of the imaginative. And it is defined thus: the vegetative is that power whose function is to vegetate. Indeed it vegetates elemented things just as the sensitive faculty senses either vegetated or elemented things. The vegetative transforms the elementative into its own species by way of generation; and from that it lives, grows, and is nourished. And the vegetative dies through lack of elementative, just as the light in a lamp dies out through lack of oil.

8.   THE EIGHTH SUBJECT, WHICH IS THE ELEMENTATIVE

IN THE ELEMENTATIVE there are specific principles and rules, with which it can have many species, such as gold, silver, and other similar things. And it is defined thus: the elementative is that power

[9] This is a sixth sense Llull introduced in a treatise of the same name written in 1294. In the *Tree of Science* he defines it as "that sense by which the interior conception is made manifest in speech, like a man who says and speaks what he thinks, or like a bird, as for instance when a hen calls her chicks."

[10] I have followed Llull in using an adjective in -ive as a noun. The usage is justified although rare in English (see the *Oxford English Dictionary* under "vegetative," B) as referring to the vegetative faculty or power. I have kept to this usage in the following two sections, but not in the previous two, where it seemed more natural to speak of the imaginative and sensitive faculties.

whose function it is to elementate. It has common correlatives, and what was said regarding the sensitive faculty can be applied here to its individual components, that is to say, to fire, air, water, and earth, which have their own correlatives,[11] without which these elements could not exist, just as the correlatives could not exist without elements, which constitute the ultimate foundation of said elementative.

And through these correlatives, the elementative has points, lines and figures, length, width, depth and volume, qualities and complexions, hardness, roughness, lightness, and heaviness, etc. And as a result the intellect understands that the elements are actually present in elemented things, although in a loose way; for otherwise elemented things would not have anything out of which they would be made, nor would they be of the genus of substance, nor would they have form, matter, motion, instinct, length, width, volume or appetite, which is completely impossible and absurd to maintain.

9. THE NINTH SUBJECT, WHICH IS THE INSTRUMENTATIVE[12]

THIS SUBJECT deals with instrumentality, and it can be considered in two ways, that is, naturally, like the eyes, which are the instrument for seeing, and morally, like justice, which is the instrument for judging, and a hammer for making things.

One can acquire knowledge of a natural instrument by using the principles and rules of the Art to deduce it in a specific way; similarly one can use the same principles and rules to deduce a moral instrument in its own specific way.

Natural and moral instruments differ from one another. We will, however, spare the discerning reader such a deduction or investigation; and if the mind of the artist feels the need for such an investigation, he should turn to the *Ars magna,* in which we discuss moral questions at length. But since we mentioned moral concepts in the

---

[11] Just as with the senses (see n. 8 above), each element unfolds into its correlative triad (fire, for example, into *ignitivum*, *ignibile*, and *ignire*), all four of which could be joined vertically into a common *elementativum*, *elementabile*, and *elementare*.

[12] Or "artifice" as he refers to it in other works.

Alphabet, we therefore want to define our moral instruments, so that, by means of the definitions, along with the principles and rules, the artist can gain knowledge of morality.

1. The instrumentative is the power with which a moral person acts morally.

2. Justice is the disposition[13] with which a just person acts justly.

3. Prudence is the disposition with which the prudent person operates prudently.

4. Fortitude is the disposition with which the strong in heart act with virility.

5. Temperance is the disposition that the temperate person uses in acting temperately.

6. Faith is the disposition with which a person believes to be true something he neither senses nor understands.

7. Hope is the disposition with which someone hopes for God's forgiveness and for glory, and places his trust in his good and powerful friend.

8. Charity is the virtue with which a person makes his private wealth available to others.

9. Patience is the disposition with which the patient person vanquishes and is not vanquished.

10. Pity is the disposition with which the kind person suffers for the suffering of his fellow man.[14]

11. Avarice is the disposition with which the rich man is poor and beggarly.

12. Gluttony is the disposition with which the glutton later finds himself imprisoned in sickness and poverty.

13. Lust is the disposition with which a man uses his powers wrongly and counter to the order of matrimony.

14. Pride is the disposition with which the proud man tries to make himself superior to other men, and it is contrary to humility.

15. Accidie is the disposition with which the accidious person grieves over another's good fortune and is joyful over his ills.[15]

16. Envy is the disposition with which the envious person unjustly desires another's possessions.

[13] *Habitus* in the original, for which see Part x, "Hundred Forms," no. 21 below.

[14] These last two virtues are new, with respect to the classical seven of the quaternary phase (see the chart on p. 79), having been added, like the last two vices, so as to be able to accomodate them to the nine-letter alphabet.

[15] For "accidie," see *Gentile*, Bk. ii, n. 8.

17. Ire is the disposition with which the irate person shackles his thinking and his freedom.

18. Falsehood is the disposition with which the liar talks or gives testimony contrary to the truth of a thing.

19. Inconstancy is the disposition with which a fickle person is changeable in many ways.

So much for the nine subjects, about which the artist can gain knowledge by examining them in the light of the principles and rules of this Art.[16]

---

[16] Which is precisely what is done in the corresponding section of the *Ars generalis ultima*.

PART X, WHICH TREATS OF APPLICATION

APPLICATION is divided into three parts. The first is when the implicit is applied to the explicit. The second is when the abstract is applied to the concrete. The third is when a question is applied to places in the Art. Let us first of all discuss the first part.

1. If the terms of the question are implicit, they should be applied to the explicit[1] terms of the Art, as when one asks whether God exists or whether angels exist. And the same is true for others applied to goodness, greatness, etc., such as: Whether it is a great, good, etc. thing that God exists and that angels exist.

2. The second part is as follows: if the terms of the question are abstract, they should be applied to concrete terms, such as goodness to good, greatness to great, color to colored, and so on. And in this way one should see how an abstract and a concrete term are related to one another, as one examines them by means of the principles and rules.

3. The third part deals with application to specific places, and it is divided into thirteen parts,[2] as follows: (1) First Figure, (2) Second Figure, (3) Third Figure, (4) Fourth Figure, (5) Definitions, (6) Rules, (7) Table, (8) Evacuation of the Third Figure, (9) Multiplication of the Fourth Figure, (10) Mixture of Principles and Rules, (11) The Nine Subjects, (12) The Hundred Forms, (13) Questions

The subject matter of the questions must be applied to these parts according as it is suitable to them. For if the subject matter of a question is relevant to the First Figure, then it must be applied to that figure, and the solution drawn from the text of that figure, by affirming or denying in such a way that the text is not violated. And what we have said about the first figure can be said about the others,

[1] Thus in the early printed sources and some MSS; three other MSS have "explained"; the rest of the MSS have "applied," which seems hard to justify in the context.

[2] After "specific places" the correcting hand in the Milan Catalan MS adds a helpful "of this Art." These thirteen parts, plus the previous two paragraphs, constitute the fifteen parts into which the corresponding section of the *Ars generalis ultima* is divided.

each in its own way. Since we want to be brief, this should be enough concerning application; if, however, the reader would like to know more about applying terms, he should turn to the *Ars magna,* where we discuss the matter at length.

12.   THE HUNDRED FORMS[3]

IN THIS PART the reader will find a hundred forms with their definitions, so that a given subject can be made to reach the intellect. For by means of the definitions of the forms, the intellect will be conditioned to examining them by the principles and rules.[4] And through such an examination the intellect acquires knowledge of the forms discussed in the questions. Here now are the hundred forms with their definitions:

1. Entity is the cause by reason of which one thing causes another thing.[5]

2. Essence is the form abstracted from and sustained in being.[6]

3. Unity is the form whose function is to unite.

4. Plurality is the form that is an aggregate of many things differing in number.[7]

---

[3] The Hundred Forms make their appearance in the years 1295–6, first in the *Tree of Science,* and then in a somewhat different guise, in nos. 101–200 of the *Proverbs of Ramon.* They reappear in the *Logica nova* (1303), and finally in the *Ars consilii* (1315). Note that all these lists are different, except for those here and in the *Ars generalis ultima,* which are identical.

[4] The corresponding definitions in the *Ars generalis ultima* usually point out *which* principles or rules are to be used for investigating each "form." So, in effect, the Hundred Forms constitute a method for investigating—or showing *how* to investigate—a series of topics external to the Art.

[5] In the corresponding "form" of the *Ars generalis ultima,* Llull illustrates his point: "as goodness is the reason why some good does good," and "as greatness is the reason why goodness is great."

[6] In the *Taula d'esta Art* (*ORL* XVII, 393), Llull relates "essence" (*essentia*) and "being" (*esse*) in slightly different terms: "essence is that by which being exists, just as humanity is the essence by which man exists." That this definition ties them in with the previous pair is confirmed on the same pages of the *Taula d'esta Art* where Llull says that "entity (*entitas*) is the essence of a thing (*ens*), which constitutes its act," to which he adds, in the corresponding "form" of the *Ars generalis ultima,* "Since entity and essence are convertible, therefore so are being and thing. And what we said [above] about entity and thing, we can say [here] about essence and being," after which he goes on to say that essence is the (superior) abstract, and being its (inferior) concrete.

[7] As with "unity" and "plurality" here, many of these Hundred Forms can be grouped in pairs or triplets. Llull is more explicit about this in the *Tree of Science,* where they are presented individually the first time around (at the end of the "Elemental Tree") and in groups the second time (at the end of the "Sensual Tree").

5. Nature is the form whose function is to naturize.[8]

6. Genus is something widely applicable and very indefinite, which is predicated of many things differing in species.[9]

7. Species is something that is predicated of many things differing in number.[10]

8. Individuality is the term farther from genus than any other thing.[11]

9. Property is the form with which the agent acts specifically.[12]

10. Simplicity is the form that is farther from composition than any other thing.

11. Composition is the form that is an aggregate of many essences.

12. Form is the essence with which the agent acts in matter.

13. Matter is simply passive essence.

14. Substance is a thing existing by itself.[13]

15. Accident is a form not existing by itself, nor one related principally to its own end.

16. Quantity is the form by reason of which a subject is quantitative and with which it acts quantitatively.[14]

17. Quality is that by reason of which principles are of the sort they are.

18. Relation is a form existing with respect to many different things, without which it cannot exist.

19. Action is a form inherent in whatever is passive.

20. Passion is the thing underlying and inherent in action.[15]

21. Habit is the form with which a subject is clothed.

---

[8] "Naturize" (*naturare*) is defined in the *Oxford English Dictionary*, as "to invest with a specific nature."

[9] The definition in the *Logica nova* (see Part IV, n. 10 above) pp. 42–3, is similar to that here, but adds, "just as animal is predicated of man, lion, eel, etc."

[10] The *Logica nova,* pp. 50–1 adds, "like Socrates, Plato, etc. which are predicated beneath the human species, and this and that lion which are predicated beneath the leonine species."

[11] Instead of "term," some of the early printed sources have "thing."

[12] In the *Tree of Science*, Llull adds, "just as pepper has the property of heating, rhubarb"— an important medicinal plant in the Middle Ages—"of attracting choler, a magnet of attracting iron, and a lion of begetting a lion."

[13] We now begin with the ten Aristotelian categories or predicaments, which were divided into substance and accident (nos. 14–15), under which latter term the nine remaining categories (nos. 16–24) are usually listed.

[14] . . . *est quantum . . . agit quantum*, where *quantum* means literally "how much." For "quantity" see Part IV, Rule F above, as well as *Gentile*, Bk. II, n. 5.

[15] The early printed editions have, "Passion is the thing [underlying action, and] sustaining it," with the Zetzner editions omitting the words in brackets.

22. Position is the disposition of parts, properly and duly arranged in a subject.[16]

23. Time is the entity within which created beings are begun and renewed. Or: Time is that thing made up of many nows with reference to before and after.

24. Place is the accident by which things are located. Or: Place is the surface immediately surrounding and containing the inner parts of a body.

25. Motion is the instrument with which the mover moves the thing moved. Or: Motion is that which knows the nature of beginning, middle, and end.

26. Immobility is that thing having no inclination to move.

27. Instinct is the figure and likeness of the intellect.

28. Appetite is the figure and likeness of the will.[17]

29. Attraction is the form with which the thing attracting attracts the thing attracted. Or: Attraction is a form having the instinct and appetite to attract something to a subject.

30. Reception is the form with which the thing receiving receives the thing received. Or: Reception is a form having the instinct and appetite to receive something in a subject.

31. Fantasy is a likeness extracted from things by means of the imagination.[18]

32. Fullness is the form far from emptiness.

33. Diffusion is the form with which the thing diffusing diffuses what is diffusible.

34. Digestion is the form by means of which the thing digesting digests what is digestible.[19]

35. Expulsion is the form with which nature expels those things which are not suitable to a subject.

36. Signification is the revelation of hidden things indicated by a sign.[20]

---

[16] Besides "position," *situs* can also be translated as "situation," "posture," or even "disposition."

[17] Second definitions added to both nos. 27 and 28 in the early printed sources are doubtless later additions, since they appear in none of the medieval MSS.

[18] *Phantasia* was the Greek word whose usual scholastic translation was precisely the word *imaginatio*, also used here, for which latter see Part IX, n. 7 above.

[19] "Digestion" must be taken in the general sense of the assimilation of any kind of nourishment.

[20] Cf. Gentile, Bk. III, n. 17.

37. Beauty is a lovely form received by the sense of sight or of hearing, or by the imagination, thought, or sense of pleasure.

38. Newness is the form by reason of which a subject is clothed with new characteristics.

39. Idea, in God, is God; in creation, however, it is creature.[21]

40. Metaphysics is the form with which the human intellect strips substance of its accidents.[22]

41. Potential being is a form existing in a subject without motion, quantity, quality, and so on.[23]

42. Punctuality is the essence of the natural point, which is the smallest part of a body.[24]

43. A line is a length made up of many connected points and whose extremities consist of two points.

44. A triangle is a figure with three acute angles enclosed within three straight lines.

45. A square is a figure with four right angles.

46. A circle is a figure enclosed by a circular line.

47. A body is a substance consisting of points, lines, and angles.

48. A figure is an accident made up of position and habit.[25]

49. The general directions are six, with the body at the center of diametrical lines.[26]

50. Monstrosity is the deviation of natural motion.

51. Derivation is the material foundation by which the particular descends from the universal.[27]

---

[21] The *Ars generalis ultima* ties this concept in with the previous one: "Idea in eternity is God; in newness [thus, instead of 'creation,' in many of the early printed sources of the *Ars brevis* as well] it is creature, just as the shape of a box in a carpenter's thoughts can be old, but when it is brought from potentiality to act, then it is new." See also Form 57 below.

[22] Many of the sources have "mathematics" instead of (and even sometimes alongside) "metaphysics," but from the definition here, Llull must surely have meant "metaphysics."

[23] In the *Ars generalis ultima* Llull adds, "like the seed, in which the tree exists potentially."

[24] "Punctuality" in the literal sense, from *punctum*, "point." In the *Ars generalis ultima* Llull adds that it is indivisible and cannot be grasped by the senses or by the imagination.

[25] *Constitutum ex situ et habitu*; see Forms 21–2 for the last two terms. To this definition of "figure," the *Ars generalis ultima* adds, "With color a figure is a visual object, and with lines and angles, and without color, it is a tactile object; with all of these things it is an object of the imagination, which shows us that the imagination is a power superior to sense, and more general than sight."

[26] For these pre-Cartesian coordinates, see *Gentile*, Bk. II, n. 4.

[27] The early printed sources have "general" for "material." The *Ars generalis ultima* adds, "like a stream from a spring, a line from points, a triangle from lines, a child from parents . . . a conclusion from its premises, a consequence from an antecedent, and knowledge from things [*scientia a rebus*] by means of the mind."

52. Shade is the state of privation of light.

53. A mirror is a transparent body arranged so as to receive all the figures presented to it.

54. Color is a condition contained within a figure.[28]

55. Proportion is the form whose function is to proportion.

56. Disposition is the form whose function is to dispose.

57. Creation, in eternity, is idea; in time, however, it is creature.

58. Predestination, in God's wisdom, is idea; in creation, however, it is creature.[29]

59. Mercy, in eternity, is idea; in something predestined, however, it is creature.

60. Necessity is the form that cannot be otherwise; but the necessitated subject is the thing containing it.

61. Fortune is accident inherent in a subject; but the fortunate person is one disposed toward it.

62. Order is the form whose function is to order; he who is ordered, on the other hand, is his own subject.

63. Counsel refers to a proposition open to doubt, and the person counseled is where it comes to rest.

64. Grace is a primary form, placed in the person receiving it without any merit on his part.

65. Perfection is the form whose function it is to perfect in a perfect subject.

66. Explanation is the form in which the intellect finds rest after making distinctions; the person enlightened is its subject, in whom the clarification is a condition.[30]

67. Transubstantiation is the act of nature in what is transubstantiated, which is stripped of its old form and clothed in a new one.

68. Alteration is the form born in the thing altered.

69. Infinity is that form having infinite activity and removed from anything finite.

70. Deception is the positive state of the deceiver, and it is the privative state of the person deceived.

71. Honor is an active state in the person honoring, but passive in the person being honored.

---

[28] In the *Liber de univseralibus* (*ROL* xii, 160), Llull adds that "there are four general colors, to wit, lightness [*luciditas*], transparency [*diaphanitas*], whiteness, blackness."

[29] See n. 21 above.

[30] "Clarification" is *declaratio*, and "the person enlightened" is *declaratus* in the original.

72. Capacity is the form with which something is capable of containing and receiving as much as is allotted to it.[31]

73. Existence is the form with which the thing existing is what it is. Agency is the form moving the thing existing to its terminal point.[32]

74. Comprehension is the semblance of the infinite, apprehension, of the finite.[33]

75. Discovery is the form with which the intellect discovers the thing discovered.[34]

76. Semblance is the form with which the thing assimilating assimilates to itself the thing similar to it.[35]

77. The antecedent is the form giving rise to the consequent; the consequent is the form in which the antecedent comes to rest.

78. Power is the form with which the intellect apprehends the object. Object is the subject in which the intellect comes to rest. Act is the connection between power and object.[36]

79. Generation, in creatures, is the form with which the agent brings about new forms. Corruption is the form with which the thing corrupting undoes old forms. Privation, moreover, exists between them, in the middle.

80. Theology is the science that speaks of God.

[31] Llull uses this word both in its physical and metaphorical senses. The latter is illustrated by the definition in the *Logica nova*, pp. 180–1: "Capacity is the habit with which possibility is clothed, so that the doer and the doable (*agens et agibile*) have the proper proportion and disposition in relation to one another."

[32] Or as defined in the *Liber de universalibus* (*ROL* xii, 162): "Existence is the essence of the thing [*ens*] which exists; agency is the being of the thing doing [*est esse agendi*], which doing [*agere*] is the act of existence, like heat heating or good doing good."

[33] In scholastic terminology, "apprehension" was contrasted to the act of grasping something in its totality, which was "comprehension," a contrast exemplified in the classic phrase that we can apprehend, not comprehend, God.

[34] *Invenire* (Catalan *atrobar*), the usual scholastic translation of the Aristotelian εὑρίσκειν, meant both "to find, find out, discover," and "to devise, invent." Llull used it in both meanings, the first in the sense of canvassing the various parts, or combinations of parts, of the Art to "find" a solution to a problem; the second in the sense of "devising" various conclusions or arguments from some component or set of components of the Art. It was a concept central to Llull's method, as we can see by such titles as *Ars compendiosa inveniendi veritatem* and *Ars inventiva veritatis*.

[35] Llull uses the word *similitudo* (Catalan *semblança*) in three different senses. One is that of "similitude, similarity, resemblance," as here; another is "image, likeness, semblance" ("Semblance is the image of another [thing]"—*Proverbs of Ramon*, §156); and lastly that of "simile, example, metaphor, allegory," thus constituting a pillar of his analogical methods.

[36] This important trio is a fundamental paradigm for the correlatives; see the "Life," n. 83 above. Llull even wrote a *Liber de potentia, objecto et actu*, which, along with the *Vita coetanea* and the *Ars brevis*, le Myésier used as the backbone of the *Breviculum*.

81. Philosophy is the subject by means of which the intellect concentrates on all the sciences.[37]

82. Geometry is an art devised for the measuring of lines, angles, and figures.[38]

83. Astronomy is the art by which the astronomer knows the influences and movements that the heavens effectively exercise over inferior things.[39]

84. Arithmetic is the art devised for the counting of many units.

85. Music is the art devised to arrange many voices so they may be concordant in a single song.

86. Rhetoric is the art with which the rhetorician adorns and colors his words.

87. Logic is the art with which the logician finds the natural connection between subject and predicate.[40]

88. Grammar is the art of finding the correct way of speaking and writing.

89. Morality is the disposition toward doing good or evil.

90. Politics is the art with which townspeople work for the public good of the city.[41]

91. Law is the well-ordered act of a man possessing justice.

92. Medicine is the method with which the doctor looks after the health of the patient.

93. Government is the form with which a prince governs his people.[42]

---

[37] Forms 80–1 along with 91–2 defined what Llull called the "four sciences." Note that, since the Elemental Figure of the quaternary phase was the basis for Llull's discussions of medicine, they correspond to the four figures discussed in n. 6 to the introduction above.

[38] Forms 82–8 comprise the seven liberal arts. The form corresponding to this one in the *Ars generalis ultima* constitutes a minitreatise on geometry.

[39] Some MSS have "astrology" for "astronomy." The corresponding text of the *Ars generalis ultima* begins, "Astronomy is the art with which astrologers . . ." It would be wrong to impose our modern separation of astrology (as superstition) and astronomy (as science) on the Middle Ages or even the Renaissance. Most of the great minds, from Aquinas and Roger Bacon to Tycho Brahe, Kepler, and Galileo accepted the astrological worldview inherited from classical times.

[40] In the *Ars generalis ultima* Llull refers the reader back to his discussion of the middle term (cf. Part II, n. 1, and Part VII, n. 6 above), to the five predicables (Forms 6, 7, 9, 15, plus "difference"), and the ten predicaments (Forms 14–24). He then compares logic to the Art, saying that the former deals with second intentions, the latter with first; the former is unstable and weak (*instabilis scientia sive labilis*) while the latter is enduring and firm (*permanens et illabilis*); the logician arrives at a conclusion by using two premises, the artist by mixing principles and rules. He ends by saying that "the artist can learn more about this Art in one month than the logician about logic in a whole year."

[41] Note the urban setting of this definition (in consonance with its etymology, from the Greek word for "city"), as opposed to the feudal one of "government" in Form 93 below.

[42] "Government" is for *regimen*, allied to *rex*, "king, ruler."

94. Chivalry is the disposition with which the knight helps the prince maintain justice.

95. Commerce is the disposition with which the merchant buys and sells.[43]

96. Navigation is the art by which sailors know how to navigate in the sea.[44]

97. Conscience is the form with which the intellect afflicts the soul for the wrongs it has committed.

98. Preaching is the form with which the preacher instructs people so they will have good conduct and avoid bad conduct.

99. Prayer is the form with which the person praying speaks to God in a holy way.

100. Memory is that thing with which things can be recalled.[45]

[43] The *Ars generalis ultima* adds, "in order to increase his wealth."

[44] The equivalent section of the *Ars generalis ultima* constitutes a minitreatise on navigation, complete with a diagram and hypothetical problems with their solutions.

[45] The peculiar use (one would expect some other term) and repetition of "thing" (*ens*, pl. *entia*) is in the original. In the *Ars generalis ultima* memory is derived by means of the principles and rules, constituting another (four-page) minitreatise.

PART XI, WHICH TREATS OF QUESTIONS

THIS PART is divided into twelve parts or headings, arranged and distributed according to the varying subject matter of the questions. For the solution to one question is indicated in one part or under one heading, and the solution to another under another. Because of this we will apply the questions in different ways to the aforesaid parts.

And this we will do in two ways, that is to say, we will solve some of the questions we propose and others not. These last we leave for the discerning artist, so that he may extract their solutions from those parts or headings to which we refer said questions, in which parts, or under which headings, he will find the solutions indicated.

For the sake of brevity we will here pose and solve few questions, for this Art is an extract from the *Ars magna,* treating it more briefly so that the intellect may grasp many things in few words. In this way the intellect is made more universal and, by means of the solutions to the questions posed and given here, is enabled to solve other questions, each in its own way.

The headings or parts to which we refer the questions are, as we said above, twelve.[1] They are, respectively: (1) the First Figure, (2) the Second Figure, (3) the Third Figure, (4) the Fourth Figure, (5) the Definitions, (6) the Rules, (7) the Table, (8) the Evacuation of the Third Figure, (9) the Multiplication of the Fourth Figure, (10) the Mixture of Principles and Rules, (11) the Nine Subjects, (12) the Hundred Forms.

And first we will discuss the first part or heading.

1 QUESTIONS RELATING TO THE FIRST FIGURE

1. *Question:* Whether there exists any being in which subject and predicate are converted into an identity of essence, nature, and

---

[1] Cf. Part x, §3 above, omitting, of course "(13) Questions." The corresponding part of the *Ars generalis ultima* only gives six, omitting the first six in the following list and starting

number throughout the entire First Figure. The answer is yes, for otherwise the conversion of subject and predicate, as well as their equality, would be destroyed absolutely, and eternity would be superior through infinity of duration, while its goodness, greatness, power would be inferior through finiteness, which is impossible.

2. *Question:* What is that being in whom subject and predicate convert? To which one must answer: God is that being, for such a conversion cannot exist except in infinite and eternal subject.[2]

3. *Question:* Whether divine goodness has in itself as great bonification as the divine intellect has intellection.

4. *Question:* Why is the agency God has in Himself as great as His existence?

5. *Question:* From what does God derive power equal to His being?[3]

6. *Question:* Why do man and animal not convert? To which one must reply: Because conversion cannot be carried out between greater and lesser, but only between equal things.

7. *Question:* Whether an angel's power, intellect, and will convert. To which one must reply: No, or otherwise it could have an act as infinite and eternal as God's.

2. QUESTIONS RELATING TO THE SECOND FIGURE

QUESTIONS relating to the Second Figure can be formulated in three ways, like a man and a lion, who through difference differ in species, through concordance accord in genus, and through contrariety are contrary to each other, that is, through what is corruptible and incorruptible. And so on for the other questions, each in its own way.

1. *Question:* Whether difference is more general than concordance and contrariety. To which one must answer that it is, since

---

directly with the Table. This seems to be the only place where the *Ars brevis* is in fact more complete.

[2] The convertibility of the dignities in God (for which see "Llull's Thought," p. 50) can turn around and act as a *definition* of God.

[3] The answer in the *Ars generalis ultima* (*ROL* xiv, 209–10) is "from Himself and in Himself."

whenever there is concordance and contrariety, there is difference; but the converse is not true in all things. For in many things one can find difference and concordance, without their naturally contraining any contrariety, as with spiritual things.

2. *Question:* Which is the greater principle, concordance or contrariety? The answer is concordance, for from concordance positive principles are derived, whereas those that derive from contrariety are privative.

3. *Question:* Whether a definition such as, Man is a manifying animal, or, Man is that being whose function is to manify, is more ostensive than the following one: Man is a rational, mortal animal. And one must reply that it is. The reason for this is that manification is something only proper to man, whereas rationality and mortality are proper to many things.[4]

By means of the triangle of beginning, middle, and end one can formulate questions in three ways. The first is when one asks:

4. Why is there one first cause and not several? To which one must reply: For the reason that there must exist one end which is infinite.

The second way is when one asks:

5. Whether the middle existing between subject and predicate is of a continuous or discrete quantity. And one must reply that it is of a continuous quantity with respect to the middle between extremes, while it is discrete with respect to the middle of conjunction and that of measurement.

The third way is when one asks:

6. What is the final end in a subject? And one must answer that it is its own proper end, and not an appropriated one.

By means of the triangle of majority, equality, and minority one can formulate questions in three ways. By means of majority one can ask:

7. Why is God above angels, and angels above man? To which

---

[4] For this definition, see Part IX, subj. 4 above; the same definition is defended in greater detail in the *Logica nova*, pp. 22–5. It is important to realize how this definition, with the phrase "whose function it is to manify" (*homificare*), implies the entire correlative structure of man, not only his senses and his elemental nature (see Part IX, nn. 8 and 11 above), but also the three powers of his soul (with the intellect, for example, unfolding into *intellectivum, intelligibile*, and *intelligere*). This is confirmed by what Llull says about "power and its specific act" in Section 6, Question 2 below.

one must reply that God is above angels because divine goodness, greatness, etc., are far from quantity as a result of infinity, and far from time as a result of eternity, whereas an angel's goodness, greatness, etc. are not. But the latter are above man's goodness, greatness, etc., since the subject in which they exist is far from division and succession,[5] whereas the goodness, greatness, etc. of a man's body are not.

The second way is when one asks:

8. Why in the soul are the intellect, will, and memory essentially equal? To which one must answer: because the first cause, through the equality of its goodness, greatness, etc. is equally intelligible, memorable, and lovable. And as a result of this, the intellect realizes that a demonstration can be made in three ways: by cause, by effect, or by equivalence.[6]

The third way is when one asks:

9. Why is sin closer to nothingness than to anything else? And one must state that this is because it is most incompatible with the purpose of being.

10. *Question:* Whether the difference between sensual and sensual is greater than that between sensual and intellectual, and than that between intellectual and intellectual.

11. Furthermore, whether the difference between beginning and middle is greater than that between middle and end.

12. Similarly one can ask about the difference between substance and substance, etc. And one must reply by means of those things signified in the above-mentioned triangles, and this subjectively and objectively using the Rule of B.

3. QUESTIONS RELATING TO THE THIRD FIGURE

I T   W A S   S A I D in the Third Figure that each principle can be applied to the other. And thus one may ask:

---

[5] Many of the sources, both manuscript and printed, have *susceptione* ("receiving, accepting"?) instead of *successione*.

[6] The first two are the classic Aristotelian proofs of *propter quid* and *quia*; the third, *per aequiparantiam*, is an invention of Llull's. It was based on the "equivalence" between the

1. Whether contrariety is as applicable to goodness, greatness, etc. as is concordance. To which one must reply that it is not, for contrariety is applied to them by depriving and opposing, whereas concordance is applied by affirming and according.

In the Third Figure it is stated that goodness is great. And therefore one can ask:

2. What is great goodness? And one must reply that great goodness is that goodness which, without contrariety and minority, accords with all the principles and their correlatives.

3. *Question:* Where is goodness? Turn to the compartment of B I and extract its meanings.[7]

4. *Question:* What does goodness consist of?

5. *Question:* How is goodness? Turn to the compartments of B D and B K and extract their meanings. And so on for others.

6. *Another question:* When is the intellect universal, and when is it particular?

4.   QUESTIONS RELATING TO THE FOURTH FIGURE

1. By the compartment of B C D one can ask: Whether any goodness is as infinitely great as eternity. To which one must answer yes; otherwise all the greatness of eternity would not be good.

2. By the compartment of B E F one can ask: Whether God is as powerful through His goodness as through His intellect. Turn to that compartment and take from it the things it signifies along with their correlatives and definitions.

3. *Question:* Whether an angel, since it is superior, begets an angel, just as man, who is inferior, begets man. One must answer that it does not, for an angel does not receive any addition to itself

---

divine dignities and their acts, and has great importance in Llull's system of demonstration (see the *Ars demonstrativa* in *SW* I, 317–8, for more details).

    [7] As Marçal (see introduction, n. 24 above) points out in his scholium on this passage, the compartment of B I referred to is explained in the *Ars generalis ultima*, Part VI, where Llull says that it exists in itself, in its own good and true concrete things. The compartments of B D and B K in the following Question 5 should also be sought out in the same Part VI of the *Ars generalis ultima*.

from the outside, since that would empty it of its essence; man, however, does, by reason of his body.

5. QUESTIONS RELATING TO THE DEFINITIONS OF PRINCIPLES

1. *Question:* Whether God is a necessary being.

2. *Question:* Whether unity can be infinite without an infinite act.

3. *Question:* Whether there exists a single God.

4. *Question:* Whether God can be evil. Turn to the definitions of goodness, greatness, and eternity, and keep in mind what they signify. For if goodness is great and eternal, then it is necessary that goodness be the reason, with respect to what is good, great, and eternal, for producing something good, great, and eternal. And similarly for other questions that can be asked in relation to the definitions of principles.

6. QUESTIONS RELATING TO THE RULES

1. *Question:* Whether believing precedes understanding.

2. *Question:* Which definition is better and clearer, the one given in terms of a power and its specific act, or the one given by genus and difference? To which one must reply, the one given in terms of a power and its specific act, for by means of such a definition a person can have cognition of the subject and its specific act; whereas by means of the other one cannot, but only of its parts.[8]

3. *Question:* Whether power acts outside its essence.[9]

4. *Question:* Whether the intellect is active in memory and passive in will.

5. Whether the intellect can apprehend an object without the senses.

---

[8] Another defense of Llull's definitional doctrine; cf. n. 4 above.

[9] Almost all these questions are answered in Marçal's scholia. This one here is answered directly—negatively—in the *Liber correlativorum innatorum* (*ROL* vi, 133, line 127).

6. Whether God's power can have infinite action.

7. Whether an act can exist without difference.

8. Whether the act belongs to the power or to the object, or to both.

9. Whether substance can exist by itself without its causes.

10. Whether the will has, in the intellect, the ability to believe, as well as the intellect to understand in the will.

11. Whether will and memory are equal in the soul.[10]

12. Whether the intellect without its correlatives can be either universal or particular.

13. Whether the intellect, when it acquires knowledge, does so by means of property and difference.

14. Whether the intellect disposes a person to love and remember, and conversely.

15. Whether the intellect can, at one and the same time, believe and understand.

16. Whether the intellect can acquire knowledge by itself.

17. *Question:* How does the intellect establish a species?

18. Whether the intellect, through its species, causes the will and memory to be objects with respect to that species.

And just as we have applied the questions having to do with the rules to the intellect, so can they be applied to the other powers, each in its own way.

7. QUESTIONS RELATING TO THE TABLE[11]

1. *Question:* Whether the world is eternal. Go to the column B C D and maintain the negative. In the compartment of B C T B you will find that if it is eternal there are many eternities, differing in kind, and they are concordant by the compartment B C T C against the compartment B C T D, which is impossible. It therefore fol-

---

[10] Many of the MSS have "unequal" instead of "equal."

[11] Here the text of the *Ars generalis ultima* (see n. 1 above) reconnects with that of the *Ars brevis.* Notice that here we have one question for each of the seven columns of the Table.

lows that one must maintain the negative answer to the question, and this is proved by the Rule of B.

2. *Question:* Whether God can be as infinite by His greatness as by His eternity. Turn to the column of C D E and to the compartment of C D T C, maintaining the affirmative against the compartment of C D T D.

3. Whether God can do as much through His eternity as through His intellect. Turn to the column of D E F and to the compartment of D E T D.

4. Whether God is as powerful through His power as through His understanding and loving. Turn to the column of E F G and maintain the affirmative by means of the compartments of E F T E, E F T F, E F T G, etc. until the entire column is used up.

5. Whether, in God, His intellect and His will are greater than His virtue. Go to column F G H and maintain the negative throughout all the compartments of said column, extracting the meanings of those compartments.

6. Whether divine truth is as virtuous through equal correlatives as is divine will. Go to column G H I and maintain the affirmative throughout all the compartments of said column.

7. Whether, in God, His virtue, truth, and glory have the wherewithal to be equal, and to be remote from time, place, and minority. Go to column H I K and maintain the affirmative throughout all the compartments of said column.

8. QUESTIONS RELATING TO THE EVACUATION OF THE THIRD FIGURE

IN COMPARTMENT B C it was said that goodness is great. Now we ask:

1. Whether goodness is great, and
2. What is its greatness? and
3. In what do goodness and greatness accord? and
4. Whether they can accord without any difference.

To all this one must reply, that goodness is great, as is clear from the definition of greatness, and its greatness resides in its possessing its correlatives, as is clear from the Second Species of Rule C. And they accord because goodness is great through greatness, and conversely. But it is impossible for them to accord without the difference of their correlatives.

And this, for the sake of brevity, is enough about the Evacuation of the Third Figure. For from what we have said about it, the artist can formulate and solve questions using the other compartments.

9.   QUESTIONS RELATING TO THE MULTIPLICATION OF THE FOURTH FIGURE

1. *Question:* How can the intellect be conditioned to being general for the sake of general understanding? Turn to the Multiplication of the Fourth Figure and see how the intellect multiplies conditions, thereby multiplying objects as well as its own understanding, so that it will be general and clothed in many different ways for the sake of much and greater scientific knowledge.

And this, in the interest of brevity, is enough about the Multiplication of the Fourth Figure.

10.   QUESTIONS RELATING TO THE MIXTURE OF PRINCIPLES AND RULES

1. *Question:* Whether goodness can be investigated by means of greatness, duration, etc., and conversely. To which one must reply yes, by making the subject into predicate, as was shown by the Third Figure.

2. *Question:* What is goodness in greatness, duration, etc.? To which one must reply that in greatness it is great and in duration enduring.

3. *Question:* What does goodness have in greatness, duration, etc.? To which one must reply that it has its correlatives which are great in greatness, and enduring in duration. And what we have said

about goodness applies equally well to the other principles, each in its own way.

And this, for the sake of brevity, is enough about Mixture.

11.   QUESTIONS RELATING TO THE NINE SUBJECTS

11/1.   Questions Relating to the First Subject, Which is God

1. *Question:* Whether God exists. The answer is yes, as was proved in the Questions relating to the First Figure.

2. *Question:* What is God? To which one must reply that God is that being whose intrinsic activity is as great as His existence.

3. By the Second Species of Rule C one asks, What does God possess coessentially in Himself? To which one must reply that He possesses His correlatives, without which He could not possess immeasurable and eternal dignities.[12]

4. By the Third Species one asks, What is God in something else? To which one must reply that He is creator, governor, and so on.

5. By the Fourth Species one asks, What does God have in another thing? To which one must say that in the world He has power and dominion, and in men judgment, as well as the acts of grace, mercy, humility, patience, and pity.[13]

And this, for the sake of brevity, is enough about God.

11/2.   Questions Relating to the Second Subject, Which is Angel

1. *Question:* Whether angels exist. The answer is yes, for if that which seems to be less similar to God exists, then all the more so will that which seems to be more similar to God exist.

---

[12] The early printed sources have "essentially" for "coessentially." As in Part IX, n. 3 above, the original of "dignities" is here also *rationes* (Cat. *rahons*).

[13] The Zetzner editions have, "To which one must say that in another thing He has power and dominion, and in all things judgment, as well as the act of grace, mercy, patience and pity."

Moreover, if something composed of body and intellect exists, all the more so will something composed of intellect and intellect exist.

Furthermore, if angels did not exist, the ladder of difference and concordance would be empty, and therefore the world too, which is impossible.

2. *Question:* What is an angel composed of, and whose is it? To which one must reply, by Rule D, that it is composed of itself, for its essence cannot be made up of points and lines. By the Second Species of the same rule, it is composed of its spiritual correlatives, that is to say, of its -tives, -ibles and infinitives.[14] By means of its -tives it is active, by its -ibles it is receptive, and the infinitive is the act existing between the -tives and -ibles. By the Third Species one must reply that an angel is God's.

And this, for the sake of brevity, is enough about angels.

11/3. Questions Relating to the Third Subject, Which is Heaven

1. Whether heaven moves itself. The answer is yes, in order for its principles to have their own substantial correlatives by means of its constellations.

2. Whether heaven moves in any direction. The answer is yes, in a circular direction in itself and with respect to the things beneath it, but not outside itself. The reason for this is that there is no action it has or can have outside itself.[15]

3. Whether an angel moves the heavens. The answer is no, because if it did then the -tives of its correlatives would be inferior and its -ibles superior, and thus it would not move the elements or elemented things by means of its form, but by means of its matter, which is impossible.

4. *Question:* Whether heaven has a motive soul. The answer is yes, for otherwise the sensitive and vegetative powers would not have motive souls, and the elements would have no motion.

---

[14] *De suis -tivis et -bilibus et -are*; see Part IV, n. 4 above.

[15] As Marçal points out, Llull does not mean to deny the influence heaven exercises on things here below, but rather he means that it cannot send any part of itself outside its own sphere.

5. One asks by the First Species of Rule E, Why does heaven exist? To which one must say, because it is made up of its own form and matter.

6. By the Second Species of Rule E one asks, Why does heaven exist? To which one must say, in order for things below it to have motion.

And this, for the sake of brevity, is enough about heaven.

11/4. Questions Relating to the Fourth Subject, Which Is Man

1. *Question:* Whether a man can have greater knowledge of God by affirming or denying. The answer is, by affirming, for God does not exist by means of those things without which He exists, but by means of those things without which He cannot exist.

2. *Question:* Why does man act by means of a specific form? Turn to the Second Species of Rule E, where the solution is implied.

3. Whether a man, by increasing his acts, increases his essence. To which one must reply that no man can act upon himself.

4. *Question:* When a man wants to remember and cannot, which is more deficient, his memory or intellect? The answer is his memory, for it naturally restores former species sooner to the intellect than to the will.

5. *Question:* In what way do body and soul constitute a man? The answer is that in man bodily and spiritual goodness make up a single goodness, and so on for the others.

6. *Question:* What is the life of man? To which one must reply that it is that form which is composed of the vegetative, sensitive, imaginative, and rational powers.

7. What is the death of man? The answer is the dissolution of the elementative, vegetative, sensitive, imaginative, and rational powers.

8. *Question:* Whether man is visible. The answer is no, for sight can only see colors and figures.[16]

---

[16] The explanation of this seemingly mysterious question and answer can be found in the corresponding part of the *Ars generalis ultima,* where Llull says, "Whether man is sensible. The answer is no, for accidents are sensible, whereas substance not at all; it is, however, intelligible."

9. *Question:* Whether in man intellect and memory are one and the same power. The answer is no, for if they were, the intellect would not be successive in its acquisition of species, nor would it be able to forget them. Also, it would be too strong against free will in an object.

And this is enough concerning man.

11/5. Questions Relating to the Fifth Subject, Which Is the Imaginative Faculty[17]

1. *Question:* Whether the imaginative faculty imagines imaginable things in the same way that the sensitive faculty senses sensible things.

2. *Question:* Why is it that the imaginative faculty abstracts species from sensible things?[18]

3. *Question:* What is the imaginative faculty?

4. Whether the imaginative faculty has correlatives.

5. Whether the imaginative faculty increases by increasing its activity.

6. Whether the imaginative is a higher power than the sensitive.

7. Whether the imaginative has a specific instinct and appetite.

8. In what way does the sensitive impede the activity of the imaginative?

9. Why is the imaginative not as strong in sensed things as the sensitive? Turn to the subject of the imaginative faculty.

10. *Question:* Whether the sensitive senses the imaginative. To which one must answer that the inferior powers do not act on the superior ones.

11/6. Questions Relating to the Sixth Subject, Which Is the Sensitive Faculty

1. *Question:* Which of the following powers feels hunger and thirst—that of taste or touch? To which one must reply, the one most related to the object.

---

[17] See the corresponding Subject 5 of Part IX above (as well as the section corresponding to *that* in the *Ars generalis ultima*) for answers to the questions of this section.

[18] Here Marçal quotes the *Ars generalis ultima*: "If imagination did not exist, there would be no knowledge of past things, nor would an animal know how to return to a spring, and so on" (cf. *ROL* XIV, 239).

2. Whether taste uses instinct and appetite to perceive hunger or thirst, in the same way that sight uses color to perceive a colored object. Turn to the Second Species of Rule E.[19]

3. *Question:* With what does the sensitive faculty sense the things it senses? To this one must answer that each individual sense senses its sensible thing by means of its specific form, just as a colored subject which lies beneath a crystal colors that crystal.

4. Whether the sensitive power has quantity in terms of points and lines. To which one must answer that the sensitive power attains its object as readily from far as from near.

5. Whether the sensitive faculty, in the same way that it has a common sense, also has a common power, instinct, and appetite.

6. What is the sensitive faculty?

7. Through what things is the sensitive faculty common and particular?

8. From what does the sensitive faculty live and what nourishes it?

9. Whether the sensitive faculty is sensed. Look under the subject of the sensitive faculty.

11/7. Questions Relating to the Seventh Subject, Which Is the Vegetative

1. Whether the vegetative acts by means of its own species.[20]

2. If there is any reason by which the vegetative is common and particular, like the sensitive faculty.

3. Whether the quantity of the vegetative is expressible in terms of points and lines.

4. *Question:* What is the vegetative and what does it possess in itself, according to the Second Species of Rule C?[21]

5. *Question:* From what does the vegetative live, gain its nourishment, and grow, and in what subject is it planted?

6. What constitutes the death of the vegetative? Turn to the subject of the vegetative, in which the solutions to the above questions are implied.

---

[19] Some of the MSS and all the early printed sources have "Rule C," which is surely wrong.

[20] Marçal adds, "The answer is yes," after Questions 1 and 3, which the two eighteenth-century Majorcan editions copied as if these replies were part of Llull's text.

[21] The "D" of the last three Zetzner editions is clearly a mistake. Also mistaken here is the text of *ROL* XII, 249, which tacks this last clause onto the beginning of the following question.

11/8.   Questions Relating to the Eighth Subject, Which Is the Elementative

1. What is the elementative?

2. Whether the elementative, like the sensitive, has many species.

3. Whether the elementative has its correlatives.

4. Whether the candle's flame elementates the wick of the lamp when it lights it.[22]

5. Whether the candle's flame lights the wick by means of air just as sight sees a colored object by means of light.

6. Whether the elementative is the special cause of length, breadth, depth, and fullness.

7. Whether the elementative is the common species of the elements.

8. Whether the elementative can exist in a subject when the elements themselves are removed from it.

9. Whether the elementative can be the source of points, lines, and figures.[23]

10. Whether the elementative impels itself as naturally with its instinct and appetite, lightness, heaviness, heat and so on, as man does artificially with his feet.

11. Whether the elementative can have a nature without substantial correlatives.

12. Whether the elements exist in act in elemented things.

13. Whether the elementative is continuous in quantity everywhere in the sublunary world.

14. Whether there exist two heats, two drynesses, two whitenesses, and so on. Turn back to the Subject of Elementative, and extract from it the solutions,[24] with the intellect conditioned and fashioned by this Art.

15. Whether there exists a fifth element. The answer is no, for in elemented things four complexions suffice.

---

[22] That is, impregnates the wick with an element (see "elementate" in the *Oxford English Dictionary*), in this case of course, fire. Marçal points out that both this and the next question should be answered in the affirmative.

[23] Instead of the *fons* ("source") of the early printed sources and many MSS, many other MSS have *finis* ("end, purpose").

[24] With this plural, Llull is presumably referring not only to this question, but also to the previous thirteen of this section.

11/9. *Questions Relating to the Ninth Subject, Which Is the Instrumentative*

Since above we have already formulated questions concerning natural instrumentality we will here formulate those concerning morality.

1. *Question:* What is morality?

2. *Question:* What is justice, prudence, etc.?

3. *Another question:* What is avarice, gluttony, etc.? Turn back to the Ninth Subject of Instrumentative, and do what that treatise indicates.

4. *Yet another question:* Whether justice is good. The answer is yes; for if it were not, injustice would not be evil.

5. *A further question:* Whether justice has correlatives. The answer is yes; for if not, there could exist no just condition, nor any things in which it could be sustained and situated.

Following these examples, one can formulate questions relating to justice by means of all its principles and rules. And what we have said about justice can be applied to the other virtuous conditions.

6. Whether the vices are simply privative principles. The answer is yes, for they have no concordance with the virtues. In the virtues, for their part, the doer, the doable, and the instruments are in accord in the virtuous object.

And this, for the sake of brevity, is enough about moral matters, especially since in the *Ars magna* we have dealt with them at length.[25]

12. QUESTIONS RELATING TO THE HUNDRED FORMS

QUESTIONS relating to the Hundred Forms can be formulated in as many ways as each form is different in accordance with the Nine Subjects, like "entity," for instance, which is one form in God, another in angel, yet another in heaven, etc., as when one asks:

---

[25] There Llull gives two sets of questions (*per principia* and *per regulas*) for each vice and each virtue.

1. Whether God's entity is the origin of all other entities. The answer is yes, because His goodness is the origin of all goodnesses, His greatness of all greatnesses, His eternity of all durations, etc. The same, however, cannot be said of an angel's entity, that of heaven, etc. And thus a form, according to how it is different from others, must be examined by means of its own principles and rules.

2. *Question:* Whether essence and being are convertible. To which one must answer that in God they convert with one another, for in God nothing is superior or inferior. In angels, heaven, etc., however, they do not convert, since being exists in them through essence, and not conversely, and therefore in such things essence is superior and being inferior.

Questions can be formulated in one way concerning God's unity, and in another concerning an angel's unity, in another concerning the unity of heaven, etc., as when one asks:

3. Whether it is the function of God's unity to unite the infinite. The answer is yes, for if that unity did not unite the infinite, then it could not itself be infinite, because its power would be finite and constrained, and it would be idle in eternity, and the same could then be said of divine goodness, greatness, etc., which is impossible.

4. If, however, one asks about an angel's unity, whether its function is to unite, the answer must be in accordance with the conditions of its unity. That is to say that an angel can, in a moral, objective way of speaking, be united to another in a single loving, a single understanding, and a single bonifying.[26] I do not say, however, that an angel can become one with another angel, since it cannot, as has already been explained. Nor can heaven become one with another heaven. The unity of heaven, however, is the effective cause of inferior unities. But the unity of man is not like this, for one person can join another to produce a third. And similarly with other things, each in its own way.

5. Whether there is plurality in God. To which one should answer yes, with respect to His correlatives as exemplified in the Second Species of rule C, without which He could not have in

---

[26] Instead of *bonificare*, the Zetzner editions have *homificare* ("manifying"). The previous "moral . . . way of speaking" (*moraliter*) should probably be taken in the sense of "figurative," or even "spiritual" (as opposed to "physical"); cf. the *Book of the Lover and the Beloved*, n. 5.

Himself an infinite and eternal operation bonifying, magnifying, eternalizing, etc., as a result of which His dignities would be constrained and idle, which is impossible. The plurality of an angel, however, is not like this, for an angel is composed of -tive and -ible with respect to God's simplicity. And likewise heaven is more composite than an angel, and man more than heaven.

6. *Question:* Whether in God there is a nature. To which one must answer yes, so that He may have natural remembering, understanding, and loving, as well as natural goodness, greatness, etc.; also so that these very dignities may be natural to Him in order for him to produce infinite and eternal good for the purpose of naturizing. An angel's nature, however, is not like this, for it is finite and newly created. It does, however, have the function of naturizing, since it has innate and natural species with which it objectively and naturally objectifies. And thus one can also speak of the nature of heaven in its own way, as well as according to its principles and its natural and specific rules, with which it naturally and specifically acts. And similarly one can discuss the other subjects, each in its own way.

From what we have said above, the artist can formulate questions concerning the Hundred Forms and solve them in accordance with how the questions are variously treated and derived by means of the Nine Subjects which differ from one another, by observing for each Form the definition of it we gave above. And thus the intellect learns in what way it can be most general in formulating many questions and solving them by the method indicated in the Evacuation of the Third Figure and in the Multiplication of the Fourth Figure. As a result, who could possibly enumerate all the questions and solutions that could be thus formulated?

And this, for the sake of brevity, is enough about questions relating to the Hundred Forms.

PART XII, WHICH TREATS OF HABITUATION[1]

THIS PART deals with habituation to the Art, and it is divided into three parts, the first of which is itself divided into thirteen parts corresponding to the thirteen divisions of the Art. And the artist of this Art should become familiar with them, so that he may know how to apply a question to that place or those places which are related to the question, in accordance with how analogous they are to the matter of the question.

The second part states that he should become familiar with the method and procedure of the text of this Art, keeping to the method of the text for proving and solving other questions, that is, using the method by which they are presented in the text, just as one example can be used to exemplify and explain another.

The third part states that he should become familiar with the method for multiplying questions and solutions towards one and the same conclusion, as is indicated in the Third and Fourth Figures and in the Table.

And this, for reason of brevity, is enough about habituation.

---

[1] This word could also be translated as "(learning and) mastering the Art," although I have kept the English homonym to connect it with "habit" (see Part X, "Hundred Forms," no. 21 above), and sometimes used "become familiar with" in the text itself.

PART XIII, WHICH TREATS OF THE METHOD FOR TEACHING THIS ART

THIS PART is divided into four parts.

The first part states that the artist should know the Alphabet by heart, as well as the figures, definitions, and rules, along with the arrangement of the Table.

The second part states that he should explain the text well to his students, by rational means, and not bind himself by the authority of others. And the students should read through the text, and if they have any doubts, they should ask the artist or teacher about them.

The third part states that the teacher or artist should formulate questions in front of the students and solve them rationally, according to the method of the Art. For without reason the artist cannot make proper use of the Art. And it should be understood that the Art has three friends, which are subtlety of intellect, reason, and good intentions, without which no one can learn this Art.[1]

The fourth part states that the artist should put questions to the students, so they may answer them; and he should have them multiply their arguments toward one and the same conclusion. Moreover, they should find[2] the places by reason of which they will know how to answer and multiply. If, however, the students do not know how to answer, multiply reasons, or to find the right places, then the artist or teacher should teach them the above-mentioned things.

---

[1] Le Myésier quotes this phrase twice in the *Electorium*.
[2] For this use of *invenire* (Cat. *atrobar*) see Part x, n. 34 above.

EPILOGUE

THE END OF THIS ART

TO THE HONOR and praise of God and for the public good Raymond finished this book in the monastery of San Donnino[1] of Pisa in the month of January of the year 1307 of the Incarnation of our Lord Jesus Christ.[2] Amen.

[1] The "Saint Dominic" usually printed here seems to be an error (a *lectio facilior*) introduced by later scribes.
[2] January 1308 by our reckoning.

Suggestions for Further Reading

FOR THE READER who wants to delve further into Ramon Llull, the larger anthology from which this one is extracted—*SW*—has not only a greater range of works, but has much more extensive bibliographies, and at the end a complete catalogue of Llull's works.

The standard modern work on Llull in English is J. N. Hillgarth, *Ramon Lull and Lullism in Fourteenth-Century France* (Oxford: Oxford University Press, 1971). More specialized are the two seminal essays by Frances Yates, "The Art of Ramon Lull: An Approach to It through Lull's Theory of the Elements," *Journal of the Warburg and Courtauld Institutes* and "Ramon Lull and John Scotus Erigena," both printed in the *Journal of the Warburg and Courtauld Institutes*, the first in vol. 17 (1954), 115–73, and the second in vol. 23 (1960), 1–44, and both reprinted in her *Lull & Bruno: Collected Essays, vol 1* (London: Routledge & Kegan Paul, 1982). Of Robert Pring-Mill's many important writings on Llull, the only two in English are "The Analogical Structure of the Lullian Art," *Islamic Philosophy and the Classical Tradition: Essays Presented to Richard Walzer on His Seventieth Birthday* (Columbia, S.C.: University of South Carolina Press, 1972), pp. 315–26, and "The Trinitarian World Picture of Ramon Lull," *Romanistisches Jahrbuch* 7 (Hamburg, 1955–6), 229–56. More recently in English there has appeared Mark D. Johnston, *The Spiritual Logic of Ramon Llull* (Oxford: Oxford University Press, 1987). The earlier writings of E. Allison Peers, such as his *Ramon Lull, a Biography* (London, 1929; reprint Leiden: Brill, 1982), his briefer *Fool of Love* (London, 1946; reprint Havertown, Pa., 1973) and his translations of *Blanquerna* (London, 1926) and other works, are now quite dated, especially in his lack of sympathy for the central body of Llull's thought, which he tended to treat as the unfortunate aberration of an otherwise inspired mystic and poet. Much more trustworthy and interesting is the edition of the medieval translation of the *Book of the Order of Chivalry*, ed. Alfred T. P. Byles, in the Early English Text Society (London: Oxford University Press, 1926).

In other languages, the basic works are the still valuable article by E. Longpré, "Lulle, Raymond (Le Bienheureux)" in the *Dictionnaire de théologie catholique* 9, 1 (Paris, 1926), cols. 1072–1141; the monumental and still indispensable T. & J. Carreras y Artau, *Historia de la filosofía española: Filosofía cristiana de los siglos XIII al XV*, 2 vols. (Madrid, 1939–43); the more recent E.-W. Platzeck, *Raimund Lull, sein Leben, seine Werke, die Grundlagen seines Denkens (Prinzipienlehre)*, 2 vols. (Rome and Düsseldorf, 1962–4); and the collection of essays by Eusebi Colomer, *De la Edad Media al Renacimiento: Ramón Llull—Nicolás de Cusa—Juan Pico della Mirandola* (Barcelona: Herder, 1975). In Catalan, and now also in Spanish translation, I and Lola Badia have tried to give an up-to-date survey in *Ramon Llull: Vida, pensament i obra literària* (Barcelona: Empúries, 1988; Spanish translation, Barcelona: Sirmio-Quaderns Crema, 1993).

For good surveys of specific aspects of Llull's thought and influence, on his mysticism there is Louis Sala-Molins, *La philosophie de l'amour chez Raymond Lulle* (Paris and the Hague: Mouton, 1974); on a fundamental structure of his system Jordi Gayà, *La teoría luliana de los correlativos: Historia de su formación conceptual* (Palma, 1979); on his influence on Renaissance thought Paolo Rossi, "The Legacy of Ramon Lull in Sixteenth-Century Thought," *Mediaeval and Renaissance Studies* 5 (1961), 182–213; and finally his influence more specifically on Renaissance metaphysics Charles Lohr's chapter on "Metaphysics" in the *The Cambridge History of Renaissance Philosophy* (Cambridge: Cambridge University Press, 1988), pp. 539–57, 586.

As for editions and anthologies, in addition to those given in the list of abbreviations at the beginning of this volume, there are in Catalan the interesting Ramon Llull, *Antologia filosòfica*, ed. Miquel Batllori (Barcelona: Editorial Laia, 1984). In Spanish there are three other anthologies, in all of which the same Miquel Batllori has had a hand, and all of which are good: Ramon Llull, *Obras Literarias* (Madrid: Biblioteca de Autores Cristianos, 1948); *Antología de Ramón Llull*, 2 vols. (Madrid: Dirección General de Relaciones Culturales, 1961); Ramon Llull, *Obra escogida*, trans. Pere Gimferrer (Madrid: Alfaguara, 1981).

Finally a complete bibliography from 1480 to 1868 can be found in Elíes Rogent i Estanislau Duràn, *Bibliografia de les impressions lul·lianes*, (Barcelona: Institut d'Estudis Catalans, 1927; reprint Palma: Miquel Font, 1989–91), a work which has been continued in

Rudolf Brummer, *Bibliographia Lulliana: Ramon-Llull-Schriftum 1870–1973* (Hildesheim: Gerstenberg, 1976; reprint Palma: Miquel Font, 1991), and finally in Marcel Salleras, "Bibliografia lul·liana (1974–1985)", *Randa* 19 (1986), 153–98. There is also a specialized journal with articles, bibliographies and reviews: *Estudios Lulianos* (Palma, 1957–), since 1991 retitled *Studia Lulliana*.

Index of Llull's Works

Works are listed alphabetically according to the first significant word in the title. The square brackets following the title contain the number of the work in the catalogue of *SW* II, 1257–1304, brought up to date in *OS* II, 539–89 (if there is any difference of numeration, that of *SW* follows the word "formerly").

APOCRYPHAL WORKS

General Index

MYTHOS: The Princeton/Bollingen Series in World Mythology

J. J. Bachofen
MYTH, RELIGION, AND MOTHER RIGHT

George Boas, trans.
THE HIEROGLYPHICS OF HORAPOLLO

Anthony Bonner, ed.
DOCTOR ILLUMINATUS: A RAMON LLULL READER

Jan Bremmer
THE EARLY GREEK CONCEPT OF THE SOUL

Joseph Campbell
THE HERO WITH A THOUSAND FACES

Henry Corbin
AVICENNA AND THE VISIONARY RECITAL

F. M. Cornford
FROM RELIGION TO PHILOSOPHY

Mircea Eliade
IMAGES AND SYMBOLS

Mircea Eliade
THE MYTH OF THE ETERNAL RETURN

Mircea Eliade
SHAMANISM: ARCHAIC TECHNIQUES OF ECSTASY

Mircea Eliade
YOGA: IMMORTALITY AND FREEDOM

Garth Fowden
THE EGYPTIAN HERMES

Erwin R. Goodenough (Jacob Neusner, ed.)
JEWISH SYMBOLS IN THE GRECO-ROMAN PERIOD

W.K.C. Guthrie
ORPHEUS AND GREEK RELIGION

Jane Ellen Harrison
PROLEGOMENA TO THE STUDY OF GREEK RELIGION

Joseph Henderson & Maud Oakes
THE WISDOM OF THE SERPENT

Erik Iversen
THE MYTH OF EGYPT AND ITS HIEROGLYPHS IN EUROPEAN TRADITION

C. G. Jung & Carl Kerényi
ESSAYS ON A SCIENCE OF MYTHOLOGY

Carl Kerényi
ELEUSIS: ARCHETYPAL IMAGE OF MOTHER AND DAUGHTER